# THE SCHOOLED SOCIETY

# THE SCHOOLED
# SOCIETY

## THE EDUCATIONAL
## TRANSFORMATION
## OF GLOBAL CULTURE

## David P. Baker

Stanford University Press
Stanford, California

Stanford University Press
Stanford, California

Printed in the United States of America on acid-free, archival-quality paper

Library of Congress Cataloging-in-Publication Data

Baker, David, 1952 January 5- author.
The schooled society : the educational transformation of global culture /
David P. Baker.
pages cm
Includes bibliographical references and index.
ISBN 978-0-8047-8736-9 (cloth : alk. paper)
--ISBN 978-0-8047-9047-5 (pbk. : alk. paper)
1. Education--Social aspects. 2. Social change. 3. Education and globalization.
I. Title.
LC192.B35 2014
306.43--dc23
2014006099

ISBN 978-0-8047-9048-2 (electronic)

Typeset by Bruce Lundquist in 10/15 Sabon

*To Gero and John for their generous mentoring
in the ephemeral city of West Berlin so long ago.
It made all the difference.*

# Contents

List of Figures and Tables     ix

Preface     xi

Introduction: A Quiet Revolution     1

PART I

DIMENSIONS AND ORIGIN OF THE SCHOOLED SOCIETY

1   From Education Revolution to the Schooled Society     23

2   Constructing Culture: Academic Intelligence,
Social Status, and Human Rights     41

3   The Incredible Longevity of the Western University     58

4   Mass Education and the Super Research University     83

5   Constructing Reality: Ice Cream, Women's Studies,
and the MBA     99

PART II

SOCIETAL CONSEQUENCES OF THE EDUCATION
REVOLUTION

6   The Educational Transformation of Work     125

7   Credentialing in the Schooled Society     156

8   The Transformation of Knowledge and Truth Claims     184

9   Failure, Redemption, and the Construction of the Self     219

10   An Educated Polity: The Universal Solvent
and the Political Paradox     247

11   An Educated Laity: The Education-Religion Paradox     261

Conclusion   The Schooled Society and Beyond:
Ubiquitous, Formidable, and Noisy                          275

Notes                                                      303

References                                                 311

Index                                                      339

# Figures and Tables

FIGURES

I.1 Traditional perspective on the relationship between education and society 9

I.2 Schooled society (neo-institutional) perspective on the relationship between education and society 11

1.1 Number of students in primary, secondary, and higher education worldwide 24

1.2 How long can children expect to stay in school? Average school life expectancy, in years, for primary to secondary education, by country, 2001 26

1.3 Examples of synergistic cultural meaning from core values of education as an institution 34

4.1 Growth trends in university graduate study in the U.S., 1970–2004 95

6.1 Proportion of total employment of professional, technical, and kindred workers, 1910–2000 134

7.1 Four processes of institutionalization of educational credentials within the occupational structure 163

7.2 Educational credential requirements among growing and declining U.S. occupations, 2004–2006 164

7.3 Percentage of U.S. workers in licensed versus unionized jobs, 1950–2006 166

7.4 Impact of educational degrees versus years of schooling on occupational prestige in the U.S., 1950–2008 180

8.1 Mean number of problem-solving strategies and their conceptual abstraction in U.S. mathematics textbooks 193

8.2  Distribution of upper secondary academic tracks/programs
worldwide, by historical period                                    197

8.3  Decline of classical language and rise of foreign languages
taught in national curricula worldwide                             203

8.4  Prevalence of foreign language education in grades 1 to 8,
circa 2000, by world region                                        204

9.1  U.S. high school regular diploma and GED completion rates
by age 24, 1930–2000                                               224

9.2  Attainment of high school diploma by 1992 of national
sample of 1980 U.S. high school sophomores, by race               240

### TABLE

7.1  U.S. architects, professional associations network:
Constructing and intensifying educational credentialing
via licensure                                                      167

# Preface

NEVER BEFORE IN HUMAN SOCIETY have so many individuals dedicated so much time, energy, and resources to becoming educated. What social scientists call the education revolution has caused unprecedented growth in the number of people going to school throughout the world. With each new generation the amount of education and required academic degrees spiral upward, so that what our grandparents' generation considered a normal education would now be woefully inadequate. In just 150 years, or across four generations of a family, formal education has gone from a special experience for the few to an ordinary one for most all. While it is now routine for children and youth to spend thirteen to seventeen-plus years sitting long hours in classrooms doing the cognitive work of schooling, it is a remarkable anthropological change.

It is obvious that the world is becoming more educated; what is not so obvious is how much this revolutionizes human society. When the big picture of the education revolution is considered, it is frequently underappreciated. The common opinion, including that of most intellectuals, is that all of this schooling has occurred because society has changed and one "needs it" to live in a complex and sophisticated world. Or more darkly, that education is mostly a myth and serves the purposes of the powerful to reproduce a world where they win. But both opinions miss the real story behind the education revolution: the ubiquitous massive growth and spread of education has transformed our world into a schooled society— a wholly new type of society where dimensions of education reach into, and change, nearly every facet of human life. Formal education, from early childhood to the upper reaches of the university and into lifelong learning programs, has become such an extensive undertaking that society is influenced by its logic and ideas more than the other way around, and this has been so for some time. In fact, it will be shown that along with large-scale capitalism and representative political democracy, the education revolution should be thought of as a key founding social revolution of late modern and postindustrial forms of global society.

Unfortunately, the scholarly dialogue about what caused the rise of complex, nontraditional human societies is mostly silent about the impact of educating large numbers of people; intellectually the education revolution is a distinctly quiet one. To end the silence, four decades of research by social scientists is leading to a new way to think about the effects of education on society, opening up a much broader appreciation of how education transforms everyday life. Supported by an innovative theoretical perspective known as neo-institutionalism, a radically new assessment of the quiet revolution's transformation of society is emerging, where education not only transforms individuals—a considerable feat in and of itself—but also produces a widespread culture of education having the legitimate power to construct new types of minds, knowledge, experts, politics, and religions; a new definition of personal success and failure; new conceptions of profit-making, work, and workplaces; new ways in which social mobility occurs; a new privileging of a narrow range of human capabilities; and more. At the same time, like all robust social and moral orders of the past, the emerging schooled society takes no prisoners: increasingly one either plays the education game or risks being marginalized with a wounded self-image. Similarly, the schooled society has edged out older, traditional ways of understanding many central things of life, and some once valued ways of living have disappeared as a result. And because the same general form of education has surfaced most everywhere, the cultural transformation and the demands of the education revolution are a global phenomenon; for better or worse, the education revolution constructs and sustains significant understandings and meanings of the global culture.

To appreciate the dimensions of the emerging schooled society, one needs to dispense with the usual ways of thinking about education and the state of society. Too often, and paradoxically, education is considered either the savior or the whipping boy of postindustrial society. On the savior side, one hears the expectation that education will make the better individual and the better society, to the point that education has become the accepted master solution to all manner of personal and social problems. Low-income nations and foreign aid agencies invest heavily in human capital development, as governments across the world make education one of their largest expenditures. Parents incessantly discuss their children's educational progress and their local school's challenges and their remedies. Sophisticated nations with long historical-cultural heritages often condemn their own future if they think their system of formal education is not world-class. Subpar universities are assumed to leave a nation out of the coming knowledge society and the global construction of new economies.

At the same time, an uneasiness about education and its role in post-industrial society exists in some quarters. It always seems to be inadequate or dumbed down from unspecified past glories. It is frequently considered as only ineptly meeting the needs of an evolving world, and the routine assumption is that there is too much education for too many people, or too little access to quality basic schooling for it to matter much. And universities are faulted for offering a watered-down version of essential knowledge needed for the common good. Business leaders routinely complain of an ill-trained workforce, and on any given day public pundits suggest that education problems jeopardize our very future.

As the seemingly incompatible visions of savior or whipping boy vie for our attention, they inadvertently promote the same assumption about education and society: the former blindly follows changes in the latter, and thus mostly just trains (or indoctrinates) individuals for positions in society. Yet this assumption is increasingly inadequate to understand the growing array of educational phenomena and their impacts. This book turns the assumption on its head by arguing that widespread education and the values, ideas, and norms that it fosters make it a robust primary institution that now uniquely shapes society far more than it reacts to it. Indeed it is education's success in shaping culture that creates the tandem savior and whipping boy images: massive secular faith in education along with frustration at unmet, albeit unrealistic, grand expectations do not come from a weak derivative institution; rather, just the opposite.

The theoretical perspective here is about how major social institutions constitute society, and how they guide behavior and emotions and influence the conscious experience of society. After a long decline in empirical support for the original institutional theory (essentially functionalism), neo-institutionalism emerged over the past decades as a viable alternative to Marxist accounts of the origins and persistence of the structure of society. Although fruitful in shaping a productive research agenda about the effects of education on society, as a theory neo-institutionalism is mostly an insider's game, not very accessible even to other social scientists and analysts of education. A major objective here is to explain in a comprehensive fashion, as well as critique, this perspective as a working theory about the rise and consequences of the education revolution.

A challenge in examining such a vital and common institution as education is to find a way to understand what is historically unique about the everyday normal. This is undertaken in two ways. The first part of the book describes the dimensions of the education revolution and why education grew into the vigorous institution it is today. These chapters argue that the schooled society's roots are in the historical development of the university, specifically the unique social charters and functions of its Western form. Over the course of the education revolution, schooling and society in general have been pulled towards the knowledge-production and educational logic of the university. Examined here is the now extensive knowledge conglomerate of the university, its shaping of new knowledge and its credentialing of people who in turn gain the authority to enact such knowledge in everyday life; in particular, this process was intensified over the past fifty years by a supercharged form of the research university and mass higher education. This is illustrated through analyses of three research fields, their academic degrees, and the resulting occupations, all created by the university—one example each from the sciences, the social sciences, and business and formal organizations. The conclusion is that the university, with an eight-hundred-year development of its institutional charters, is perhaps the single most dynamic creator of cultural understandings in postindustrial society.

The second part explores the argument that if education is a primary founding institution of society, then there should be ample evidence that it influences non-educational institutions. Analysis of such influence on six institutions finds that the schooled society is the foundation on which many mega social trends (some thought of as good; others, as disconcerting) have been built, and with some highly ironic results. The much heralded knowledge society, the rise of new economies, and the growth in professionalism of many jobs and the workplace are direct results of the education revolution. So are the growth of contentious politics and the politicizing of ever more issues of everyday life. A world made up of an expanding population of massive formal organizations, business and otherwise, rests directly on the capacities and sentiments of educated individuals, and also on the ideas fostered by a culture of education. In religious arenas, the schooled society has not caused widespread secularization as much as it creates capacity for mass religious belief and practice. Concepts of the self, along with understandings of personal failure and success, are increasingly defined by the logic of education, as are mechanisms to ensure a normal life. And all types of traditional ways for individuals to find a place in society have been supplanted by the logic behind academic degrees. These, and other major trends, are all upon us as a result of the schooled society.

I have thought about, and played with, the ideas here ever since my graduate student days at Johns Hopkins. Numerous collaborators and colleagues over the years have helped me develop the arguments, and I owe all of them much gratitude. Almost a decade's worth of graduate students in my seminars on the sociology of education were hapless audiences to many rehearsals of the arguments herein; I appreciate their patience and generous, constructive feedback. I also thank Stacey Bielick, David Bills, David Brown, Henry Brzycki, Claudia Buchmann, Regina Deil-Amen, Roger Finke, David Frank, Saamira Halabi, Floyd Hammack, Gillian Hampden-Thomas, Michael Hout, David Kamens, Hugh Lauder, Gero Lenhardt, John Meyer, Justin Powell, Alan Sadovnik, Daniel Salinas, Maryellen Schaub, Evan Schofer, Thomas Smith, William Smith, Manfred Stock, Armend Tahirsylaj, Kate Wahl, Alex Wiseman, and Michael Young for helpful comments on earlier drafts. And a special note of appreciation goes to Emily Anderson for pulling it all together at the end; to Adrienne Henck and Haram Jeon for bibliographic assistance; and to Emily Smith Greenaway for completing the occupational prestige analysis. Lastly, portions of Chapters 6 and 7 were previously published in the *Journal of Education and Work* and *Research in Social Stratification and Mobility*, respectively (Baker 2009, 2011).

# THE SCHOOLED SOCIETY

# Introduction

## A Quiet Revolution

The education revolution is as important as the industrial and democratic revolutions have been.

TALCOTT PARSONS, *The System of Modern Societies*, 1971

Education systems themselves are ideologies. They rationalize in modern terms and remove from sacred and primordial explanations of the nature and organization of personnel and knowledge in modern society.

JOHN MEYER, *American Journal of Sociology*, 1977

A REVOLUTION IN EDUCATION has thoroughly transformed human society over just a century and a half. Along with a few other major global phenomena, such as large-scale capitalism and representative democracy, schooling whole populations for ever more years changes both individuals and the institutions at the core of society. Intensifying right up to today, what is called the "education revolution" is a cultural phenomenon more than a material or political one, although it has major material and political consequences.

At the heart of the education revolution are two intertwined, powerful social forces, one obvious but often misinterpreted, and the other underappreciated. The first one is that formal education has historically progressed from a privilege for the few to a mandatory essential for everyone. Widespread schooling, or "mass schooling" as it is now known, has spread to all populations in the world, and the standard of educational attainment spirals upward with each new generation. This relentless and ubiquitous expansion of formal education is witnessed most recently in the waves of youth entering universities and other higher education institutions, in residence and online, to earn a dizzyingly wide array of degrees, often going into considerable debt and postponing adult life to do so. It is a stunning development when over the span of about 150 years the world changed from being populated by mostly unschooled illiterates to having an estimated 80 percent of all adults schooled at least to the point that they can write and read a short statement about their life—this is a new global condition thought improbable as recently as fifty years ago (UNESCO 2002).

Accompanying this great inclusion of the world's population into formal education is the creation of an extensive and robust culture of education that has come to influence all facets of life. This second powerful force justifies and intensifies the now widely held belief that formal education is the best way to develop all humans and their capacities; an idea that surpasses centuries-old notions unrelated to education about how to raise children, make productive employees, and create effective citizens. This powerful cultural influence is what sociologist of education John Meyer insightfully recognized (in the epigraph) as education's *ideology*. For example, as a consequence of the education culture, formal education continues to expand at both ends of the life-course, with considerable public sentiment that it is the "right thing to do." Over just a few decades, the American kindergarten has become significantly more academically oriented, while the worldwide campaign for mass pre-K schooling has gained strength. Adult education and the idea of "life-long learning" make going to school normative well into adulthood, and hence currently one third of the entire U.S. labor force is required annually to enroll in continuing education as a condition for employment (e.g., Jacobs and Stoner-Eby 1998).

From early childhood up through graduate training and adult education, extensive access to schooling in postindustrial society, sustained by deeply held ideas and values, imbues society with a culture of education. Well beyond merely training individuals for jobs, the education revolution has produced a world where education is an independent social institution that shapes significant parts of *all other* core institutions in society. Major transformations of social institutions at the hands of education abound, many of which will be explored here. For instance, the education revolution is transforming the nature of the workplace and work itself into an image of itself. It is also narrowing and intensifying the societal value of certain types of cognitive skills while displacing other human talents. An educated polity transforms the terms of political mobilization and civic behavior, while an educated laity changes the dimensions of religion, including essential images of God. And the growing and influential global network of large formal organizations, for-profit and otherwise, is a direct consequence of the increased organizational capacities and sentiments of educated populations. Some of these changes are thought of as positive and others as negative, but all are substantial sociological transformations.

Equally transforming is the impact of the education revolution on individuals. To a degree unknown in past societies, outcomes of formal education in the form of achievement and earned degrees have come to both subjectively and objectively define individual success and failure. Increasingly, individuals with a less-than-average education see themselves as failures—less than fully actualized persons—and assume that only more educational attainment will make them successful. At the same time, for a growing number of jobs, occupational credentials are structured by the terms and meanings of formal education to the point that education dominates the very essence of individual social mobility in postindustrial society. And beginning just a few decades ago, among cohorts of young adults, academic attainment now diminishes or even eradicates any impact of their parents' social status on their own future standing.

Yet for all of the societal influence wielded by mass education, the education revolution is a distinctly "quiet revolution" underappreciated in many ways. In other words, compared to other massive social forces, the societal effects of the education revolution have received very little intellectual attention. As a routine subject of daily life, education is certainly discussed everywhere, just as the study of its parts, such as teaching, curriculum, and learning, is a large intellectual enterprise. But rarely is the education revolution thought of as a founding force behind the historical transformation from traditional society to modernity and on to the postindustrial society. Instead, intellectual prominence is given to other major social forces shaping human society: industrial production, technology, science and medicine, capitalism, the rise of the nation-state and democratic politics, large-scale warfare, decline of religious authority, the culture of individualism, changes in the nature of the family, and the rise of rationalized bureaucracies. These, and not the spread of formal education throughout the world's population, have won the lion's share of study.

When mass education is considered as a major social force, it is frequently thought of as some sort of collective mistake, too much "unneeded" education resulting in educational credential inflation. From this perspective the education revolution is readily dismissed sociologically as a relatively trivial event or, worse, as troubling educational inflation that wastes peoples' time and energies. For example, in the late 1960s the notion of overeducation became a topic of intense concern—it was assumed that too many children were receiving too much education and would become frustrated and alienated when they could not find suitable jobs for their eventual education credential, while jobs requiring little skill would increasingly go to those with more education than needed. Economists, professional educators, sociologists, and other experts all proclaimed that the education revolution was a threatening and growing social problem.

Yet these negative consequences never came to pass. And as described later, there was no revolt against expanding education among the world's populations. Indeed, people from all cultural heritages and national governments of all stripes have embraced the idea of formal education as both a personal and a common good. Since the overeducation debate forty years ago, the presumed inflationary educational bubble has failed to burst; rather, the rise of a sturdy culture of education has changed ideas about society. Economies and society in general did not remain fixed as education expanded; instead, they themselves were changed by this phenomenon. As argued here, education and society have developed a unique cultural affinity with each other, a mutual and dynamic accommodation. Symbiosis, not inflation, is the best way to consider the effects of the education revolution. But symbiosis implies that education, as a social institution, is far more robust and sociologically independent than is usually assumed, a realization that gets lost in the persistent dialogue about education's supposed failure.

Hence is the interesting paradox about the usual image of schooling's role in society. On one hand, many powers are attributed to formal education—teaching children to read, to understand mathematics and science, to practice and enjoy the arts, to memorize the historical development of a nation, and now even to know about the development of human society across time and place—which are all routinely thought of as what schools do to transform children into functioning adults. These are indeed part of the bigger story here. On the other hand, schooling and university training are frequently portrayed as failing modern society in fundamental ways. It is this paradox that leaves the education revolution underappreciated.

Why does this paradox exist? First, most people do not recognize the full scope through which mass schooling transforms society. Formal education has become so common, so ubiquitous that it is often simply assumed to be a natural outcome of a complex, technological, global society. Also, many people, even professional educators and scholars of education, become overly fixated on specific aspects of the system at the exclusion of perceiving its formidable total impact—they lose the forest for the trees. And observers of education often do not consider the substantial qualitative ways schooling has changed over recent history, which serve to intensify the broad effects of education examined here. Lastly, and perhaps the most problematic, most intellectual accounts take a limited view of schools, colleges, and universities by seeing them as little more than "helping" institutions that only socialize and train (some say oppress) our children to join society.

Whether or not formal education should be even more effective at what it does is a major topic of debate, but it is a debate rarely informed by a full sociological accounting of the institution itself and its complete impact on society. Therefore calls for better education are of secondary concern here. The focus of this book is on the larger picture, regardless of supposed shortcomings and limitations: to what degree does this revolutionary practice of formally educating everyone in society change society itself? Contrary to the well-worn cries of failure, it can be argued that as a social institution, schooling—from kindergarten through the upper reaches of higher education—continues to be one of the major success stories of the times. It profoundly transforms who we are, what we can do, and what we believe to be true.

## THE UNDERAPPRECIATED EDUCATED MODERN INDIVIDUAL

What has all of this new education done *to* individuals? Education does many things *for* the individual, such as training, credentials, and social status, but how profoundly it changes a person is a crucial question for assessing the total impact of the education revolution. Because today even a high school dropout has received, historically speaking, an extensive education, it is hard to judge how much people are transformed by formal education. Most people today are so surrounded by the effects of education that it can appear as if there are no effects at all. But this is fundamentally not true.

Social scientists were on to part of the answer about fifty years ago as the education revolution was creating mass schooling in many nations for the first time. But unfortunately, the results of this research, and evidentially the question itself, were dropped, further eluding an appreciation of the education revolution in intellectual thought about the development of modern and postindustrial societies. The major consequence from this intellectual negligence is illustrated in a prominent investigation of what makes individuals modern; the study all but ignored exceptionally rich evidence for a broad societal consequence of many children attending school.

In the late 1960s, researchers at Harvard University collected extensive information about young men living in what were then six developing countries where, at this time, education and economic development were even lower than in most developing nations today. For the times, these cross-cultural data were innovative and rare; included were basic demographic information and a survey measuring the men's attitudes, values, and beliefs (Inkeles and Smith 1974). The data showed that in each nation a small minority of men exhibited, in addition to the functional skills of literacy and numeracy, distinctly modern attitudes and preferences, such as openness to new experience, independence from traditional authority, belief in the efficacy of science and modern medicine, abandonment of fatalism, interest in the rational planning of their lives, and strong interest in civic affairs and national and international events. These all characterize how education as an institution has transformed postindustrial society, which is described in the chapters to come.

When the data were analyzed to see which young men held modern attitudes, values, and beliefs, the researchers found that hands down, educational attainment was the best predictor of individual modernity. Exposure to formal education, even just primary schooling, was 50 percent more powerful as a predictor than the influence of working in what the researchers assumed to be the strongly transforming industrial job (versus farming) (Inkeles 1996). Yet in the researchers' discussion of the findings it is perplexing to read how they talk themselves out of their own results, retreating instead to a clear bias for the influence of industrialization over that of mass education. The fact that young men with more formal education were significantly more likely to embrace modernity was dismissed by the strange argument that since schooling had "full time control over the pupil's formal learning, [why] does it not perform [as an effect] a lot *better* than it does relative to the factory?" (Inkeles 1969, 139). So although the education effect is the largest one in these data, because it is not even larger, one should then ignore it? Further too, factory work is controlling over long hours, so that faithfully following where the findings lead, the implication is the exact opposite: Why does not industrialized work produce individual modernity to the same degree as mass education? But this question is never taken up, and the senior investigator for the project all but admits that they plan to marginalize the education effects, as he boldly states: "the slogan for our project became, 'The factory can be a school—a school for modernization.'" (139). Perhaps, but why ignore the obvious and stronger influence of real schools on psychological modernization?

*Becoming Modern*, the title of the study's main book, became a widely read classic in sociology, engendering much debate about the impact of industrialization from both the supportive technical-functionalist argument and from Marxian critique; but the overwhelming evidence for the education effect remained buried throughout. This investigation and others, based on some of the most scientifically sophisticated observations of the distinctly new world emerging at the middle of the last century, pushed aside, ignored, and underestimated the sweeping impacts of a worldwide education revolution.

The intent here is not to criticize just one book or a few sociologists—and to be fair, it should be noted that Alex Inkeles later acknowledged the causal importance of schooling for fostering modern attitudes (Inkeles 1974, 1996). The larger point is that in the midst of the rising schooled society worldwide, the mentality within sociology and related intellectual fields was to study the political and economic implications of postindustrial society instead of recognizing that the education revolution was also a significant and sociologically new part of this society. Even in the face of considerable empirical evidence that education was transforming society, the view of the emerging postindustrial society was described from the rearview mirror perspective of the structure of nineteenth-century Western society, well before education was to emerge as a mass institution. This was a particularly ironic oversight given that this generation of intellectuals missed a major transforming educational process occurring right under their noses in the expanding secondary schools from whence they had come and the increasingly vigorous and expanding universities where so many of them professed for a living. In many ways this mentality continues today. So with the results of nearly four decades of research on education and a new theoretical perspective, it is time to resurrect from the intellectual junk pile the prematurely discarded education revolution and hypothesize that it has had a significant independent influence on postindustrial society.

### ASSESSING A QUIET REVOLUTION

As already noted, the vast majority of scholarship on education and society assumes that education blindly follows changes in society, that it just prepares individuals for predetermined social roles, jobs, and experiences. This common view of education is as a secondary institution, a derivative of other institutions, that acts in support of other supposedly more dominant institutions such as the economy and the state. Developed here is an alternative argument: The education revolution has independently transformed postindustrial culture into a *schooled society*. The schooled society is a wholly new social order where dimensions of education reach into and define nearly every facet of human life; in short, education has become a central, primary institution. In a number of nations an advanced version of the schooled society is already fully evident, and throughout the rest of the world the same trend is occurring and the education revolution will likely intensify everywhere into the future.

In the late 1960s, as the prominent social theorist Talcott Parsons pointed out (in the epigraph), some intellectuals foreshadowed the idea of a schooled society as they observed the takeoff of mass higher education in developed nations, as well as the rise of "big science" and the "knowledge conglomerate" across the world's research universities. Mass education was predicted then to become a central institution in postindustrial society. And although some early speculations on the consequences of this change proved to be overblown (e.g., a fully rationalized, technological, narrow expert society), the overall idea was prophetic. Yet for the most part, the thesis that the education revolution was a leading force of advanced modernity was dropped over the ensuing decades in the rush to embrace a limited argument that education is merely the handmaiden of capitalist society or is the "natural" outcome of a technological society, and in either case has little independent sociological impact of its own. Now, though, there is enough empirical evidence to judge whether the education revolution deserves a place in the discourse about major independent events shaping human society. Research alone, however, is not sufficient to accomplish this task. Armed with an innovative theoretical perspective known as "neo-institutionalism," a new perspective on education and its role in society is possible.

The usual, or what will be referred to here as the "traditional," way people think about the role of formal education in society is that schooling chiefly plays a helping role in creating social and economic complexity; hence the notion of education as mostly a *reproducer* of society.[1] As shown in Figure I.1, the main arrow of influence runs from society to schooling: education only functions to train and credential people to "fit into society."

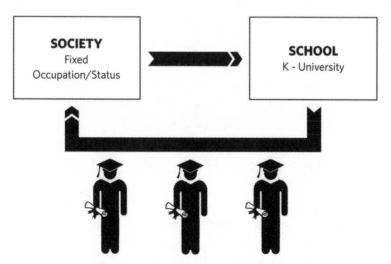

FIGURE I.1 *Traditional perspective on the relationship between education and society.*

Also it is assumed that social and economic positions allocated to adults on the basis of educational credentials are more or less fixed by the society at large, that is, by other social institutions, not education. In this picture, schooling serves the larger needs of society by educating people to take positions in society; hence schooling reproduces society in the next generation.

Among intellectuals the primary reason the traditional perspective remains so popular is because two major, albeit contrasting, arguments about the function of education in society rely on the assumption that education follows the contours of society. Human capital theory assumes that education mostly imparts work skills determined by the economy; while Marxist theory assumes that education mostly indoctrinates workers to the conditions of capitalist production and its social-class inequalities. But while there is no doubt that formal education involves training for the labor market and is increasingly the arena in which social status is determined, these theories minimize what education has become and overlook its full impact on society. If ones steps back from the traditional perspective and considers how common formal schooling through adulthood has become and how dominating a part of nearly everyone's life it is, a second and broader image of schooling emerges.

In contrast, neo-institutional theory hypothesizes that education has grown to such proportions that it has become a separate and enduring social institution; thus the education revolution *socially constructs* significant portions of the culture of modern society, rather than merely reproducing it. Not only are people trained and credentialed through schooling, but the institution itself changes other social institutions and the entire culture of society. As shown in Figure I.2, in what will be referred to here as the "schooled society" perspective, the main arrow of influence flows from education to society, and carries along with it a host of new ideas and new human capabilities, as well as changing and expanding social and economic positions.

Neo-institutional theory does not assume that the people who populate education, from students to teachers to administrators, explicitly intend to create all of this social change. Just as with the transformational influence of intensifying, large-scale capitalism on economies, or the influence of representative democracy on polities, education as an institution pri-

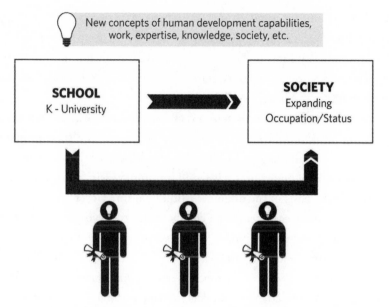

FIGURE I.2 *Schooled society (neo-institutional) perspective on the relationship between education and society.*

marily focuses on the matter within its own institutional domain, namely, education (Luhmann 2013). But with the education revolution, this relatively new anthropological activity of formally educating the majority of a population has major ripple effects on important aspects of society. In the parlance of neo-institutionalism, the real essence of the education revolution is that formal education has steadily become more *institutionalized*, creating the condition by which it has considerable influence on the social construction of society.

Much sociological theory rests on the notion of an institution accompanied by the process of institutionalization.[2] Institutions are the building blocks of human society at any time or place. Animated through individuals, a social institution is conceptual and cognitive, not physical (although it has many physical consequences); it is powerful in its control of human behavior through the production of shared meaning in all realms of human existence (e.g., Berger and Luckmann 1966). In a sense, institutions are clusters of cultural meaning and values concerning how to think, feel, emote, and act in the everyday world. Individuals and collectives, whether formal organizations or informal groups of humans, experience reality through their cultural meanings (e.g., DiMaggio 1997). From this perspective, education is an institution in the same way modern medicine and the family are social institutions: sets of cognitive maps for how to behave, feel, and think in particular sectors of life.

As a theory, neo-institutionalism is essentially a new way to look at the older concept of social institution by placing far greater theoretical emphasis on institutions' production of widely shared cultural meanings instead of as only consisting of highly prescribed and structured social roles and norms, which was the basis of the original institutionalism (Meyer and Jepperson 2000).[3] Institutions construct and channel culture as everyday knowledge made up of conceptions or models of the everyday world, also referred to as scripts, scenarios, and schemata, which people use to form a collective sense of reality (Eslinger 1998). As the fundamental product of institutions, culture is made up of these cognitive models by which people derive meaningful action, motivations, and emotions (Meyer and Jepperson 2000). From neo-institutional theory the very essence of social change is institutional change: greater or lesser institutionalization of a particular set of cultural meanings equals greater or lesser impact on perceived reality (e.g., Berger, Berger, and Kellner 1974). And, as has occurred over the course of the education revolution so far, the process of greater institutionalization means simply an intensification of the meaning of actions, motivations, and emotions around a particular sector of life by a particular institution.

To recognize formal education as a primary institution is like focusing and refocusing on the blended images of an Escher drawing, where birds turn into fish in contrasting relief. What at first appears as a common image contains a surprising counterimage that is revealed only through a new perspective. The trick to appreciating the schooled society model of education's societal role is not to think of schooling's impact as limited to its immediate influence on individuals, but to refocus on how the institution of education constructs influential ideas, social statuses, and new human capacities, and then on how these become a significant reality in postindustrial society.

Institutions can differ in their impact on cultural meaning over time and place, and several important geohistorical trends behind the origin of the education revolution are explored in later chapters. Yet even though formal education organizations may adapt differently from nation to nation, or even from region to region within nations, at a deeper level the global expression of education is strongly affixed to the same everyday ideas about what the institution is, and how it should operate. So as the process of institutionalization advances, though individual schools and universities are influenced by their local, regional, and national context, the basic ideas behind schooling are now defined in the same way globally and have been intensifying in a common direction over recent history (Baker and LeTendre 2005). Consequently, the organizations of national school systems are now also influenced by supranational forces that are beyond the control of national policy-makers, politicians, and educators. This is not to say that some world governing body, or even a powerful multinational agency, overtly forces nations to think and act similarly when it comes to schooling; rather, that the globalized institutionalization process is more encompassing. Education as a primary, culture-constructing institution joins just a few other similarly robust institutions responsible for producing worldwide society through a set of "legitimating ideas [that] are often much more than values and norms resting in sentiments: they are accounts of how the reified parts of the social world fit together and function and have a cognitive status" (Meyer 1981: 897).

Indeed, this is exactly the advantage of the neo-institutional theory as a way to think about how education as an institution constructs society. From legitimating ideas and meanings occurring within schools and universities and in the everyday actions of students, teachers, professors, scholars, administrators, and policy-makers, widespread cultural understandings flow out to other institutions, particularly now that just about everyone in fully schooled societies is heavily exposed to these similar understandings. The education revolution has resulted in an acceptance of an amazingly rich and far-reaching set of ideas that, beyond just educating individuals, shape the culture of society. All of this has come about in a soft, almost imperceptible, taken-for-granted way, which when examined with the right focus shows the institution of education in postindustrial society to be a dominating force.

## EXAMINING THE DIMENSION AND ORIGIN
## OF THE EDUCATION REVOLUTION

The five following chapters comprise the first part of the book, examining the symbiotic demographic and cultural forces of the education revolution and their origins. Chapter 1 chronicles the degree to which formal education engulfs the time and energies of individuals and full populations alike; plus it considers how this change has come about over a remarkably short historical time. This chapter also introduces the notion of the institution's cultural impact by describing some of the core ideas that the institution of education promotes: universalism of educational merit; educational development of individuals as a collective good; academic achievement as supreme achievement; belief in academically derived knowledge; and cognition as master human capability. Chapter 2 then considers how these components combine to form powerful cultural assumptions that are at the heart of the schooled society and that help to explain its wider impact. Three examples of widely held assumptions are examined: one, that what can be called "academic intelligence" is the superior human capability; two, that formal education is a human right; and last, that formal education is the most legitimate and socially just way to organize social mobility and differential occupational positions in postindustrial society.

A significant amount of research initially investigated the education revolution through analysis of growing primary and secondary school enrollments over the past century and a half (e.g., Fuller and Rubinson 1992). While being an obvious and productive approach, the impression remains that the education revolution came out of midair with few cultural ties to prior developments, thus trivializing to a degree the study of the independent influence of an expanding education sector on society. Recent scholarship suggests, however, that the origins of the education revolution were shaped over the long historical development of the Western university. Therefore, based on this research, the last three chapters of this part place the university, with its extraordinary institutional charters, at the center of the creation and deepening of the culture of education within the schooled society. This argument and its causal agent give the education revolution a clear social history, a feature lacking in earlier accounts of the origins of the phenomenon.

The argument across Chapters 3–5 focuses on the long historical development of the university's complex charter to produce knowledge, create associated degrees, and then train and certify individuals in the control, further production, and use of this knowledge across society. In this way *the university becomes a central cultural institution of modern society* out of which many of the cultural values of the education revolution were hatched, legitimated, and disseminated. Further, it will be shown that these functions interact with one another in a dynamic fashion, supercharging the primacy of universalized knowledge and academic degrees awarded in mass numbers, thus producing a self-reinforcing dynamic. The result of this dynamic charter is the creation of reigning meanings in society, reinforced by the now legions of university-trained and degree-certified experts who make up so much of contemporary society, and who in turn perpetuate the legitimacy of university-generated knowledge. Also it will be argued that the expensive knowledge conglomerate found in a growing set of super-research universities worldwide is neither a fluke of history nor some rare event. Instead, it comes right out of the success of the schooled society with its wide belief in education. It is a predicable outcome of the trends of the education revolution, whose ideas were initiated during the rise of the Western university centuries ago.

## SOCIETAL CONSEQUENCES
## OF THE EDUCATION REVOLUTION

If this account of the education revolution's origins and its ability to make new culture is of theoretical value, there should be evidence of significant influence of the education culture on other major social institutions in contemporary society. The six chapters of the second part of the book explore this thesis for selected institutions. Until John Meyer's (1977) reframing of the essential relationship between education and society along these lines, few considered this prediction. And since the traditional perspective has been, and still is, the most popular one among intellectuals, exploring the effects of education on other institutions has not been an explicit research agenda. So these chapters explore uncharted territory. While there is some useful research deriving explicitly from the schooled society perspective, one has to rely on marshalling relevant evidence from other research agendas, even though these are often theoretically ambiguous or agnostic in their assumptions about the relationship between education and postindustrial society. One also has to confront the residue of decades of traditional theorizing about education and society; many myths, half-truths, and overlooked paradoxes have worked their way into a number of otherwise useful research literatures and need to be weeded out. For each chapter's selected social institution, then, in addition to examining how the education revolution has changed the institution, the discussion critiques past theory and research and mixes in new interpretations of existing empirical findings. A fuller test of the educational transformation of social institutions awaits, but each chapter provides a beginning. While there are many possible institutions to examine, the most challenging to the argument are major social institutions that have in their own right considerable "institutional power" within the culture.[4]

At the core of the traditional perspective on education is that the economy, as an institution, significantly dictates the form and nature of formal education. So to begin, the first two chapters of this part turn this well-worn argument around and describe the educational transformation of work in advanced capitalist economies, including the structuring of jobs, occupational credentials, and profitable skills. Chapter 6 attempts to put to rest the twin ideas that education either merely follows the demands of jobs or is an out-of-control process expanding education into a pandemic of overeducation. Then, exploring a considerable amount of recent research on labor economics, firms and organizations, and neo-institutional analyses of education, this chapter finds that the education revolution is changing the qualities, the ideas, and expectations about work, workers, and workplaces; this is seen in rising cognitive complexity of jobs, managerial requirements, and professionalization, particularly in the growing sector of employment within large organizations.

Just as the education revolution transforms work, it transforms the nature of the connection between educational degrees and occupational placement. While education has been tied to access to occupations for some time, the pace of educational expansion and its cultural impact have vastly increased the strength and salience of the connection. Chapter 7 examines first how the growing intensity of the schooled society increases the phenomenon of educational credentialing for occupations and deepens the meaning and value of educational degrees in the economy. The dominance of educational credentialing for occupations is a central consequence of the education revolution, both in terms of the educational requirements themselves and in supporting a pervasive logic by which educational credentialing becomes evermore legitimate, pushing aside older, non-educational forms of credentialing. An integration of multiple sets of new findings about education, occupations, and work shows that the common negative notion of runaway educational credentialism, or degree inflation, does not fit empirical trends in the schooled society. Second, as a function of widely held beliefs about education in postindustrial society, the chapter describes and illustrates, with empirical observations and analyses, four institutional processes by which educational credentialing continues to be deeply integrated into the occupational structure.

Chapter 8 puts forth the argument that the knowledge society is fundamentally predicated on the schooled society. This chapter examines how the education revolution has changed the nature of knowledge, and truth claims by which new knowledge is validated, and in turn exponentially increases the worldwide production of authoritative knowledge. This foundation for the knowledge society, spread throughout populations by schooling from the earliest years into adulthood, consists of the growth and intensity of science, rationalized inquiry, theory, and empirical methods, all influenced and reinforced by an overarching cognitization of academic intelligence considered to apply to all humans in all of their endeavors. The educationally produced culture of cognition, scientization, and universal nature of knowledge have also led to the death of long-celebrated classicism as well as the old assumed need for vocationalism as guiding principles of formal education before the maturing of the education revolution.

Economies and knowledge production are obvious choices to explore the impact of the education revolution, but to demonstrate its institutional reach, three final chapters examine areas of life not often considered heavily influenced by education. Chapter 9 examines the impact of the education revolution on the self through its construction of personal and public identities of success and failure, as illustrated through the much noted and discussed mass phenomenon of the school dropout (and now the college dropout) and the growing use of an educational process (i.e., the GED) as a way back into the schooled society. The school dropout phenomenon is neither trivial nor media-created; it demonstrates the depths to which the education culture extends to individuals' self-image in the schooled society.

Since democracy and civil society are often acknowledged as an institutional pillar of postindustrial society, Chapter 10 explores the role of education in generating mass democracy and its current chaotic political environment. Using recent neo-institutional research, this chapter shows that many of the paradoxes about modern politics in the United States, such as the decline of old party politics, older forms of nationalism, technocratic issue politics, and the alienation of some citizens, are actually the result of expanding higher education and the pervasive culture of the schooled society. It is also argued that the education revolution is responsible for a different, vibrant global civic culture that generates a globalized polity among youth in many nations as overt nationalism recedes among the newly educated.

The last chapter on consequences, Chapter 11, examines how education increases a thriving culture of mass religion worldwide. These are two institutions widely considered to be antithetical to one another. The culture of education has transformed belief and organized religion in ways not predicted just half a century ago. Many social theorists assumed that mass education would make for a more secular, even irreligious, society. But religion continues to flourish. On the basis of new research on education and religion at the individual, congregational, and cultural levels, the chapter argues that while the education revolution has challenged religious authority, it can at times be very symbiotic to organized religion and individual spirituality. Mass education transforms, and even intensifies, religion in its own image more than it causes religion to decline.

In light of all the presented evidence, the Conclusion returns to the main issues addressed above. It assesses how much the idea of a schooled society can explain the phenomena of the education revolution, and their consequences. The conclusion is that this heretofore intellectually quiet revolution should be placed on the short list of prominent transforming causes of postindustrial society. In failing to consider the consequences of a pervasive culture of education, many social phenomena are misinterpreted. The discussion ends by considering the future of the schooled society and briefly speculating on negative and positive influences of the education revolution.

# PART I

# Dimensions and Origin of the Schooled Society

# From Education Revolution
# to the Schooled Society

My parents told me to keep coming to school even if I am killed. The people who did
this to me don't want women to be educated. They want us to be stupid things.

SHAMSIA HUSSEINI, seventeen, who returned to school in Afghanistan despite

being disfigured in an acid attack to keep her from attending;

*New York Times*, August 17, 2009

GOING TO SCHOOL and attending for a considerable number of years
is demographically a relatively new and massive change in the behavior of
children and youth. Driving this change is the central belief that schooling
should be for all people. Over the course of the education revolution this
belief, as reflected in the courage of Shamsia Husseini to attend school,
takes on increased meaning and wields a growing impact on an individual's future, as it supports significant growth in the participation in formal
education in all parts of the world.

In premodern society, before the profound changes of industrialization, urbanization, and political national consolidation that intensified in
the nineteenth century, there was no widespread mass education. Formal
education, particularly beyond just a few years of basic literacy training, was reserved for a small proportion of the population. But once the
schooling of larger numbers of children and youth began, about 150 years
ago, the phenomenon grew rapidly worldwide. While the exact political
and cultural histories of the adoption of mass schooling vary across regions and nations, the basic temporal pattern of the worldwide education
revolution is similar.

Over a few generations, the education revolution proceeded through a
stepwise pattern, first of access to primary schooling, then by the opening
up of secondary schooling, and lastly in the expansion of tertiary education. Advanced sectors of education have been spurred on by the growth
of the previous sector during an earlier generation. This progression began

in wealthier nations and since the middle of the twentieth century spread globally with less and less time between each stage of educational development as educational attainment in more nations converged (e.g., Benavot and Riddle 1988; Fuller and Rubinson 1992; Dorius 2013). Notably, too, while opening access to each new level of schooling began slowly, once begun, expansion proceeded rapidly. As worldwide enrollment in levels of schooling illustrates (Figure 1.1), throughout the nineteenth century and over the first decades of the twentieth, enrollment in primary education levels expanded, but by 1940 enrollment burst into a logarithmic climb. Twenty years later, as primary schooling reached large numbers of children, enrollment in secondary schooling turned sharply up in the 1960s. And in the early 1970s enrollment in higher education began a similar ascent. Today, in many developed nations, 70 percent of individuals have obtained at least an upper secondary education degree, and a third of 25–34-year-olds have participated in higher education (OECD, 2009a). The most recent wave of the education revolution is the expansion of higher education at both the undergraduate and graduate levels. At the turn of

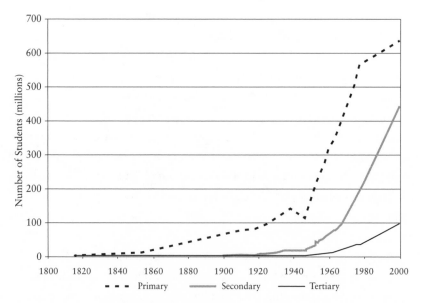

FIGURE 1.1 *Number of students in primary, secondary, and higher education worldwide.*

Source: Reprinted from Schofer and Meyer (2005). Used by permission.

the nineteenth century less than 1 percent of university-aged youth across the world attended; now 20 percent, or approximately 100 million, attend some kind of higher education setting, and the awarding of graduate degrees continues to increase in many nations (Schofer and Meyer 2005).

This rapid increase in enrollment is not just a function of population growth. What education demographers call "gross enrollment rates"—the percentage of school-aged children and youth attending schooling—have grown steadily over this time period, and only the most extreme social or political events have retarded growth at certain times in some nations (e.g., Baker, Köhler, and Stock 2007). Similarly, the average length of individuals' school attainment continues to rise worldwide. In wealthy and middle-income nations average educational attainment across the entire population is now slightly over twelve years of schooling; and tellingly, a large group of lower-middle- and low-income nations have expected attainment of over nine years (UNESCO 2001). The multilateral campaign to bring basic schooling to all children worldwide continues on with some major challenges to full implementation, but with wide political support nevertheless (Lewin 2009). As shown in the world map of average length of school careers, in Figure 1.2, the world is rapidly becoming a schooled society.[1]

The education revolution did not happen overnight, but it did unfold at striking speed compared with how long most human institutions take to develop. It is a revolution that began with younger children in the middle of the nineteenth century in the nations of Western and Northern Europe and their wealthier former colonies, so that by the last two decades of the nineteenth century, nations in Western Europe and Australia, Canada, and the United States were enrolling 50–70 percent of children aged five to fourteen (Benavot and Riddle 1988). And although older forms of education, centered on the religious indoctrination of children of elite castes, had been established in Asia, North Africa, and in Mayan, Aztec, and Incan societies well before the nineteenth century, as each of these regions was touched by Western nations, through peaceful contact and forcible colonization alike, their earlier indigenous systems of education gave way to mass Westernized education (Craig 1981).

The overarching idea propelling this sea change in people's attitude and behavior towards formal education is that schooling is useful, appropriate,

**School life expectancy in years**

No data available | <5 | 5 to <7 | 7 to <9 | 9 to <11 | 11+

FIGURE 1.2 *How long can children expect to stay in school? Average school life expectancy, in years, for primary to secondary education, by country, 2001.*

Source: UNESCO Institute of Statistics (2004). © UNESCO Institute of Statistics. Used by permission. http//www.unesco.org/education/docs/EN_GD2oo4_v2.pdf

and valuable enough to require all children to attend. Ideas about education create the belief that it is good that one's own children are schooled, as well as everyone else's children. In particular, how the education revolution unfolded in the United States illustrates the speed at which these cultural beliefs can saturate a nation with education.

## THE AMERICAN EDUCATION REVOLUTION

The United States has largely led the way in developing mass education. At the beginning of the twentieth century, about one half of all school-aged children were enrolled, and within the next forty years that proportion rose to 75 percent; over the next twenty years it rose to almost 90 percent (U.S. Department of Education, NCES 1993). Today, of course, mass schooling is so ubiquitous that looking back on schooling early in the twentieth century, one can easily criticize it for having reached only a portion of school-aged children. Yet this early wave of enrollment was actually at the vanguard of a radically new way to raise children and help youth into adulthood, which rapidly caught on. For a society to grow schooling by 50 percent in just forty years and then reach almost full enrollment two decades later is an astonishing feat reflecting widespread acceptance of the notion of schooling for all children.[2]

The way mass schooling grew in America illustrates the mechanics of the expansion of schooling children across generations. As each sector of schooling grew, its success propelled the development and subsequent expansion of the next sector. As each new generation of parents attained more education, their "demand" for even more education for their children intensified, and the "supply" of opportunities for more education moved along with that demand. In the final decades of the nineteenth century and early decades of the twentieth, the United States rapidly built a public primary system, so that by the beginning of the Second World War attaining schooling through the eighth grade became the average among American adults; just thirty years later the average had advanced to the completion of high school (U.S. Department of Education, NCES 1993). As the primary system graduated larger and larger proportions of children, a public secondary system was built, and as that system graduated larger proportions of youth, enrollment in higher education began to climb. Therefore the average amount of schooling of each successive generation of Americans substantially exceeded that of the preceding generation.

For example, just before the Second World War, of ten American adults over the age of twenty-five who were representative of their era, one of them would have attended little or no schooling, five of them would have attended just primary education, three would have attended just high school, and one would have attended higher education (and only one out of two of these people would have attained the baccalaureate or a graduate degree). Thirty years later, as most of the middle of the baby-boom generation passed through high school and as older adults with lower levels of schooling died, less than one American adult out of ten had attended little or no schooling, two would have attended just primary schooling, five would have attended just high school, and two would have attended higher education, one of these having earned the baccalaureate or higher. In another thirty years, at the beginning of the twenty-first century, the education levels of ten representative American adults would look strikingly different from either of the earlier groups: all of them would have attended primary schooling, only one would not have moved on to high school, four would have only completed high school, and five would have attended higher education, of which two would hold the baccalaureate or higher. As a consequence, a number of major American cities, such as Seattle, San Francisco, and Washington, are now places where one half of all residents have the BA or higher. Enrollment in higher education is at an all-time high (20.6 million students in 2010) and is expected to increase 14 percent by 2019 (Hussar and Bailey 2011).

Perhaps nothing is as telling of the power of the sweeping force that drove America to be a schooled society as the rate at which schooling was developed for the most disadvantaged children at various times. For example, slavery, Jim Crow segregation laws, and other oppressive measures by the dominant white society kept enrollment rates among African American children considerably lower than native-born whites throughout the nineteenth century and into the twentieth. But even within this environment of formal and informal racism, African American enrollment began to grow at a rate similar to that of white students from 1910 onwards (U.S. Department of Education, NCES 1993). And the hard-won battles of the civil rights struggle, which not surprisingly were in large part focused on achieving equal educational opportunities, added considerably to the growth in schooling for African Americans after the middle of the century (e.g., Rury and Hill 2011). The educational consequences have been stunning: within one generation the average African American, completing only some primary schooling, would most likely see her child finishing high school (10–70% increase in high school completion from 1940 to 1970), and just like whites, her grandchildren's likelihood of enrolling in higher education has continued to rise.

A similar story is true for the children of immigrants from Southern, Central, and Eastern Europe who poured into America from 1880 onward. At first their rates of schooling were very low; for instance, school attendance among Italian American children was lower than the rate among African Americans living in northern cities in the early part of the twentieth century (Lieberson 1980). Many of these groups also struggled with poverty and bigotry, which limited educational opportunity. But just as with African American children, in a relatively short time their enrollment rates began to look like native-born white children's. This growth was in large part due to the ability of these mostly Catholic families and the American Catholic Church to build a parallel, large-scale system of schools. In almost all ways American Catholic schooling developed just like the public system, and the logic to supply schooling to all children was foremost in its intentions (Baker 1999). What is particularly noteworthy about schooling for these two historically disadvantaged groups is that even through all of the poverty and oppression and struggles (and because of them in some cases), a version of the education revolution happened for these groups.

Not only has the idea that all children should be formally educated meant the incorporation of children and youth into schools; it also represents a massive societal commitment to, and investment in, what happens during school. In the case of the United States, the sheer growth in the nation's population has meant the development and funding of a currently huge system of schools. The public system of primary and secondary schooling grew about 600 percent over about a century and a half, from 7.6 million students just after the Civil War to 48.8 million students in the school year 2004–2005 (U.S. Department of Education, NCES 2006). And this has been accompanied by a growing intensity of schooling; for example, the length of the American school year grew from about six and a half months just before the beginning of the twentieth century to the current nine months of schooling, representing an increase of over a third in instruction time (U.S. Department of Education, NCES 1993). Also, as the average student/teacher ratio declines, one can assume that the resources and intensity of education are increasing, and this ratio has fallen steadily from the end of the nineteenth century, so that by 2007 nationwide there were an estimated 15.4 public school pupils per teacher (U.S. Department of Education, NCES 2008). In constant dollars, the average total expenditure on a public school student grew from only $355 in 1919 to an average of $9,518 for every student in fiscal year 2004 (U.S Department of Education, NCES 2006).

The education revolution has also expanded the notion of who can and should go to school and the idea that formal education is appropriate for all ages. For example, a full third of all students in higher education are twenty-five years or older, and a recent assessment of adult education in the United States finds that 40 percent of adults in the nation participated in some formal education for work or, notably, for reasons of personal growth (Hussar and Bailey 2011; U.S. Department of Education, NCES 2003). Lastly, as will be described later, the expansion of higher education continues in American two-year institutions, four-year institutions for the BA, and now in graduate schools, in proportions never before seen.

While rates of educational expansion can vary some, and poverty and political turmoil can slow the process, inevitably the education revolution unfolds worldwide. Beginning later in history in other regions than in North America and Western Europe, the education revolution is also occurring in Eurasia, Africa, the Middle East, Latin America, and Southeast Asia. The demography of education has been apparent for some time; what has not is how much this is a new cultural construction in human society. A description of the deeper dimension of this cultural transformation illustrates this.

## THE CULTURE OF THE SCHOOLED SOCIETY

Culture is essential to the construction of the social world, but its actual components can be hard to pin down and describe. Robert Fiala, a neo-institutional sociologist, had an ingenious idea for how to get at the widely believed ideas behind the education revolution by examining archives of national documents (prepared for international agencies) describing the aims of national education systems. He and a colleague first investigated changes in the stated national aims of education from 1955 to 1965 (Fiala and Lansford 1987); recently, Fiala has updated the sample to include changes from 1985 to 2000 (2006). There are some telling developments, from the early phase of the education revolution, when many wealthy nations were just starting to expand secondary education to wide parts of the youth population, to the present, in which formal education has spread worldwide.

There are three notable changes from 1955–65 to 1980–2000 in the educational aims of countries, reflecting historical intensification of the core values that are building the schooled society. First, most nations today openly claim the personal, emotional, and cognitive development of the individual as a main, multidimensional aim of education systems. While individual development was an aim in the earlier periods, its continued elaboration to include multiple facets of the individual is a clear indication of the intensification of mass education. Second, there has been a shift away from both elite education for the few and vocational development for the academically less able; these were still aims in the early period of the education revolution but gave way to newer and broader notions of general employability, development, and higher levels of mathematics, science, and language knowledge for all students. Lastly, educational aims around equality and democracy for all political, ethnic, religious, and social collectives have significantly intensified in most nations across the time periods (see also Dreeben 1968).

The aims described by Fiala foreshadow deeper global cultural dimensions of the schooled society, or what is sociologically referred to as education's *institutional values*. If the education revolution has become a transforming social institution beyond its role in educating individuals, these values should be obvious, widely potent in their influence beyond education, and considered highly legitimate. While there is still some debate over exactly how many institutional values are at the core of the global culture of education, four values capture most of the scholarly discussions so far and will reappear frequently in the descriptions of the broader consequences of the schooled society in later chapters. As is the case with all institutional values, these four are abstract and somewhat removed from the usual images of education and society.

*Education as a human right* is a value deeply embedded in the culture of the schooled society. Obvious today, this idea is a central product of the historical course of the education revolution. As a human right, education takes on broader and more salient meaning well beyond just skill training to encompass the mandate that schooling is essential for full development of the individual. This value also lends extensive credibility to the logic of education for all children at the heart of mass education. And this value is applied to the rationale of expansion for each new level of education. Once education is valued as a human right, to deny it, or even to externally limit it, is deeply troubling.

*Universalism of educational merit* equates equality of educational opportunity with social justice. Inculcated in mass education up through higher education, the idea of equality of educational opportunity leads to a relatively new dimension of social justice based on access to "opportunity to achieve," often centered on educational opportunity (Kett 2013). From the rise of "student" as a modern status that all are entitled to and must conform to comes the idea that all people are educable (Meyer 1977). In its attempts to educate all, mass schooling, at least formally, ignores noneducational social statuses of individuals, such as gender, ethnicity, religion, family wealth, clans, and so forth. What were once highly legitimate identities lose authority within the institution of schooling, particularly as they might be used to limit access to opportunity for the future development of the person (e.g., Ramirez, Suárez, and Meyer 2006). In other words, when these non-educational qualities are linked to opportunities, it is now increasingly construed as an insidious form of social injustice. As the institution of education becomes the main arbitrator of access to opportunity, it is easy to make the extension to the norm that educational performance can, and should, act as primary access to occupational opportunity and general adult status. While a culture of pure educational merit–that is, school achievement and the earning of academic degrees without any influence of non-educational social factors—is never fully realized, it is assumed to occur to a substantial degree and hence is widely believed to exist and to be socially just (Bills 2004).

*Development of modern individuals as a collective good* is a core educational value closely aligning human development with societal development into one symbiotic process new to human society. It stems from, and in turn reinforces, the modern notion of the individual as the basic social unit of society (Meyer and Jepperson 2000). Not only is everyone educable, but an educated population as an aggregation of schooled individuals is widely assumed to be essential for the collective economic and social good of society. Versions of this core value range from the imagery of human capital theory, where education is rationalized personal investment, to political development theory, where education is citizenship formation (e.g., Wiseman, Astiz, Fabrega, and Baker 2011). Thus earlier ideas about manpower planning and differential educational opportunities are replaced by the value of general development of all individuals through common and comprehensive academic experiences (Baker and Lenhardt 2008; Baker, Köhler, and Stock 2007). Surpassing traditional institutions of socialization such as the family, formal education comes to be seen as the essential institution by which individuals are developed as humans, and as such are defined as able to make the greatest contribution to the common good. Therefore, with greater institutionalization of this idea, education becomes generalized beyond notions of vocational training as tightly linked to occupational skills, and instead emerges as the proper and most effective arena for the development of the individual, with accompanying repercussions for all aspects of the person and society (e.g., Meyer 1977). Educational outcomes have thus come to objectify and codify progress towards human development and actualization. In postindustrial society, social stratification, including selection to the elite, is certainly still a central mission of schooling, but the larger logic behind schooling itself is to educate all for a wide host of assumed benefits to all. This idea, hatched and intensified over the course of the development of the university, is the main idea sustaining the supply of ever more formal education by citizens, nation-states, and multilateral agencies worldwide.

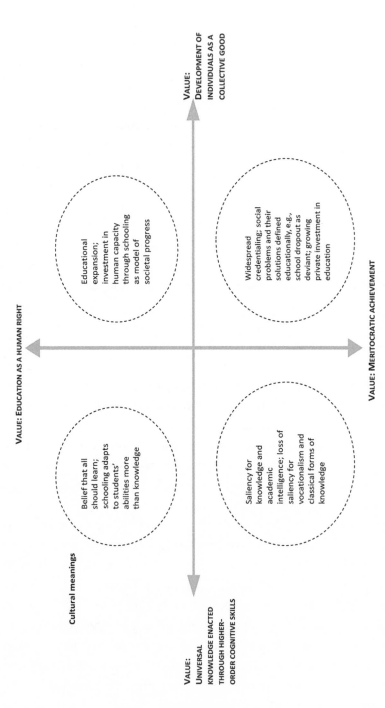

FIGURE 1.3 *Examples of synergistic cultural meaning from core values of education as an institution.*

*Universal knowledge enacted through higher-order cognitive skills* extends well beyond requirements for school advancement; the education revolution equates academic skill with general cognitive skill and privileges it as the master human capability creating high value on cognitive performance. At the same time, know-how from non-educational sources becomes less legitimate. The value in universal knowledge stems from the institutional dominance of the university as the arbitrator and producer of valued knowledge and the chartering of degrees connected to this knowledge (Meyer 1977; Meyer, Ramirez, Frank, and Schofer 2007; Collins 1979). Institutionalized educational authority, expressed through a hierarchy of academic degrees, constructs categories of educated experts entitled to apply specialized, academically derived knowledge. An educational credential is required not only to perform many occupations; it becomes in the schooled society the singular legitimating symbol of capability to perform itself. Formal education controls the entitlement to enact authoritative knowledge, such as what it takes to remove a tumor, teach a student, design a building, or forecast an economy. Socially constructed through earned degrees, educationally gained knowledge is increasingly valued as synonymous with the potential for occupational performance; this results from a tightening of the connection between educational degrees and acknowledged expertise. At the same time, official school curricula all over the world have converged towards a similar academic model over the past century; requirements for advanced cognitive skill are infused throughout, and those who master these curricula are defined as "smart and accomplished" even before any posteducational achievements (e.g., Benavot, Cha, Kamens, Meyer, and Wong 1991; Schaub 2010). Educational performance becomes synonymous then with the individual's cognitive ability, which is viewed as generalized ability that is assumed to be crucial for posteducational life.

As these institutional values about education have intensified over the past 150 years, they have dynamically combined into elaborate cultural meanings that shape the common understandings, aims, goals, and even the organization of schooling from kindergarten through advanced graduate training. Figure 1.3 illustrates some of these cross-products. For example, the core values of *education as a human right* and *development of modern individuals as a collective good* combine to generate irrepressible educational expansion as educational investment becomes the main societal logic for creating social progress. Just when one stage of educational expansion becomes saturated and many think it is all that is possible, another cycle of expansion begins.

Another example of institutional values producing major attributes of the culture of education is at the intersection of *universal knowledge enacted through higher-order cognitive skills* and *universalism of educational merit*. A robust notion of what can be called "academic intelligence" supports (see next chapter) the practice of young primary school students doing sophisticated thinking exercises for ever greater amounts of time, and more of the curricula at all levels of schooling demanding active learning and student-as-scholar behaviors. As explored in Chapter 8, the teaching of cognitive skills, particularly related to what can be grouped together as higher-order skills, has been on the rise historically. This intersection of values not only changes what fundamentally occurs within classrooms and seminars, but there is much evidence that it changes many other institutions as well.

A final example is how the intersection between the core values of *universalism of educational merit* and *development of modern individuals as a collective good* generates—along with widespread use of credentials and social status defined educationally—unprecedented amounts of private investment in education as seen in a rising culture of "academic achievement at any cost" and the intensification of consumers' attention to school and university quality. This cultural product is clearly at work in the power that schooling has on changing notions of good parenting and the well-adjusted child (Schaub 2010). Also, as will be argued, this imagery provides a high degree of universality to educational degrees, as well as supplying the logic by which traditional (i.e., non-educational) forms of social status become taboo because they are considered socially unjust, in turn largely because educationally determined status is seen as offering a legitimate social hierarchy.

While these values and their cross-products are abstract, the meanings they hatch work themselves into observable, everyday, yet powerful qualities of education. Three of these are examined in the next chapter.

## FROM THE LAST EDUCATED FEUDAL
## TO THE EDUCATED EVERYONE

The full cultural and demographic impact of the education revolution is hard to appreciate because of the common assumption that education does not change much in its content, intentions, and goals; it just expands. While it is obvious that there is more education now for more people, the deeper, subtle changes in the very nature of education are less known. And when changes are evident, the rush to make moral judgments, usually of the nature that "older forms of education" are superior, hinders a clear understanding of the changes themselves. The usual view of the long history of Western formal education is one of a strong connection from early classical Greek education. And it is true that large, successful civilizations of the past had a version of formal education and held ideals about the educated person. Given this, it is often assumed that modern schooling is (or should be) a natural extension of these ancient forms. Yet except in a few small ways, it is mostly not. Although the education revolution's origin can be found in the development of the medieval Western university, the cultural ideas and practices hatched in this unique institution have led to many subsequent changes in education at all stages. Because these influences are now so ubiquitous, a little historical context is useful.

The idea of a continuum of formal education from antiquity to the modern period is mostly a myth maintained by classical-leaning educators. Instead, starting in the early decades of the nineteenth century, a radical set of ideas about formal education—forerunners of the cultural values just described—qualitatively changed everything, and a distinctly different kind of education was born. The difference is made a little clearer by a comparison to what it meant to be educated in earlier eras before the education revolution. Consider education in the late Roman Empire. The historian of late antiquity Peter Brown aptly describes the classical education of the fourth-century C.E. Catholic philosopher (and future saint) Augustine of Hippo as aimed at producing an orator who could wield an argument with verve and with pleasure to his audience. Technical skills, problem solving, analytic strategies, and all the common ideals of education in the schooled society were not part of the classically educated person. A uniform way of communicating in a learned fashion, and not the attainment of degrees, established who counted in society, so that even some four hundred miles across the Mediterranean Sea from Rome in the hinterlands of North Africa someone educated like Augustine could

Maneuver, with infinite precision, in the cramped but supremely well-charted environment of an age-old tradition. Such a man could communicate his message to an educated Latin at the other end of the Roman world, merely by mentioning a classical figure, by quoting half a line of classic poetry. (Brown 2000, 24)

The educational goal was to train a relatively small number of individuals who could communicate in a "rigidly-defined traditional standard of perfection." And those few that received this schooling became a successful caste unto themselves by serving the empire, much like similarly classically educated mandarins of imperial China (Marrou 1956). This traditional approach lasted well into the second millennium (Suen and Yu 2006).

To put the schooled society's ideology in further historical perspective, consider the example of the education of the early-sixteenth-century Briton Sir Thomas More. Dubbed a "man for all seasons," More rose from an elite, yet minor aristocratic family to the very pinnacle of the kingdom as King Henry VIII's lord chancellor (a kind of chief of staff, attorney general, and secretary of state all rolled into one), in large part because of the skills he had developed through formal education at a school named St. Anthony and then at Oxford University (Ackroyd 1999). Before More was beheaded for his strong spiritual commitment to Catholicism, he was a star product of a feudal education, and his educational experience marks how radically different education is now.

In school and the university More learned preset forms of communication used to demonstrate one's learnedness and considered as an initiation to the culture of the educated elite, which Augustine would have fully recognized some twelve hundred years earlier. Public discourse, performed only among the elites, was chiefly oral and in Latin—the common language of the educated—and often involved statements made in set poetical forms. Even public writings took this oral, rhetorical form; More and fellow students were expected to memorize rhetorical discourse such as simple syllogisms, proverbs, and apothegms, which were to be learned through oral repetitions in class and routine performances in public (Ackroyd 1999). Even the form of debate about matters of the state was highly ritualized and formulistic; like other educated people, More mastered polemics, refutations, confutations, and dialogues to use in his professional oral and written communications as the lord chancellor.

At the core of More's education was the belief that the total sum of knowledge was fixed (ultimately by God as the absolute authority on truth) and that to be educated was to master this fixed corpus of knowledge as a hierarchical taxonomy of truth, which would serve as the foundation of the educated feudal mind (Ackroyd 1999). In this period the curriculum was based on a fixed set of ideas, starting with the trivium (grammar, rhetoric, dialectics), then the quadrivium (geometry, arithmetic, astronomy, music), and then Christian theology along with canon law (Durkheim 1938/1977; Aries 1962). There occurred little research within academic settings as happens today, and scholarship was limited to subtle and minute exegeses of biblical texts. Although by this period formal knowledge was not something to be kept secret and preserved for the initiated few, as it often had been during antiquity (in both the West and the East), knowledge was nevertheless not considered intended for any and all members of society (Marrou 1956). Among educated feudals, Christian theology directed all matters, and learning was mostly performed orally for an audience: there was no room for individual takes on this truth, and knowledge was a closed system; so was education. This is not to imply that educated feudals were unintelligent or trivial; just like the highly educated today, they employed their ideas about knowledge in matters of the state and Church, with major consequences. But they were a product of the ideology behind the educational institution of the times, which reinforced a worldview of stability, ultimate single truth, and a social order where the supreme educational goal was to prepare one to emulate classical form. To overtly attempt to change or add to this system of knowledge and its expression would have been considered disruptive and dangerous to society.

This is in marked contrast with the education ideology that has developed over the course of the education revolution and now so thoroughly infuses contemporary culture. As will be described in subsequent chapters, the current assumptions about what education is, and what it should do, are the exact opposite from the education ideology of the feudal period and both Western and Eastern antiquity. For example, resulting from the astonishing success of the university in the West, knowledge in the schooled society is considered to be opened-ended, discoverable by humans, and unpredictable and potentially mutinous to fixed taxonomies. So too, formal curricula are interlaced with the overt demand for cognitive skills such as problem solving, active inquiry, scientific method, and openness to the knowledge production process. The student is considered not as an emulator of classical forms but is on the route to fuller development and actualization. At the same time, the societal functions of education have broadened and now dominate social status, employment, and many other social institutions in ways that would have been unimaginable by More and his contemporaries.

As the young More finished his formal feudal education, the seeds of what would become the education revolution were already growing in the universities and they were nurtured by humanists, who eventually included the adult More himself. A shift was occurring in the ideas and values behind education that would set it on the long road to dominating present culture. Good examples of this are the rise of academic intelligence; the rapid emergence of formal education's near total dominance of the process by which society's power, prestige, and riches are distributed; and formal education as a route to social justice.

### CHAPTER 2

# Constructing Culture

## *Academic Intelligence, Social Status, and Human Rights*

THE INSTITUTIONAL VALUES OF EDUCATION, like those described in the preceding chapter, have intensified over the course of the education revolution, and together they create elaborate cultural products shaping the nature of education and its construction of society. Illustrative of this process are three primary cultural products that are readily obvious and diffuse through the educational culture and hence the wider society. The first is the cultural belief that cognitive skill, particularly as promoted in schooling, is the essential human capability for all types of jobs and social roles, and remarkably even has come to define the successfully developed person. The second is the belief that educational performance, as reflected in academic achievements such as degrees attained, is the chief, and rapidly becoming the sole, legitimate factor on which to base social hierarchy within society. And lastly is the belief that formal education is not a privilege; it is increasingly a basic human right and is socially just, in the same way food, shelter, and security are considered universal human rights.

It should be noted that education's institutional values do not always combine in some smooth, copasetic fashion. While they often symbiotically combine into cultural meanings, as described below, they also cause competing, even conflicting goals and priorities in the politics, funding priorities, and administration of formal education. In fact, most of the debates internal to the day-to-day operation of formal education at all levels are about the balance among central values stemming from the education revolution. The values themselves have become so robust in their influence on meaning about education that they vie for independence with one another, and the scholarship on educational systems and their operations is brimming with descriptions of these battles. But since the goal here is to understand the broader cultural dimensions that make the overall institution of education the central one it has become in postindustrial society, the synergistic products among the values will be the focus. And, of course, all three resulting complex cultural products play major roles in the consequences of schooled society described in Part II.

## THE RISE OF ACADEMIC INTELLIGENCE AND PRIVILEGING A HUMAN CAPABILITY

All questions have answers, the answers are the same for everyone, the answers can be figured out by individuals, and these individuals can and should do it alone. Nothing in social life quite parallels, in purity, the constructed world of the test and the school.

JOHN MEYER, "Reflections on Education as Transcendence," 2000

Over the past seventy years every new generation has been getting smarter, at least in terms of IQ.

JAMES FLYNN, public address, October 2004

The education revolution creates a culture where there is wide belief that academic achievement reigns supreme for the making of a productive and broadly capable human. This function of schooling is so taken for granted that it is often overlooked when social and behavioral scientists examine the impact of education on society. What is missed is how the education revolution has changed the very nature of academic achievement, and how this in turn changes society. The education revolution has given rise to, and imbued with considerable meaning, what can be called "academic intelligence," a capability that just a century ago would have been considered narrow and perhaps of dubious benefit to all but a few.

Academic intelligence is a distinctly different type of academic achievement from the past, and it has become valued as the central human capacity of the schooled society. It is metacognitive skills, or what psychologists refer to as "domain-general cognitive skills," such as problem solving, higher-order thinking, abstraction, informed interpretative skills, reasoning, generating new ideas, and critique. All of these are thought to be essential to today's curricular and instructional invitation to all students to be active participants in academic subjects from kindergarten through graduate study. Literacy, numeracy, and mastery of other academic subjects still are seen as skills needed for adult life, but over the course of the education revolution a thorough "cognitization" of formal education has occurred. Academic intelligence becomes an objective in and of itself

42

as well as a publicly celebrated quality of the individual that is verified via school success. Also, schooling inculcates a sense of empowerment in the individual to use these kinds of cognitive abilities in presumably all life activities, making cognitive skill the most valued central human capability in postindustrial society (Martinez 2000). Of course, intelligence expressed in cognitive forms has always been valued in human society, but the schooled society intensifies this to the point where intelligence, enhanced and validated through formal education, is assumed essential for the performance of social roles of all types, from work to modern soldiering to parenting, and is even the key to a fulfilling life in general (e.g., Nisbett 2009; Labaree 1986; Meyer 2000). Building on John Meyer's point about the academic test (in the epigraph), academic performance in the schooled society transcends itself into an all-encompassing image of human capabilities. And of course, nonacademic skills, particularly those furthest removed from domain-general cognitive skill, become correspondingly less valued.

At the same time, the effects of this culture of cognition run in the other direction too; academic intelligence has become such a dominating cultural construct that it shapes our ideas about general human intelligence (Baker, Salinas, and Eslinger 2012). Academic achievement, and its everyday manifestations as grades, test scores, teacher recommendations, and educational promotions, is the central currency of formal schooling, so much so that a person's intelligence is now largely publicly judged through indicators of his schooling performance, such as formal degrees attained: one's intelligence has become merged with one's performance of academic achievement. Other areas of schooling are increasingly subjugated to the march for academic intelligence; curricular activities like music and visual arts, which in the past were considered necessary for the worldly, well-rounded, educated individual, are now justified by educators and parents alike because of their supposed collateral benefit to students' thinking skills (e.g., Schaub 2013). All of the attributes that were once the valued goals of good parenting and earlier forms of education, such as moral character, ability to work hard, and even erudite knowledge, are surpassed by the value of the smart youth who does well in school, or more accurately phrased, the one celebrated as smart because she achieves in school.

In the schooled society, academic performance becomes synonymous with the successfully developed person (e.g., Richardson and Powell 2011). And by extension everyone should attempt to capture as much achievement as they can. Those who do are valued because they are an accomplished academic achiever, a status that follows them for life. Note how often adult acclaim is prefaced by notable academic accomplishments regardless of how long ago they were achieved. An individual with considerable academic achievement who later fails in adult society is described as wasting a high level of education—meaning the wasting of valued cognitive ability among other things.

Each wave of new students comes to value academic intelligence as generalized human potential. For example, a recent Norwegian study of youth considering their future in a system with an extensive set of connections from upper-secondary schooling to narrow but otherwise good jobs found that many youth were turning away from these in favor of a less specified academic option, giving the rationale that "it is a waste of good grades to go for vocational programs" (Geir, Norwegian adolescent, as quoted in Hegna and Smette 2010). Similarly, American parents of college-bound high school seniors proudly and publicly celebrate the status of admitting colleges as confirmation of their child's academic prowess, and by inference their parenting of such achievement.

The importance placed on academic intelligence and how this has led to a thoroughly cognitized education demanded of all students is a direct outcome of education's institutional values described earlier. All four values contribute to the rise and centrality of academic intelligence in the schooled society. Yet this pronounced feature of formal education is so ubiquitous that it is difficult to observe its historical intensification over the course of the education revolution. There is, however, an observable, interesting social phenomenon that is a likely consequence of this aspect of the education revolution.

## THE INTRIGUING FLYNN EFFECT

Encountering James Flynn's remarks (in the epigraph) for the first time, many might find it questionable and maybe just plain silly. Look at all the problems in the world, each brimming with examples of stupid things done by apparently uninformed and unthinking people. Yet the fact remains, there is considerable evidence that populations of humans have gotten more cognitively competent over the course of the twentieth century and continue to do so; and there is equally compelling evidence that the education revolution has played a major role in this phenomenon.

"More cognitively competent" in this sense means that the whole distribution of IQ (intelligence quotient) scores in tests administered to large swaths of the adult population has shifted upwards with each succeeding generation over the past seventy years (Flynn 1984, 1987, 1998, 1999). IQ scores average 100 points with 15 points as a standard deviation, so that two-thirds of all people will have a normed-score (a standardized score of types) between 85 and 115. Normed-scores can conceal historical trends, but when unnormed IQ scores are compared over history, a growing average IQ trend is evident, and to an amazing degree: compared to the average person in 1930, the average person today scores two full standard deviations higher, at 130. Successive generations have been gaining about 15 IQ points over the preceding generation. While 15 IQ points may not seem like a lot, it represents going from mere "average" intelligence to "superior" intelligence, and of course people with superior intelligence (120 plus) in the preceding generation are matched by people in the succeeding generation with "exceptional" scores (135 plus). This trend has been dubbed the "Flynn effect" after the political scientist who originally reported it in the 1980s. Because of its potentially important consequences for the study of human intelligence, its validity as a substantive trend has been verified by a commission of psychologists and sociologists at the request of the American Psychological Association (Neisser 1998).

For those scientists who consider human intelligence to be a highly stable and basic genetic quality and who also assume that IQ tests accurately measure this deep and relatively unchangeable trait, the confirmation of the Flynn effect is potentially a major challenge to their paradigm. One or the other—the notion of a deep trait or the accuracy of IQ tests—is at stake. How much IQ tests reflect intelligence is often questioned, but most of the debate over the Flynn effect concludes that at the very least these instruments accurately measure an expression of intelligence, and that this expression is rising. At the same time, though, prior generations obviously were not of such low intelligence that over half of them would have been classified as mentally retarded, nor is it true that the rising generation of children and youth is mostly gifted with intelligence, with a good fourth functioning in the genius range.

By and large, psychologists have been at a loss to explain the Flynn effect. While most cognitive scientists agree that human intelligence is a product of genetics and environment, the speed and size of the change across generations prove difficult to explain. Certainly the trend has occurred too rapidly for some fundamental genetic shift in the population, but similarly a host of environmental factors (e.g., nutrition, television, social complexity) hypothesized as environmental causes have been shown to be mistimed or too weakly associated with intelligence to explain the historical trend (Neisser 1998). As proof of the intellectual underappreciation of the potential for the education revolution to transform society, increasing mass formal education, an obvious candidate as a cause of the trend, was until recently dismissed as too ineffective and dumbed down to be considered. But interestingly, two qualities of the trend of rising IQs point directly to the education revolution as a cause (Blair, Gamson, Thorne, and Baker 2005).

First, all the evidence uncovered indicates that the Flynn effect has occurred so far only in nations that have been economically developed for some time, like the United States, Japan, and Western European countries (Flynn 1987). As already described, these nations were the first to experience the expansion of formal schooling to ever wider proportions of their populations.

Second, one part of IQ has had the most dramatic historical increases, namely, "fluid IQ." In general, IQ is described as consisting of two large sets of capabilities. One set, known as fluid IQ, are the abilities to solve novel problems by planning approaches to complex tasks (executive functioning); being able to keep important facts in mind as one solves problems (working memory); processing information in an effective way (inhibitory control); shifting the mind's attention to parts of problems in an effective manner (attention-shifting); and understanding spatial relationships—all of which are central to domain-general intelligence. For example, fluid intelligence skill would be activated if one were asked to describe the next figure in a patterned series of complex abstract figures of varying shadings, geometric shapes, and sizes. Indeed, much of the data behind the Flynn effect are from the IQ test called Raven's Progressive Matrices, made up of exactly these pattern problems.[1] A real-life application of fluid IQ would be the cognitive skills one would use in a workplace to plan an approach to a new and complex set of problems. The other set of cognitive skills, known as "crystallized IQ," are the abilities to remember and understand facts and routine solutions to problems. If an adult were asked, for example, to name the first four presidents of the United States or how to calculate a sphere's surface area, solving these problems would use crystallized skills.

While there is some evidence of a modest historical rise in crystallized skills, rising fluid skills are driving the Flynn effect. And over the education revolution these are precisely the kinds of cognitive skills that make up academic intelligence, that have grown in prominence within curricula, and that are now so intensely valued and celebrated in the schooled society. Since academic intelligence is considered a necessary skill that all students are now expected to master, mass schooling through the highest reaches of college and university has promoted academic intelligence as the primary learning goal of an education.

A likely cause of rising fluid IQ is that of the wider and deeper exposure of populations over time to the distinctly cognitively rich experience of schooling. It is not, of course, that schooling has changed populations' genetic endowments to their neurological capacities; rather, over successive generations formal education has made a certain set of cognitive capabilities extremely important and accessible, and these have been mastered across populations. This seems especially true for the functions that provide domain-general resources for planning, organization, working memory, and integration of experience, knowledge, and skills for goal-directed behaviors (Baker, Salinas, and Eslinger 2012). Seen this way, the Flynn effect makes sense, not as some artifact of IQ testing nor as a radical challenge to our understanding of the genetics of human intelligence, but instead as a function of a powerful social institution privileging particular applications of innate intelligence. In fact, one of the central conclusions from the now sixty-year-old scientific endeavor known as the "cognitive revolution" is that cognitive development is an epigenetic process, meaning that both genetic and environmental factors play a symbiotic role with each other. So it is not true that past generations were mentally impaired because most did not attend school, nor is it true that future highly schooled generations will have many more geniuses. Rather, the education revolution, in terms of both wider access and qualitative changes in content, has produced population-wide improvement in a set of cognitive skills that have also come to be highly valued and believed as essential to all kinds of human endeavors. Moreover, the Flynn effect is not trivial; it has real consequences for individuals and other social institutions, as populations with higher levels of fluid IQ skills change many aspects of society. This will be described in Part II.

This is not to argue that schooling, then or now, functions optimally in all respects, or that all students master these skills equally in some kind of educational utopia. There is much evidence and everyday experience that belies such an image. Yet a case can be made that the effects of schooling are strong enough and so thoroughly infused into the educational culture to influence most people's cognitive functioning in ways never before witnessed in human society. Reading, writing, and understanding numbers and basic operations are themselves transforming skills, but there is evidence that in the process of learning these skills, domain-general cognition is enhanced as well (Baker, Salinas, and Eslinger 2012; Ceci 1991). For example, in the 1930s, when large numbers of unschooled Russian peasants lived alongside those who had had access to some schooling as children, noted Soviet psychologists Luria (1976) and Vygotsky reported evidence that adults with even small amounts of exposure to formal school showed greater propensity to use cognitive abstraction and reasoning to solve new problems, while unschooled adults tended to rely on their concrete experiences even at the risk of finding an incorrect solution. Since this initial finding, the impact of schooling on the ability to reason more abstractly and problem-solve in new and unique situations has been demonstrated in related research in other cultures (Cole 1996; Stevenson and Chen 1989; Tulviste 1991). For instance, employing a natural experiment among Ghanaian subsistence-level farmers who as children experienced different levels of schooling, psychologist Ellen Peters and colleagues, including this author (2011), found substantial schooling effects on measures of domain-general cognition, decision-making skills, and new problem-solving tasks. Lastly, sociologists of education Douglas Downey, Paul von Hippel, and Beckett Broh thought of a creative way to compare what students gain academically over the school year versus the summer vacation, when many have little contact with schooling; they report significant net schooling effects beyond a host of other social and material conditions of students and their families (Downey, von Hippel, and Broh 2004).

As mass schooling spread during the twentieth century and its cognitively intense environment reached greater portions of the world's population, more individuals were exposed not only to the specific skills of literacy and numeracy but also to reasoning and new ways of thinking. It is not surprising then that domain-general cognition shows significant improvement across populations of adults over successive generations during the past one hundred years. Understandable too is evidence that differences in cognitive skills across socioeconomic statuses and even occupations among cohorts born after 1945 have decreased relatively and absolutely (Weakliem, McQuillan, and Schauer 1995).

With the coming of the schooled society, the cognitive capacities that make up academic intelligence are routinely considered an objectified good, often in surprising contexts not seen before in society. For example, increasingly, measures of academic achievement of national student bodies are thought to indicate the economic and social health of nations (e.g., Ramirez, Luo, Schofer, and Meyer 2006). Widespread reactions to the results of international academic achievement tests, comparing students from a host of nations, mirror the deep reverence modern society holds towards school-certified smartness. Witness the condemnation in many nations over poor national scores and the rhetoric of societal doom and gloom in the media that accompanies this; or conversely, the international celebration of academically high-performing nations (e.g., Baker and LeTendre 2005). It is an amazing occurrence when large nations with huge labor forces, complex economies, technological militaries, celebrated histories, and other indicators of national prowess condemn their own future on the basis of an eighth- or twelfth-grade math test! But it happens often. Such are the proportions to which academic achievement has grown in the modern psyche via the education revolution.

But the reactions to these international or national test results often lead to claims by pundits and experts that schooling has gradually been dumbed down, made easier, and filled with many pursuits not immediately related to achievement. This begs the question, for if schooling is becoming less academic, how has it produced such a culture of academic achievement? Often the answer given to this question is that some kind of desperate conspiracy is afoot—as futures are ever more directed by academic performance, schools and educators are increasingly irresponsible (or withholding) in providing what students need in this new world. But conspiracies are complicated to pull off, particularly in such a widespread activity as modern mass schooling. Maybe the simpler alternative is true, namely, that formal education has produced this laser-like focus on achievement at least in part because, contrary to the pundits and experts, schooling has gotten more demanding, particularly in those loftier pursuits known as higher-order thinking skills.

It is easy to ask whether schooling has gotten more demanding over its history, but it is a hard question to answer. One approach is to examine the kinds of things students were taught and asked to learn, at which grades and during which historical periods. As will be described fully in Chapter 8, a recent study did this by systematically examining a century of primary school mathematics curricula as represented in popular and widely used American textbooks (Baker et al. 2010). In particular, the analysis looked for shifts in the cognitive demand of curricula in terms of textbook problems and examples that emphasize more-fluid thinking skills and mathematic concepts as opposed to rote arithmetic and repetitive computation. Overwhelmingly, the findings are that over the twentieth century mathematics instruction has not been dumbed down; rather, since at least the mid-1960s its reliance on the cognitive skills of academic intelligence has increased significantly.

The widespread enhancement of fluid thinking skills across generations is an excellent example with which to consider the transforming power of the education revolution. Schooling has considerable power to create on its own new ideas, behaviors, and values. Mass schooling has produced and distributed a unique definition of intelligence, and in a relatively short time has made this intelligence universally accepted as not only useful but essential to being a fully developed individual prepared to participate in society. Schooling, through its everyday activities, has created a new model about what is important for effective human development and performance, one based primarily on cognitive skills. Certainly debates within the education research community will continue as to whether advanced levels of schooling add to cognitive achievement, but compared to little or no schooling, there has been major change in populations' cognitive skill levels over the course of the education revolution (e.g., Arum and Roksa 2011). Learning to read, write a language, and use numbers, even under rudimentary conditions, results from considerable abstract cognitive exercise that likely transforms how schooled individuals think, reason, and problem-solve. Also, schooling progressively engulfs students in a cognitive process uniquely different from subsistence-level farming, early industrial factory work, and other premodern activities. The effect of the schooled society in this regard is so extensive that when qualities that are less related to cognitive ability are used to make educational decisions about students, it becomes publicly controversial, litigious, and ultimately taboo (Hammock 2010).

What is sociologically new here is not that schooling influences how students think; after all, that has been known for some time. Rather, what is new is that the education revolution, in intensifying the time-consuming common activity of going to school, has brought massive attention to certain types of human capabilities, making them seem as if they were always central capabilities and thus making it "natural" for so many to focus on cognitive skills and academic achievement as never before. Obviously, across the some 200,000 years of *Homo sapiens*'s existence thinking capabilities have been central; but until just the past century, most human existence was a base physical one and the type of reified and abstracted thinking that is now poured into students' heads in school was not common or useful, or even much valued in everyday contexts. In a few generations this has all changed, and thus the cultural product of academic intelligence will find its way into many of the later chapters concerning the effects of the education revolution on other social institutions.

THE NARROWING EDUCATION ROAD
TO SOCIAL STATUS

As long as "equality of opportunity" is a value in American society, increasing the proportion of workers with college degrees benefits society by making occupational opportunity independent of social origins for a large percentage of the work force.

MICHAEL HOUT, *American Journal of Sociology*, 1988

South African secondary school students preparing for competitive entrance examinations to university riot because their teachers are too frequently absent (Dugger 2009). South Korean families spend millions of dollars on after-school tutoring for their children (Byun and Baker 2013). A young American convict granted early parole asks to serve his complete sentence so that he can take full advantage of the prison's classes to help him prepare for the GED test for a secondary school diploma (*Centre Daily Times* 2009). What would appear at first to be strange stories makes sense when thought of from the second major cultural product of the schooled society. Increasingly, formal education has become the main—and may soon be the sole legitimate—route to adult social status. Educational achievement, degree attainment, and credentials dominate social stratification and social mobility, superseding and delegitimizing all non-educational forms of status attainment. Four decades of sociological research point to a future society where education performance will be the singular, predominant factor in occupational and social status attainment. In fact, to a large extent this has already happened in a number of nations.

From historical accounts of social mobility, it is clear that prior to a century and a half ago, formal education played almost no role in the process of intergenerational mobility. For example, although in late European feudal society, as described in the case of Thomas More, a small stratum of elite and semi-elite positions for individuals was allocated on the basis of university training, the vast majority of positions were not defined by educational attainment. Much later, just before the advent of the education revolution, a variety of decidedly non-educational criteria and routes to adult status dominated intergenerational mobility in preindustrial and early-industrial societies, criteria such as family origin and position in a social stratum, status inheritance, sinecure, marriage,

age, gender, religious charisma, guild training, patronage, caste, and land ownership. But starting in about the midnineteenth century in economically developed nations, these non-educational routes were receding and increasingly replaced by education routes to status (e.g., Collins 1979; Hogan 1996). Also, the ageless process of transferring wealth and position through the inheritance of family businesses and farms was in decline, and when it did occur, it was seen increasingly as a less valid alternative to education for reaching one's eventual adult status (Bledstein 1976). As will be described in Chapter 7 on credentials in the schooled society, attainment of diplomas was becoming the chief way to adult social status for a growing middle class.

By the 1960s, when modern statistical methods first were applied to analyze social mobility data from large samples of individuals, the education revolution was in full swing. Not surprisingly, the groundbreaking research of Blau and Duncan (1967) showed that educational attainment had become a causal factor in adult status attainment to a degree unique in human society, and the same pattern was evident in other heavily schooled nations (e.g., Breen and Luijkx 2007; Hout 1988; Ishida 1993; Shavit and Blossfeld 1993; Treiman and Ganzeboom 1990). While older forms of intergenerational reproduction (i.e., parents passing on their status to their children) were still evident, formal educational attainment had become the main route to an individual's adult status across the population; this happened in two ways once thought mutually exclusive (Hout and DiPrete 2006). Educational attainment was influenced by an individual's social origin, but also by schooling factors independent of social origin, namely, academic merit (success or failure at schooling based on effort, intelligence, and motivation). The next historical shift witnessed an even greater saturation of education in the social mobility process. Sociologist of social mobility Michael Hout's landmark study (1988; see also 1984) found that by the late 1980s, direct intergenerational influence of origin had completely vanished among individuals completing the BA, and had substantially declined among individuals with a high school degree. Recently, in a comprehensive study of American social status attainment, sociologist Florencia Torche (2010) replicated Hout's findings and found that the trend has continued since the late 1980s; it has also been found in

Sweden, France, and Germany (Brand and Xie 2010; Vallet 2004; Breen and Jonsson 2007; Breen and Luijkx 2007).

Thus once one is in the higher education arena, success becomes based chiefly on educational achievement, such as better academic performance in college, majors selected, and perhaps the influence of educational and prestige differences among higher education institutions.[2] Of course there remains the influence of a person's origin on his educational attainment, even up through higher education (e.g., Duncan and Murnane 2011). But parental socioeconomic status is itself increasingly a function of earlier educational attainment. Consequently, over just several American generations, education has thoroughly saturated intergenerational mobility; given the increasing homogenization of schooling's influence, the educational dominance of social mobility is or will soon be global.

Often the shift towards education's role in status attainment is attributed merely to greater economic and social complexity, particularly from both social-class reproductive and human-capital theories, which employ the traditional model of education as a secondary institution. Certainly economies have changed and family-owned farms and small businesses have declined; yet replacing age-old social mobility mechanisms in such a rapid and total fashion as the education revolution has done has taken far more sociological change than accounted for by greater economic and social complexity. With the exception of the apprenticeship, the non-educational mechanisms of status attainment listed above are not well known to most in modern society. Yet before the education revolution, these were deeply embedded in societies and considered legitimate ways by which individuals gained access to occupations and social status. The rise of education as the near sole arbitrator of access to adult status has been so complete that these former processes—sinecure, occupational inheritance, marriage, religious charisma, guild training, patronage, caste—appear now as exotic social relics.

While formal education controlled access to a few elite positions in some traditional societies, the fact that it now singularly does so for nearly the entire status hierarchy would have been an alien idea just one hundred years ago. Education's role in the attainment of social status may seem to many contemporaries as natural, but it is in fact a sweeping sociological

construction at the foundation of postindustrial society. As such, it produces a strong belief in the power of education to the point that individuals
and families pursue its prizes in exhaustive and elaborate ways. The riots
of students against unaccountable teachers, the growth of a worldwide
multibillion-dollar tutoring industry, and the decision of a young convict
to stay in prison to pursue a degree are all understandable and reasonable
reactions to a schooled society and its acceptance of education as the legitimate source of access to occupations and social status.

## EDUCATION AS A HUMAN RIGHT

Sometime around 50 years ago a great mental tide began to sweep across the world. . . .
They have a certain template of what a "normal" country looks like—with democracy
and openness—and they feel humiliated that their nation doesn't measure up.

DAVID BROOKS, editorial on Tahrir Square reform protests in Egypt;

*New York Times*, February 1, 2011

Mass schooling was initially a distinctively Western cultural product, which
because of its powerful transforming properties and founding philosophical
tenets has, for better or worse, subsequently pulled the rest of the world
toward a Western model of society; it creates and disseminates internal-
ized global templates that David Brooks describes as driving so much social change. At the same time, growing mass education at all levels has
produced the cultural belief that formal education is more or less a taken-
for-granted human right, an essential part of what national societies, not
clans or families, should provide for all children and youth; in doing so,
education is an entitlement integral to achieving the good society (Baker
and LeTendre 2005; Meyer 1999). The converse influence of the education
revolution on the politics of nations is taken up in Chapter 10, but in the
present discussion an important cultural product of the schooled society
is mass formal education as a state-sponsored human right.

Therefore an important partner of the education revolution has been the
modern nation-state. A hugely transforming institution itself, the emerging
nation-state, from about the eighteenth century onward, became the sole
legitimate political organization of human society. It rapidly replaced empires big and small, colonies, tribal lands, and other older traditional ways

by which humans organize the landmasses on which they live (Anderson 1991; Soysal 1994). And much like their public education systems, nation-states have spread rapidly as a political form and are now incorporated universally worldwide. This major political change has not come about without considerable violence and strife, from colonial oppression and struggles for freedom to world wars based in large part on extreme forms of nationalism. But at the same time, the nation and its global status is the context by which a new view of humans and their political, social, and economic contribution to the common good has come about. At the heart of this transformation is state-sponsored, state-financed public schooling. Without the spreading political form of the nation-state, the worldwide education revolution would likely not have been possible (Meyer and Hannan 1979; Fuller and Rubinson 1992).

Providing widespread educational opportunity for nations' populations is not only thought of as desirable; it is now approaching the cultural status of a basic human right, not unlike nutrition, health care, and civil rights. Following a trend starting immediately after the Second World War, multilateral agencies began assisting nations in economic development, which also included educational development (e.g., Heyneman 2005). For example, representatives from major agencies such as the United Nations, UNICEF, the World Bank, and UNESCO in alliance with the governments of most nations, and international nongovernmental organizations (INGOs) such as Oxfam and Action Aid, gathered together at an international conference in Jomtien, Thailand, in 1990, where they not only once again declared that education is a basic human right, but set forth a plan of action to make education universal worldwide (the Jomtien Declaration). This process was updated and intensified in 2000 at a similar international conference, "Education for All," in Dakar, Senegal (UNESCO 2002). During each conference attendees affirmed the need for all children to have access to quality education within the near future, for the good of nations and also for the good of the worldwide society. Although ambitious, the conferences laid out clear steps to meet this goal throughout the developing world.

The prominence of the cultural idea of education as a human right is tellingly reflected and embodied in a special office of the United Nations' UNESCO dedicated to monitoring worldwide progress towards education for all, in reports chronicling the progress of the education revolution nation by nation. Basic schooling is now so widespread and successful that as the world's enrollment rate of all school-aged children approached 85 percent in 2005, achieving the final 15 percent takes on a do-or-die urgency to eradicate undereducation, like the inoculation of the world's population with a vaccine against a deadly global disease. UNESCO reports are full of estimates of the undereducation of children, including girls, ethnic minorities, and the physically challenged, who have lagged behind in school attendance in developing nations (UNESCO 2000, 2002, 2004, 2010). The report titles alone tell the story: *The Right to Education: Towards Education for All Throughout Life*; *Education for All: Is the World on Track?*; *Gender and Education for All: The Leap to Equality*; and *Reaching the Marginalized*. This purposeful, political, final drive towards universal primary education in every corner of the world attests to the full influence of 150 years of the educational culture at the core of the schooled society.

While its status as a fundamental human right supported by most nations of the world shows how far the education revolution has traveled, its origins reside much further back in the history of Western society to the invention of a particular type of institution of higher learning.

### CHAPTER 3

# The Incredible Longevity
# of the Western University

Higher education is, and has been, the central cultural institution of modern society.

JOHN MEYER, FRANCISCO RAMIREZ, DAVID FRANK, AND

EVAN SCHOFER, "Higher Education as an Institution," 2008

HOW COULD ANY SCHOLAR make such a sweepingly positive statement about the university and higher education in society today? The complaints about the university worldwide are all too familiar, composing a litany of failures to assist society. For example, it is frequently pointed out that the large American higher education system is very uneven in cost, prestige, and in many people's belief, quality. As more students than ever try for admission to elite institutions, competition soars while the tuition prices continue to skyrocket. It is now three times more difficult to gain admittance to a Harvard, Stanford, Oberlin, or Caltech than just four decades ago. Humanists grumble that the once classical curriculum of the academy has been gutted and all but discarded. For seemly arbitrary reasons, occupations once dominated by the lesser-educated are increasingly pulled into higher education's orbit. The constant increase in the proportion of secondary students entering some form of higher education has made the remedial course as commonplace as the pundits who question whether all these youth really need a higher education.

A virtual cottage industry of books critical of the American university spills forth from the neo-conservative political perspective, charging that political correctness and multiculturalism have become valued over "real learning"; while books from a leftist perspective warn that collegiate traditions have lost out to the march of corporatism, the fear of litigation, and a crude rationalization of teaching and scholarship by a growing nonacademic corps of administrators. And criticism is not limited to U.S. higher education, as there are criticisms of the university worldwide. Germany, the home of some of the best universities during the nineteenth century, has been in the throes of a quality crisis over its universities for the past several decades.

From the traditional perspective of education as a *secondary institution*, the usual assumption is that the university "serves society." From here it is a short jump to the image of an institution that requires constant realignment with societal change lest it risk stepping out of its bounds and becoming ineffectual and irrelevant. Even the much-valued research and technology development functions of the university are frequently cast in the light of a weak institution. For example, the university's mission of generating new knowledge is often criticized as being irrelevant and out of sync with the "needs of society," as if the university and its scholarship were wandering dangerously afield of its exogenously determined path to aid in social progress. Various versions of the weak university argument assume an institution that has perpetual tendencies to be ever more irrelevant (the ivory tower problem), trivially relevant (the closing of the mind problem), or too commercial (the privatization-marketization problem). All of these visions see an institution in crisis because of an inability to effectively follow and serve society (e.g., Bloom 1987; Slaughter and Rhoades 2009; Tuchman 2011; Washburn 2005; Watson, Hollister, Stroud, and Babcock 2011). But by contrast, the schooled society perspective turns the vision of the weak university on its head.

There is another way to look at the university, namely, as a major institution at the foundation of Western society that has had a profound and lengthy impact on the culture of education, which is now increasingly globalized.[1] Over its long history, the university has become a *strong primary institution*, producing and granting authority to a considerable number of the ideas about the nature of knowledge, individuals, humankind, and indeed the entire cosmos—all of which form the bedrock cultural beliefs and values that drive the schooled society to ever larger proportions worldwide (Meyer, Ramirez, Frank, and Schofer 2008). In short, this picture is one of the university producing not only new knowledge through scholarship and research but also, and crucially so, the very ideology and beliefs that underpin the experienced reality of modern society. If this argument is correct, as a growing number of neo-institutional studies indicates, then the university is the primary institution behind the wide-ranging educational transformations of society.

This argument builds off an interesting paradox about the development of the university in the West and its subsequent success as an institution: if the university has been so successful, why is it often thought to be a weak or failing institution in society? Fellow neo-institutionalists David Frank and John Meyer (2007) convincingly argue that the first part of the paradox is true—the university has succeeded in postindustrial society. The extraordinary global diffusion and expansion of universities and associated enrollments, the similarity in their curricular and knowledge-production goals, and the considerable isomorphism in organizational structure across thousands of universities worldwide all attest to their success. Perhaps, then, the fallacy in the paradox is the assumption that the university is a weak or somewhat isolated institutional player in society. The solution to the paradox is to instead see the university as a successful form in and of itself *and* as a major transforming force within global society. Following Frank and Meyer, this and the next two chapters argue that human society, simply put, has come to take on the cultural meanings of the university more than the other way around.

It is not that universities do all of this cultural construction in some heavy-handed, edict-issuing way. In fact, when universities try to shape peoples' everyday worlds directly, they look inept and indeed usually are ineffectual. The power described here is subtler but extremely pervasive. This argument then should not be confused with an older one that proclaimed that because the university trains elites, it is a powerful institution passing information down from on high.[2] This is part of the story, of course, yet this image, being overly functional and grandiloquent in tone, confused the charter to train elites with elite status itself; it also perpetuated an untrue picture of the university as some manifest commander of society through a naïve assumption of the inevitable power of science. The institutional power of the university is neither omnipotent nor conspiratorial. It is, nevertheless, deeply embedded in the everyday life of the schooled society.

Instead of sending down scientific facts and trained experts from its ivory tower, the university has come to be fully integrated within the schooled society through its claims to produce knowledge that is not so much esoteric as it is imbued with a power to influence all kinds of every-day activities. Universities generate and sustain an overarching ideology that pervades all things, often employing the methods of science but always relying on an epistemological mandate that rests on original methods of scholarship having deep roots in Western culture. The process described here by which the university influences so much of our thinking about reality is not based on an elitist view of the institution. In fact, rising higher education enrollments worldwide, or what university watchers sometimes refer to as the *massification* of the university, are a major driving force in intensifying the power of the institution in modern society.

Placing the cultural origin of the education revolution within the development of the Western university is not to deny the considerable research showing the facilitating and funding of mass public education by the nineteenth- and twentieth-century nation-state. There are many excellent accounts of the historical development of the relationship between mass education and the state (e.g., Fuller and Rubinson 1992; Archer 1979). But none of these can provide an account of the broad cultural origins of the ideology driving the education revolution—this requires an analysis of the university in the schooled society.

Further, there is some debate and contradictory empirical evidence over whether the university is *the* primary origin of new ideas or whether it also creates awareness and gives a unique form of authoritative legitimacy to new ideas that arise from other institutions in society. This debate awaits future research. Either way, the underlying image is of the university as a strong institution through its unique, multifaceted charter to systematize ideas (universalistic scholarship), distribute them (new knowledge and the teaching of it), and authorize enactment of knowledge via certification of graduates in particular domains of everyday life (education degree credentialing).

What is meant by "knowledge" in this case needs to be defined. Implied here is a much broader definition than usual. Many university watchers often underestimate the scope of knowledge production by sufficing it to mean only new text interpretations, scientific information, techniques, technology, and all types of humanistic scholarship. All of these kinds of knowledge are of course part of the university-generated knowledge package; but to assume that they are the only kinds would miss the deeper sociological impact of the university. Over the centuries the university has come to create, sustain, and legitimate *ideologies*—guiding bodies of knowledge about truth—that define all things human, as well as the physical universe. Knowledge evolves over time, of course; yet, over a long development stemming from feudal Europe, the university has become a major (if not the main) arbitrator of ideologies.

This arbitration is not necessarily wielded in a prescriptive, conspiratorial, or even technocratic fashion; indeed, scholars at universities are rarely aware of their role in arbitrating central ideologies about reality. Instead, what they see themselves doing is manifestly producing "new" truth, albeit one small piece at a time. Whether the new truths are a scholar's new interpretation of a central text, a new scientific discovery, a new theory, or indeed this very monograph, these "discoveries," each arbitrated by standards of scholarship, reinforce an overall ideology about the nature of human society and its universe at any particular time. By definition, truth is open to discovery by anyone and new knowledge comes from both outside and inside the university; but the university's charter organizes, validates, and legitimates all knowledge and claims about how we know something to be true (e.g., scientific method), and hence it forms bedrock ideologies about reality. The oft-made claim that modern universities are special organizations *because* they generate new knowledge shows the power of their institutional charter; no other institution in modern society makes such a claim so unabashedly. The assumption that all things can be submitted to rational scholarship appears today as natural, but at its inception it was a strikingly radical idea.

## ORIGINS OF THE EDUCATION REVOLUTION
### IN THE WESTERN UNIVERSITY

Even in light of contemporary criticism, in many ways it is obvious that the Western university has been an effective cultural institution from its founding in medieval Europe over the twelfth and thirteenth centuries.[3] Tellingly, most of the longest-existing organizations in the world today are universities (Kerr 1987). For example, the earliest universities founded in medieval Europe are still functioning today; the universities of Paris,

Bologna, and Oxford are all about eight hundred years old.[4] And just as tellingly, these extremely old universities, and many others like them, are not merely propped-up museum pieces; they are vibrant, dynamic organizations of learning and scholarship.

Contrasting the circumstances of the earliest universities with those of the most successful today illustrates how much the institutional form has flourished. When first formed, universities were little more than collections of scholars who banded together to protect their common interests in medieval society. These early universities often had no official buildings or common grounds, and they borrowed private residences or existing public buildings for teaching. Students paid individual scholars directly to teach, and in some cases fined scholars who did not teach up to their expectations. Indeed, early universities were such semivirtual communities that they could, and sometimes did, completely decamp for another location as part of a strategy to win resources and freedom from local powers. Compare these humble beginnings to the epitome of the successful contemporary university. In the United States, to be counted among competitive, research-intensive universities having an extensive portfolio of scholarship and research (including a medical research center) requires minimally about 1.5 billion dollars in annual funding (Baker 2008a). Commanding and sustaining this level of resources (from both public and private funds) would be virtually impossible if the university were a weak secondary institution. Though many universities are funded at levels unimaginable a few decades ago, the earliest universities, established to meet a unique set of needs in medieval society, have led directly to the strong primary institution of today.

In many accounts of the role of the university in society, the medieval history of the Western university is referenced as an interesting aside. Yet the role that the university initially played in medieval European society foreshadowed what it continues to play, powerfully, in worldwide postindustrial society. Further, the longevity of the university in a world where so many other institutional forms have died out attests to the staying power of its original function.

In the early 1990s, Phyllis Riddle, sociologist of education and neoinstitutionalist, undertook an extensive study of the founding and rise of the Western university as the basic model for universities worldwide. Meticulously amassing the founding dates of every Western university (including those that went out of business along the way), from the form's inception up to the modern era, she found that during the six hundred years from 1200 to 1800, over 160 universities were founded throughout Europe. From the beginning of the nineteenth century and lasting until now, growth has continued apace, as there are now thousands of universities across the world essentially operating along an institutional model set in motion eight hundred years ago.

Analyzing the pattern of the founding of the earliest universities, Riddle showed that the places and specific time periods in Europe where occurred the earliest and fastest growth in the number of universities were *not* necessarily times and places experiencing the greatest population or economic growth (Riddle 1993). This is an important, counterintuitive finding, because if the university were a weak secondary institution the opposite should be true. Instead considering the university as a robust primary institution, Riddle hypothesized that universities were founded most rapidly in times and places where political and religious authorities were striving for legitimation in competition with similar authorities; in other words, the founding of the Western university was at the heart of a transition to a new society.

This is in fact what Riddle's exhaustive archive of founding dates confirms. In the specific places and times where elites in authority were more decentralized, fragmented, and in competition with one another, as in the regions of the Holy Roman Empire or in the feudal city-states of Italy, universities were used to help establish legitimacy of power and hence were important tools in winning struggles among competing political authorities. It is not surprising then that universities were frequently established in many German princedoms, since they were competing among one another within the Holy Roman Empire under only the loosely coupled authority of the emperor. In all, thirty-five successful institutions were begun in these areas, or about 20 percent of all Western universities founded in this initial period; by the late 1600s more universities were operating in the empire than anywhere else in Europe (Riddle 1993). The same is true among the Italian city-states, where thirty universities were founded during this period, and in the kingdoms of France and Spain, where another fifty-five universities were created; thus over 60 percent of newly founded universities came from these four regions. Along with a growing number of political historians, Riddle argues that while there was centralized political power in France and Spain during this period, there was also significant internal, interprovincial competition and other conflicts among groups of elites divided by language, custom, and geographical boundaries (Cobban 1975; Kagan 1974; Riddle 1993). By contrast, the more centralized and internally less divided realm of England established only two universities (Oxford and Cambridge) between 1200 and the early 1800s. Even though England experienced a substantial growth in population and economy starting in about 1520, it did not found another university until some three hundred years later (Stone 1972).

Many questions are yet to be answered about Riddle's hypothesis, such as why she finds no detectable impact of widespread conflict between Catholic and Protestant elites after the Reformation, or to what degree was the comparatively more centralized kingdom of France really open to internal competition among elites. Whether or not her hypothesis completely holds up to new historical research, what is clear from this research is that universities did not simply grow to the economic or demographic rhythms within European society; other factors were involved, and political authority seems to be a very likely one. Yet this story is not simply one of competition over authority. At a time and place already rife with wars fought for political power, why would medieval universities be considered so important to the legitimizing of power and authority that princedoms and city-states would spend so much of their treasuries to establish them? The earliest universities, after all, were essentially little more than communities of scholars held together by common interests in obtaining rights, position, and resources from the papacy and emperor to fend off material exploitation and official arbitrariness by the local municipality and local ecclesiastical officials (Rüegg 1992). Furthermore, most of the medieval population consisted of uneducated peasants with only a thin layer of experts between them and the rulers; so why establish universities? Yet within this tiny segment of experts lies a clue to the puzzle over why so many feudal authorities sought and financed this new kind of institution, and subsequently why this new institution became so successful.

A significant player in the initial creation and success of the Western university was the Roman Catholic Church. This fact is often interpreted to mean that these early universities were directly part of the Church and owed their support completely to the Pope, but this was not the case. Although the Pope did fund early universities through prebends (grants) to priests and monks so that they could attend, the feudal university was never solely part of the Church. Instead, historical analysis of the origins of universities clearly shows a symbiotic relationship between the Church and the earliest universities, which were growing in capacity to do new things in society. In exchange, many universities received crucial papal endorsement and funds that were unencumbered by local lords or by bishops' interests and restrictions (Cobban 1975). Papal sponsorship also gave the first universities distinct transterritorial status to the point that students and scholars could move from university to university under the protection of the Pope against the considerable risk of danger for travelers of the period (Le Goff 1993; Ridder-Symoens 1992).

As a strategy to extend the Church's authority, the Popes supported universities for three functions, all of which were revolutionary in their ultimate impact on European society and directly foreshadowed the power of the university in the schooled society of today (Durkheim 1938/1977; Rüegg 1992). First and foremost, the Popes had a direct interest in producing rare, highly coveted *authoritative knowledge* in the form of a rationally intelligible theological dogma for the Church to use as a bulwark against a rising tide of heretical Christian theologies and breakaway sects. Second, the Popes also wanted to form *an educated elite* for the Church—a curia (the Pope's staff of experts)—to help solve theological, administrative, and legal problems. Third, the Popes hoped to combine these innovations to create *experts defined by use of authoritative knowledge* to strengthen the authority of the papacy and ward off the increasingly powerful and secular nobility, who threatened the exclusivity of the Church's power.[5]

What gave further impetus to the founding of universities during this early period was that the Church's rival secular authorities also recognized the benefits of a university to bolster their own authority in a strategy parallel to that of the Church. Histories of early universities established by nonreligious authorities reveal a secular version of the same three perceived benefits of the university. Alongside scholarship on religious dogma and the training of a curia for the Church grew legal scholarship and text interpretation aimed at developing orderly legal and administrative codes for secular power, and the training of cohorts of legal experts to enact this authoritative knowledge. Indeed, after the initial period of the early university, there was a long era during which Church and secular authorities (increasingly organized into nation-states) competed for ultimate authority over the university, the secular winning out in many places by the seventeenth century (Riddle 1993). Since Riddle's study, subsequent extensive historiography of the early Western university is compatible with the argument advanced here (e.g., Ridder-Symoens 1992; Rüegg 1992; Rubenstein 2003).

Universities from their inception were about the production and distribution of ideas, and because these ideas originated from this special institution they were considered authoritative to the point that university scholarship became equated with a "search for truth." Interestingly, this coupling occurred well before any notions of scientific research and technology development in the university were in place. Furthermore, from the beginning, the graduates of these institutions were chartered with the expertise to interpret and act upon these university-generated ideas in the outside world (or generate more knowledge as the next generation of university scholars), thus joining together authority of ideas with the authoritatively endowed expert. Since its inception, the university has not been aimed at vocational or technical training; instead, a fundamental universalism came to underlie its training. Early forms of effective legal scholars and ecclesiastical experts, not better farmers, artisans, or merchants, were the expected products of this new institution, but later, as described in Chapter 5, the university's charters transformed these and other occupations too. The initial coupling of special knowledge and experts yielded a powerful innovation that slowly, then more rapidly, expanded into the schooled society of today.

For eight hundred years the university has done more than survive; it has flourished. First through outright cultural imposition by European and American forms of colonialism and then through a globally embraced model of social progress, the Western model of the university has spread to the extent that by now every nation has at least one university operating within its borders (Schofer and Meyer 2005). The modern university searches for, discovers, and disseminates central cultural ideologies and meanings that form the everyday experience of reality. Or as Riddle concludes her large study, "universities inherently make universal claims" (1993). And the university imbues its graduates with the authority to enact the ideologies and meanings based on these universal claims into ever growing aspects of human life. This cultural power is at the heart of the later education revolution.

## THE UNIVERSITY AND ORIGINS OF ACADEMIC RATIONAL INQUIRY

What had first been nurtured in the Church's intellectual hothouses of monasteries prior to the thirteenth century shifted to this new organization of the university. Interpretation of early Christian texts (i.e., not the word of their God, but the Bible and its patristic commentaries) and the study of the rediscovered ancient writings of Aristotle (preserved by Islamic scholars) by the earliest Western university scholars are the forerunners to secular academic scholarship, including the large-scale scientific and technical research at the core of the modern version of the university. This is not merely historical coincidence. In significant ways the rise of science and indeed the whole epistemological heritage of modern society owe their existence to the earliest university scholarship (Rubenstein 2003). The development of the university for specific scholarly needs of the Church created a unique form of rational inquiry that once in place within the institution of the Western university intensified and spread throughout the schooled society. Through a long line of early church scholars from St. Augustine to St. Aquinas the Church became convinced that the unique human ability to think and reason is the primary godly gift that *should be used to its maximum potential* to know God and his world. Put into modern terms, along with faith, higher-order cognition is the way to God. For education in general and the early university in particular, this was a powerful belief with wide-ranging and long-term ramifications. Scholarship, and the university as the place where it was chiefly produced, were at the center of the Church's development and maintenance of theology, an ideology that by the second millennium was the dominant cultural reality of at least the elites, across vast parts of Europe. As sociologist of religion Rodney Stark observes, "official Church theology enjoyed a secure base in the many and growing universities, *where reason ruled*" (2005, 8, emphasis added).

On the basis of numerous recent historical analyses of the rise of science in Europe, current scholars speculate that Western science had its roots in Christianity and developed primarily within universities well before the much celebrated Scientific Revolution of the sixteenth century (e.g., Stark 2005; Huff 2011). By worshiping a divine rational being that has a means-ends calculated plan of salvation (i.e., human progress), Christians connected together faith and science. If God is rational, then his creation of the universe is "necessarily a rational, lawful, stable structure, *awaiting increased human comprehension*" (Stark 2005, 12). In contrast to the traditional assumption that Christianity and science were antithetical, unique qualities of their deity led Christians not only to produce early scholarly inquiry, but also to anticipate the scientific method as a way to more fully appreciate the world God created and his plan for believers. It is a short jump from placing the origins of science in Christian scholarship to envisioning the early university as playing a major role in knowledge production right from its Christian beginnings; science is "the culmination of many centuries of systematic progress by medieval Scholastics, sustained by that uniquely Christian twelfth-century invention, the university" (12).

Moving forward historically, German sociologist Gero Lenhardt's extensive institutional analysis of the historical rise of the university and its development in Germany from the seventeenth to the twentieth centuries carries this idea further in documenting a long period of conflict with various political authorities, during which the university survived and intensified its role as the dominant source of knowledge (2002, 2005). He argues that over its evolution the university transformed simplistic text-reading and copying into a form of scholarly interpretation and intellectual inquiry that became the epistemological foundation of the modern university, a quality Lenhardt and other sociologists refer to as *universalism*. This term summarizes the nature of scholarly knowledge and the related authoritative role of preparing learned scholars, as described above.[6]

Most importantly, universalism implies that the university, activated by its professors and students, has the right, freedom, and competency to "pursue and question and investigate any object," physical or metaphysical (2002, 277). It is this sweeping claim and the freedom to act upon it that has propelled the original form of the university to its current position as the cultural generator of the schooled society. Lenhardt's central point about universalism is considerably more than just freedom from political retribution against university scholars for their political opinions. It is that, but much more too. Universalism underlies the university's extensive power to give authority to ideas, knowledge, and now experts, all of which are at the conceptual foundation of everyday beliefs and meanings; or in short, the university's ability to produce a significant proportion of society's basic culture.

Lenhardt goes on to demonstrate through the specifics of the German case that down through its historical development the Western university has experienced continual tension, and sometimes outright conflict, between its universalistic claims to the production of knowledge versus particularistic claims by economic, political, and theological interests of various authorities who strove too vigorously to control and harness the university for their own immediate ends. Over its history there have been many attempts to instrumentalize the university, meaning to turn the inquiry and education process into an instrument of some particular need or power external to the university. Ironically, these struggles have been with some of the university's otherwise ardent supporters; in each case the idea of universalistic inquiry and the academic freedom that it implies eventually won out. In struggles with first the Church, then European absolutist rulers, then the modern nation-state, and perhaps lastly with large-scale capitalism, the basic model of universal inquiry has become institutionally stronger within the university. It is an interesting historical trend much in keeping with the argument of the university as a strong primary institution: at each stage the university became allied with the next rising political authority, and as a result its universal claims to knowledge production and expert training were incrementally strengthened at each turn.

These struggles lasted a long time, and specific universities, depending on which political authority they had support from in a given era, fared better or worse in holding on to their universalistic core. There are a number of examples of these struggles. For instance, universities of imperial Germany were prohibited from teaching and doing scholarship on liberal radical versions of political economy, and even for awhile newly developing empirical scientific research was "condemned as value free and positivist" (Lenhardt 2002, 277). These new ideas and methods of inquiry were deemed as too universalistic and threatening to the conservative social order. The same particularistic control occurred in training experts and cultural elites; for instance, Jews and members of social democratic political parties at all universities, and Catholics at Protestant universities, were prohibited from becoming faculty in imperial Germany. But in these examples of restrictive particularism one sees the power of the institutional model of the university. These restrictions were not the result of crude exclusion or psychological prejudice; rather, the logic of the imperial rulers was such that they fully believed that the German university produced truth and trained scholars of that truth; therefore, ideas and people from outside, or at best on the margins, of German society should not be part of this crucial core undertaking. It was because the university was considered capable of providing this central role that official exclusion was necessary; exclusion from a weak institution would not have been worth the effort.

Another example of the twists and turns of the development of the university is how some political authorities have tried at various points to create new institutions that are particularistic alternatives to the university. France's *grandes écoles* and Germany's *Fachhochschulen* were created at the height of nationalistic (read particularistic) control over higher education in Europe; the former removed elite expert training and the latter removed applied scientific research and training from the university. In both cases these state-created institutions weakened the development of universities in these nations over the twentieth century, and in many ways they are at the root of the crisis of the European university that has been occurring over the past several decades (Baker and Lenhardt 2008). But here too one can see the eventual emergence of the university's claim of universalism. In Germany, as around the world, schools of applied science continue to press for university status and attempt to emulate the latter's universalism; meanwhile, there are no known cases of demands going in the opposite direction, away from university status. Such efforts to become a university would not be undertaken if the university were a weak institution (Lenhardt 2002, 2005).[7]

Taken together, the arguments of Riddle, Stark, and Lenhardt place the university at the center of cultural production, from the rise of Western civilization in medieval Europe to today's global schooled society. As each scholar shows, at many points the university could have taken a different path of development, leading ultimately to less impact on society; instead, over the long span of eight hundred years the university has intensified its original charter to the extent that today it is more supranational and global in scope, as well as more central to the basic ideology of society, than at any time in its history (Baker 2008a).

Three elaborated examples of this process are presented later, but a brief case in point of the university's charter to arbitrate knowledge is Edward Said's late-twentieth-century scholarship done at Columbia University. This influential work challenged an entire political-cultural ideology called "orientalism" in its status as the recognized canon about the people, lands, and cultures of the Middle East (e.g., 1978). Orientalism was itself an intellectual product of European universities and state institutions in the eighteenth and nineteenth centuries. Said's scholarship, based of course on prior scholarship and accepted empirical methods, argued that the ideology of orientalism is not a true view of the region; as such it supported a degrading colonial influence that retarded a dynamic and balanced understanding of a large part of the world. Whether the newer version is truer is not the point here. Rather, it is noteworthy that by virtue of being a product of academic knowledge, the now discarded original ideology had had considerable lasting power in Western culture; just as Said's ideology (now carried forward by many other scholars) is now the widely acknowledged correct and accepted image (i.e., reality) of this region. On the basis of the arbitration of university scholarship, Said's new ideology is taken as true; and as would be expected, this academic arbitration continues (e.g., Lewis, 2004).

With intellectual universalism at its core, the modern university now creates, legitimizes, arbitrates, and distributes a common global culture, which makes the university the ultimate transforming institution of the schooled society, just as Meyer and colleagues suggest in the epigraph. Though there are many examples of this transforming power, the university's role in developing what is perhaps the largest cultural domain of rational inquiry—science—is often underappreciated, and therefore of particular interest.

### THE UNIVERSITY AND A SCIENTIZED WORLD

Science, with its close cousin, technology, drives significant creation of postindustrial society; yet, from the traditional picture of education as a secondary institution it is easy to assume that science and technology derive from society at large, while the university only follows along and, according to some accounts, even gets corrupted in the process. However, this image does not hold up to recent historical analysis of the origins of science and technology, and it inhibits a clear understanding of what is arguably one of the university's most dramatic impacts on current world culture.

From the traditional perspective on education and society, the story about science and the weak university goes as follows. As a result of the intellectual freedom experienced during the Renaissance in Europe, scientific findings and methods increased during the sixteenth century, which led to a scientific revolution and growing adoption of this new form of thinking within society. Only a long time afterwards do universities catch up and become the place where scientists are trained and where most of the work of science happens. For the most part, science is considered a powerful separate entity that finds the university and makes it its home. As the story continues, the university becomes such a good home for science and technology research (presumably because science radically changes the old classical university) that these completely come to dominate the modern university.

The university part of the story ends with one of two versions depending on the teller's opinion about the impact of science and technology on the common good. In a dark version, domination of the university by science epistemologically corrupts the former, killing classical inquiry in the humanities and stifling the essential philosophical and moral education required for any successful modern civilization to offset runaway science and technology (e.g., Bloom 1987). In a brighter version, the once mostly irrelevant university is fortunate to have been found by science and technology, and its rightful obligation to society is to assist the two in achieving the greatest possible progress of human society (Clark 1962; Kerr 2001).

Neither the basic story nor the endings are correct, however, because each assumes the university plays a passive role as it follows behind in support of an independently scientizing, technological society. As already described, a number of historians now question the independent rise of science because their scholarship places the roots of science and rational inquiry further back in history within the culture of early second millennium Christianity (e.g., Grant 1986; Huff 1993a). Most important for an analysis of the role of science in the Western university is the evidence that the seeds of rational inquiry were *within* the earliest universities. Similarly, both Riddle's and Lenhardt's studies point to forerunners of the modern research university in specific universities at Halle (1694), Göttingen (1734), and Erlangen (1743), each of which had enough state support to move universalistic inquiry in a distinctly secular direction without significant interference. The authors' point is that when a political authority provided some protection for the university, without attempting to force too many particularistic functions upon it, universities tended to intensify universalism, not because they saw it as support for science but because of the freedom and ultimate authority a universalistic approach to inquiry won for them. Following this, a major consequence of the pursuit of universalistic inquiry was the creation of the highly rationalized methodology of science, something that many authorities were wary of at the time.[8] Now if this strong version of the role of the university in the production of scientized culture is taken seriously, what is the accurate ending of the story about science, technology, and the university?

Institutional scholars Gili Drori, John Meyer, Francisco Ramirez, and Evan Schofer in *Science in the Modern World Polity* (2003) provide clues to the answer. In this multifaceted study of the rising role of science in the global culture, they show a scientized reality spreading through all kinds of major social institutions. By "scientized culture" they mean that scientific rational inquiry takes on a singular authority which is a widely believed ideology applied to everything from the nature of the cosmos to the minutiae of everyday life. The argument is that science does not so much provide all answers to all questions in a top-down, technical fashion as it provides a widespread belief (ideology) in the assumptions behind science—empirical observation, logical and non-supernatural explanations of phenomena (theories), and generalized rational inquiry (experiments as the highest form)—assumptions that become widely held and are routinely at the base of shared public reality.

Starting with the earliest social theorists, there is of course an already large scholarly literature on how Western culture shifted its base from Christian ideology to, increasingly, rationality, science, and technological discovery. Indeed the descralization of society and what replaced religious dogma as commonly held, public truth is one of the overarching intellectual themes of Western culture (see the paradoxical role of education in religion discussed in Chapter 11). Therefore, Drori and her colleagues' thesis is not particularly new, but how they go about testing it is.

By using historical data about the rise of science and its relationship to authority in many countries, the authors analyze an indicator of the growth of scientized culture across time and place. They find that as the production of science increased over the twentieth century in terms of the number of scientists, scientific publications, expanded scientific training, and the scientific labor force, so too was there an increase in the number of countries with national science policy organizations (e.g., ministries of science and related agencies), a growth in the use of scientific authority within governmental bureaucracies, and more economic and social policy directly connected to the ideology of science and technology as the path to social progress. Drori and colleagues argue that "the coevolution of science and modern social institutions solidified the link between science and various progressive agendas in society" (224). They go on to show that currently and globally, "science includes everything from improvement of individual life (psychologically, medically, politically, morally) . . . to social organization (including the polity, family life and law) . . . to improved human understanding of all aspects of nature (astronomy, physical anthropology, environmental studies)"; or simply put, the reigning cultural ideology of the postmodern world is, for better or worse, thoroughly scientized.

Therefore science, and technological innovation through the application of science, is the embodiment of rationality that has penetrated so deeply into present-day culture. The fact that this process of scientization of life is directly related to the rise of universities is not lost on Drori and her colleagues. While they might have done more analysis of their data from a strong-university perspective, they do show that the expansion of higher education and extensive institutionalization of science go hand in hand. Their interpretation of this link is in line with the arguments above: universities are "more than just a site of professional training, [they] serve to institutionalize the content of science by sustaining a particular set of disciplines"; in other words, they create and sustain new knowledge (224).

The observation that science and universities are linked is also not a new one as a number of higher education watchers noted this as early as the takeoff of large-scale, university-based research in the 1960s (e.g., Ben-David 1971). And since by and large everyone involved in knowledge production at the university and most everywhere else (e.g., independent scientific laboratories, research and development centers in corporations, think-tanks) in society has received extensive specialist training at the university, in many ways it is an obvious observation. But a question remains: Are universities truly at the core of the schooled society through their claim of the lion's share of universalistic inquiry that has created our scientized world?

One way to answer this is to analyze what has happened to the production of "basic and applied research" in universities over the past several decades. Basic research is at the heart of universalistic inquiry, and it is thought to lead to new theory-based knowledge generated by empirical, usually explicitly scientific methods; hence, it is closer to the direct production of scientized culture than is applied research and knowledge, which includes for example the development of a particular technology. Recent analyses of the basic/applied research trends present an intriguing paradox. Many science production observers suggest that a host of factors point to a future when most basic research will be done outside the university; at the same time, it is acknowledged that universities' impact on knowledge production has not diminished, as was widely predicted. Those who focus on the first part of the paradox predict that the university will become increasingly less relevant to the production of science and other basic research. They see the oft-noted trends of greater proliferation of research technologies, increased demand for economic and social relevance in research, and larger shares of research and development moving towards industry all as signs of a declining role for the university in the production of scientific and technological knowledge.

This supposed decline leads to another commonly told ending to the story about science and its university home, which goes as follows. Although initially the modern university was a good home for science and technology development, the newfound bond between science and technology, and considerable success over the past decades, has them outgrowing their university home. Since in a scientized world so many social institutions have become involved in scientific and technical knowledge production, the once cozy home provided by the university now cramps the new style of science and technology and a larger, more suitable mansion is needed. No one knows exactly where this mansion will be, but those who tell this version of the story all agree that the old university home is fading out of the picture.

Those who see it this way argue that a once successful process of knowledge production has been transformed into a revolutionary new one. They claim that the older process, portrayed as negatively antiquated, unfolded long ago in a university environment characterized by the advancement of theory within traditional academic disciplines, "small science," and a linear, one-way transfer of scientific knowledge out of the university to technology development in industry. The new process, in contrast, occurs in a context of social and economic application marked by transdisciplinarity, heterogeneity of knowledge production, and an interchange between science and technology that leads both forward and beyond the university. The brave new world of the new process has been termed "Mode 2 knowledge production," while the supposed antiquated process is called "Mode 1 knowledge production" (Gibbons et al. 1994; Nowotny, Scott, and Gibbons 2001).

Starting in the mid-1990s, predictions of an emerging Mode 2 process made a splash in science and university management circles, particularly since they forecasted that the university's role in knowledge production would radically diminish in the near future. Mode 2-ers reasoned that the success and growth of science and technology development had reached such proportions that they would destabilize the university; in the coming knowledge society, the university must widely share its claim to universalism and rational inquiry or essentially fade into a training facility (Gibbons et al. 1994). This is essentially a new wrinkle on the usual weak-institution picture of the university; apparently the university was strong enough to support universal knowledge production, but over time was not strong enough to withstand its own growing institutional success.

Interestingly, the trends that initially motivated Mode 2 predictions are all true: there is a constant growth in knowledge and in access to it, considerable growth in knowledge producers, and economies are increasingly driven by new knowledge production. Furthermore, it is also true that non-university organizations such as private firms and government research centers have gotten into the research game in a big way. And too, large parts of the world operate on more and more generated knowledge that can have major social and economic implications. The problem with the Mode 2 interpretation of these trends is that it unnecessarily jumps to the assumption that universities will therefore produce less and less basic research.

In reality, the writing on Mode 2 science is equal parts critique of Mode 1 and fantasy about how the world should be, so the argument about why the university will decline (or has already) in basic knowledge production is a bit odd. The coiners of Modes 1 and 2, Gibbons and colleagues, first correctly note that "the massification of higher education provides the base for which knowledge industries could emerge [and] higher education . . . had the effect of supplying the continuous flow of trained manpower for the industrial system" (1994, 85). But they then argue that all of this training and even the past success with research have destabilized the university, rendering it less effective in producing knowledge:

This process supposedly harbours an instability. By providing increasing numbers of scientifically literate graduates, the universities are continuously working to their own disadvantage by ensuring that the number of able trained people outside universities rises continuously, relative to the number of those within . . . universities [who] will comprise only part, perhaps only a small part, of the knowledge producing sector. They are no longer in a strong enough position, either scientifically economically or politically, to determine what shall count as excellent in teaching or research. (85)

But why assume this? Unless there is a major shock to the system, the successful social institution usually breeds more success. It is hard to imagine why the university, the developer of universalistic knowledge over eight hundred years, would suddenly, on the cusp of perhaps its biggest and most widespread success, be overwhelmed and then recede. The problem is that proponents of Mode 2 knowledge production begin by assuming that the university is a relatively weak institution. From this position it is easy to speculate that new organizations taking part in a rising tide of science and technology production would diminish the university's role. However, what ultimately transpired within universities as these new trends in science and technology unfolded tells a very different story, which is understandable only from the perspective that universities are the main creator of basic research and that their successful model is rapidly spreading and transforming applied science into the more universalistic image of basic research.

Historian of American higher education Roger Geiger's cogent analysis of basic research production over the second half of the twentieth century solves the paradox. The production of science and technology in the United States is the largest among all nations, so arguably what occurs in that country has a large impact on science and technology worldwide (U.K. Royal Society 2011). Examining patterns of research funding, Geiger first shows the consequences of the trends that originally motivated speculation about Mode 2 knowledge production (2004).[9] The federal government's share in funding research (once the source of most university-based research) declined dramatically over the twenty years from 1980 to 2000, from almost one half to just over a fourth of the nation's total expenditures on research and development (of technology), referred to as R&D. What gained proportionally during the same time were private firms, which now fund 70 percent of all U.S. R&D. Furthermore, the funding for basic research, which is predominately carried out in universities, grew only from about 14 to 18 percent.

So, on the surface it would appear that basic research and the university's share of it are in serious decline just as suggested by the Mode 2 argument—if it were not for two other related trends that prove otherwise.

First is the trend that the overall growth of U.S. R&D from 1980 to 2000 kept pace with the rapid growth of science and technology that the world has experienced since the seventeenth century (de Solla Price 1963). Combined university-based and non-university-based R&D (basic research and expensive technology development) spending from 1980 to 2000 more than doubled in constant dollars from about $115 to $248 billion. Second is the fact that within this rapidly expanding R&D climate the university has held its share of about one half of all basic research. While federal support for research to American universities has declined, it has been replaced by private economic sources; overall, academic funding as a share of GDP grew by 50 percent in twenty years to an amazing $28.2 billion in 2000, and by 2009, the year after the large market devaluation, when total U.S. R&D expenditure had grown to $400 billion, the university had almost doubled its 2000 expenditure (National Science Foundation 2012). The Mode 2-ers are thus correct in observing that more non-university funding and research organizations are in the research game, but they missed the staying power of university-based basic research, which expanded right along with a dramatically growing R&D pie (Geiger 2004).

Further, Geiger identifies an emerging *knowledge production conglomerate* in American research universities consisting of this robust funding situation plus existing trends in the organization of university research and scholarship, which are aimed at interdisciplinary scholarship, the proliferation of research institutes, and "raising the bar" for expected faculty research and new knowledge production. This muscular academic approach to knowledge generation stems from a broad consensus in the United States (and most everywhere else) around the idea that university research is crucial to economic global competitiveness (Geiger and Sá 2008). While being a narrower argument than the one developed here about the university and the schooled society, it is nevertheless consistent with the primacy of the university and the intensification of its original institutional charter in the creation of knowledge. So too, the university has been deeply involved in developing new inquiries strategies. Certainly, the older Mode 1 of traditional academic disciplines, "small science," and one-way transfer of scientific knowledge continues, but at the same time universities have adopted and in many cases innovated on many of the Mode 2 rallying cries for transdisciplinarity, heterogeneity of knowledge production, and an interchange between science and technology development.

The ability to maintain its share and ride a growing wave of R&D expansion is evidence of the university's enduring ability to generate universalistic inquiry and produce fundamental knowledge that feeds an ideology of rationality and science into world culture. Counter to the Mode 2 hypothesis and more compatible with *all* the empirical trends is the view that over the past fifty years Drori and colleagues' developing scientizing world has been driven in large part by the education revolution, for which the university provided much of the original ideology. From this perspective, one could argue that much of what underlies the knowledge society is really the schooled society with the university as its strongest and furthest-reaching institution. (This interpretation is developed further in Chapter 8.) Rapid worldwide growth in higher education obviously produces more individuals who are scientifically literate, but broadly this growth imbues a large proportion of the globe's population with a culture of rational inquiry, giving that culture unprecedented legitimation which in turns fuels the university's multiple-tiered charter.

Admittedly, this historical institutional analysis skims over a lot of detailed history about the university and its objectives at various times. There were, of course, many historical zigzags in the development of the Western university into what it is today. Particular regions and nations developed traditions that emphasized only certain aspects of the overall institutional model. The Germanic Humboldtian model was a precursor to the research university; the British version embodied by the ideas of John Henry Newman emphasized limited training of cultural elites; and the French Napoleonic model broke off elite training from the university altogether. Plus, there were dead ends in some nations during some eras, resulting in a fair number of failed universities. Nevertheless, the university has become the model for all formal education and, by extension, a model for the schooled society itself. Perhaps most supportive of the strong-university argument is that the university's original functions—knowledge production, training of experts in this knowledge, and a dynamic synthesis between them—are not only still intact today but remaining at the core of this primary institution in society.

The explosion of science and technological development at the turn of the twenty-first century may seem a far cry from Stark's thirteenth-century Christian scholars searching for a reasoned way to their rational God or from Lenhardt's eighteenth-century professors extending universalistic inquiry right under the noses of local political authorities. Yet these early developments towards rational inquiry were the vanguards of an institution that now is the global model for nearly all universities. It is also the embodiment of the institutionalization of science and as such is ultimately the wellspring of our scientized schooled society. This has not destabilized the university as an institution; quite to the contrary, and as described in the next chapter, the massification of higher education is a key factor driving the growth of an unprecedentedly resourced research-intensified university.

### CHAPTER 4

# Mass Education
# and the Super Research University

The university has already become the most important . . . focus of modern society, and is likely to become still more important in the future, superseding even the business firm and the governmental structure. . . . We now have by far the largest-scale institutionalization of change in important parts of the cultural system that . . . has ever existed.

TALCOTT PARSONS, "Higher Education as a Theoretical Focus," 1971

AMERICAN MEDIA routinely enjoy pointing out that famous success stories, such as those of Thomas Edison, Bill Gates, and Albert Einstein, can happen without much basic education, like Edison, or without the now routine undergraduate or MBA degree, like Gates, or without being on the faculty at a research university, like Einstein during his early discoveries.[1] Although these stories make good copy, they are frequently misinterpreted as meaning that education is only vaguely relevant to successful innovation, business, and even scientific genius. But it is the rarity of these exceptions that illustrates the point about the dynamic relationship between university knowledge generation and the training of experts. In the schooled society, the vast majority of high-level success stories rest on a foundation of formal education, usually culminating in one, and increasingly two or more, graduate degrees. This is not because of some natural outcome of learning technical material alone; rather, education as an institution constructs ideas of expertise and the knowledge that the expert is entitled to wield, and the university is at the heart of this construction as well as its wide dissemination throughout postindustrial culture.

A symbiotic relationship between educating and knowledge production as a cultural force is hardly new in the history of the university. What is new though is the unprecedented intensification and acceleration of both—the extension of university (and related) training to ever larger proportions of youth, and the immense increase in resources applied to the university's claim to generate new knowledge. As described in the preceding chapter, as the knowledge society emerged the university did not recede in its influence nor did it narrow its degree-creating and -granting functions. Instead, as Parsons predicted forty years ago, a claim can be made that the university has become the central cultural institution in society because of its multiple-tiered charter to generate the universal knowledge that forms basic ideologies and creates academic degrees and expertise around these ideologies. If true, the university would have had to intensify its original charter to a level unimaginable even at the start of the education revolution. Therefore, is there evidence of this? One way to approach this question is by examining recent dynamic interactions among the parts of the charter. Here is described the dynamic between an upsizing of the university's knowledge production conglomerate and the proliferation of universities and access to them. The following chapter will examine the intensifying interaction between knowledge production and degree creation.

## THE SUPER RESEARCH UNIVERSITY
## AND THE KNOWLEDGE CONGLOMERATE

Over the past several decades, two major transforming trends in higher education have been occurring, which reflect the intensification of the university's charter. These are widely observed yet only rarely in relationship to each other. In fact, among many observers of higher education these two trends represent polar opposites, which on the surface seem to create more conflict than harmony within the university. One trend, already noted, is the continuation of the education revolution in the form of unprecedented expansion of higher education in most nations. The other trend is the rise and flourishing of what can be called the "super research university," initially in the United States but increasingly as a model aspired to by many research universities throughout the world (Mohrman, Ma, and Baker 2008). Often the former trend is dismissed as pedestrian while the latter is celebrated, but what is not appreciated is that they are related, symbiotically, to the point that each would likely not be happening if not for the other. Together they take the cultural impact of the university to a whole new level.

The advent of the super research university (hereafter, "super RU") over the past several decades, primarily in the United States, is a stunning educational development (Cole 2009). While it has its detractors and supporters, most agree that the super RU is an intensification of a number of unique qualities of the Western university, resulting in a small but growing number of institutions that have the capacity to generate unprecedented levels of science, technology, and knowledge about human society and the physical universe. Sometimes identified as "world-class universities," these institutions lead the establishment of an emerging model of the university that is rapidly becoming the accepted standard by which institutions will undertake graduate and professional training within the context of research production.[2] As already described, the particular characteristics of the super RU can be traced back to the earliest of universities in feudal Western Europe, but the expanding resources dedicated to these aspects and the prominence given to them within the university and the culture at large mark a new era for knowledge production. Some debate continues among university watchers about what the exact model of the super research university of the future will be, but most agree on a set of characteristics that are emerging as a foundation which will take the institution into the future (e.g., Altbach and Salmi 2011; Chait 2002; Geiger 1993; Mohrman, Ma, and Baker 2007; Pelikan 1994).

First and obviously, super RUs strive to be ever more research-intensive, not only in science and technology but also in the scientization of disciplines traditionally outside the sciences, such as the now thoroughly scientized study of humans (e.g., behavioral and social sciences) (Drori, Meyer, Ramirez, and Schofer 2003; Drori and Moon 2006). The intensity of research far exceeds past experience and drives worldwide competition for students, faculty, staff, and funding. Like the universities that house them, research projects are often global rather than just national in reach. Similarly, more research explicitly uses strategies aimed at multi- and transdisciplinarity to generate teams and larger external funding streams. What was once a dominant focus on individual scholarship has been transformed into large-scale scientific research done with teams of faculty and graduate students in expensive, state-of-the-art laboratories. This "big science" model has spilled over into all parts of the faculty as social scientists and even traditional scholars in the arts and humanities are encouraged to adopt as much of the model as possible. Moreover, a priority pertains for theoretical knowledge that can lead to marketable products (Pau 2003). In a practice often termed "dual integration," research universities are developing science parks, research incubators, technology transfer offices, and spinoff businesses to carry products to market.

The intensity and spread of a scientific model of research is one of the most controversial aspects about the impact of the super RU on higher education. For example, faculties in the humanities declare their own immunity to many of these transformations, but nonetheless, escalating expectations of scholarly productivity are evident in these fields too. Similarly, faculty, seen now more as producers of new knowledge than as traditional scholars, are assuming new roles, shifting from traditional independent patterns of inquiry to becoming members of team-oriented, cross-disciplinary, and international partnerships. Research in the super RU is now directed, at least on the surface, more often toward perceived real-world problems than purely scholarly interests (Altbach 2011). Like all characteristics of the super RU, its intensification of research holds perceived costs or benefits depending on the perspective of the observer. For instance, in observing American super RUs, many point out the benefits of interdisciplinary research, resource leveraging, and greater collaboration in the production of knowledge, but at the cost of teaching, graduate training, and diversity in scholarly approach.[3] Much of the explicit justification for supporting the super RU rests on the assumption that investment in human capital is good for society and that new knowledge leads to a better world. The emerging cultural model holds that nations and society-writ-large can harness a rational process of knowledge production through public investment in the research university, and super RUs are widely considered a key ingredient in the recipe for managed social and economic progress (Frank and Meyer 2007).

A second characteristic of these institutions is that they see themselves among a set of universities whose mission is not local or even national, but explicitly global. In transcending national concerns, the super RU's image of its fundamental mission is the antithesis of the older national-flagship university, which focused on the production of successive generations of national elites. Further, instead of considering itself a passive bystander or even a critical reactor, the super RU prides itself on being an active participant in the process of globalization of knowledge. Ironically, the assumed small set of elite universities is not very small, at least in view of self-nominations and organizational expectations. Universities worldwide are now openly and unabashedly declaring their intention to be among the most influential and best research universities in the world, even in the face of restricted resources and lack of full autonomy (Mohrman, Ma, and Baker 2007). This goal is accompanied by the explicit assumption that the frontiers of knowledge are broader—universal—than national boundaries, and the guiding image is that communities of scholars of all disciplines transcend national borders. While this has always been the case, from the earliest Western universities on, the new super RUs see themselves as especially active organizational players in the global production of knowledge, and thus they explicitly dedicate resources to be global. Therefore, the model behind these institutions is that a wide competition for the discovery of new knowledge exists and that this competition is global (i.e., among super RUs worldwide, not just among individual scholars).

Third, with the expansion of the super RU's mission and its intensification of research, expectations for the faculty role also expand and intensify around research. So professors are evaluated in large part on their success in getting external funding for scholarship and on the publication of research results, especially in English-language (meaning globally accessible) journals. Even on campuses quite different from leading research universities, the demands on faculty for research publishing have increased dramatically. Faculty are expected not only to conduct publishable research but also to teach graduate and undergraduate students, provide service to their universities, and use their knowledge for the benefit of local, national, and global communities. In addition, institutions seek to extend their research emphasis to graduate and undergraduate students, engaging students in research projects earlier in their education than ever before. There is evidence that many undergraduates think they gain from this and future students will come to expect these opportunities (e.g., Seymour, Hunter, Laursen, and DeAntoni 2004). This process certainly ratchets up the expectations and standards for direct research involvement of students throughout the higher education system.

In a related vein, super RUs in particular and all kinds of universities in general are adopting worldwide recruitment strategies for students, faculty, and administrators. Well-recognized super RUs have thoroughly international faculty; for example, the London School of Economics, ETH Zurich, and the University of Hong Kong each have more than 80 percent of their faculty originating from outside their national borders. A number of other universities, especially British and Commonwealth institutions, report that more than half of their professors are citizens of other nations. Universities in Western Europe and North America, long the magnet for students from other parts of the world, have a tradition of persuading their best Ph.D. students to remain in country as scholars and teachers—and many of those bright graduate students want to do exactly that. But at the same time, ambitious universities, eager to move into the international higher education scene, recruit professors from other countries to bring instant upgrading, and often prestige, to their campuses.

Fourth, the model behind the super RU has significantly upped the complexity of the internal organization of institutions. In recent years, research universities have expanded substantially, often desiring to become more comprehensive and integrated by adding new programs to existing departments, establishing professional schools, launching new research centers, encouraging interdisciplinary units, creating offices focused on corporate research projects, and developing science parks to collaborate with businesses in an effort to take academic research to the marketplace. The expansion of its charter to create new knowledge is matched by the university's internal organization to make such knowledge and distribute it. Well-known examples of this increased internal complexity in the research-intensive super RU are the Jet Propulsion Laboratory at Caltech and the Applied Physics Laboratory at Johns Hopkins. There are similar complex units in the medical and social sciences at many super RUs. This growing complexity transforms the nature of large-scale academic scholarship. Such units take faculty as researchers out of traditional departments and supply them with facilities, scientific colleagues, and other assistance to develop bigger, interdisciplinary, and very expensive science. The availability of competitive funding for scientific R&D has made such units essential for any institution that aims to become a high-quality research university. Through their autonomous research role inside the university, these organized research units have intensified the knowledge production capabilities of their institutions (Geiger 2004).

Fifth, the model of the super RU is driven by, and in turn deepens, the participation of universities in an interesting mix of competition and cooperation, which thereby intensifies networks of universities. The proliferation and importance of even crudely done rankings of universities in terms of knowledge production is one clear indicator of this trend (this system will likely become more sophisticated in the near future). At the same time, universities increasingly enter into some degree of cooperation, particularly for obtaining very large funded projects. The global aspirations and growing similarities across universities worldwide propel both competition and cooperation (Meyer, Ramirez, Frank, and Schofer 2007). Manifesting the transcending mission of the global institution is the growth of international university associations that offer a forum for these complex organizations to appraise their structure and performance vis-à-vis other like-minded members. An example of this is the European Union's Erasmus Mundus program, a cooperation and mobility initiative promoting the European Union as a center of excellence in learning around the world. Another example is the Association of Pacific Rim Universities, involving thirty-seven comprehensive, research-intensive institutions on all shores of the Pacific. A recently organized group, the Intensive Research University Association, is highly selective, permitting only super RUs to join. The explicit member benefits of these international associations of universities are multiple: to share information, to establish formal programs of student and faculty exchange, to improve access to international resources, to facilitate collaborative research, and to provide a global dimension to the curriculum. These global organizations also provide a validation of international stature, lending significant prestige to member universities.

Lastly, what has caught the most public attention about the emerging model of the super RU is the extreme level of funds required to support its activities. Research funding has rapidly moved to levels unimaginable even a few decades ago. On the research side, estimates of required annual funding to support a super RU with a medical center are $1.5 billion plus. Some universities have annual costs far beyond this, such as Johns Hopkins with its 2011 total budget of $4.4 billion and research grant revenues of $2.5 billion (The Johns Hopkins University 2011). Not surprisingly, few institutions can compete at these levels of funding. Approximately thirty U.S. universities have budgets of at least this size, while as of yet no European institution can match such resources (Ward 2005). In the United States, such institutions receive about 20 percent of their budget from state tax revenues and another 30–40 percent from competitive research grants; meanwhile, the share of private funds pouring into both public and private universities in the United States is unprecedented. As governments flatten higher education expenditures, all universities increasingly raise money through different strategies, including private donors, increased tuition and fees, grants for research and technical innovation, profits from spinoff businesses, contracts with corporate entities, recruitment of international students for higher fees, and so on. Finally, the strength of the super RU model is such that it increasingly shapes what many universities do and strive for, even less-funded institutions, which may never have the potential to be truly research-intensive.

### MASS EDUCATION MEETS
### THE SUPER RESEARCH UNIVERSITY

The United States currently has the highest number of universities with the characteristics described above, and these institutions produce considerable amounts of new knowledge across many fields (U.K. Royal Society 2011). For example, systematic assessments from a few years ago indicate that of the ten universities worldwide having the highest rate of research productivity and quality, eight are U.S. institutions, while many other American universities are above the world average.[4] Similarly, the majority of universities capable of generating enough money to sustain the super RU model are today American.

What is missed in observations of the super RU's origin is its relationship to mass higher education and considerable societal support. The usual take on the American case—private money, low central control, and high tolerance for between-institution inequality—is not why so many of the super RUs are found in the United States. The root cause is not just that the super RU model is expensive to pursue and thus requires a wealthy society. Nor is it that private money now makes up a substantial part of funding in the United States; nor even that many super RUs are privately controlled. While these factors certainly have enhanced the development of the super RU model, they are not its origin. Instead, the cause is found in the way the American society has generated widespread societal support for higher education, including and culminating in research universities. In other words, formal education in the United States has been an early leader in the movement towards mass higher education and all that its development entails. Instead of assuming that mass access to higher education and the model of the super RU are mutually exclusive, zero-sum forces, what the American case illustrates is that these two trends support each other, as well as some coming world trends.

This fundamental symbiotic relationship is not the product of some intentional central plan; rather, it grew out of a unique set of historical conditions. These conditions become more obvious as the model for the American super research university becomes attractive to other nations, leading higher education in many nations to mimic certain aspects of the model—including faculty working conditions, competitive-based governmental support for research, a large private-sector basis, and so forth. Yet what is frequently missed in these efforts is the exceptional societal support the United States has been able to generate for education, and for higher education specifically.

It has achieved this support for essentially two reasons: first is the nation's comprehensive system of secondary education, which graduates youth who in turn aspire to and expect more education; and second is its long history of a relatively open and comprehensive higher education system. This yielded the relatively early belief within American society that the university, particularly the super RU, is not an elitist or esoteric enterprise; instead, it is perceived to a remarkable degree as a democratic and useful institution. The fact that so many Americans attend some institution of higher education and have deep connections to these diverse institutions translates into wide societal support for the funding of the super RU, even if only a small proportion of Americans will attend one. As with the expansion of mass and comprehensive (nonstratified) elementary and secondary education, the country has led the way in mass higher education with the idea that more and more types of people can develop as individuals (and not just as workers in the narrow sense) through extended formal education. Today about 60–70 percent of American youth with a secondary school diploma enroll in some type of higher education; while many other nations have caught up and more will, the United States has been the leader in higher education expansion. Further, what the research university has long thought to do for American society by its public in turn legitimates continued expansion of education for all, and this has foreshadowed current trends in many other nations.

The tremendous level of private support for higher education in the United States is not only a reflection of rising tuition; it also reflects how higher education and specifically universities are thought about in the country. The lack of an exclusive, state-controlled set of universities and other institutions of higher education has led to robust and broad support of individual institutions, and of the entire sector to a considerable degree. Certainly, rising tuitions and private funding is a trend that has upper limits, and implications for unequal access; in some ways the trend is a product of diminishing public funds for higher education. But the idea of societal support is broader than just the shifting split between public and private funding; in the United States the resource pie continues to grow for higher education.

The land-grant model of the research university, which developed in America in the nineteenth century, sowed the seeds of the future of American higher education, and in many ways the future of global higher education. A case can be made that land-grant institutions presented the forerunner of the model that now drives the super RU, especially in terms of the symbiotic relationship between the university and society; it is a model representing a major intensification of the past institutional trajectory of the university in Western Europe (Lenhardt 2005). The model joined together several strands of ideas into one institution for the first time—scientific knowledge, rational social progress, wider non-elite human empowerment, and the privileging of universalistic knowledge—which became embedded within the authority of the university; today, this authority, based on an intensification of these ideas in the modern world, drives the support of the super RU model in the United States (see also Geiger 1993; Meyer, Ramirez, Frank, and Schofer 2007). Ironically, given all the hype about "world-class" universities as elite organizations, the model of the American super RU thrives on waves of support from the public for the university as a democratic, mass institution in American society (Baker 2008a, 2008b; Ross 1942). This has meant that the knowledge production conglomerate is extremely expansive in the nation. In turn, the considerable American capacity to produce science, technology, social science, plus all other scholarship rides upon the expanding educational dreams of the average eighteen-to-twenty-one-year-old undergraduate!

An illustrative counterexample is the current state of crisis in the German university and its role in society (Baker and Lenhardt 2008). The decades-long crisis and calls for change run through nearly every aspect of the German university (Enders, Kehm, and Schimank 2002). The cost of reunification of East and West Germany produced an acute shortage of funds even as enrollment increased (national enrollments have more than doubled since the 1970s) and demand rose for greater higher education services. Stagnation of public funds is particularly damaging to efforts towards fostering internationally competitive basic research in the universities, as they receive only a relatively small share of the entire national research budget and they must contend with a healthy, budget-capturing sector of extra-university research organizations, such as the Max Planck Institutes. Problems with inflexible teaching loads have raised concerns about the quality of instruction, inadequate time for research, and a growing student discontent with the institution (e.g., Enders and Teichler 1995). Similarly, problems of ineffective mentoring, inordinately long periods of dependency on full professors, and adherence to the feudal *Habilitation* (i.e., second thesis) system of access to professorships hamper the development of junior faculty and young university scientists, which is needed to sustain the university's research tradition (e.g., Holtkamp 1996). What had been an innovative and internally competitive system of universities in the nineteenth century is now described as "institutionally immobile," exhibiting many of the opposite tendencies from those that once made it a world model (Ben-David and Zloczower 1991). Mini-steps are now being taken by the German higher education system to reform the university, but these are far from the extreme levels of qualities that are driving most super RUs in the United States and elsewhere.

As in the United States, many in the German system fail to appreciate that access and internationally competitive research are symbiotic, because they represent two parts of the underlying intensified model of the university at the heart of the schooled society. The ideas behind the American comprehensive secondary system and its relatively open higher education system—ideas that encourage wide societal support—have yet to transpire in Germany (Baker, Köhler, and Stock 2007).[5] Along with several other Western European nations, Germany holds on dearly to the older idea of "manpower planning" supported by a highly stratified secondary system crowned by the *Gymnasium* and the university as the source of society's elite.[6] It is no wonder that the German higher education system finds it difficult to capture the funding (public or private) to compete globally in its research universities. Why would people who were cut off at the early stages of education—fourth through sixth grades—from the *Gymnasium*, which leads to the university, support the latter, individually or collectively? The logic behind this sentiment is aptly reflected by an offhand remark from a German higher educationalist, who on hearing a thorough description of the efforts and success of American super RUs to raise funds through alumni gifts said, "for a German, university-trained or not, being asked to give money to a university would be like asking him to give a gift to the post office!"[7]

Another counterexample comes from the American system itself. When the multiple institutions of the City University of New York (CUNY) were differentiated in the 1990s, resulting in a certain amount of segregation of research and access to mass undergraduate education, a number of problems and a general institutional weakening of CUNY occurred (Bastedo and Gumport 2003; Gumport and Bastedo 2001).

Precisely during the era of the American (and soon worldwide) super RU, a growth in university graduate training also increased, directly in-graining a larger proportion of the population than ever before in the university's knowledge conglomerate. Obviously, universities have been training experts ever since their inception, for positions within and without the university. From the thirteenth century onward, most Popes were themselves university-trained, as were many of the cardinals that made up the Church's central bureaucracy of the Curia (Rüegg 1992). For a considerable part of their long history universities have been explicitly about training experts, professionals, and what might be called social elites, often as one and the same.[8] Educating and certifying lawyers and the learned religious as professionalized experts in secular and religious contexts are the earliest examples of the use of university training in developing authority that soon spread to related positions of authoritative social control, such as medical doctors. This training of authority continued and slowly expanded over the course of the university's development, but since at least the 1970s in the United States, and increasingly elsewhere, the commingling of the university's knowledge production and advanced-degree granting has accelerated to a level unknown over the past eight hundred years. For example, as shown in Figure 4.1, both enrollment in all graduate programs and completion of master's degrees have increased by substantial amounts. Over this time, the growth rates in the number of people completing a master's or a Ph.D. is 140 percent and 50 percent, respectively. Similarly, professional degrees, such as in law, medicine, and dentistry, have increased by over 100 percent over the same period.[9]

Postbaccalaureate training in the United States has grown along with an expanding proportion of secondary school completers enrolling as undergraduates. For instance, in the academic year 2006–2007 the entire U.S.

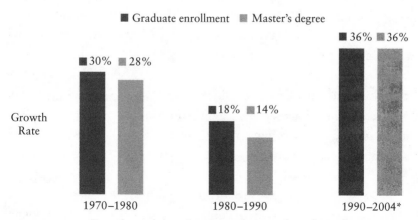

FIGURE 4.1 *Growth trends in university graduate study in the U.S., 1970–2004.*
* Note fourteen-year period.
Source: National Center for Education Statistics, "Digest of Education Statistics" (2005)

higher education system graduated just over 1.5 million students with the baccalaureate (hereafter, BA for all forms) *and* another 755,000 students with graduate degrees, for a ratio of about one graduate degree for every two BA degrees (U.S. Department of Education, NCES 2008). Since the early 2000s, individuals earning advanced degrees have had the highest rate of increase in U.S. history; over the past decade new Ph.D.s grew by 1 million (45%) and masters' by 5 million (43%) (U.S. Census Bureau 2012).

Included in this unprecedented growth in graduate degrees are not only cohorts of experts filling the scientific and technical expectations of a scientized world but also scores of experts trained for a rationalized and universalized world that includes every sector of society. For example, as discussed in the next chapter, the largest share of master's degrees is the MBA. At the same time, more individuals are attaining multiple graduate degrees. The U.S. Department of Education followed a nationally representative sample of 1992–93 BA completers over the following ten years: four out of ten enrolled in some graduate study during the decade, and one fourth of these enrolled in multiple graduate degree programs of which half were for two or more masters' in different disciplines (U.S. Department of Education, NCES 2007).[10] Among BA degree holders from private research universities, where a significant amount of the spectacular success of American research universities has been, over five out of ten BA completers enrolled in graduate programs and over a fourth of these enrolled in more than one degree program. Similarly large numbers of BA holders envision themselves as completing a graduate degree or two sometime in their future; and the U.S. study reports that at the time of BA completion a full 85 percent expected to undertake graduate training over the ensuing decade. Of course, this did not happen (yet) for about one half of these individuals, but the implications are clear: graduate training at the university is becoming more normative with each passing decade. This (along with early childhood education) is the newest wave of dynamic educational expansion.

What was once the reserve of the elite students in the United States and elsewhere is rapidly turning the corner towards mass graduate schooling. For example, many American universities already have extensive programs to recruit and assist in graduate degree completion by underrepresented students from socially disadvantaged backgrounds, even though these prospective graduate students, having all completed the BA, would hardly still be disadvantaged in terms of educational attainment. No doubt the usual cycle of contrasting reactions (mostly unfounded, as discussed in Chapter 6) to this wave of education will follow rapidly on its heels; indeed, one can almost hear the inevitable public lament about the dashed dreams of graduate education of so many BA holders, right along with dire predictions of the effects of too many people holding graduate degrees!

Many assume that with higher education expansion comes a dumbing-down towards a secondary school model in universities, but there is evidence that mass undergraduate training adapts to the historical university model, blending a university education with the value of education for all. For example, consider the large numbers of remedial courses now offered to undergraduates and aimed at assisting the academically challenged student to finish the BA; these are not a way to shunt students off onto lesser educational routes, nor a way to usher them out of the university altogether. Also, about one hundred U.S. public universities and colleges now have special programs for "intellectually disabled youth" (the current phrase for youth with Down syndrome or other forms of mental retardation) to experience university life and in some cases earn credits towards a degree. As a parent of one university-enrolled daughter with mental retardation reports, "she would so many times say, 'I wish I could go to college'; she loves to learn, and she has missed it ever since high school stopped" (*Chronicle of Higher Education*, 2005). Increasingly, too, degrees that merge the undergraduate and graduate together in various five-year programs are on the rise, as is the university's reaching into secondary schools and their curricula via distance learning and credit for advanced courses.

The advanced stage of the education revolution invites all into the university, from whence its core ideas came, as the university creates a powerful ideology that supports universalism of individuals and of knowledge. The medieval Popes' Curia and secular advisors like Thomas More were members of a razor-thin social stratum of university-trained and -chartered experts, which since has grown into a broad, encompassing portion of the population of postindustrial society. This is not a result of an expanding elite as much as mass higher education's development of a successful model of knowledge, credentials, and experts. Together, the expanding knowledge conglomerate and mass higher education form a major avenue by which the ideologies that the university facilitates enter into everyday culture— a phenomenon, as described next, that is rarely driven by purely external influences such as technology, capitalism, or newly perceived societal needs.

### CHAPTER 5

# Constructing Reality

## *Ice Cream, Women's Studies, and the MBA*

From the fuel economy of cars to getting pregnant, from stealth technology in war to teenage rebellion [all are] to be understood in a day-to-day basis around basic natural-scientific understandings. The process at work here is the reverse of that which gave rise to the applied sciences over the century. In [that] case, society penetrated university sciences . . . now [university] sciences penetrate society.

DAVID FRANK AND JAY GABLER, *Reconstructing the University*, 2006

The new B.A. that we're going to be offering will be called "The Management of Aging Services" . . . it will integrate management science with public policy with gerontology.

KEVIN ECKERT, Dean of the University of Maryland's newly endowed School of Aging Studies, May 2006

THE MOST COMMON IMAGE of knowledge that underpins our sense of reality is that it is objective, natural, and waiting out there somewhere to be found. When a new piece of this knowledge is found, it moves from the unknown pile to the known pile and never the other way, so that ever more of the unknown becomes known. Scientific discoveries are often talked about in precisely this fashion—"what was not known before but now is." Yet this turns out to be a naïve perspective. Volumes of inquiry and thought about the philosophy and sociology of knowledge contend that humans socially construct knowledge (e.g., R. Collins 1998). Yet the notion of social construction does not imply some flimsy, willy-nilly, or idiosyncratic process; instead, it refers to a widely shared process of social construction through the inner workings of social institutions (Berger and Luckmann 1966). Social construction of knowledge also does not mean that physical facts can be willed in or out of existence. Insistence on the belief that the apple will *not* fall from the tree invokes images of insanity—the belief in nonreality—not to mention a very real bump on the head. Certainly, facts are facts and new ones are discovered all the time, but how humans interpret these and weave them together to form explanations of a broader understanding of their reality is what is meant by the observation that *knowledge is socially constructed* (e.g., Berger and Luckmann 1966; Young 2008).

Probably the most accessible illustration of this is to contrast a society that is based on a religious account of reality with one based on a secularized, rational, scientific account. Both societies exist in the same physical world, but widespread belief (knowledge) within one society that a deity (or deities) causes the apple to fall, versus the other society's belief in a godless (or at least divinely unmediated) law of gravity is a matter of social construction within the main social institutions of each society. Of course, diverse modern societies contain overlapping constructions of knowledge, so that even though secular rationality and all that it implies is now the driving approach to knowledge worldwide, many individuals and a few institutions continue to carry alternative religious explanations.[1] But even so, there are clearly dominant forms of knowledge behind the understanding of reality that are widely shared and accepted as such. For well over one hundred and fifty years the main trend in the socially constructed reality of worldwide society has been toward rationalized explanations and away from religious ones, or what Max Weber so appropriately referred to as the disenchantment of the reality of modern life.[2]

The preceding two chapters demonstrated the central role the university plays in the social construction of ideologies; explored here is how its charter to connect knowledge production and degree creation is intensifying, and interjecting its authoritative ideologies into ever more aspect of daily life.

### THE UNIVERSITY AND BELIEFS ABOUT REALITY

Neo-institutionalists of education David Frank and Jay Gabler undertook a sweeping study of the transformation of the university's core knowledge production over the twentieth century to address the connection between the development of the university and its impact on modern cosmology and ontology (2006; see also Drori and Moon 2006). Their basic argument is similar to one developed here: "university knowledge maps reality" (17).

To illustrate this, they began by amassing an archive of numbers of faculty, by departments, and course rosters from 159 universities worldwide in 1915 up to 711 universities by 1995.[3] In what most would overlook as historical trivia, Frank and Gabler creatively saw a way to trace trends in faculty disciplinary makeup (i.e., assignment to academic departments) and course content as indicators of the type of knowledge being produced, sustained, and mapped over the century by universities. They argue that these data reflect broad shifting trends in the social construction of knowledge in universities over the century.

They examined three branches of the curriculum and the accompanying number of departmental faculty: (1) the humanities, such as philosophy, literature, linguistics, the arts, and classics; (2) the natural sciences, such as physics, biology, geology, and early on, botany; and (3) social-behavioral sciences, such psychology, economics, and sociology. They also divided the curriculum and faculty between basic subjects, or those fields that produce "knowledge for knowledge sake," and subjects that represent an expansion of an academic approach to things not originally within the purview of the university; in short, a distinction between a faculty and curricular emphasis on classical subjects versus an academic approach applied to new elements in everyday society.

While various parts of what Frank and Gabler find are well known, the whole picture is striking as to how much core knowledge production at universities has changed across just eighty-five years (e.g., Brint 2002). As represented by the distribution of faculty across the three branches, early in the twentieth century the university's knowledge base was apportioned as follows: about 60 percent in the natural sciences, 33 percent in classics and humanities, and the small remainder in the social sciences. But by the end of the century the university's intellectual core had dramatically shifted: just half of faculties were in the natural sciences; fewer than 20 percent were in the classics and humanities; and 30 percent were in the social-behavioral sciences. Over the century, humanities and the natural sciences had dropped by 41 and 12 percent, respectively, while the social-behavioral sciences had grown by 222 percent! And a significant shift had occurred between faculty and courses dedicated to classical subjects versus subjects aimed at topics new to the traditional university menu: early in the century the percentage split was about 60/40 between classical versus new incorporation; by the end of the century this had flipped to 40/60, and most of this change was due to the unprecedented growth in widely applied social-behavioral sciences (meaning bringing basic social-behavioral science into the understanding of everyday life, as in the epigraph) plus a modest 13 percent growth in natural sciences applied to ever more topics. Subsequent analysis of course rosters verified these trends as well.

The researchers' interpretation of these findings is equally innovative. What these trends show is a profound shift in the social construction of knowledge, and hence reality, at the hands of the university—a change in what Frank and Gabler refer to as the "story of origins or the cosmology [of reality]" and the "story of being or the ontology [of reality]" (20). The origin of life shifted to neo-Darwinian evolution, while the logic of being shifted from theology to a rationalized world in which science is the main claim to truth. They argue that the influence of precursors to later empirical social sciences (such as Hobbes, Locke, Rousseau, Marx, Durkheim, and Weber), and their "discovery of society" or, better, their "invention of society" as a manifest entity worthy of intellectual inquiry, formed a profoundly new way to conceptualize origins of human life and its nature as a collective reality (Collins and Makowsky 1998).

Nothing short of an epistemological revolution, this change led early sociological, anthropological, and economic thinking toward a conception of society as a global phenomenon, with all its contributing processes now available to rational inquiry within an increasingly scientized reality. Thus, social stratification becomes the domain of sociology, material production the domain of economics, leadership the domain of political science, language and culture the domain of anthropology, consciousness and behavior the domain of psychology, and so on. Similarly, there was rising emphasis on the study of individuals, not as before, in the traditional classics sense of the individual as the pinnacle of a divinely created biological and social existence, but instead as a social animal that is an equal participant, along with all other organisms, in the biological and social world. Underneath all the emerging social and behavioral sciences lies this same conceptual logic, one that represents humans as rational actors in societies who therefore can (and should) rationally pursue progress.

Against this new construction of knowledge and knowing, intellectual accounts of divine creation and divine actorhood wane in the face of a strong belief in biological evolution and humans as the main actors of society (Meyer and Jepperson 2000). Over the twentieth century scholars within and without the university (but increasingly within) have rationalized universal humans and their collective life in society to a wholly new level. For example, Hobbes was trained at Oxford and was a tutor to the elite, who were headed to the university. Karl Marx was initially trained as an academic, but was banned from German academia because of his then radical ideas on society and social class, ideas which are now commonplace in university courses about society. Durkheim and Weber had academic careers very similar to contemporary faculty. Of these examples of some of the founding social theorists of the new ideology only Rousseau had neither a university education nor a position at a university. The subsequent rise of faculties within the disciplines of the social-behavioral sciences sustained and added to this transformation of reality and now distributes the implications of it widely.

This change also explains the century-long fall in faculty share of the classics and humanities, a lamented trend among classicists and fine arts scholars. Frank and Gabler observe that much of the humanities and the arts of the older university were based on a Western classical cosmology and ontology of the human and his society as the highest form of a divinely inspired universe. Thus, the works and lives of the great artists and humanists (mostly from the Western antiquity and feudal periods), representing the pinnacle of a divinely inspired mankind, were singularly worthy of university-based inquiry and imitation. But over the century, as this older cosmology and ontology was replaced, so too the emphasis on the classics and the humanities within the university waned; and as shown later in the impact of the education revolution on the knowledge society, this set the stage for the long slow death of classicalism as the basic ideology behind knowledge.

All types of academic disciplines have adopted a basic social-behavioral ideology: history, cultural studies, literature, and so forth focus on essentially social-behavioral aspects of society, often employing the ideas and terms of social-behavioral sciences (Camic, Gross, and Lamont 2011). As in the case of the death of orientalism, the new ideology envisions a profound equality among humans and among societies; prior ideas of hierarchies die out, while notions of panworld social justice underpin the knowledge that counts versus that which does not. An image of world society and its environment made up of networks of interrelated actors—humans and other organisms—emerges as the best (read, truest) way to think about the world (Meyer and Jepperson 2000). So too, the new ideology opens the door widely to universal knowledge as the best foundation for all aspects of life. And the frequent calls for reform of university knowledge production that stress more relevant, applied knowledge under various brave new labels—service learning, public scholarship, engaged university, intellectual advocacy, translational research, research collaboration, and so on—are really echoes of what the university as a strong institution has already set into motion, namely, an intensification of the universalization of knowledge towards assumed social progress.

The cosmological and ontological shift within universities is carried deep into society through the millions of graduates educated to think about themselves as budding experts, experiencing firsthand a rationalized and scientized world and imagining a role in its progress. The tension during the early development of the university between particularistic interests outside the university and the institution's claim to universalism vanishes as the university extends itself widely, mostly not through outside pressure but through the deepening acceptance in modern society of the logic of the schooled society that universalism is the best way to find new knowledge and train experts to use this knowledge.[4] In a nutshell, *the institutional triumph of the university is the central triumph of formal education as the basis for our cultural reality.* As the massive university-based knowledge conglomerate churns away, this is the future that Frank and Gablers' history of a university-based shift in the cosmology and ontology underpinning society would predict.

Yet many university detractors misinterpret this process as greater vocationalism (more specific job types) creeping into the academy, and hence a devaluing of the institution (e.g., Grubb and Lazerson 2005). In reality, the institution has transformed its true feudal vocationalism—theology, law (canon and civil), medicine, and philosophy (for intellectuals)—which Riddle's research showed to be so important to its initial societal charter and success, into a generalized epistemological approach to nature and society that transcends a late narrow vocationalism. Or as aptly described by Frank and Meyer:

The "knowledge society" that results is distinguished by the extraordinary degree to which the university is linked to society. But it is also distinguished by the degree to which society is organized around the university's abstracted and universalized understandings of the world and its degree-certified graduates. (2007, 287)

Consider several examples of how the university as an institution reconstructs pedestrian phenomena into authoritative universal knowledge, and then, through linking such knowledge to expertise, expands participation in higher education. This in turn increases the institutional power of the university specifically, while more generally making the institution of education the model of society itself.

### A THEORY OF ICE CREAM

For most of us nothing tastes better than a bowl of delicious ice cream. The older ones among us can remember back when the quality of homemade ice cream varied by the maker's skills, quality of ingredients, and imagination in blending-in tasty things. While making quality ice cream back then was considered to depend on skill and knowledge, they were thought of as utterly practical skills and everyday know-how. Since then ice cream has become big business worldwide and is mostly made on an industrial scale. Either way, ice cream making is well removed from what is thought as the exalted knowledge of philosophy, science, and the social-behavioral sciences of the university. Yet even this mundane topic has been transformed by the university's knowledge conglomerate into authoritative, state-of-the-art knowledge and as such has been added to the university's repertoire of degree granting and expert training—the point being that if the university can enact its charters on ice cream, there is little else it could not include.

At the author's university, a large public land-grant institution that fully aspires to (and mostly achieves) every aspect of the super RU model, there is a research and graduate training program in frozen confectionery—in everyday language, ice cream (Stout 2009). There is a lightheartedness to the program (and one might also add, a certain democratization), as one flavor was developed in honor of the university's former popular football coach ("Peachy Paterno"); equally telling about the universalization of ice cream is that another flavor ("Keenie Beenie Chocolate Chip") celebrates the program's founding professor—read scholar of ice cream.[5] Originating early in the twentieth century, by the mid-1960s the program had become fully transformed as a university subject. Today, a dozen Ph.D. faculty connected to the program are expected to publish, like any others in the university, on the science (universalization) of their topic, and they routinely do so under such titles as "Chemical and Thermal Characteristics of Milk-Fat Fractions Isolated by a Melt Crystallization," "Characterization of 'Flavor-Fade' and Off-Flavor Development in Roasted Peanuts," and "Viscosity of Molten Chocolate with Lactose from Spray-Dried Whole Milk Powders" in scientific journals such as the *Journal of Food Science* and the *Journal of the American Oil Chemists' Society*, which regularly publish research findings from university-based scholars in some two dozen ice cream programs at American research universities. Further legitimation is supplied by professional associations and funding from manufacturing-related organizations such as the American Cocoa Research Institute.

Of special interest here is the fact that an accompanying expert training program has developed right along with the production of authoritative knowledge on ice cream. This training takes on two forms, each of which demonstrates a different aspect of the dynamic power of transforming everyday things into authoritative knowledge and the credentialing of trained experts entitled to use such knowledge. The first training route, the more standard of the two, turns out new generations of knowledge producers in the area of ice cream, or more broadly in the area termed "food sciences." This includes related graduate training at the master's and Ph.D. levels. Second is what is called the "ice cream short course," combining training in the business with an introduction to a university-produced science of food. The second program, run by Pennsylvania State University, is very popular and reaches significant numbers of people. Here is how a 2000 press release from the program describes the course's popularity:

All kinds of people want to go into business for themselves. The Penn State Ice Cream Short Course often attracts entrepreneurs for its special *"ice cream mystique."* Now entering its 109th year, the course continues as the nation's old-est, best-known and largest educational program dedicated to the science and technology of ice cream. [At] this year's seminar . . . attendees will get to see the *"mystique"* in action. (italics added)

Evident in this marketing statement is the dynamic process forged out of a self-reinforcing link between university-based science and ice cream as a potential business; but one should not assume too narrowly that this process is driven by outside capital forces. The whole point of the short course, and hence the promise to see the "mystique in action," is to in-troduce the would-be ice cream entrepreneur to expert knowledge about the business *and* science of ice cream. Additional evidence of this is how basic (theoretical) research interests easily expand into the ice cream pro-gram. For example, this university's Physics and Aerospace Engineering departments conduct thermoacoustic research on ice cream, as a "cross-fertilization of device development, meticulous laboratory experiments, and numerical simulations using parallel processing has fostered a deeper understanding than could have been achieved if these approaches had been explored in isolation."

Regardless of how mundane a topic is thought to be, or whether it is in the domain of everyday know-how, the university has the singular com-bination of charters to transform anything into authoritative knowledge and integrate it with the creation of experts who then carry the new under-standings about the topic into everyday life. Undertaken over and over again, this process constructs the wide dimensions of the schooled society.

While food science and frozen confectionary training have clear con-nections to the scientization of knowledge and industrial technological development, the next case is informative precisely because it is mostly *not* about science, industry, or technology.

### THE UNIVERSAL WOMAN

Compared to the eight-hundred-year development of the modern university, thirty-five years is a mere drop in the bucket, but it took only these few years for university scholars throughout the world to develop the subject of studying women as a formal universalized academic topic, complete with feuding theoretical camps, dedicated journals, empirical research, and all other hallmarks of academic scholarship. Starting in American universities then spreading out, women's studies programs of scholarship and expert training emerged in the late 1960s, and by the late 2000s there were some seven hundred academic programs, departments, and research centers at institutions of higher education—an amazingly large and rapid development of new knowledge and expert training potential.[6] Furthermore, while many of the American programs are for undergraduates, a significant number of research universities offer master's and Ph.D. degrees in women's studies, ensuring future cadres of experts who will continue to produce and consume future academic studies of women. This development of new knowledge and expert training has been a global one too, as universities in fifty-nine nations have started a women's studies program since 1970 (Wotipka and Ramirez 2008).

The newly produced academic knowledge about women is distributed just as rapidly. In 1969 there were only seventeen courses on women's studies in the whole of American higher education, but at the end of the following decade there were an estimated thirty thousand such courses dispersing universalized knowledge about women to hundreds of thousands of students (Howe 2000). Also, the expanding knowledge conglomerate at American universities led to a booming capacity to undertake research in conjunction with training in women's studies: by 1984 there were 247 full degree programs in women's studies, many of them at major research universities (Gumport 2002).

The extensive and rapid development of women's studies within the university is a particularly interesting case because the resulting knowledge base is not about science, such as in the food science example above, nor technology development, as in the multiplying academic fields related to emerging nanotechnology. While surely some of the field's growth flows from the same logic behind the growing dominance of the university-led scientization of society, there has never been a widely held assumption that women's studies is a natural science or even purely a social-behavioral science. But just as with science and technology, the rapid development of women's studies shows the university's expansive influence on authoritative knowledge that feeds into central ideologies about reality. Further, while certainly gender and the female expression of it are essential parts of human life, there is nothing obviously utilitarian, commercial, techno-logical, or even moral (other than the issue of social inequality between the genders, which is a cornerstone subject of the field) in this academic study of gender with a focus on females. In short, as recent research finds, this new field comes out of the institutional logic of the university more than from any particular external forces.

From its beginning, much of the field's substance was the study of social, political, and economic elements and the status of women in human society, both historically and contemporarily. Journals such as *Signs: A Journal of Women, Culture, and Society* or simply *Women's Studies*, created by early women's studies scholars, published articles with titles illustrating the early eclecticism at the heart of the field—"On the Power of the Weak" (Janeway 1975), "On Masochism: A Contribu-tion to the History of a Phantasy and Its Theory" (Lenzer 1975), "Eco-nomic Determinants of Volunteer Work by Women" (Mueller 1975), and "Contraceptives for Males" (Bremner and Kretser 1975). Although this mixture of topics, theory, and methods continues today in scholarship on women, as women's studies matured into a knowledge area within the university it became a somewhat narrower discipline than its broad name might imply. The inception of the field was accompanied by a fer-vor within the university rarely seen in the contemporary expansion of scientific fields. Both the field's founding proponents and its opponents considered the subject the leading edge of female faculty's struggle to join the male-dominated ranks of the professoriate. Consequently, there has been controversy and some resistance to the field's establishment, and not surprisingly a fair amount of scholarship has been done on the develop-ment of women's studies itself (along with race and ethnic studies) (e.g., Boxer 1998; Howe 2000; Rojas 2007).

Unfortunately most of this literature relies on some version of the weak university as a highly penetrable institution. The standard plot in most of the scholarship chronicles the political feminist insurgency from out-side the university's walls struggling against the sexism of the academic old guard. While there is some truth in an impact of outside changes, recent research on the field's rapid academic success belies much of the notion of an outsiders' insurgency pushed upon the university. A more accurate way to think of the rise of women's studies is as part of the process by which the university creates, sanctions, and embraces new knowledge. The speed and thoroughness at which the university does this is further indication of its power in the schooled society.

This crucial point is demonstrated by two recent studies on the institutional origin and growth of women's studies. The first study, by neo-institutionalists Christine Wotipka and Francisco Ramirez (2008), statistically analyzes what caused the spread of the field from nation to nation from 1970 to 2000. First and tellingly, they find *no* support for the notion of an outsiders' insurgency; variation in female participation in higher education had no impact on the spread of programs. This is notable, since obviously the field was founded by members of the first sizable generation of female scholars in the academy; yet beyond this presence, women's studies did not spread as a function of a growing proportion of female students in higher education attempting to bring their world into the university.[7] What did increase the spread into more nations was first and foremost the number of women's studies programs in operation in universities worldwide, and secondly the impact of three high-profile international conferences of the United Nations Human Rights' Committee on the Elimination of Discrimination Against Women starting in 1982—an international attempt to improve the social and economic status of women. While nominally "outside" the university, these highly legitimating international events relied heavily on newly constructed academic ideas about women already developed and dispersed by university-trained experts on women's studies and related fields. In other words, the rise and spread of women's studies was more of a university-based diffusion; once it got started by a few universities, it continued along on its own academic logic.

This is further illustrated by the second study, a richly detailed qualitative investigation of the first and second generation of women's studies scholars. Authored by sociologist of higher education Patricia Gumport (2002), this is an innovative comparative analysis of the intellectual struggle and success of women's studies in universities; it provides a rare chronicling of the progression of knowledge production newly applied to a common facet of everyday life. Gumport describes an array of factors inside and outside the university that led to the establishment of women's studies, but overall her findings support "inside" more than "outside," because the university dominated the process at each turn.

Gumport aptly names the founding scholars of women's studies "pathfinders," and from interviews with a small sample of them weaves a complex story about their role in the rise of the field. Although narrating stories about feminist awakenings and struggles with the vestiges of crude sexism on the part of older male faculty, the pathfinders present themselves more as pioneers discovering new territory (knowledge) than as revolutionaries breeching the university's walls. As American women slowly matriculated into graduate programs in the mid-1960s, a generation of pathfinders was formed, and what is striking here is how initial political motivations and personal struggles with sexism gave way to more-traditional academic paths. For example, Gumport describes that in hindsight most of the pathfinders saw their careers as "guided primarily by academic commitments . . . or saw politics as present but subordinate to academic commitments" (2002, 86).

This is not to say that the politics of feminism had no influence on women's studies, for clearly it did. And so did parts of the women's movement and new left politics in the United States, which partially came from outside the university; also, certainly many of the pathfinders' motivations were shaped by the larger social upheavals at universities during the late 1960s (e.g., Lipset 1971). Nevertheless, the rise of social science and its related influence on the new epistemological ideology was fully underway by the 1960s, and hence the major outcome of the pathfinders' struggles ended up not being explicitly political (see also Berkovitch and Bradley 1999). There was no formation of a women's party or political lobby by these scholars as a collective; instead, the main outcome was, and still is, the production of new knowledge redefining women and their world as an academic topic, accompanied by scholarship shaping main cultural images of gender and women, along with the training of future experts in this endeavor. The advance of women scholars into the institution met with some resistance from the male-dominated faculty, to be sure, but in the final analysis it was remarkably flimsy and it fell quickly in face of the logic of the university's charter to universalize all topics. Not an insurgency, the pathfinders primarily focused on making women the subject of new theory and even attempted to invent whole new gendered methods of inquiry in history, sociology, and philosophy.

The second generation of women's studies graduates—the "pathtakers"—were themselves heavily influenced as undergraduates by the rapidly multiplying courses and academic literature on authoritative knowledge about women's studies. While often individually dedicated to feminist politics, this second generation of graduates received training and developed academic careers in ways very similar to faculty in any other academic discipline. The feminist fervor and any notion of an insurgency from without had receded, and "the Pathtakers [could now] regard feminist ideas with indifference and simply assume their right to central places in the scholarly life of their disciplines" in the university (Gumport 2002, 150).

Women and their role in society is obviously a topic ripe for knowledge development by the modern university given its ideology of a human-constructed society for rational action and social progress, which certainly would explain the relatively short time needed to establish women's studies as part of the body of authoritative knowledge. Further, as expected, women's studies programs at some universities have started to expand toward the subject of maleness, and so the university-driven cycle starts again.

### THE RISE OF THE MBA AND THE SCIENTIFIC MANAGEMENT OF EVERYTHING

The worldwide growth in the master's of business administration (MBA) and the scholarly transformation of business into an academic topic of professional management, occurring seemingly in concert with the intensification of capitalism by ever larger and more rationalized firms, could be held up as the quintessential example of the institutionally weak university following outside trends. But most university watchers focus only on the explosion in training and credentialing of the MBA phenomenon, and therefore miss the full influence of the university. Behind the hundred thousand annual MBA degrees are a thousand schools of business in universities with thousands of faculty, who as scholars and researchers have transformed this once most practical of topics into universalized authoritative knowledge.

Business and its administration could not be further from classical subjects at the heart of the original university; during the first seven hundred
years of the Western university, commerce was considered the epitome of a
practical, particularistic, nonintellectual activity antithetical to academics
(Lenhardt 2002). Even through the nineteenth century, as capitalism grew
in scope and complexity, what business administration there was to be had
was considered little more than a clerical, lower-level endeavor, and hence
training in it occurred in rudimentary business-related schools mostly at
the secondary education level (Knepper 1941). But this all changed in the
twentieth-century university.[8] One hundred and twenty years following
the first founding of a university-based professional management degree,
at the University of Pennsylvania in 1881, more than one thousand business schools and more than two thousand stand-alone MBA programs
were operating within universities worldwide. Further, while there was
consistent growth over the first half of the twentieth century, since the
1960s the number of degrees awarded and business schools founded in
U.S. universities grew exceptionally fast: for example, from 1967 to 1977
annually awarded MBA degrees expanded by 176 percent, from about
18,000 to 47,000, and by 1996 to about 94,000, for a total increase of
over 400 percent in just three decades, a trend that continues in the twenty-
first century (Moon 2002). Within the expansion of all kinds of graduate
degrees now being awarded in the United States, an estimated one in four
masters' awarded are MBAs, making this degree the leading edge of mass
graduate training.

The capacity of the university-based knowledge conglomerate now
aimed at business management is enormous. For example, the oldest
and largest scholarly management association, the Academy of Management, has 18,878 members, almost none of whom are actual managers in
business but are instead university-based faculty from 111 nations. This
peak association holds an annual conference where thousands of academic papers on aspects of management are presented; new Ph.D.s from
business schools seek jobs in other business schools; and the community
of scholars of business generally celebrates itself as a manifest success.
Evident too of the robustness of scholarship on business management
is how widely these scholars and their authoritative knowledge reach

across society, in many cases well beyond commerce and profit-seeking firms to what is emerging as an all-encompassing scholarship about the extensive formal-organizational nature of modern society (Drori, Meyer, and Hwang 2006).

The Academy of Management lists two dozen subfields (divisions of the association) that members can join. Included are diverse names such as Business Policy and Strategy; Conflict Management; Gender Diversity in Organizations; Management, Spirituality and Religion; Operations Management; Organizations and the Natural Environment; Public and Non-Profit; and Research Methods. Further, while there is wide application of academic scholarship on organizational management of all kinds, the epistemological goals of each subfield are similar, mostly using a lexicon mixing the methods and theory of organization in the social-behavioral science. For example, compare the chartering statement of Business Policy and Strategy, the subfield most closely aligned with the practicalities of business management, with that of the subfield Management, Spirituality and Religion:

[Business Policy and Strategy involves the study of] the roles and problems of general managers and those who manage multi-business firms or multi-functional business units. Major topics include: strategy formulation and implementation; strategic planning and decision processes; strategic control and reward systems; resource allocation; diversification and portfolio strategies; competitive strategy; cooperative strategies, selection and behavior of general managers; and the composition and processes of top management teams.

[Management, Spirituality and Religion focuses on] the study of the relationship and relevance of spirituality and religion in management and organizations. Major topics include: theoretical advances or empirical evidence about the effectiveness of spiritual or religious principles and practices in management from approaches represented in the literature including religious ethics, spirituality and work, and spiritual leadership, as well as applications of particular religions, and secular spiritualities to work, management/leadership, organization, and the business system; and evaluation studies of the effectiveness of management approaches that nurture the human spirit in private, non-public or public institutions. (Academy of Management 2012)

Foreshadowing the later discussion of the influence of the schooled society on the workplace, chartering statements of the Academy of Management frequently refer to humans as *resources*, not labor; organizations as *flat*, not hierarchical; and workplaces as *creative*, not controlling.

Yet as is well known, the expansive boost in MBAs from the 1970s onward occurred well after the major transformation of private firms into large, multidivisional, complex organizations with correspondingly sizable managerial staffs (e.g., Chandler 1977). Therefore one could argue that the capacity to undertake business and management scholarship does not necessarily mean that the university originated this ideology but rather that it was just a robust response to the rise of a new business environment. Still, the longer historical record of the scientization of management tells a more nuanced story.[9]

Robert Locke's historical studies of the epistemological development behind the study of management uncover the early roots of the topic, which extend back to the nineteenth century (Locke 1984, 1989). He notes that the faculties of even the earliest business schools in the late nineteenth century were more interested in the scholarship of management than its practical application in the emerging large industrial firms in the United States: "The business school program . . . reflected the gap between science and vocationalism, [the latter] characterized the old paradigm in [non-university] business training" (1989, 5). By the late nineteenth century, the mostly empirical, descriptive "historical-institutional school" of economics gave way within the university to a formal neoclassical approach, which derived knowledge about economic activity from a set of postulates about a system of exchange. Or in the language of the preceding chapter, at the hands of academicians business as a topic was moved to an even more abstract level of universalistic knowledge. This paradigm shift led to the use of mathematics as a way to represent and hence study the internal logic of the exchange system, a major intellectual technique that in turn rested on the ideas of George Boole at Ireland's Queen's College, starting in the late 1840s, which mathematized the language of logic.[10]

A neoclassical microeconomic theory influenced the university-based science of management in three ways (Locke 1989). First, it oriented universalistic inquiry towards the behavior of the individual firm and from there towards the behavior of the individual entrepreneur within the firm. Second, in doing so, not only the firm but also the individual entrepreneur were seen as operating in the same economic system of exchange, and hence business behavior (decision making) was analyzable by the same mathematized form of economic theory. And thus, most importantly for the future development of a science of management, the central postulate of neoclassical economics—the marginal utility theory of profit-seeking—was conceptualized as a function of the entrepreneur following the same (read theorized) rules of profit. Third was the somewhat parallel development of econometrics from the eighteenth- and early-nineteenth-century university-based development of the mathematics of statistics and the conceptual "fusion between [sic] statistics, mathematics, and neo-classical economics" developed by Irving Fisher at Yale University and by others during the first half of the twentieth century (1989, 20). This combination advanced the idea that behavior could be modeled mathematically, which is one of the central conceptual foundations upon which the rise of the social-behavioral sciences within the university has occurred over the past century (Weintraub 2002).

Alone these conceptual leaps did not form a complete science of management, but they did set the stage for the notion that the entrepreneur made managerial decisions that could be analyzed within the mathematics of marginal utility theory, and opened the question of what managers do and how their behavior might be analyzed through a logical-mathematical system. As Locke states it:

In short, the marginalist theory of the firm is outward-looking, the entrepreneur's viewpoint inward looking, for the theory of the firm treats the operations within the firm as a black box, an unknown, a problem that has already been solved. Because it assumes that the entrepreneur knows how to run his firm efficiently, it stops at where the entrepreneur wants analysis really to begin. (1989, 15)

Locke goes on to trace the development from this beginning through to the second decade of the twentieth century when John von Neumann developed, first at several German universities and later at Princeton University, the mathematics of game theory as a way to model human decisions around competition and cooperation, and then on to the idea that management could be studied as a universalized topic, a science in this case:

Game theory drew a straight line from modern mathematics . . . through economics, to management to show how entrepreneurs, in conflict situations, could, under certain assumptions, act so as to be guaranteed at least a certain minimum gain (or maximum loss) by following the algorithm. (1989, 20)

Locke points out that it was a relatively short leap from here to the use of linear algebra, topology, and probability theory to give "scientific status to economic knowledge and make it more operationally understandable to management" (20). This line of intellectual work joined the emerging social-behavioral sciences within the university, and together they used the instrumentality of mathematics to universalize the study of management.

This is not to say that intensifying capitalism had no impact on intellectual development; increasingly, larger and more complex corporate capitalism was also a major transforming institution of postindustrial society over the twentieth century. Certainly, without this change the MBA would not have been developed to the mass proportions that it has. The successful growth from the late nineteenth century on of hierarchies of management in multiform corporations, first in the United States and then worldwide, was a kind of new social technology that went hand in hand with the growth of a science of management as the forerunner to what now can be called the *mass* MBA degree (Chandler 1977). The point here is that the construction of management as a universalized academic topic appropriate for empirical research comes from a long development within the university, which eventually shaped the very essence of management in all types of organizations, from profit-seeking to nonprofit.

This is further, and somewhat ironically, illustrated by observations that some of the first products of the new mathematized science of management did not necessarily help managers in practical situations (Locke 1989). For example, midcentury offshoots of scholarship on management, such as operations research and the science of management applied to governmental bureaucracies (e.g., the Planning Programming Budgeting System), had notorious practical failings. In practice, management is a messy process, more one of just sufficing than an exact science. An observer of the rise of the science of management and practical managing astutely notes this:

The manager's job is actually of an unprogrammed character: [he or she] . . . is not much concerned with the flow and rational use of "hard" information, his information is distorted, incomplete, his job is ambiguous . . . he is not primarily a decision-maker, a planner but an "inspirer," a fire fighter, and a rationalizer after the fact. (Glover 1978, as quoted in Locke 1989, 40)

It is unlikely that if the university had been merely following society at large it would have so independently developed a science of management that at times could be so alien to practical applications.

The institutional power of the university in this respect is that (through the charter of faculty scholarship) it constructs universal topics without the limitation of immediate practical application. This is followed by the creation of expertise spread through the training of more experts, so that universalized knowledge comes to replace preuniversalized practical know-how with its own definitions and understandings; in short, the university constantly creates the reigning ideologies of the schooled society. In the final stage of the process, those become the "way it is done." This is not to imply that the older "know-how" methods were somehow naturally better than the methods based on universalized knowledge; there is certainly much evidence that new capabilities of organizational complexity can lead to profit levels that never could have been achieved with pre–management science approaches. Rather, the point is that the understandings and models for managerial action become heavily shaped by the ideas developed within the university over many decades. As the academic development of management science continued over the century, it is clear that later applications of scientific management had positive effects on business, particularly as the ideology shaped the latter stages of the industrial revolution.

Locke's earlier study, a sweeping historical examination of the effect of higher education on levels of entrepreneurship in Germany, France, and Great Britain, is aptly titled *The End of the Practical Man* (1984), as it gives some insight into the transformation of knowledge from know-how to universalized knowledge, and the latter's use in national economies. He argues that during the second industrial revolution, from 1880 to 1940, which was caused by intensified use of technology and new management strategies, German economic performance was better than French performance, and that both in turn were better than British performance. The major reason for this, he argues, was the national difference in higher education training of the key new experts—engineers, accountants, and managers—for an emerging industrial world whose increased productivity chiefly derived from contributions of technology (e.g., results from applied scientific research) and new managerial techniques (e.g., standard cost accounting). These educational differences accompanied significant differences in economic outcomes.

At one extreme, British higher education did not train expert engineers, accountants, and managers for their jobs; instead, men learned these skills on the job, making them the "original practical man" of the first industrial age, who were rapidly vanishing during the second industrial age—notably, a period that exactly coincides with the beginning of the education revolution. By contrast, French higher education developed a more formalistic curricular approach to training engineers, accountants, and managers, combining it with elite education for prestigious state civil service positions; hence, the training was encyclopedic, downplaying more-active laboratory work in favor of passive lecturing. While the French approach was far more academic than the British one, its lack of active research and involvement of students in knowledge production ultimately yielded an inferior training experience compared to that in German higher education. With stronger ties to academia and to knowledge production of faculty in both applied science and managerial technique, the German engineering professions rapidly embraced (because of being taught) scientific management and research-based engineering, which they then carried into firms throughout the nation. The German research university of the nineteenth and early twentieth centuries was emulated by fledging American universities, and the successful German experience with higher education and the transformation of industrialization was a forerunner to the influence of the research university on management science today.[11]

Perhaps the trajectory of management science from the university to the boardroom is best summarized by Rollin Ford, CIO of Wal-Mart, one of the biggest global retailers, which employs 2.1 million workers worldwide, who said, "Every day I wake up and ask, how can I flow data better, manage data better, analyze data better?" ("Data, Data Everywhere" 2010). Armed with considerable university training in the science of management, managerial consultants analyze mountains of data and advise clients often across diverse industries and organizations; these consultants consider themselves and act as university-credentialed professionals (McKenna, 2006).

Indicative of the argument here is neo-institutionalist Hyeyoung Moon's innovative study of factors leading to the founding of new MBA programs from 1880 to 2000, in which she finds the worldwide "population" of these programs grew under the influence of three main factors at the national level (2002). The first founding condition, as would be expected given the rise of the schooled society over roughly the same period, is an expanded mass education system, specifically in the spread of university and higher education systems in nations. This education factor is followed by the influence of a rationalized business environment as measured by the existence of stock exchanges and organized firms. And lastly, especially after 1960, there is a broad contagion effect as programs spread, particularly in nations that have numerous international ties and diplomatic activities. While it is true that the modern MBA did not become one of the engineering fields at the center of postindustrial technology development (fields that are also highly academically developed), the MBA and related knowledge production have focused on the managerial side of the postindustrial transformation, and now produce the main ideology of all business and commerce for the twenty-first century.

Lastly, the MBA's current curriculum intertwines business, social science, and an abstract notion of organizational leadership. Business topics such as accounting, finance, supply chain management, and business environments are mixed with social processes of organizations and basic social science areas such as leadership and communication, team processes, statistics, power and influence, and economics. At the author's university, for example, 60 percent of the regular two-year MBA curriculum can be classified as business topics such as the former, while 40 percent are about general processes within formal organizations and social science such as the latter. Additionally, of the eight required "special intensive-training activities" spread throughout this two-year degree, seven are about team processes, community service, travel abroad, and individual career plans, while only one is directly related to "real" business problems and is the last part of an overall team process experience that runs through the whole two years. Also, many of the business courses are taught from a research/ scholarship, theoretical perspective, and considerable amounts of reading on the social science of management are mixed in.

While there is evidence that MBA programs adapt to some local or national factors, for the most part this American university's model is the generic one that has spread globally. And it is a model that also spreads to ever more types of formal organizations. These programs and their faculty are the platform on which new ideas about management, such as those behind the "new public management" for the huge sector of nonprofit and government organizations, are staged and distributed throughout universities worldwide (e.g., Mazza, Sahlin-Andersson, and Pedersen 2005; Sahlin-Andersson 2001). Finally, in partial overlap with the development of the MBA, there is a similar story about the rise of economics as a university subject and research domain, and its transformation into a universal transnational expertise aimed at national economic development (Fourcade 2006).

All three of the cases in this chapter illustrate the dynamic charter of the university at the core of the education revolution. John Meyer's original formulation leading to the schooled society perspective predicts this key point:

Education not only creates "economic knowledge" which must be taken into account by rational actors. It is also a structure helping to create the role of economist, to justify economists' authority claims in society, and to define precisely who is an economist. Education thus creates, not only psychiatry, but psychiatrists; not only modern management ideology, but MBA's. The rational actor must take into account medical knowledge, and to do so he must consult a doctor. Thus, the modern organizational structure of society incorporates legitimated bodies of knowledge by incorporating the designated personnel. . . . Education helps to *create* new classes of knowledge and personnel which then can be incorporated in society. (1977, 68, emphasis added)

This formidable symbiotic cultural process will be referred to often in Part II in assessing how the education revolution reaches into and changes major aspects of society.

# PART II

# Societal Consequences
# of the Education Revolution

### CHAPTER 6

# The Educational Transformation of Work

Laborers have become capitalists not from a diffusion of the ownership of corporation stocks, as folklore would have it, but from the acquisition of knowledge and skill that have economic value.

THEODORE W. SCHULTZ, Presidential Address

to the American Economic Association, 1961

Schools used to be for educating people, for developing minds and characters. Today, as jobs depend more and more on certificates, degrees and diplomas, aims and motives are changing. Schooling has become more and more a ritualized process of qualification-earning . . . ritualistic, tedious, suffused with anxiety and boredom, destructive of curiosity and imagination; in short, anti-educational.

RONALD DORE, *The Diploma Disease*, 1976

FROM THE 1960S TO THE 1980S, as the mass education revolution heated up, enrollment rates in lower- and upper-secondary and higher education expanded, and many educators, economists, sociologists, and experts on national development predicted dire consequences from a worldwide oversupply of educated youth working in jobs beneath them. In wealthy nations the poster-boy for seemingly runaway overeducation was the embittered Ph.D. driving a taxi for a living, while in less wealthy nations it was the angry young man with an upper-secondary diploma who could not find a prestigious job in the nation's civil service.[1] As many youth entered educational opportunities formerly reserved mostly for elites, it threatened the established educational order, which was tightly connected to a small number of elite jobs. This so-called overeducation crisis was considered a looming social problem, a kind of disease on the verge of epidemic proportions. And even though the crisis never materialized, new predictions of a looming overeducation crisis are trotted out with each succeeding wave of educational expansion, such as with the current expansion of graduate education. But as will be argued here, the overeducation crisis image rarely, if ever, predicts what actually happens to jobs and economies as education expands significantly in populations. This is a good place to start to demonstrate how the education revolution transforms other institutions.

The relationship between education and work is much studied, yet one might wonder what all the fuss is about since from everyday observations education and work are clearly related. Indeed, that is what a virtual mountain of systematic research shows in nation after nation, then as well as now, and without exception across the whole literature: all else equal, on average, workers with more education earn more income than less educated workers. But why this "education premium in wages" occurs is the essential question to ask about the relationship between education and work. Up to now two contrasting arguments, both stemming from the traditional perspective on education, have suggested possible answers.[2]

The human capital theory and a Marxist theory of education are the bookends for the traditional perspective, and they are frequently applied to thinking about the relationship between education and work in postindustrial society. The human capital theorists, mostly economists, who brought education in out of the cold of classical and neoclassical economics and placed it into the mainstream of economic analysis, assume education to be directly and inseparably tied to work through the ability of individuals to invest in their own productivity through skill acquisition from either formal education or on-the-job training (e.g., Becker 1993; Schultz 1961). Although the human capital literature is full of discussions of skill, what it really means in almost every case is *skill acquired through education*.[3] The main version of the human capital argument takes education at its face value as an imparter of useful capabilities to individuals by assuming that schooling does what it is "supposed to" in an everyday sense, so this key assumption is never really brought into question (Keely 2007). As tautological as it may be, the fact that an education usually leads to higher wages in the labor market is enough for the human capital position to assume that if market forces choose workers with greater productivity then education must be the main causal factor.

The Marxist position, held by many sociologists, assumes education to be a myth, a kind of grand rip-off: schooling does not for the most part do what it is "supposed to." It does not impart useful skills as much as it serves as a rather expensive societal sorting machine indicating to employers which students have the ability and attitude to work (e.g., Spring 1988). For example, the titles of Paul Willis's and Jay MacLeod's popular ethnographies of the education of working-class British and American youth—*Learning to Labor* (1977) and *Ain't No Makin' It* (2009)—lean heavily on this imagery. Contrary to the human capital theory, this education-as-myth position considers schooling as mostly sorting and socializing people to be compliant workers and accepting of academic inequalities; what goes on in school in the guise of learning is generally economically irrelevant and perhaps even oppressive (e.g., Giroux 2000). As examined more in the following chapter, this position's explanation for the education premium is that it results from "credentialism" and class-based socialization instead of actual skill brought to jobs.

Both positions, however, ignore the power of education as an institution to not only train and allocate students, but also transform understandings and expectations for peoples' capabilities, the nature of work, and even what constitutes usable knowledge for economic value. The human capital position sees a too narrow one-to-one correspondence between education and job skill, and misses the dynamic and complicated relationship between the two. And the education-as-myth cynics have ignored the growing evidence that educating people changes their productivity and having greater numbers of such workers changes the nature of work itself. While education does of course prepare individuals, its growing independent cultural power transforms whole economies, which profit from the capabilities of plentiful educated workers in a proliferating new type of workplace that is itself fashioned around the sensibilities of the educated. So too, with greater education of the labor force and the population as a whole, new occupations are developed and old ones become more elaborate. In other words, mass education and work are symbiotically connected, and this process is changing large parts of the world economy.

This symbiosis is evident in four ways. First is how wrong dire predictions were that the education revolution would produce extensive over-education and thus social upheaval. Second, contrary to older visions of jobs and workers' skills, more waves of educated individuals flooding the workplace spread a kind of mass professionalization of work. Third, firms are adapting their profit-seeking strategies to the skills and work habits of educated employees with accompanying changes in technology in the workplace. Lastly, the schooled employee of the schooled occupation in the schooled workplace does not just come about because of changes in the individual's skill sets; it is broad cultural change occurring over a considerable time period and in many unexpected ways.

### THE GREAT DIPLOMA DISEASE
### THAT NEVER HAPPENED

In 1976, venturing out from his usual scholarly confines on the economic development of Japan, the renowned British Japanologist Ronald Dore published a book with the provocative title *The Diploma Disease*, which came to stand for a whole litany of discontent with the worldwide expansion of schooling. Along with an impressive number of experts at the time, Dore predicted that overeducated and underemployed masses of youth would eventually become embittered over the gap between their education and labor market opportunities, and that unmet expectations for a significantly better job created through more advanced schooling would cause all sorts of social problems.

The logic behind this forecast was compelling and easy for the public to grasp. With the expansion of education in the 1960s and 1970s, youth worldwide were enrolling in secondary education, particularly upper-secondary and also higher education, at unprecedented rates. What had been for the most part the sole educational arena of the elite began in a few short decades to include youth from a wide range of social and economic backgrounds. Before this, tight access to the upper reaches of formal education had been widely thought of as a more or less efficient sorter of individuals into a relatively small number of upper-level jobs; the earlier gains in primary education for the masses did not threaten this arrangement and were even welcomed for a host of assumed economic and social benefits. But this new expansion into upper-secondary and higher education was different; it did seem threatening, and a severe oversupply of educated people would surely be a social problem. If advanced schooling were offered to a much larger proportion of students, what would happen when this large group competed for limited jobs geared to higher levels of education? The thriving education revolution had completely blown the lid off an older elite education system, and as the masses edged towards formerly reserved advanced schooling, many worried about the implications for the world of work and even for worldwide social stability.

Part of the reason for the success of Dore's book was that it hit on an already circulating reaction to growing educational enrollments. For example, note how one professional observer of American higher education predicted the consequences of expansion of college as early as the late 1940s:

College students within the next 20 years are doomed to disappointment after graduation, as the number of coveted openings will be substantially fewer than the numbers seeking them. (Harris 1949, 64)

It is not surprising then that *The Diploma Disease* became an instant best seller and was rapidly translated into a number of languages; even today it remains on the list of influential works on education as a classic statement of the effects of "too much" education expansion. The book is not only about the abstract relationship between education and society; it is grounded in the debate over ideas about how poor nations can (and should) develop, since many of its chapters were intended to influence the then emerging endeavor of helping impoverished nations develop modern economies, and these arguably made the biggest policy impression of the book. For experts of international development, Dore, a prominent comparative scholar, argued what up to then had been unthinkable: that the supposed ameliorating effects of bringing light to the dark reaches of the impoverished world through education had apparently backfired—schooling had become a national disease.

Eloquent and persuasive, Dore predicted two dire consequences of the diploma disease. First, particularly among low-income nations that entered economic development relatively late, a sudden expansion would likely lead to educational "qualifications inflation"—inflation in the sense that for the same jobs, successful job-seekers will have to compete at higher levels of educational attainment as verified through examination-driven diplomas. Qualification inflation is what labor economists think of as "within-job education qualification upgrading" (or for short, "educational upgrading"); instead of upgrading skills required for a job, educational upgrading is merely credentialism, which in a rational economy is considered inefficient and wasteful. Notably, Dore argues that education is certainly an important component of national development, but runaway credential-hunting may cause more economic and social harm than good through educational upgrading, which is unrelated to skill training.

Secondly, Dore predicted that this diploma disease would corrupt education itself, because in a hypercompetitive education system, spurred on by mass enrollments in secondary and higher education, most credentialing will be reduced to performance on gatekeeper examinations. This imagery was particularly salient in the quasi-British education systems used in many former colonies that Dore had firsthand experience with in the middle of the twentieth century. He assumed that expansion would lead to downgrading of the curricular content, aim of instruction, and motivation of students because the only goal of education would be to pass examinations for credentials. As the epigraph quotes, with the spread of the diploma disease education supposedly becomes ritualistic in the sense of people only attempting to pass examinations, devalued in the sense that those involved lose the intrinsic sense of inquiry, and irrelevant in the sense that people are not educationally transformed by the mere competition for better jobs.[4]

In short order, this ultimately cynical book helped foster a mini genre of education, demography, and public policy literature on the pending consequences of "too much" education (e.g., Bowles and Gintis 1976; Clogg 1979; Freeman 1975, 1976; Rumberger 1981; Smith 1986; Witmer 1980). In one version after another, overeducation was defined as a growing social problem, with predictions of wide and disastrous proportions, in which the pessimism of each successive account outdid the last. Some went so far as to blame the threat of a whole societal upheaval on overeducation. One report stressed that frustrations of the overeducated and underemployed are nothing less than the "central dynamic for social discontent emerging in America," while another influential book claimed that the "incongruence between the aspirations of college students . . . and the labor requirements of the economy is the chief cause of student radicalism" (Blumberg and Murtha 1977; Bowles and Gintis 1976, respectively, as quoted in V. Burris 1983, 455). Even the much trumpeted international Trilateral Commission and the U.S. government got into the act, as an influential report from the latter proclaimed, "the potential for frustration, alienation and disruption resulting from the disparity between educational attainment and the appropriate job content cannot be overemphasized" (U.S. Department of Health, Education and Welfare n.d., 136, as quoted in V. Burris 1983, 456; Trilateral Commission 1975).

Though an obviously unrealistically grim picture, many did, and still do, see it precisely this way. The image of overeducation and its looming negative consequences seems to help many understand the rapid, and at times disconcerting, growth of education occurring in their midst. When one's whole sense of an educated self becomes obsolete in less than a single generation, when more family time and energy must be committed to schooling in a seemingly never-ending upward spiral, when more years in the lives of youth are devoted to studying instead of working, and when so much emphasis is placed on educational credentials in getting jobs, it is a relief to embrace some version of a diploma disease. Yet as appealing as this cynical prediction about education and the world of work might be, it turns out to be wildly inaccurate.

When sociologists searched for social unrest resulting from the education revolution, they could not find even the remotest of traces. A representative example is Val Burris's (1983) comprehensive analysis of a large nationally representative sample of working Americans, which finds no substantial differences between people who are overeducated for their jobs and those who are not in job satisfaction, political radicalism, political alienation, unionism, and allegiance to an achievement ideology (see also Spenner 1988; and Vaisey 2006 for a modest effect on job satisfaction).[5] Nor did mismatches between education and jobs cause social unrest among less wealthy nations. Nor is there much evidence that mass education downgrades its own effectiveness in curricular content, instruction, and student motivation. If anything, as described later, there is more evidence of upgrading across a certain pattern of academic content. And while the schooled society has produced intensified civic political actions that are in part responsible for recent social unrest in totalitarian societies, personal alienation because of an education and job mismatch is not the cause of this effect.[6] In short, the diploma disease, with its supposed pending dire consequences for the social contract, never happened.

Also, it was assumed that overeducation would be a mass phenomenon of expanding education, but actual estimates of how many people were involved and who they were paint a somewhat different picture. Estimates of mismatches between education level and required job skill ranged from a low of 14 percent to a high of 22 percent of employed individuals in the late 1970s and early 1980s (B. Burris 1983; Clogg and Shockey 1984).[7] And while the higher estimate represents a sizable group, most mismatches are mild and level of mismatch is rising only very slowly, particularly relative to the fast pace of the education revolution. More recent technical research on education, wages, and job satisfaction concludes that one, two-thirds of overeducated workers are only apparently so; two, more education yields higher wages than adequate education for the same job; and three, firms use education level of workers and changes in job skills as a profit-seeking strategy instead of as fixed conditions (e.g., Acemoglu 1998; Chevalier 2000; Sicherman 1991; Sloane 2002).

Further, the kinds of people most likely to experience a mismatch are illustrative of the larger picture of a changing workplace exactly due to more employment of educated workers. The greatest concentration of education/job mismatch occurs in two places in the labor market: one, among those workers having some higher education but not a college degree, and two, among people working as managers (B. Burris 1983; Clogg and Shockey 1984). In the American case, the former is most likely due to the rise of two-year institutions of higher education at the time (although participation in higher education was increasing in all developed nations), while the latter is due to rising education requirements of managers, which are discussed below. Unlike what Dore and many others predicted, the supposed largest newly "overeducated" group and potentially the most disruptive—the college graduate—experienced relatively little job mismatch despite the rapid expansion of mass higher education during this period (Schofer and Meyer 2005).

The overeducation argument underestimated how dynamic the relationship between education and the world of work became as the rising demand and supply of education became a worldwide norm. Operating on the incorrect image of a fixed structure of jobs into which education merely feeds trained individuals, it was no wonder that as Dore, and others of a similar mind-set, watched the education revolution take off into secondary and higher institutions they predicted a volatile clash in the labor market. What the overeducation image fails to account for is that with large numbers of more educated people flowing into jobs, this massive demographic change and the cultural meanings accompanying it also led, and continue to lead, to changes in the world of work. How sustainable this pattern will be into the future is open to debate, but it is clear that so far the education revolution has changed jobs and economies (Frey and Osborne 2013).

## THE RISE OF MASS PROFESSIONALISM

Why the diploma disease did not happen is illustrated in the story of the rise of professionals and managers in wealthy nations' economies. There is a vast sociological literature on the rise of the professions and professionals, a major subtheme of which is that in modern society the profession becomes a pervasive form, or more accurately a model that is spreading through the organization of work well beyond the ancient traditional areas such as medicine, law, and theology (e.g., Wilensky 1964). It is widely hypothesized that one of the cornerstones of expanding professionalization is formal education, particularly access to, and expansion of university-based education (e.g., Abbott 1988; Parsons 1971). If this is true, then as mass education expands into higher education, one should see a growth in jobs taking on more qualities of professions, as well as the roles of workers in these jobs taking on more qualities of professionalism. And this is exactly what has occurred for a substantial part of the American workplace and many other nations' workplaces.

Two economists of the U.S. Bureau of Labor Statistics, Ian Wyatt and Daniel Hecker, have compiled the most comprehensive, comparable set of information on trends in occupational groups over the twentieth century to date (2006).[8] Census data have always included information about the occupational categories (menial workers, technical workers, professionals, etc.) of jobs that U.S. workers have done over the last century, but because of changing definitions and the emergence of new job categories over time, it was difficult to accurately compare trends. Wyatt and Hecker painstakingly developed a standard set of occupational categories that can be used to compare across censuses; thus, theirs is the first full picture of changes in the U.S. labor forces during the rise and acceleration of the American version of the schooled society.

As Figure 6.1 shows, the most striking change over the century is the radical increase in the occupational group termed "professionals, technical and kindred workers," which increased its share of the overall labor market from about 4 percent in the early part of the twentieth century to 23 percent by the beginning of the twenty-first century, an expansion from 1.7 million to over 30 million workers! In other words, as described in the three prior chapters on university-generated authoritative knowledge and educational credentials connected to this knowledge, there has been a significant increase in jobs for people with special expertise, trained and credentialed through formal advanced education.

Unpacking this overall trend shows that a multifaceted transformation of the American economy went hand in hand with the rising supply of more advanced educated individuals streaming into the labor market (Goldin and Katz 1996). Technological production, particularly the introduction of computers in the workplace around 1970, and the increasing number,

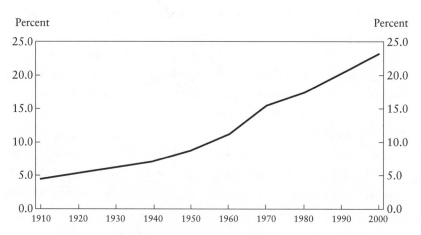

FIGURE 6.1 *Proportion of total employment of professional, technical, and kindred workers, 1910–2000.*

Note: U.S. Bureau of Labor. Data for 1930 are an average of 1920 and 1940 because original data were unavailable when article was written.

Source: Wyatt and Hecker (2006, 44)

size, and complexity of formal organizations, plus the growth in health care, education, social services, and government, each contributed to the professionalization of the workplace. Correspondingly, computer specialists grew ninety-five-fold as a proportion of total employment between 1960 and 2000; engineers grew ninefold from 1910 to 2000; accountants and auditors grew by a factor of thirteen over the century; health care professionals, by five; educators at the university level, by twelve; and teachers, a large single category of white-collar workers, by 1.4 (Wyatt and Hecker 2006). Certainly, a proportion of this expansion is due to increases in technical components of jobs, as discussed below, but a fair amount of it is due to the growth in jobs that take on professional, read educated, qualities.

Among Wyatt and Hecker's list of labor market transformations most relevant to the education revolution and the mass spread of professionalization is the growth in complex formal organizations, where jobs are now increasingly located. Such organizations use formal decision making, explicitly articulated rules and universalistic principles, and office holders, and they operate under general bureaucratic and highly rationalized means/goals procedures, as opposed to informal organizations such as traditional small firms, families, and clans. A major facet of modern society is its density of formal organizations, interconnected with one another, operating in a similar fashion, and organizing all kinds of human activity to a degree unknown in traditional and early modern societies (e.g., Boli and Thomas 1999; Carroll and Hannan 1999; Chandler and Mazlish 2005; Dobbin, Meyer, and Scott 1993; Drori, Meyer, and Hwang 2006). The earliest scholars of this trend barely envisioned what has come to be, but even then they were confident that the emerging schooled society constructed the bedrock upon which a proliferation of formal organizations would flourish. For example, two founders of the study of organizations in postindustrial society, Arthur Stinchcombe and James March, insightfully observed that a schooled society raises "practically every variable which encourages the formation of organizations and increases the staying power of new organizations" (1965, 150).

The vast army of late-twentieth-century educated professionals and technicians worked predominately in formal organizations versus being self-employed or in small family-run businesses. For example, in 2010 over 50 percent of the U.S. labor force in just the private sector worked

in organizations with over 250 employees, and 38 percent worked in organizations of over 1,000 employees; the percentages are no doubt higher
among workers in the public sector (U.S. Bureau of Labor Statistics 2011).
Included here, of course, are industrial, blue-collar jobs, but these have declined even while jobs in large organizations continue to grow. This means
that more people work within formal organizations, including all for-profit
corporations and other economic organizations as well as nonprofit organizations. The emergence and spread of the modern organization coinciding
exactly with early waves of masses entering secondary and postsecondary
institutions changed the nature of the workplace along qualities that now
are widely expected by individuals with advanced education.

Organizational sociologist Walter Powell's assessment of the emerging
institutionalized organizational design of corporations—the landscape of
so much work—finds "how rapidly the social technology of organizing
work has changed" over the past fifty years (2001, 68). And the dimensions of this new social technology have recently been thoroughly docu-
mented in an insightful multipart study of the globalization of formal
organizations by Gili Drori, John Meyer, Hokyu Hwang, and nine other
neo-institutional scholars (2006). They find that the new modern organization has three central components largely based on the schooled society's
leveraging of the organizational capacity of humans. The first component,
and the one that is most obviously a direct result of the schooled society,
is the extensive "personnel professionalism" permeating the modern organization. Personnel professionalism means two things. First, not only are
the leading, core professionals of the organization educated and formally
credentialed; so too are many others working there. Education provides
people with the skills to function in the modern organization, and it certi-
fies them as such. Educational credentials control access to sets of activities and management responsibilities inside formal organizations, and a
hierarchy of academic degrees has become thoroughly blended with the
internal hierarchy of the modern organization.[9] Second, with the notion
of personnel professionalism comes a workplace based on the idea of personnel as responsible individuals who are "thinking and choosing actors,
embodying professional expertise and capable of rational and creative
behavior" (Luo 2006, 230), all qualities that have become embedded in

the education systems of most nations as attributes expected of everyone. This is in direct contrast to the average workplace earlier in the twentieth century, where workers were seen as "adjuncts of machines, coarse, unclean, unreliable, and prone to drunkenness" (Common et al. 1921, as quoted in Luo 2006, 230).

The second component is the increase of intensive rationalization within the modern organization. Rationalization of human activities as an explicit organizational strategy flourished in the early bureaucracies of the nineteenth century, and the social technology of the modern organization now applies rationalized means/ends activity with ever more authority to ever more aspects of the social order (e.g., Perrow 1986; Weber 1978). Just as the modern organizational form is applied to a wider set of human activities once considered outside the reach of formal organizations, intensive rationalization is applied to ever more internal aspects of organizations. The rise of accounting and auditing, fundraising, elaborate legal contracts, corporate (or in the public sector, organizational) social responsibility, human relations, and strategic planning are just a few examples of now heavily rationalized internal activities of formal organizations, in which an expert culture reigns supreme. An underlying core belief in the schooled society is that these rationalized domains are to be trusted only to educationally credentialed individuals in university-created areas of expertise with accompanying special knowledge bases (e.g., Fogarty 1997). Instead of being some "natural outcome" of organizational need, in actuality intensified rationalized internal activities come directly out of the consequences of the education revolution. Accountants, auditors, fundraisers, legal staff, corporate social responsibility experts, directors of planning, and so forth are increasingly educationally credentialed professionals assumed to have similar educationally accredited operational approaches and common understandings, and who consider themselves as a specific kind of professional first and an employee of a specific organization second. By the same logic each type of profession captures, and legitimately holds control over, certain sets of activities within organizations, often with major resource and strategic implications. Accountants, for instance, who are so by virtue of a specific university degree, are considered specialists—experts with a standard and up-to-date technical method, who control accounting functions and budget flows within a specific organization. Thus, although these new organizational professionals are embedded within organizations, their educational credentials and accompanying charters transcend any particular organization (Drori, Meyer, and Hwang 2006; Shanahan and Khagram 2006).

The third component of the modern organization is that it has become horizontal in its authority structure. Authority and responsibility are far more widely distributed within organizations than in the past, thus "the relative authority, autonomy, and degree of responsibility for people and things"—in short, managerial skills of various types—grow as parts of job descriptions across occupations (Howell and Wolff 1991, 488). For example, this has meant that Americans employed as managers grew from 6.5 percent of the workforce in 1910 to 14.2 percent in 2000, or an absolute growth from 2.5 million to just over 18 million managers (Wyatt and Hecker 2006). While the full implications of this for understanding the impact of the education revolution on work are discussed below, this change is likely a symbiotic process interacting with the growth of the MBA and its specialized university-generated knowledge base.

Predictably, the organization of classrooms has similarly changed over the twentieth century. Comparing teachers and the nature of classrooms from 1890 to 1990, educational historian Larry Cuban finds that classrooms late in the twentieth century were less hierarchical and more informal and flexible; oriented towards the strengths and deeper learning capacities of students; and focused more on high-level cognitive capacities and students interacting in small groups (Cuban 1993, 2009). Also, in many current workplaces, accepted managerial styles and the rhetoric supporting them contain considerable reference to teacher-like mentorship and an education-like development of employees for the future well-being of the economic enterprise (Scott and Meyer 1991). In the schooled society, the cultural power of education as an institution makes the classroom a prominent model for the workplace, instead of the reverse, as traditional images of schooling and capitalism would have it (Bowles and Gintis 1976).

No doubt those still faithful to the overeducation image will suggest that the rise in new professionals through the expansion of formal education is an ersatz professionalism, a phony accommodation to growing rates of higher education enrollments, and thereby a type of whitewash that somehow fools the newly educated into taking the same old jobs merely wrapped in the trappings of an educated professional. Yet like the literature on the supposed crisis of overeducation, this falsely assumes that jobs represent some fixed order, or even less accurately, some naturally fixed order. But this has never been the case. Jobs and their labor requirements in centuries past were no more fixed than now.

This is perhaps the central insight of Karl Marx, arguably the founding sociologist and economist of work, who observed that the organization of work is intricately constructed by, and tied to, a society's social order. Since Marx, this is what so much historical sociology on work and social order illustrates. If it was true then, there is no reason why it should not be true now. Therefore, as a large part of the emerging social order over the twentieth century was dominated by educational expansion, it is not surprising that the workplace and work take a corresponding significant degree of personnel professionalism, rationalization, and managerialism. If for some strange reason jobs and the workplace had not been changed by the effects of the education revolution, one could envision, along with Dore, numerous and extreme mismatches in education and jobs, which would have produced some degree of social unrest. What happened instead was not widespread overeducation; rather, the very nature of work changed with the qualities, ideas, and schooled capabilities of the educated worker.

### EDUCATION AS MYTH?

If it can be argued that the schooled society has created many jobs in many workplaces that are compatible with the educated worker, it should also be true that the very content of jobs themselves has changed with the education revolution. Such a thesis though has been suppressed by the popularity of the education-as-myth perspective, which assumes that job content moves mostly towards deskilling through a pernicious combination of technology and profit-seeking to the point that education matters little to the real content of what is done at work. If educational upgrading happens at all, it is only a byproduct of a bias on the part of employers in favor of pliable social sensitivities of the educated rather than a need for advanced skills (e.g., Bowles and Gintis 1976).

This perspective originated with sociologist Ivar Berg's *Education and Jobs: The Great Training Robbery* (1971), arguing, as its provocative title suggests, that virtually no connection pertains between education and jobs beyond vacuous credentialism (educational upgrading), and hence the education revolution is some sort of societal rip-off. Written five years before Dore's monograph, the book has come to stand for the education-as-myth perspective and is still routinely referenced today. But its prowess as a standard citation aside, *Education and Jobs* is mostly a diatribe interspersed with empirical demonstrations, the weaknesses of which actually illustrate the problem with the educational upgrading argument. For example, one demonstration is responses from a small survey of senior managers at moderate-sized private firms at the time, showing that managers did not keep an account of the productivity of workers by their educational attainment and hence did not know if there was such a relationship. From this Berg infers that managers believe more in education than in actually knowing about its real impact on work, and in part he is right. This belief is an important part of the institutional impact of education on the workplace that is discussed in the following chapter on occupational credentials. But a belief in something does not in and of itself suggest that it could not also be true. From forty years of research on organizations and their use of rational strategies, it is well known that all kinds of disconnections happen among organizational actions, beliefs, and information (e.g., March and Simon 1993). In light of this, the fact that some managers do not know if a relationship exists between education and productivity in their production sites is not surprising, nor is it much evidence either way about a relationship between education and job skills.

Similarly, when Berg does present some direct evidence about education and productivity, his resistance to considering its full implications leads him away from a richer evaluation. For example, analyzing data about productivity and education among workers in six technical engineering and scientific firms, he finds the usual education wage premium of increasing salary from lowest to highest levels of education but with some variation in the absolute size of the premium across firms. From this, Berg claims that there is a lack of real skill differences by education level. Perhaps, but there could be many reasons for some variation across firms in the education wage premium, such as age differences in the labor force, regional differences in availability of people with certain education, and so forth. In and of itself, cross-firm variation does not prove a disconnection among education, job skill, and productivity.

Furthermore, in an accompanying table Berg presents some intriguing information contrasting the salary averages by education in these firms between workers of ordinary performance and workers of highly valuable performance (as judged by management).[10] Although the table plainly shows that across each education level valuable performance is rewarded with higher salaries, Berg ignores this and instead makes much of the fact that the payments on performance are larger for workers with Ph.D.s versus those with master's degrees and so forth on down through the education levels. Even if one were to ignore the fact that this observed pattern is exactly what a human capital hypothesis would predict—wage premium by productivity rate due to education—nothing in these results points to a dramatic degree of educational upgrading that is unrelated to skill or productivity levels. In fact, the whole table is a kind of minitestimonial to the opposite claim from that of Berg's!

The final type of evidence presented is what the book has become best known for among the proponents of the education-as-myth idea. Using what was for the time an obscure federal archive of information about jobs, Berg examines the historical shift in skill levels across many jobs in the U.S. economy. The U.S. Department of Labor's "Dictionary of Occupational Titles" (DOT) documents direct assessments of the educational and vocational preparation needed for the skill requirements of thousands of jobs (U.S. Department of Labor 1956, 1965, 1977). From the middle part of the twentieth century until 1986 the DOT undertook various updates and hence provides a historical record of direct measures of skill requirements for detailed jobs. Berg, like most researchers who have examined this archive, focused on the three submeasures of the component "general educational development" (GeD; not the same as the GED diploma)[11] in each job's requirements; namely, language, mathematical, and reasoning skills. Contained too in the DOT are measures and indicators of the physical demands of the job, requirements for interpersonal skills, autonomy versus control, and the job's overall substantive complexity (Spenner 1983). To ensure independence between job skills and education, the DOT explicitly states that the job skills are assessed irrespective of education levels of workers who might have these skills; therefore, just the skills needed to successfully do the work of the job are recorded, and the GeD levels are not simply a tautological reflection of education levels—although of course they are related (Fine 1968). Exactly how they are related and whether the relationship is only one of educational upgrading or represents skill upgrading is the question to which Berg applies these data.

Examining just the change from 1956 to 1966, Berg takes only the highest score among the three submeasures of the GeD to represent the change in skill requirements, completely ignoring the considerable information contained in the other submeasures (as is examined in the more recent research discussed below). Yet even with his rather crude approach to the data, contrary to the education-as-myth perspective—which he wants to support—Berg finds considerable skill level upgrading; indeed, about one third of the four thousand jobs examined underwent skill upgrades in just one decade. Instead of recognizing the implications of this, Berg juxtaposes this decade of job skill changes with changes in educational attainment of American workers, and declares the results to indicate mostly skill-less educational upgrading. It is not clear what his analysis really shows. As best as one can tell, for Berg never explicitly describes his logic, he reasons that if skill upgrading has moved somewhat slower than educational attainment in the labor force, then educational upgrading must be occurring. This assumption, particularly as it is based on such a short time frame, does not really add up; none but the hardest-core human capital enthusiast would expect a perfectly matched rate of increase between the two.

Berg goes on to demonstrate that depending on how the analyst decides which GeD levels (mathematics, language, and reasoning skills) match to which education levels, the data can be made to show some mismatch—but they can also be made to show considerable matching. Astonishingly enough, after all of this modeling of the data, Berg concludes that there is more match in the data than mismatch! He concedes that there is just not much proof of runaway educational upgrading due to increases in educational attainment of Americans over this decade. What his analysis does show, and he even notes this, is that there is substantial upgrading of the low-level jobs to expanded-skill jobs for more educated workers:

It is possible that this consolidation reflects actual upgrading of a number of low-level jobs. We can speculate that employers, *having access to better-educated workers, have in fact expanded the scope of some jobs.* (Berg 1971, 48, emphasis added)

As an argument about extensive educational upgrading, *Education and Jobs* would be unremarkable if it had not become one of the standard sources for the opinion that education and skill, as well as education and the workplace, are not very related. As readers go beyond the title and unfounded assumptions, they find that the best and most relevant DOT data support the opposite conclusion: job skills and education *are* related and there seems to be more than just runaway educational upgrading happening historically. To think that the education revolution is some kind of societal rip-off is to assume some "natural" world of work where educational attainment is rarely meaningful. The labor market in Berg's view is mostly fixed, and therefore large-scale changes on the education side must for him be trivial at best, or may even become a major social problem. We come full circle to the essentially unfounded conclusion of the overeducation crisis. Ironically, the way out of this view is captured in Berg's own words above: a useful way to look at the rising skill requirements in the American labor market is as an outcome of a supply of workers with increasing levels of education, not as phony credentialism but as a real adaptation to what educated people think about themselves, how they have come to think about their world, and how they expect to work, and even as the market adapting to higher levels of productivity by educated workers.

What if the world of work is not mostly fixed in some preconceived, natural fashion and instead expands and adapts in response to large-scale changes in the characteristics of the workforce? Demand for skilled labor means more than just a change in recruiting and training; it means redesigning the jobs themselves to fit the capabilities and mentalities of highly skilled—read highly educated—workers. Recent research on shifting job skills and their relationship to the education revolution shows precisely this.

ACADEMIC INTELLIGENCE AND JOB SKILLS

Newer analyses of the American job market and its shifting skill requirements show the opposite of the education-as-myth perspective. Working with the same job skill information but with the longer time series of 1960 to 1985 and with a detailed systematic approach to the measures, two labor economists, David Howell and Edward Wolff (1991), find that across a consistent set of 264 occupations and sixty-four industries three major changes occurred over the past four decades. First, not surprising, is a persistent decline in the demand for physical motor skills in American jobs. Second, no doubt part of the education-fostered managerial revolution, is a sharp rise in interactive skills for working with coworkers. And last is the growth in the on-the-job need for greater cognitive skills of analytical reasoning and synthetic reasoning.

This last finding is particularly telling of the wider impact of education on the workplace. The rise of academic intelligence as a major cultural product of the schooled society is among the most fundamental impacts that mass education has made on modern society. It would be a strange world if, after most people were exposed to formal school instruction lasting from twelve to sixteen-plus years of their lives, during which they learned these skills that are so valued and have such payoff within the schooled society, the world of work did not reflect this change. "Reflect" here means more than the mere addition of some higher-level cognitive jobs. Instead, given the large-scale transformation that the education revolution has brought in how people think about thinking, one would expect a similar transformation of the entire workplace. And this is what Howell and Wolff find (see also Levy and Murnane 2012).

Benefiting from earlier research on the DOT (e.g., Spenner 1983; Zuboff 1988), these researchers calculate two measures of the cognitive skills required in jobs: one is the combined GeD measures (mathematics, language, and reasoning skills) to form an indicator of analytical reasoning; and the second is a measure of the substantive complexity of the job to form an indicator of synthetic reasoning, that is, putting different ideas and concepts together in new ways (also referred to in the science of cognitive development as effortful thinking and new problem solving). It is notable that both of these skill sets rely heavily on the components of fluid

IQ that have been so thoroughly institutionalized as key academic intel-ligence capabilities through mass education (Blair, Gamson, Thorne, and Baker 2005). Howell and Wolff find that from 1960 to 1985 occupations with the highest level of substantive complexity grew from 20 percent of all studied occupations to just under 30 percent; over the same time, jobs with the lowest levels of substantive complexity dropped to 15 per-cent. Similarly, the jobs with higher cognitive complexity attracted large gains in employment growth. Added to these trends over this period is the growth of the entire service sector, which has higher-than-average skill re-quirements relative to the manufacturing sector (Howell and Wolff 1991, table 6). Lastly, among the industries with the greatest growth in cognitive job skills is found the least amount of inequality in skills across jobs—in other words, "upgrading of cognitive skill is associated with narrowing cognitive skill requirements across jobs" (498). This is true even though the American labor market continues to have areas of significant inequal-ity in wages and job conditions. As mass education has spread an ideol-ogy of the universal individual in possession of developed thinking skills, changes in the nature of some jobs have reflected this shift.

Even though the education revolution has made cognition a valued capability that lowers inequality among jobs in many parts of the labor market, this is not always the case. For example, there is also growing in-equality in income across education levels; the segregation of females into lower-paying part-time jobs (many demanding considerable cognitive skill levels); and growing inequality between low-skilled and high-skilled parts of the labor market (e.g., Massey and Hirst 1998). It is also true that those who have not played the education game well for any number of reasons increasingly suffer in the labor market. Starting in the late 1970s and continuing into the 1990s in the United States, the real wages of workers with twelve or fewer years of schooling fell by 26 percent and have never recovered. A similar pattern has clearly happened throughout the labor markets of other economically developed nations and most likely is now happening in less-developed economies too (e.g., Berman, Bound, and Machin 1998; Hanson and Harrison 1995). In the current world economy, the once embittered taxicab driver with a Ph.D., the symbol of what turned out to be the benign diploma disease of the 1970s, is now likely employed in a higher-level job at a good wage, and it is the undereducated cabdriver taking him to work who is at much greater risk of economic uncertainty than before. As education expands in national labor markets globally, this process repeats itself, including renewed media images of the evils of a supposed overeducation crisis; note, for example, the recent wave of Chinese media attention on a graduate student who took the civil service test for a menial job within the public sector because of the difficulty of finding stable, high-paying private-sector positions for the highly educated, when she said, "If I had to die, I'd rather die a street cleaner within the system" (*China Business Morning News*, January 4, 2013). Certainly unevenness among educational expansion, job content, and economic adjustment ebb and flow to a degree, but in the near future it is likely that highly educated street cleaners in China will be an overeducation myth.

Compelling evidence indicates that the content of jobs has changed and that a substantial portion of this change is exactly as one would predict from the growing emphasis on cognitive skills in mass education. Contrary to what Berg intends his analysis to show, most studies using the DOT find an observable skill upgrading of existing jobs and in the creation of new jobs, particularly in terms of more cognitive skills (see Spenner 1983). So the question becomes: What causes job skills and the workplace to change given the presence of ever more educated workers? The answer lies in examining the dynamic relationship among education, jobs skill, and technology.

EDUCATION, JOB SKILL, AND TECHNOLOGY

Perhaps the reason the education-as-myth perspective has gotten so much traction over the past decades is that up until now there has never been a thorough investigation of the relationship *among* education, job skill, and technology. Research literatures exist on the relationship between any two of these, but not all three together. The human capital argument often assumes, but without any further elaboration, that the three are tied through market forces. This is certainly true, but why firms choose to react one way, say through deskilling, instead of another way, say through job skill upgrading through technology, and make accompanying decisions about the desired education level of employees, is more complex than just maximizing profit, which is a given in any case. Recently, though, research has begun to untie the complicated knot among these three forces, and the findings shed further light on the way the education revolution transforms work. Before examining this new research, it is helpful to understand the brief conceptual history of considering all three factors together.

A whole generation of American sociologists of education cut their conceptual teeth on Randall Collins's first book, titled *The Credential Society* (1979). In the late 1970s it attempted a third possible sociological argument besides the Marxian image of formal education as the handmaiden of capitalism and a theoretically problematic technological functionalism (somewhat related to the human capital model), and it remains a classic in the intellectual development of a sociology of education. It is best known for advancing thinking about credentialing and the emerging schooled society at the time (the ideas of which initiate the discussion of the educational domination of labor market credentials in the succeeding chapter). In addition, the book also initiated the idea that educational growth, job skill change, and technology are related and together form a relationship key to understanding the schooled society. Further, it rejected a "myth of technocracy," namely that society and hence education chiefly follow where technological advances take them (similar to the traditional perspective here). Instead, Collins was the first to argue that educational degrees become a method to capture control over the vast resources (monetary and social) that advancing technology yields, as described above in how education and large organizations interact. While not yet acknowledging the full impact of the schooled society, the book is an earlier version of it, where education has its own robust influence on work and the workplace.

Innovative for its time, unfortunately the book ends up falling back on Berg's (and Dore's) content-less educational upgrading of jobs. Other than producing the social and physical resources that are the much sought-after prizes, technology and educational upgrading in Collins's version lead only to credentialism. But this flies in the face of so much observation of work, education, and technology; the modern workplace and its production process are brimming with technology that changes, sometimes radically, with new innovations that are directly related to real change in job skills. Can it really be the case that mass education has no impact on this process other than to capture control of it through formal degrees? As insightful as Collins's observations about credentials and resources are, his reliance on education-as-myth assumptions handicapped subsequent institutional inquiry about the impact of education on technology, which looms so large in postindustrial society. Instead, there is growing evidence that the rise of the schooled society has created a dynamic and self-reinforcing interaction among education, job skill, and technology.

An emerging research literature since the late 1970s indicates that expanding education has had a profound impact on the incorporation of technology into work. Largely in the pages of the *Quarterly Journal of Economics*, economists of labor and national development present empirical findings about the relationships among education of workers, technology, and the organization of work inside firms. This research is motivated in part by an intriguing counterintuitive finding about the expansion of higher education and what economists refer to as the "college wage premium," a reference to the salary of college-educated workers being consistently larger than that of less-educated workers (Autor, Katz, and Krueger 1998). The background is as follows: in the United States from 1940 to 1970 college-educated workers in the labor force grew by 2.73 percent each year, and then from 1970 on increased annually by 3.66 percent. As the large American baby boom was finishing high school and heading to university and college, these rates represented a massive change in the educational composition of the labor force, which continues into the present. To economists it made sense that as the supply of college-educated workers rapidly increased, starting just before the Second World War, their skills became less unique, and so, following the law of supply and demand, the college wage premium fell as expected from an advantage of 55 percent more wage for a college graduate than a high school graduate in 1970 to 41 percent by 1981. The puzzling finding is that as the supply of BAs in the workforce rose even faster after the watershed year of 1970, the college wage premium did not continue to decrease; paradoxically, it turned and increased, so that by 1995 college graduates were earning 62 percent more than high school graduates. Given the relationship between labor supply and demand (as reflected in wages), this should not have happened. Why did it?

A big part of the answer to this paradox is what education does to individuals and in turn what that means for the use of technology in the workplace. Recently, labor economists have been exploring a phenomenon known as "complementary technology," or the process by which the educated worker transforms the workplace through what she is capable of and hence through the technologies that will be most productive and profitable (Acemoglu 1998). When most people think about the relationship between technology and the skill capabilities of workers, they envision technology as mostly replacing, not complementing, workers. A long history of just such a (deskilling) relationship can be read throughout the eighteenth century, when most innovative technology—the spinning jenny, weaving machines, printer cylinders, the later assembly lines, and so on—replaced workers (1998). The same process can still be found in today's workplaces, as for example when computers replaced some skilled jobs that are now done by less-skilled workers. But this is not the only way technology can influence the workplace. There are now a number of examples of technology complementing the rising education of workers, making employing them more profitable.

Moreover, it is not just any technology that is complementary with more educated workers; rather, it is what labor economists refer to as "pervasive skill-biased" (read pervasive education-biased) technology (Autor, Katz, and Krueger 1998; Berman, Bound, and Machin 1998; Murnane and Levy 1996). This is what a number of studies of firms, technology, and worker education have shown. Research on complementary technology started with the simple-enough finding of a positive relationship between an educated workforce and computer adoption in production, as well as findings that the addition of more nonproduction employees—that is, managers—is associated with the adoption of more computers in the firm (e.g., Autor, Katz, and Krueger 1998; Dunne and Schmitz 1995). In an attempt to sort out the direction of causality, in other words, to answer whether the educated workforce drives adoption of technology or vice versa, Dom, Dunne, and Troske (1997) show that firms that adopt new factory automation technologies hire more educated workers. When firms under study replaced traditional teams of draftsmen and model-builders, who developed new products, with computer-automated design workstations, their labor force reorganized towards higher levels of education. The effects can be substantial: compared to firms with the lowest level of technology adoption, firms with high levels of technology had workforces that included four times more higher education degree-holders and twice as many managers. Most telling about the question of education's impact on technology, the study also finds a longitudinal pattern of hiring and technology adoption which suggests that firms that already have an educated workforce are more likely to incorporate advanced technologies in production than firms with a less educated workforce. The relationship between complementary technology and the educated labor force appears symbiotic, or as Murnane and Levy summarize about their case study of computers and higher education of workers in a bank:

The development of computerization, the design of jobs, and the recruitment of college graduates—three sides of the same coin—are not fully played out [at this bank] . . . experience suggests that an increased demand for skilled labor means more than just a change in recruiting or training. *It means redesigning the jobs themselves to maintain the interest of higher-skilled workers.* (1996, 262, emphasis added)

Does the pattern of a falling and rising education wage premium in the United States then defy the law of supply and demand? No. Instead, after a certain point, when a type of education becomes more widespread, as the growth of BAs did in the United States, firms see that capitalizing on the increased capabilities of workers through more advanced production technology is profitable; they then pursue these kinds of workers, pay them wages to retain their skills, and redesign jobs that are more compatible with them. But only by considering education as a skill-transforming process—as a real transformation of the individual beyond simple screening (essentially education-as-myth)—does the law of supply and demand hold true.

Perhaps the best example of this phenomenon is research on how the American version of the education revolution symbiotically interacted with industrial development over the course of the late nineteenth and early twentieth centuries. Two other labor economists, Claudia Goldin and

Lawrence Katz, have shown that much of the nation's economic development has been a spiraling interplay between rising human (educational) capital and technological change (1996, 2008). Noting ironically that virtually the entire American literature on labor history rarely mentions the education of production workers, they find that the education-biased process that seems so newly pronounced in recent decades actually began in the turn of the twentieth century, in manufacturing.

Certainly, many types of industries developed during this period in a widely recognized classical progression from collective skilled artisan production to mass unskilled labor forces in assembly lines using Taylorist production. In these cases, technology and capital intensification during the first industrial revolution deskilled many jobs in cotton, wool, silk textiles, footwear, lumber, stone, clay, and cement. Yet what has tended to be overlooked is that during the same era, a number of industries moved beyond unskilled mass production by using new continuous-process and batch production technologies in petroleum refining, dairy products, paints, chemicals, rayon, and nonferrous metals. In these industries as well as in those like radio production, which began to use significant amounts of electrical power and incorporated advanced technology of the time, there is clear evidence of an educational expansion of workforces, that is, more employment of workers with secondary education and more nonproduction managers. Various new managerial strategies also added to this emerging complementary relationship between education and technology in the first half of the twentieth century (Chandler 1977). Firms that intensified capital through these "hard and soft" technologies hired significantly more high school graduates (the wave of masses on the leading edge of educational expansion during this era), while many other firms continued to invest in the traditional formula of deskilled mass production.

Goldin and Katz's review of federal archival documents on labor from the second decade of the twentieth century illustrates that transforming industries wanted to recruit the more educated worker not for his middle-class sensibilities and habits, as the education-as-myth perspective insists, nor for narrowly defined vocational skills, as a traditional human capital perspective suggests, but rather for the cognitive skills found in the emerging curriculum of academic intelligence that went hand in hand with educational expansion and increased production. As the authors describe it:

Cognitive skills were valued in various trades. High school graduates were sought because they could read manuals and blueprints, knew about chemistry and electricity, could do algebra and solve formulas and . . . could more effectively converse with nonproduction workers. . . . Blue-collar positions requiring some years of high school or a diploma were described as needing cognitive skills such as "good judgment," "skilled in free-hand drawing," "special ability to interpret drawings [and] chemical formulas," "general knowledge of chemicals used," "[ability] to mix the chemicals" . . . "knowledge of electricity and electric wire sizes and insulations," and "general knowledge of photography." (Goldin and Katz 1998, 718; quoted texts are from U.S. Department of Labor reports from 1918 to 1921)

The third cycle of the revolution—the spread of mass higher education—has not been unique in its transformation of the current workplace; the earlier cycles of schooling expansion also played a role in transforming the workplace of one hundred years ago.

In reflecting on the causes of this earlier trend, Goldin and Katz speculate that the jobs created in these technologically changed industries created a demand for more educated workers and people undertook more education as a result. Certainly this was, and is now, true to a degree, but it may leave out a broader process. An additional promising hypothesis is that expansion of education occurs for many reasons, not just job requirements, and once a symbiotic process among education, technology, and job skill upgrading begins, the three likely feed one another. This is what the underappreciated findings of the transforming power of education already began to show in developing nations in the 1960s and what continues now worldwide (Inkeles and Smith 1974).

Since the education revolution is worldwide, its impact on economies should be observed worldwide. Economists of an older generation speculated that opening trade between rich and poor nations would greatly favor unskilled workers in the latter; skilled workers would suffer and hence be more likely to emigrate. But over the last two decades there are indications that the workplace in less-developed nations is also being upgraded through the educated worker and her ability to use advanced technology. For example, an international study of manufacturing firms and their production plants by Berman, Bound, and Machin (1998) suggests how this is happening. A rising supply of more educated people entering the labor market leads to more extensive use of education-biased technology, so that jobs within plants are rapidly being upgraded through a complementary relationship between education and technology. It is important to show, as the authors do, that this is happening across nations within both the same industries and the same plants within those industries, as this helps to rule out exogenous factors that could influence the composition of the labor force. The trend is significant; for example, in many developed nations examined over just eight years, from 1979 to 1987, there was a 71 percent shift to more-educated workers within plants, and this increase in educated workers generated eight times more profit than increased trade (1998). And of course all of this is occurring even while more educated workers receive higher wages. Further, there is still cross-national variation in the rate of the education-related skill upgrading in the manufacturing workplace. This makes sense, as the rates of educational expansion, while all in a positive direction, vary cross-nationally as well. This parallel is a further indication of the transforming power of education in the workplace (Gottschalk and Joyce 1998). It would not be correct to conclude, however, that technology is used only for more enlightened production; there is considerable evidence that computers (and the expert-managers behind them) are also used for command-and-control functions in firms (Brown and Lauder 2009).

## TOWARDS THE EDUCATED WORKPLACE: HUMAN CAPITAL OR MYTH?

Education goes well beyond the training of individuals in its influence on society. Research examined here indicates that the schooled society's workplace continually adapts to the ideas of personnel professionalism within an expanding model of the formal organization as the main context of jobs, while major control of the massive resources and power generated by technological production goes to educationally credentialed and legitimated experts. Professionalism, technical expertise, general cognitive capability, and managerial skills are the defining components of the twenty-first-century job. And there is significant job skill upgrading along these lines, particularly in terms of complex cognitive skills and synthetic reasoning, which were more or less unheard of in the average workplace one hundred years ago. The ability of ever-expanding mass formal education to redefine people and their capabilities, as well as technical innovation and information, in turn shapes work to an unprecedented degree. Neither Dore's diploma disease, nor Berg's education-as-myth and fears of a mass duping of people about schooling have come to pass. If the education revolution transforms the very basics of work, what is to be concluded about the two contrasting models—traditional human capital and education-as-myth—that have so long dominated most intellectual discussion of work in modern society?

Most of the research reviewed here is more critical of the education-as-myth perspective than the human capital theory, but the latter does not go unchallenged. In fact, while the emerging educated workplace supports some of the basic ideas behind the human capital perspective, it points to a number of theoretical limitations as well. Human capital argumentation reads as if there is a natural order of productivity that increases as workers gain more skill. The broader institutional view of the schooled society argues that there is no particular natural order of skill; rather, as mass education is unleashed on society, it makes a new ordering of job skills. Collins's vision of a credentialed society was on to this important insight; it just stopped short of its full implications, namely, that education fashions a new type of work in society. Educated workers become "productive" in an educationally defined fashion, but not as the education-as-myth perspective would have it, as phony or merely an indoctrination; instead, because there are real ramifications of this new educational order of work. This ability of education to reshape the workplace, particularly in the large formal organization, along the dimensions of cognitized abilities, personnel professionalism, and mass managerialism in the aggregate is underappreciated by the human capital perspective. It hypothesizes tight, one-to-one efficiencies among new skill, wages, technology, and productivity, running from jobs to education, but these are not so routinely evident, as the relationships are more dynamic. There is considerable evidence that changes brought on by mass education of workers influence job content and economic strategy (see also Carnevale and Rose 2011). The usual human capital perspective must be expanded to take into account how formal education, both as individual human capital and as a mass phenomenon, interacts with the modern economy in the schooled society (Crespo Cuaresma, Lutz, and Sanderson 2014; see also Bills 2003).

The research here also suggests that the education-as-myth view stemming from the traditional perspective of education needs to be put to rest, at least in its crudest application. It censors the full extent of insights of a neo-institutional model of education and work. There is no reason why a perspective on education and work cannot hold the ideas of education as transforming work and the elaboration of an educated workplace together. Schooled individuals are capable of (accustomed to and expect to use) certain kinds of skills, particularly those flowing from academic intelligence, which less-schooled or unschooled individuals tend not to be. Work is increasingly organized around these skills, and this process is sustained by formal organizations that contain significant numbers of jobs. This is not to say that the educated worker is a "naturally" more productive worker in every type of workplace, as cruder versions of the human capital view suggest. Rather, the educated worker is *the* definition of productive in the educated workplace. Workers and jobs dynamically change together as the full impact of the education revolution unfolds.

### CHAPTER 7

# Credentialing in the Schooled Society

Whereas the class position of most Americans in 1840 was almost entirely a
function of their ownership of property, a century later educational credentials
had become the primary and proximate determinant of class position for most
people by virtue of the capacity of educational credentials to regulate access to the
occupational structure.

DAVID HOGAN, *History of Education Quarterly*, 1996

I misrepresented my academic degrees when I first applied to M.I.T. 28 years ago and
did not have the courage to correct my résumé when I applied for my current job
or at any time since. I am deeply sorry for this and for disappointing so many in the
M.I.T. community.

Public apology of the resigning Massachusetts Institute of Technology Dean of
Admissions for educational credential fraud; *New York Times*, April 27, 2007

WITH ITS VAST CULTURE OF EDUCATION, a distinctive feature of
postindustrial society is the primary requirement of formal educational
training for access to increasingly more occupations. Over time and across
many occupations, educational credentials have gone from mostly irrelevant, or at best supplemental, to ascendant over non-educational credentials. Before formal education was widely practiced, traditional forms of
access to occupations—such as prior experience, audition, repute, sinecure,
simony, sponsored apprenticeship, artisanal training, tutelage, praetorship,
personal letters of reference and introduction, family membership, marital status, age, gender, "traditional school tie" (attendance at a particular
institution), rectitude, guild or union membership, patronage, ownership,
and position in a social stratum—dominated, and among them were few
qualities of formal schooling. Yet over a relatively short sociological period, as historian David Hogan observes, formal education generated the
capacity to regulate access to occupations, and in so doing has weakened
the legitimacy of traditional forms to the point that for many occupa-

tions their use is taboo. Taboo, now too, are fraudulent representations of educational credentials, even in the face of exceptional, posteducation, on-the-job performance, as the precipitous professional fall of MIT's talented admissions dean illustrates.

Not only has formal educational credentialing become widely interjected into the occupational process, but the nature of educational credentialing itself continues to intensify. Expanding beyond mere participation in schooling is an emerging normative assumption in the labor market and society that an individual's educational training should be solely chartered through the attainment of formal academic degrees. Secondary school degrees, educational training certificates, vocational degrees, associate degrees, the bachelor's, and all sundry graduate and professional degrees are salient social constructions supplanting lesser and older educational training distinctions such as partial participation in schooling and even charters from specific elite educational institutions. This process includes much more than just narrow credentialing; educational degrees are fast becoming universally synonymous with human capacity in the occupational structure and are a prominent reflection of the cultural impact of the education revolution on other institutions.

Oddly, with only a few notable exceptions this distinctive and expanding feature of education in postindustrial society is generally underappreciated, underanalyzed, and undertheorized in the sociologies of education, occupations, and social stratification. If appreciated, educational credentialing is seen as only playing a supporting role in interoccupational conflict; if analyzed, educational credentials are considered as a mere technical adjustment to statistical modeling of the process by which individuals attain adult status; and if theorized about, educational credentialing is considered a minor phenomenon and taken at times to be an indicator of overeducation. Yet this anemic sociology of educational credentialing flies in the face of the immense practice of educational degree attainment by ever increasing proportions of each new generation, and the ensuing pervasive belief in the power of degrees to both allocate individuals in the labor market and serve as job requirements in the occupational structure. No doubt the weakness in the scholarship about education and occupational credentialing is an outgrowth of the weakness of the traditional perspective on education as an institution. It misses the centrality of the dominance of education over occupational credentialing in postindustrial society and what this means for the transforming nature of the education revolution. Interesting in its own right, this trend is also a supporting symbiotic process in the educational transformation of economies and work described in the preceding chapter.

Assembled here is evidence for how over the past century a rapid and robust educational transformation of occupational credentialing has occurred and what the current intensification of this trend means. Similar to the educational transformation of other institutions, the dominance of educational degrees stems from the cultural ideas that mass education as an institution has instilled into the culture of postindustrial society. Most germane are four beliefs that form the socially constructed logic behind the growth of educational degrees as occupational credentials. First, belief in equality of opportunity as a form of social justice lends the quality of merit to educational credentials for the individual, the labor market, employers, and occupations. Second, belief in the development of modern individuals as a collective good justifies educational degrees as codifying progress towards human development and actualization beyond preparation for specific jobs, and this also supports the process by which educational degrees become synonymous with the broader social status of the individual. Third, with the belief in academic intelligence and its wide application, educational degrees become indications of individuals' cognitive ability, the central generalized ability that is widely assumed to be crucial for posteducation life. Lastly, belief that a diversity of academic degrees is synonymous with a diversity of specialized knowledge and expertise tightens the connections among educational degrees, occupational expertise, and the entire university knowledge conglomerate.

Evidence of this change is illustrated by four empirical examples of the central institutionalizing processes that are driving educational credentialing and its assumptions deep into the occupational structure. These are followed by examples of how misrepresenting educational credentials, once a trivial omission, has in a short time become defined as a major form of social deviance. Lastly is a brief empirical demonstration of how the rise of educational credentialing adds another important institutional dimension to education's dominance of social mobility. Before a consideration of the evidence, however, the popular education-as-myth image applied to educational credentials known as "credentialism" will be shown to be an inaccurate explanation of how growing education transforms occupational credentials.

## CREDENTIALISM LAID TO REST

Along with its aliases "hollow credential," "diploma mill," "sheepskin effect," and "paper chase," "credentialism" is essentially another pejorative term for educational upgrading of jobs without any substantial change in required skills. As described in the preceding chapter, skepticism about expanding formal education led to the belief that credentialism is inevitable (Bills 1988, 2003, 2004). From the traditional perspective of the relationship between formal education and society, if education is chiefly to serve the interests of external institutions, then its rapid expansion is assumed to be unneeded and wasteful. Therefore, if as is usually found there is a larger payoff to degrees than equivalent years of schooling and if the payoff for the same level of schooling significantly changes over historical periods, then credentialism is assumed to be occurring (e.g., Park 1999; Bills 2004; Ferrer and Riddell 2002). Supposedly, individuals pursue educational degrees beyond just years of schooling because of this disproportional payoff, which in turn drives up the collective use of valued degrees as labor market credentials, hence creating skill-less educational upgrading over time. Firms are thought to use educational degrees only as a signal for suitable employees, and this also contributes to credentialism (e.g., Thurow 1975). Consequently, educational degrees as occupational credentials have been thought of as a function of changes in occupations and the economy that are external to the system of education, and this supposed secondary nature of the institution produces credentialism if it expands beyond assumed external needs.

In keeping with the argument about the educational transformation of work, what has not been considered before is the hypothesis that educational credentialing is mostly driven by the greater institutionalization of education and its corresponding greater share of cultural understandings.

Educational credentialing flows from the institutional logic of the extensive culture of education of the schooled society. Thus, non-educational credentials decline while educational ones increase because education as an institution transforms reigning theories of personnel, the nature of work, the increased formal organization of society, and valued human capabilities. Expanding educational credentialing is not mostly a function of rampant overeducation or skill-less educational upgrading. While all observers agree that growing educational credentialing sweeps non-educational credentials aside, expansion does not mean that credentialism is the best way to theorize about the relationship between education and access to occupations. Also a pervasive belief in the inevitability of credentialism retards intellectual thinking about educational credentials as a broader institutional phenomenon. If—because education has considerable transforming power over work and the workplace—the over-education crisis did not, and usually will not, happen, then credentialism will not either. The notion of credentialism should be laid to rest so that the broader hypotheses about widespread educational credentialing in the schooled society can be considered.

In many ways Collins's 1979 *The Credential Society* foreshadows these broader hypotheses, but prophetic as the book's message was for the time, even it could not predict what has occurred to credentialing in the schooled society. Collins was the first to argue systematically that the presence of educational credentials is really a whole system by which educational degrees become the main legitimate route to power and access to resources within an increasingly professionalized and formally organized society. The culture of education has been directly interjected into the growing personnel professionalism of large formally organized, white-collar workplaces. The schooled society makes educational credentials ever more dominant, not only for individuals but also in how the prodigious resources and riches from a technological world are legitimately divided up.

Seen this way, educational credentials essentially codify the entire package of access, control, and rights of usage of authoritative knowledge generated by the university. Credentialing becomes the embodiment of an educationally constructed everyday world of expertise and the expert, and is the manifestation of education's unique institutional privilege in modern society (Bills 2003). Educationally credentialed lawyers, accountants, human resource specialists, economists, psychologists, engineers, medical professionals, and so on capture larger roles in struggles over competition of resources (capital and power). So too managerial cadres of MBAs come to control larger shares of organizational resources, and educationally defined and exclusive groups of professionals lay claim to certain privileged functions within the ever more organized (yet fluid in competition for resources) workplace. Credentials play a central sociological role far beyond just allocating individuals; educationally generated credentials become nothing less than the central currency of social power (including material resources).[1] But the process is not limited to one of power attainment, as the logic behind educational credentialing transforms the individuals, methods, and ways activities are undertaken, and even which activities are to be legitimately undertaken.

As mentioned at the close of Chapter 5, on the university, not only does education produce and verify the expertise, knowledge, and the logic by which actors are pressed to use; it also produces new classes of personnel connected to expertise, knowledge and logic in a tight fashion. As shown later, the firm, the church, the state, the military, the family and clan, and so forth are no longer the institutions that provide the primary logic behind reigning theories of personnel; increasingly, education alone has the charter to create and sustain this process. What John Meyer predicted in 1977 has come to be a core cultural phenomenon of the schooled society. Therefore, economists, chartered solely through an advanced degree and exposure to economics from the university, become the legitimate predictors of economies, not psychologists or even experienced business managers with MBAs, for instance, who have their own entitlement to apply other knowledge to other activities; and degree-holding human resource specialists are credentialed to handle all kinds of sensitive information and personnel issues within large formal organizations, not those with an MBA in finance. This is of course training for functional differentiation, but it goes beyond purely technical demands, as the functional differentiation itself is to a remarkable degree educationally constructed and defined, as described in Part I. Propelled and reinforced by permeating cultural understandings, educational degrees are more than training; they represent agreed upon, legitimate access to special knowledge, which is enacted in prescribed activities. This cultural logic becomes self-reinforcing and in turn publicly legitimates the resulting variation (inequalities) in power, resources, and prestige.

In the face of widespread and trusted educational credentialing, all manner of non-educational logics such as prior experience, reputation, everyday know-how, and charisma pale as the way to organize occupations. Most if not all of the increasing professional, managerial, and technical occupations described in the preceding chapter are controlled through educational credentialing, thus deepening the dimensions of the schooled society. This is not to imply that a vacuous credentialism is at play, or that laws of supply and demand in the labor market are not always in force. Rather, the argument is that the schooled society results in a profound reconstructing of meanings about jobs, workplaces, and credentials along the logic of formal education, and hence the content of occupations and processes of supply and demand for labor follow along.

Unfortunately, by relying unnecessarily on the assumption that education does little to change jobs and individuals other than to credential them (a radical conclusion from what many incorrectly thought Berg's earlier book proved), Collins stops short of the broader implications of his own argument. One does not need to rely on the image of credentialism to understand what is rapidly occurring in the schooled society. So too, educational credentialing is far more than an avenue to power and resources in organizations; it is the vanguard of a full change in the nature of social organization and social stratification, the likes of which were unknown in previous human society.

### EDUCATION'S SPREAD INTO
### OCCUPATIONAL CREDENTIALING

Greater institutionalization of formal education spreads through the structure of occupations in at least four main ways, each of which is diagramed in Figure 7.1. The first can be referred to as *horizontal institutionalization*, which is evident in the historical increase in the proportion of educationally credentialed occupations. Also, if the argument is correct, the use of educational credentialing will not just pile up at the elite end of the

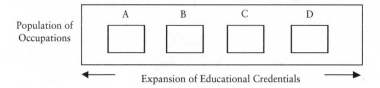

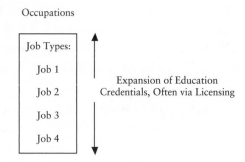

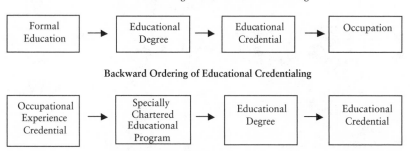

FIGURE 7.1 *Four processes of institutionalization of educational credentials within the occupational structure.*
Source: Baker (2011)

prestige spectrum of occupations, but will occur across the whole range of occupations. There will be evidence too of expanding educational credentialing in new and growing parts of the occupational structure, and conversely, vanishing occupations will have disproportionally used non-educational credentials.

An example of horizontal institutionalization of educational creden-tialing is shown in Figure 7.2, which displays required educational creden-tials for the fastest-growing occupations—that is, those with the largest job growth in both percentage and absolute growth in number of work-ers—and occupations with the largest job decline from 2004 to 2006, as compiled by the U.S. Bureau of Labor Statistics. Among the forty-five fast-est-growing occupations (in percentage job growth) in the U.S. economy, three-fourths require an educational credential and over one half require a bachelor's degree or higher. Twenty-five percent of the fastest-growing occupations require a graduate or professional degree, including medical scientists (Ph.D.), occupational therapists (MS), postsecondary teachers (Ph.D.), mental health counselors (MS), and veterinarians (first professional degree). While absolute job growth was dominated by non-educational credentialed occupations, 30 percent of the largest job growth was in oc-cupations requiring an educational credential, most among these requiring a bachelor's degree. Lastly, all thirty of the occupations experiencing the largest job decline were not educationally credentialed. This example is

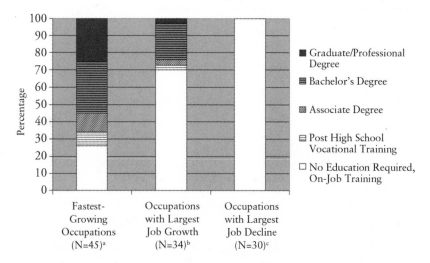

FIGURE 7.2 *Educational credential requirements among growing and declining U.S. occupations, 2004–2006.*

[a] Largest percentage growth in jobs   [b] Largest absolute growth in jobs

[c] Smallest absolute growth in jobs

Source: Author's analysis of data presented in D. Hecker (2005), and Dohm and Shniper (2007).

cross-sectional and looks at occupations experiencing the greatest changes, but it is illustrative of the degree to which educational credentialing penetrates the occupational structure.

One can make the case, as Collins and others did some time ago, that interoccupational competition certainly continues to occur and that the use of educational degrees as credentials is one weapon in that competition, but it is unlikely that this process is now the main cause of the institutionalization of educational credentialing (Collins 1979, 2002). Instead, it might be best to think of interoccupational competition as a subtype of horizontal institutionalization. In the schooled society, the logic behind educational credentialing is increasingly the normative trend behind occupational credentialing.

Second, along with horizontal institutionalization should also be evidence of what can be called *vertical institutionalization* of educational credentialing. As shown in the second diagram in Figure 7.1, educational credentialing can intensify within an occupation as more of its job types become controlled by requirements of formal educational degrees. Greater vertical institutionalization is evident by the infusion of the cultural values behind formal education and use of academic degrees in occupational access and control processes such as licensure.

Occupational licensing, including its close cousin occupational certification, is a transforming trend in the occupational structure in postindustrial society that is now fully rooted within the increase in educational credentialing (Bills 2004; Kleiner 2006; Kleiner and Krueger 2008). Prior to the schooled society, access to many occupations was controlled through labor unions and membership in other occupational associations, yet these are now in competition with the process of occupational licensing. As shown in Figure 7.3, licensed occupations have been growing over the past fifty years and now account for the jobs of one fifth of the U.S. labor force, while during the same time unionized occupations declined substantially. And although the United States probably leads the trend in licensing, there is evidence of similar growth in other national occupational structures (Kleiner 2006).

Certainly financial considerations, quality control, and competitive motivations are also behind the organizing of occupations through a licensure process, but the trend signifies a deeper motivation. Sociologically,

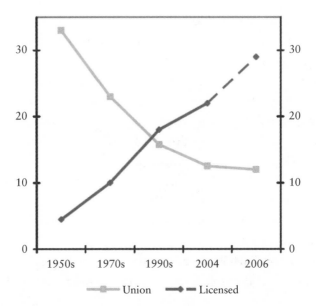

FIGURE 7.3 *Percentage of U.S. workers in licensed versus unionized jobs,*
*1950–2006.*
Source: Kleiner and Krueger (2010). © Blackwell Publishing Ltd/London School of Economics.
Used by permission.

occupational licensing can be thought of as a form of mass professionalization, described in the preceding chapter (Parsons 1971; Baker 2009).
Of course, across occupations there is varying fidelity to the high form of
the original liberal professions (medicine, law, and theology), but a major
professionalizing component is now fully integrated within the licensing
process through the establishment and maintenance of formal educational
requirements, usually verified by academic degrees, for entry and renewal
of a license to practice an occupation.

As an illustrative example of how the licensing process is a main conduit
by which educational credentialing is interjected vertically within occupations, consider the academic nature of the current network of professional
architectural associations and its influence on the intensified use of university degrees for the license to practice architecture in the United States, as
diagramed in Table 7.1. A contemporary view of the network is shown,
but its historical development, particularly as to the inclusion of academically related associations, can be inferred from the establishment dates.

TABLE 7.1  *U.S. architects, professional associations network: Constructing and intensifying educational credentialing via licensure.*

## Networks of Associations

| Association | Year Established | Affiliate / Institutional Type | Member Characteristics | Member Enrollment |
|---|---|---|---|---|
| AIA[1] | 1857 | Educationally credentialed professionals | Architects with architectural degree | 83,000 |
| ACSA[2] | 1912 | Higher education institutions | Accredited colleges and universities with architecture programs | 134 |
| NCARB[3] | 1950 | State and territorial governments | Architectural licensing board | 53 |
| AIAS[4] | 1956 | Higher education students | Students in architectural degree program | 6,800 |

## Intensification of Architectural Degree Credentialing

| Association / Requirement | Year Established | Purpose / Mission | Impacts |
|---|---|---|---|
| NAAB[5] | 1940 | Sole accrediting body for college/university architectural degree programs in U.S.; established program standards | Forty state-level boards mandate continuing education credit as condition for licensure[6] |
| EESA-NAAB[7] | After 1940 by NAAB | Sole accrediting body for non-U.S. college/university architectural degree programs | Educational credential evaluation, worldwide |

## Architectural License Requirements

| Degree / Educational Credential | Continuing Education | Board Examination |
|---|---|---|
| Bachelor's, master's, or doctoral degree from accredited or EESA-NAAB–approved program | Academic credit hours to maintain license; varies across states (5–20 credit hours annually) | Passing score on multiple-part written examination |

[1] American Institute of Architects (AIA)  [2] Association of Collegiate Schools of Architecture (ACSA)  [3] National Council of Architectural Registration Boards (NCARB)  [4] American Institute of Architecture Students (AIAS)  [5] National Architectural Accrediting Board (NAAB)  [6] Continuing education credit requirements were instituted at various times at the state level after the establishment of the NAAB.  [7] Education Evaluation Services for Architects (EESA-NAAB)

Sources: American Institute of Architects (AIA); Association of Collegiate Schools of Architecture (ACSA); American Institute of Architecture Students (AIAS); National Council of Architectural Registration Boards (NCARB); Education Evaluation Services for Architects (EESA-NCARB); National Architectural Accrediting Board (NAAB)

As shown in the first part of the table, of the four founding professional associations in American architecture, three are explicitly based on status in architectural training in colleges and universities. The first of these is the American Institute of Architects (AIA), founded in the middle of the nineteenth century, and as the oldest association in the network it has had direct influence on the founding and functioning of the other associations. Historically, the network started from the AIA and spread educational credentials throughout the occupation, transforming what had mostly been a craft with artisanal training traditions into a budding profession with specialized university-based education by the early twentieth century (Woods 1991). With just a few exceptions, currently all of the 83,000 members of the AIA are holders of one or more of three specialized higher education degrees, namely, the Bachelor, Master, or Doctor of Architecture. Many of the AIA's members are also licensed architects (68%), but licensed or not, the major commonality among members are their educational credentials.

The network's next founding association is the Association of Collegiate Schools of Architecture (ACSA), which was created early in the twentieth century to represent the interests and future development of the three architectural educational degree programs in institutions of higher education; the ACSA now represents the 134 accredited (i.e., to educate architects) higher education institutions. Third is the American Institute of Architecture Students (AIAS), established in the 1950s, representing the interests of students in these accredited architectural degree programs, most of whom will upon graduation become members of the AIA. The network's one association whose membership is not explicitly connected to architectural education, yet nonetheless has influence on educational credentialing, is the National Council of Architectural Registration Boards (NCARB), which is an association of state licensing boards that helps to promote and regulate the licensing of the occupation.

The next important feature of the network is that all four founding associations have direct influences on three processes that maintain and intensify educational credentialing of the architectural occupation (refer to the second part of the table). The first process is made up of the accreditation of new degree programs in higher education, continuing accreditation of existing higher education degree programs, and the development of educational standards (read curricula) for each degree. Created by the AIA and ACSA, the National Architectural Accrediting Board (NAAB) is a fourteen-member board composed of three representatives each from AIA, ACSA, and NCARB, two representatives from AIAS, two from the public, and an independent chair. The NAAB is

the only agency authorized to accredit professional degree programs in architecture in the United States. Although graduation from a NAAB-accredited program does not guarantee registration, accreditation is intended to verify that accredited programs achieve education standards established by NAAB in collaboration with the four collateral organizations—the AIA, AIAS, ACSA and NCARB.

The NAAB is the focal point in the network in terms of intensifying educational credentialing for jobs in the architectural occupation, as it both standardizes and universalizes architectural training. As set out in its charter statement, the NAAB "review process has become a formalized process of validation" for educational degrees, and it is broadly charged with the responsibility and charter to apply the accreditation process and revise it when deemed necessary. With the authority of the four professional associations behind it, the NAAB also develops and revises the standard curricula for architectural education, and well beyond just technical training in the skills of architecture to include general academic subjects in mathematics, natural science, social science, humanities, and human environments, which make up just under one half of the credit hours recommended for an architectural degree (National Architectural Accrediting Board 2012).

For all U.S. states and territories, the main consequence of this network is the establishment, as a licensing requirement, of the attainment of at least one higher education degree (BA, MA, Ph.D.) in architecture to practice the occupation. Currently, about 194,000 workers are employed in architectural firms nationwide, and of these, 46 percent are licensed (read educationally credentialed) architects. As is evident through the language of their publications, the associations in the network promote the belief that the mandatory educational credential will yield a standard, high-quality workforce for the occupation. Lastly, while there is technically a way for someone without an architectural degree who has prior architectural experience to become licensed, overwhelmingly all four associations advise the would-be architect to obtain education first and experience second, or as the NCARB states[2]:

A professional degree from a NAAB-accredited program is the primary means of satisfying most U.S. registration boards' education requirement and the education requirement for NCARB certification. (National Council of Architectural Registration Boards 2012)

The second process of intensification of educational credentials enacted by the network is the construction of continuing professional education requirements and programs for the maintenance of a license; continuing education requirements, which are now mandatory in forty states, range from five to over twenty credit hours completed annually. The AIA and the ACSA actively promote this idea of career-long, continuing education, duly verified through annual completion of academic credits, for the long-term development of the architect and the occupation. These associations also guide licensed architects to approved continuing education programs and opportunities.

The third intensification of educational credentials is evident in the establishment of the Education Evaluation Services for Architects (EESA), which applies the NAAB standards to assess the validity of educational credentials from nonaccredited American degree programs and from universities outside the United States. This function also serves to tighten connections between the network's accreditation process and all architectural education in the entire higher education sector worldwide; plus, it also publicly defines and condemns educational credential fraud in the architectural occupation (see discussion of credentialing taboos below).

As shown in the last part of the table, two out of three requirements for licensure depend on education (a formal degree–verified credential being the first, and continuing education the second). There are no traditional non-educational credentials listed in any state's licensure requirements (e.g., age; see discussion of cosmetology below). The third requirement, the board examination, while not explicitly a part of formal education, is itself tightly connected to required architectural education. In addition to the NCARB's development of standards for state boards' tests (many use the common Architect Registration Examination, ARE), it also publishes pass rates for all NAAB-accredited degree programs, which in a sense is a public endorsement of these degree programs. And as might be expected from a process that relies heavily on attainment of an extensive educational credential, most pass rates on the board examination are relatively high, falling in the range of 65 to 75 percent. Lastly, the NCARB, in describing the intensions of the examination, cites education as a primary component: "the ARE is a practice-based examination founded on education enhanced by experience" (National Architectural Accrediting Board 2012).

Control of educational credentials is control of occupations, as Collins and others theorized, but as the architectural case illustrates, it is not cynical control through ritualized use of educational credentials merely to limit competition and maintain tight enrollment quotas in professional degree programs. Instead, the entire associational network is saturated by the assumptions behind the education revolution applied to architects, and the network continually works to intensify these assumptions for the occupation. It is true that unlike medical training for the MD degree in the United States, architecture did not capture full control over all educational training. For licensure one can still receive the required degree from a few nonaccredited programs, although the degree must meet approved NAAB educational standards. Nor does architecture as an occupation control enrollment to degree programs, though nevertheless, entrance to and tenure within the occupation is fully influenced by formal educational training and its array of cultural constructs. Further, most research on the effects of licensing shows that beyond the incorporation of educational training and credentials, licensing has little additional impact on financial and quality control within occupations, even though they are often assumed prima facie to be the reason behind the licensure process (Kleiner 2006).

This is evidence from just one licensed occupation, architecture, but it is likely that little of the network promoting educational credentials for architecture is unique to this occupation, and most likely many other occupations have similar networks with similar consequences for intensifying educational credentialing. If the schooled society argument about educational credentialing is true, there will also be evidence that licensing in other national occupational structures rests upon educational assumptions and enhances educational credentialing. An example of this is Canada's licensing/educational credentialing network for architects, which is similar to, and affiliated with, the U.S. network.

A final form of vertical institutionalization can be seen in the transition from non-educational to educational credentials within occupations. To illustrate this trend, consider the shifting balance in credentialing for cosmetology, an occupation at the other end of the prestige and income spectrum from architecture. While educational credentials are far less institutionalized across jobs in cosmetology, the licensing process nevertheless promotes educational requirements with very few options for solely learning on the job. For example, across the fifty state cosmetology licensing boards, for jobs such as salon hairdressing and barbering, all require formal cosmetology education in accredited programs, ranging from 1,000 to 2,100 course hours, while 32 percent of states also require a formal educational degree, usually a high school diploma or GED. At the same time, some traditional non-educational credentials are still in use in some states, although they are less universal than educational credentials and often have accompanying education requirements. For example, 24 percent of states have minimum-age requirements (from sixteen to twenty-three years old); 18 percent have an apprenticeship option combined with formal training; and the state of Ohio requires moral rectitude. Finally, cosmetology also demonstrates partial vertical institutionalization of educational (versus non-educational) credentials, as the job of electrology requires more academic degrees for licensure in some states than barbering and hairstyling.

In addition to saturation of occupations with educationally based credentials, what can be called the *forward educational credentialing* process, or the idea that educational training and credentialing should occur before actual work experience in an occupation, becomes a widely held norm in the schooled society (see third diagram in Figure 7.1). While this taken-for-granted idea is rarely questioned now, this was not always the case. For example, the once widely used traditional apprenticeship mixed training and work with no particular assumption of ordering. And other processes of job training used before the emergence of the schooled society often blended training and work experience instead of following the distinctive ordering of forward educational credentialing. In Thomas More's feudal England, for example, young law clerks first worked in the profession and later received more formal educational training, and membership in craft occupations, often controlled by guilds, came first followed by training (Akroyd 1999).

This has radically changed with the primacy of the modern ordering of education before occupation. Indeed, forward ordering has become so normative that often the only predegree experience with an occupation many youth have is sponsored and organized by higher education institutions themselves. The increasingly popular and academically credited internship and related miniprofessional experiences established by many undergraduate degree programs in the United States and undertaken by approximately one half of recent graduates make for explicitly educational control over early contact with many occupations (National Association of Colleges and Employers 2011; Valentino 2011). For those already in the labor market in search of new jobs, there are now more educational credentialing options with industry certification, educational reentry, and online learning. Whether this educational diversity will disrupt the existing formal education monopoly on forward credentialing is an interesting question for future research. Nevertheless, at least in the United States, there is a pervasive norm that "it is new educational credentialing first and then a new job," and this is the increasingly acceptable way for workers to change occupations.

Even though informal cynicism about the dominance of education over experience is commonly heard in workplaces, as the normalcy of forward educational credentialing deepens in postindustrial society, so does the assumption that formal education prepares individuals for work, though not necessarily in a tight vocational fashion. For example, over the past several decades the format and content of on-the-job training itself has become decidedly more academic and broader in character, so that on-the-job *education* becomes the assumed remedy for "inexperience" (Scott and Meyer 1991). The same trend is evident by the normative occurrence of continuing education for workers in an occupation regardless of their actual experience and work skills, so that in 2005 34 percent of working American adults reported that their occupation had legal or professional requirements for continuing education (U.S. Census Bureau 2005).

The consequence of the normative strength of forward educational credentialing is illustrated by the waves of young BA-holders streaming into graduate and professional degree programs with little or no work experience in their target occupation. The student-first sequence (increasingly including an internship), which is developed, owned (tuition fees), and controlled by educational institutions themselves, is defined as "the proper and strategic path" to the world of work. All the while, older sequences, such as testing out one's affinity for a type of occupation before obtaining extensive education, are increasingly considered naïveté, a waste of time, and even a risk to future success in the occupation.

The rise of the MBA as an academic degree within the university and its dominance over managerial positions in all types of formal organizations is a perfect example of how education as an institution develops and reinforces forward credentialing in a growing number of areas of human activities. The MBA, a credential widely attained before work experience, is also the context for interesting examples of backward credentialing, the final institutionalization process of educational credentials.

As diagramed in Figure 7.1, *backward educational credentialing* is the opposite ordering: occupational experience first and then the awarding of an educational degree as a credential.[3] As irrational as it might initially seem, a popular set of educational programs occurring at various points over the rise of horizontal and vertical institutionalization of educational credentials has successfully employed this logic, with considerable demand from individuals. Some backward credentialing is little more than a ceremonial anointment of an educational credential to individuals already functioning in an occupation, but other examples involve school-like experiences, albeit condensed and cushioned to an extent from the usual academic travails and risks of failure. Ignored in prior sociological analysis of credentials, backward credentialing reflects the degree to which forward credentialing has become normative, and it represents the extent to which the educational degree is public acknowledgment and verification of successful occupational performance, including eligibility for future advancement in the same occupation.

For example, in the late 1980s and early 1990s, as the MBA increased in significance, executive education programs at a number of universities' business schools sprang up with the purpose of granting the MBA on completion of a shortened and flexible formal education program by working executives who lacked the degree (Price 2004). Considerable tuition is charged, and the already employed and presumably skilled, yet MBA–less, executive (with any amount of experience) attends specially designed classes over two-week sessions several times a year, and completes assignments and examinations online.[4] An earlier version of these programs required even less classroom time. This is pure backward-ordered educational credentialing, as individuals without considerable occupational experience are not accepted into the programs and the assumption behind the degree is partial academic credit for past occupational experience.

Why would someone with considerable occupational experience, success, and job security as a manager (companies presumably would not pay sizable tuition for an unsuccessful employee, nor for one about to leave the firm) go through the effort to obtain an Executive MBA? Obviously, manager and employer share the assumption that even a minimalist educational program renders the experienced worker with more skills, and the degree as a credential verifies this enhanced status; plus, they also likely assume that the Executive MBA degree acknowledges and substantiates past occupational experience as only a higher education credential now legitimately can within the schooled society. The reasons that employers and enrolled managers have come to think this way, and why the programs are widely successful, are telling about the rise of educational credentialing as a function of the education revolution. A big reason is that these programs were established and became popular during the take-off in forward credentialing for managerial jobs through regular MBA programs for aspiring managers. As the MBA became the standard credentialing degree and as business schools as its supplier grew in prestige, a robust logic formed about the value of formal education for the manager, which spread the desire to earn the MBA to the already experienced manager and his employer.

That significant numbers of individuals with considerable occupational experience sought out educational credentials in a backward ordering is compelling evidence of the educational transformation of occupational credentials. By the middle of the 1990s some of these programs ended their degree-awarding component as the regular MBA saturated the labor pool. But others have continued to expand backward credentialing with a degree now known as the EMBA, as is shown in one executive-degree-granting program's current description:

The Executive MBA (EMBA) Program at Columbia Business School is a 20-month graduate program designed specifically for high-achieving businesspeople that are looking to enhance their education without interrupting their careers. The EMBA Program meets on alternate Fridays and Saturdays on the Columbia University campus. The program offers both September and January entry dates.

The program's innovative curriculum and collaborative learning environment helps you apply your knowledge and skills to problems you face in today's marketplace. An outstanding faculty exposes you to cutting-edge ideas and practices—ideas and practices that others will later adopt, teach and apply.

To date, more than 800 organizations have sponsored executive-potential employees as students in Columbia's EMBA program.

Like the backward credentialing of the EMBA, similar phenomena, often dismissed as anomalies, await analysis from the perspective advanced here; these include honorary degrees, higher education academic credit towards a degree for work experience (e.g., CAEL, the Council for Adult and Experiential Learning), and alternative educational credentialing of uncertified teachers in the United States.[5] Also included among these cases is backward credentialing through university-established executive master's degrees for occupations such as in public health. Related to the strong institutionalization of educational degrees into credentialing is the mostly unstudied phenomenon of academic degree and credential fraud, which if the institutional argument developed here is true, should become a publicly punished taboo in the schooled society.

DEVIANCE IN THE SCHOOLED SOCIETY

By time-honored sociological logic, ostracized deviance reveals ubiquitous normalcy. So central and valued are educational credentials that when mass fraud is suspected it is defined as a widespread social problem; for example, the production of counterfeit degrees by diploma mills is estimated to be a billion-dollar industry (Ezell and Bear 2005). Although reliable data on the extent of fraud are virtually nonexistent and many estimates, including the one just noted, appear to be wildly exaggerated, the perception of credential fraud is salient enough that to date there have been two major congressional investigations into fraudulent educational credentials in the United States. Relying mostly on anecdotal evidence, much of the tone of the investigations is intended to whip up even greater levels of concern over fraud. And tellingly, the fear of credentialing fraud and the taboo itself has created a new line of business in the verification and investigation of educational credentials; this includes the service of translating foreign educational credentials into the American system of educational degrees (other nations now have similar businesses), which is no doubt a result of the growing globalization of upper levels of the educational and occupational structures, reinforced by worldwide convergence on the centrality of educational degrees as credentials.

In the schooled society, social costs of breaking educational credentialing taboos can be extreme, and in good Durkheimian fashion the mass media often report on the fall of the successful for misrepresenting their educational credentials, adding a measure of public shame that reinforces the value of such credentials. CEOs and CFOs of well-known corporations such as RadioShack and Bausch & Lomb; a head of the U.S. Olympic Committee; a dean of admissions at a prestigious university; and various university athletic coaches have all been the subject of recent widely publicized stories of educational credential fraud. While a systematic study of high-profile cases would be revealing as to the reach, strength, and meaning of the taboo, a few examples are illustrative.[6]

First consider how the taboo about faking educational credentials is the other side of the norm of educational credentialing, a norm that has intensified across the occupational structure and delegitimized former practices of credentialing. This is illustrated by an incident several years ago in which a newly appointed athletic coach for a high-profile collegiate sports team was fired after just five days on the job for falsely claiming he had completed a master's degree when in fact he had only attended the program. In media reactions, other coaches commented that what the errant coach had done *had in the past been common and tacitly accepted* as a relatively harmless embellishment of educational credentials, but now they saw that things had changed.

A second example shows the expansion of the logic of educational credentials to ever more forms of academic degrees. In 2008, the Iranian interior minister was dismissed after it came to light that his honorary law degree from Oxford University was a forgery. Apparently, even in an anti-West theocracy the falsification of an honorary degree from a decidedly secular university in the former colonial-master nation is not exempt from the educational credentialing taboo.

The extent to which educational credentials overshadow actual occupational performance is illustrated by several high-profile cases. One noted in the epigraph is the fall of MIT's dean of admissions, who resigned in disgrace even though she had recently been awarded that university's highest recognition for effective administration and her on-the-job performance was widely acknowledged as excellent. When the corporate board of a prominent firm found out that its very effective CEO had falsified an MBA from a prestigious business school, it chose to publicly reprimand him even in the midst of a banner year of profit and corporate health. One would be hard pressed to imagine another corporate board, enjoying a similar state of success, publicly reprimanding an effective CEO for lying about his age, marital status, or nationality. So too, in the highly competitive world of collegiate sports, where effective coaches are at a premium, the highly experienced yet credential-falsifying coach from the first example had to take a lesser job in the sport for a few years before he could be hired as head coach by another university. Finally is the case of a CEO who was performing poorly but was not fired by the board—until the publicized evidence of his educational credential fraud proved to be his downfall.

Certainly, all of these highly publicized cases of educational credential fraud involved idiosyncrasies, and of course the punishment was in part for lying and breaking trust. But in each case what is also clear is the growing centrality of educational credentialing in postindustrial society and the strength of taboos against breaking the norm of this form of credentialing. Not surprisingly, then, is evidence that public trust itself in large societies increasingly rests on trust in the credentials of strangers, which of course are increasingly based in formal education (Nock 1993).

One last example illustrates the value of educational credentials from the unusual viewpoint of the black market. In China, the official master file (*dangan*) of a student's entire academic accomplishments, including degrees earned, is a handwritten, hard-copy file that follows the student from the first days of schooling until the last days at university (for the fortunate few who make it to a university). As of a few years ago, there were no centralized or computerized records of attendance, performance, and earned degrees other than the *dangan*, and if it is lost or stolen, students are treated as if they have little or no educational credentials, or as if they themselves are attempting to falsify someone else's record. A media story reported that stolen *dangan* sell on the black market, depending on the quality of degree credential, for $3,000 to $7,000, or about one to over two times the average annual wage of a Chinese worker in 2008 (LaFraniere 2009).

Horizontal and vertical integration of educational credentials into the occupational structure, along with the spread of the norm of forward educational credentialing (including backward educational credentialing of successful occupational performance), and the increasing strength of taboos against breaking these norms, all create greater institutionalization of educational credentialing. If future systematic analysis of these processes of institutionalization yields the kind of evidence suggested by the empirical examples, the centrality of educational credentialing for the occupational structure of postindustrial society will be well established. And such evidence would be the final nail in the coffin of "credentialism" as a way to think about the phenomenon of educational credentialing.

## EDUCATIONAL CREDENTIALS' MASTERY OF SOCIAL STRATIFICATION

The shift from non-education to educationally based occupational credentialing is a major conduit by which the education revolution led to formal education's domination of status attainment and social mobility. This is illustrated in Figure 7.4, which plots the impact of educational degrees on individuals' occupational prestige compared to the impact of attending college without degree attainment, controlling for a standard set of non-educational factors about working American adults from the 1950s until 2008 (for specified model, see Faia 1981).[7] The line with diamonds represents the effects of four years of college attendance, irrespective of degree

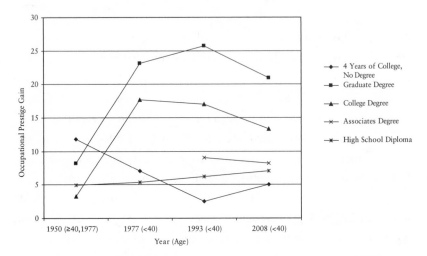

FIGURE 7.4 *Impact of educational degrees versus years of schooling on occupational prestige in the U.S., 1950–2008.*

Note: Estimates for the 1950s and 1977 are derived from Faia's analysis of the General Social Survey (Faia 1981), and using the same equation original analysis are estimates from the 1993 and 2008 General Social Surveys. Occupational Prestige scores were regressed on forty-year-olds' or younger respondents' educational degrees, years of education, and controls, including: socioeconomic status (SES), income, log income; and respondent's father's occupational prestige, SES, years of schooling, and educational degrees. Estimates from the 1950s are derived from current occupation of forty-and-older adults who entered the labor force in the 1950s. Four years of college is estimated by multiplying four times the effect of one year of college.

attained, on occupational prestige; the other lines represent the occupational prestige return from various higher education degrees attained, from the associate degree to the Ph.D. over the past sixty years. In the 1950s there were not large differences between attendance and degree attainment, but starting in the 1960s degree attainment yielded more prestige while the return from just attendance began to decline. This divergence between attendance and degree attainment became substantial by the last decades of the twentieth century (see also Denny and Harmon 2001).

In past research, this pattern of degree effects led to the popular conclusion that educational expansion creates widespread sheepskin effects—credentialism. The number of years of schooling was assumed to be the "natural" measure of educational input, and any return "above it" from degree attainment was considered phony. Yet as argued here, educational degrees have become the normative social construction, while attending school without degree completion is now considered subpar occupational preparation, and the results reflect this.

Seen in this new light, the results in Figure 7.4 raise a number of interesting questions about the dynamics of educational degree attainment and occupational outcomes. Note how similar the prestige returns were for degree attainment and just four years of college in the 1950s, before the American version of the education revolution had expanded secondary education to the full cohort (high net enrollment rates were not reached until the mid-1960s) and also before accelerated growth of higher education in the 1960s.[8] A quarter of a century later and well into major higher education expansion this all changed. Both bachelor's and graduate degrees yielded significantly more access to prestigious occupations than only attending four years of higher education. Relevant too is what happened by the end of the twentieth century. The dynamics of educational expansion made bachelor's degree attainment increasingly normative and widespread. Also, as described above, mass graduate degree attainment was well underway during this period. Interestingly, while there was still an ordered return to occupational prestige by educational degree, with educational expansion the returns dropped from the 1977 levels. Note also that the return on four years of college without a degree reached its lowest point in the 1990s.

## THE CREDENTIALED SOCIETY
## AS THE SCHOOLED SOCIETY

Not only are formal educational degrees central to individuals' social status attainment, but education as a primary institution continually bends the process of social stratification toward all things educational and away from non-educational factors. Along with the educated job and workplace, educational credentialing is now an unrelenting force enacting the tenets and cultural values of the schooled society throughout occupations. While educational credentials are a source of power within formal organizations, the change they have brought on is broader and deeper. Rooted in, and legitimated by, the university's knowledge conglomerate and degree-granting charters, the educational credential signifies not just the *capability* to apply knowledge in the everyday world of occupational roles; it becomes mandatory (even assumed) for entry into specific occupational statuses with exclusionary *control and rights* to apply such knowledge.

Trapped within a worldview of education-as-myth and credentialism as the only outcome of educational expansion, some mistakenly conclude that older modes of training and occupational access were somehow more natural and hence more effective. But did the apprenticeship or sinecure of an earlier era "really prepare" individuals for work? Yes, but no more or less than formal education does now. Does formal education, verified by an educational degree, "really prepare" individuals for work? Yes, and increasingly so, as the very essence of work and jobs is ever more defined by the skills and orientations learned and privileged in the culture of the schooled society. The point is that there is nothing natural about non-educational ways to prepare for work and obtain a position; for their time, they too were dominant social constructions.

The logic behind social stratification and mobility is also historically socially constructed (e.g., Berger and Luckmann 1966). With educational credentialing, the idea of legitimate education-based, meritocratic stratification instead of privilege-based stratification becomes embedded within the culture. Turning educational performance, reflected by academic degrees, into the dominant arbitrator of merit has not occurred all at once; indeed, a historical line can be drawn from early forms of academic talent proven in the medieval university, serving as at least modest meritocratic access to the administrative Curia for the Pope, to secular political interests up through the nineteenth-century development of manifest state chartering of elite intellectuals through selection to the École normale in France and similar educational institutions in other nations. But the pace of the education revolution over the past century has thoroughly equated educational performance with socially just merit, and the intensification of educational credentialing reinforces this process.

Of course, educationally determined status is frequently criticized by reference to the considerable volume of research showing that in practice systems of formal education rarely offer fully equal opportunity to succeed in school for everyone, for a variety of non-educational reasons (e.g., Baker and LeTendre 2005). But what is missed in the debate over an educational meritocracy is the taken-for-granted nature of its basic assumption: if fairly achieved, educational degrees are widely assumed to be, if not completely meritocratic then, at least, the most legitimate accomplishment on which to base future opportunities (albeit unequal) for *everyone*. This is a powerful and transforming belief in postindustrial society and, as shown in Part I, is increasingly evident in analyses of the mechanics of social stratification.

In a sense, the world that Michael D. Young envisioned in his 1958 dark satire, *The Rise of the Meritocracy*, has come about, although it is likely less dark, less oppressive, and less singularly hierarchical than he predicted. Importantly, merit is based today on educationally defined and controlled verifications of academic intelligence, not just on Young's notion of innate intelligence. Whether educational achievement is a measure of "true merit" is not the right sociological question to ask. Just like celebrated non-educational realms of merit in past societies, such as military prowess, superior physical ability, or masterful craftsmanship, educational ability is constructed as the supreme domain of merit in the schooled society, and spreading educational credentialing enacts this belief.[9] Over a relatively short sociological period, education has approached worldwide acceptance as the one appropriate and legitimate playing field on which to compete for merit. This normative belief could perhaps be the education revolution's furthest-reaching and most salient sociological product so far. Similarly, its most far-reaching epistemological impact has been the transformation of knowledge and the construction of the knowledge society.

### CHAPTER 8

# The Transformation of Knowledge
# and Truth Claims

Knowledge of the powerful is powerful knowledge itself.

MICHAEL YOUNG, *Bringing the Knowledge Back In*, 2008

I don't actually read other peoples' books. If I want to read a book,
I write one myself.

Irish literary critic TERRY EAGLETON's answer to the interview question,
"Have you read anything good lately?" *New York Times*, April 22, 2007

THE MUCH HERALDED "knowledge society" could have only come about because of the accumulative impact of the education revolution. Yet it is referred to as if it arose spontaneously from information-processing technology and an interconnected world; in fact, the schooled society creates the capacity for every facet of a knowledge society. While it is obvious that all past societies were based on knowledge, the amount, intensity, and use of knowledge since the middle of the twentieth century has led to wide speculation about a new relationship between knowledge (including data) and society (e.g., Lauder et al. 2012; Sörlin and Vessuri 2007a, 2007b). Of course, mass schooling supports this in the narrow sense of educating individuals to work with and understand knowledge, but equally if not more important is that the education revolution transforms the quantity *and* qualities of knowledge itself. The long development and growth of the university makes these institutions central in producing and defining knowledge and the acceptable ways that knowledge is thought to be true—what can be referred to as "truth claims" (Frank and Meyer 2007; Young 2008). How the education culture has come to imbue certain qualities of knowledge and truth claims throughout the world's population illustrates the schooled society's creation of the conditions for a knowledge society.

## ALL THE KNOWLEDGE IN THE WORLD

At the end of the fifteenth century the Hungarian feudal lord Mathias Corvinus, known as the Raven King, amassed a library in the sleepy late-medieval town of Buda, before it became the combined city of Budapest on both sides of the Danube. The library was notable for two reasons. First was its unlikely location, as Western European society considered Hungary an outpost against the invading Muslims from the east. Second was its unlikely large number of holdings. Over his long reign of thirty-two years, the passionate bibliophile Mathias collected what for then was an astounding number of books—an estimated 2,200–2,500 Latin and Greek manuscripts. On the edge of Europe, the Raven King's library was in size and scope second only to the largest collection in Christendom, the papal archive in Rome; no other library came close to these two collections (Tanner 2008).

Because Mathias' sole librarian and acquisitionist strove to satisfy the king's love of general knowledge, science, and the ancient philosophy of the Greeks and Romans, the collected two thousand some volumes represented the sum total of formal recorded knowledge in the West five hundred years ago.[1] Copied and constructed by artisans' hands, old and new manuscripts alike were so rare, so exceedingly expensive, and so hard to come by that they were indeed luxury items. A single manuscript without extensive illustration would routinely cost more than the annual income of a domestic servant at an Italian court, while extensively illustrated texts cost a small fortune (Tanner 2008). In Mathias' library the most valued manuscripts were kept chained to elaborately decorated stands, and the entire collection was meant only for the eyes of the king and a handful of visiting intellectuals.

Contrasting the Raven King's ambitious library with the holdings of current-day research universities illustrates the extensive dimensions of the knowledge society (Stehr 2004). For example, the library at the author's university holds over five million volumes, and every year it acquires over forty times the total number of books that Mathias' library collected over three decades. About five hundred library employees assist in maintaining a system of wide access to the knowledge; each year about 600,000 items are physically circulated to the university community and to other libraries and scholars, and the library's website hosts about 1.5 million annual electronic visits. Cornell University's noted sizable research library holds seven million books alone and many other items, and the library routinely acquires all books published by every university book press across the country. And of course, the mother lode of knowledge at the Library of Congress in Washington, D.C., includes over 138 million books, maps, ancient texts, and other printed materials; the book collection alone contains an estimated 15 terabytes of data ("Data, Data Everywhere" 2010). Given the ever expanding digital conversion of printed material and its electronic storage, in the not-too-distant future everyone with internet access will have the entire corpus of human recorded knowledge literally at their fingertips. This knowledge is growing at a rapid rate as reflected in expanding online databases of abstracts, or summaries, of technical papers in all kinds of fields. The database Medline, for example, contains abstracts from seven million technical articles from biomedical journals alone.

Certainly, late-feudal Europe did not fully represent the world at the time, as Chinese, Islamic, and other empires had archives of recorded knowledge too (e.g., Rubenstein 2003). But if the relative size of Mathias' library is an indicator of the amount of collectable knowledge, at least in the West, then the telling question is how society went from being able to fit all of its knowledge on several room-length bookshelves to requiring, at the Library of Congress, over 650 miles of bookshelves to store one collection, which is added to daily by about ten thousand new items (in 470 languages) and managed by what would have been a significant portion of feudal Buda's total adult population (3,700 employees).

The frequently given answer is that the knowledge society grew out of technical sophistication and complexity of society at the hands of advancing technology, class struggle, and increasing complexity, or all of them at once (Castells 1996). What is almost always left out of explanations is the potential impact of the education revolution on knowledge (Hoskin 1993; Young 2008). If it is included at all, education is seen in its traditional role as a secondary institution following a changing society. Oddly, effects of the education revolution are an afterthought relegating formal education to the production of individual capacity to consume knowledge, or at least information, but not the production of the knowledge itself, and certainly not the shaping of the qualities of knowledge and truth claims.

But this perspective misses the profound transformation of the qualities of knowledge, its production, and its truth claims that emerge in the culture of a schooled society.

The significant difference between the Raven King's ability to amass all known formal knowledge in medieval Europe through two thousand texts and the Library of Congress's mind-boggling collection is a major consequence of the rise of the schooled society. Although the prodigious scale of the schooled society's knowledge production is an important feature, the amount of knowledge is not the only new aspect here. A society intensely based on knowledge could not, and would not have occurred if it were not for the education revolution.

## MICHAEL YOUNG'S KNOWLEDGE PARADOX

As implied in the argument here, qualities of knowledge are thought to be socially constructed and true at the same time. Described in Part I, the university forms much of modern culture through its role in the production, adjudication, authorizing, and dissemination of authoritative knowledge. Seen this way, knowledge is certainly an institutional product and hence is socially constructed, but at the same time the university's production of knowledge creates a widely shared reality experienced as truth. How is it that knowledge is both socially constructed and real?

This paradox has been raised and explored by Michael Young,[2] one of only a handful of sociologists investigating the connection between education and the qualities of knowledge. Young was an early founder of the 1960s British school of the "New Sociology of Education," which focused on how schooling reproduces social inequalities through knowledge. At the heart of this school of thought is the rejection of the notion that knowledge is a natural entity (e.g., divinely given or only technically derived) and the assumption that the purpose of education is to provide the intellectual tools to appreciate inherent truth.[3] Employing for their time a radical conception of knowledge and society, the new sociologists of education in the 1960s argued that schooling is the product of powerful interests in society, and hence that what it teaches is constructed by the powerful. This equates the content and qualities of knowledge with the social position of the knower, and gives rise to a number of ideas such as the existence of privileged knowledge, social status of knowledge, and so-cial inequality created through restricted access to knowledge and its use. This theory is essentially the Marxian form of the traditional perspective on education and society applied to the curricular content of schooling: the curriculum reproduces societal power inequality.

These ideas quickly led to the premise that knowledge was completely socially constructed along the vicissitudes of shifting social power, and the powerful could reconstruct knowledge for social purposes such as increas-ing social class inequality. Note how Michael Apple, a main proponent of this position, describes the connections among schooling, knowledge, and economically derived power:

One of the ways schools are used for hegemonic purposes is in their teaching of cultural and economic values and dispositions that are supposedly "shared by all," while at the same time "guaranteeing" that only a specified number of students are selected for higher levels of education because of their "ability" to contribute to the maximization of the production of the technical knowledge also needed by the economy. (1990, 61)

Similarly, consider the now famous extreme statement by the French in-tellectuals Bourdieu and Passeron: "All *pedagogic action* is objectively symbolic violence insofar as it is the imposition of a cultural arbitrary by an arbitrary power" (1977, 5).

Over the ensuing decades a general form of the New Sociology of Edu-cation argument influenced how a lot of sociologists thought about school curriculum, and university knowledge production too. So extensive has the argument's impact been that even without any systematic empirical testing it is frequently an assumed given. It took exceptional intellectual courage then for Young to recently turn away from his own radical view of knowl-edge, condemning it as an "over-simplistic social constructivism" (Young 2008, 258; Young 1971; Young and Muller 2007). Young persuasively argues that contrary to the assumptions of early Marxist intellectuals and many current postmodernists, knowledge is not up for grabs. Its content is not a mere reflection of social power, nor can it easily be changed at will for social purposes; further, there is not a hierarchy of knowledge that parallels social hierarchy (Hoskin 1993; Young 2008). Yet Young does not retreat back to the old assumption that knowledge is natural; rather, he pushes towards what is being explored here, namely, an institutional image of knowledge (but not facts) that is humanly constructed but much more permanently and pervasively than originally thought by the New Sociology of Education. At the center of this construction is the institutional power of the schooled society. A major drawback of the New Sociology of Education is that it runs aground on the rocks of mass education and its implications for access to knowledge. As wide swaths of the world's population attain skills and empowerment through access to authoritative knowledge, the Marxist's argument must conjure up ever more complicated (and unrealistic) images of how an elite supposedly maintains its active control through the education system.

Young makes the astute observation that with mass education more people, particularly non-elites, gain access (sometimes less than perfect access) to powerful knowledge and this wide access changes not only people but, by extension, society in ways unpredicted by the Marxian position on knowledge, schooling, and power. At the same time, the robust culture of education in the schooled society transforms the qualities of knowledge and privileges certain truth claims. Young's observation is refreshingly honest about both knowledge and mass schooling: if elites truly had the all-powerful constructive license over knowledge, why would they allow such widening access to it? In other words, his solution to the paradox is well taken—*knowledge of the powerful is powerful knowledge itself*—and hence widespread access to education equals mass access to powerful knowledge. Schooling is not only a reflection of a more complicated economy or technological world; instead, formal education is a major creator of an ever more complex, knowledge-rich human society. And at the center of this creative power is nothing short of an educational epistemological revolution.

## THE EDUCATION REVOLUTION AND EPISTEMOLOGICAL CHANGE

As described in Part I, the current epistemological foundation, forged out of the university, is the normative way to think about what qualities of knowledge are important, what inquiry methods are valid, and so forth. The growth and intensity of science, rationalized inquiry, theory, empirical methods, all influenced and reinforced by an overarching cognitization of academic intelligence understood as empowering the educated to think more abstractly and assertively, are at the core of an epistemological revolution brought on by the education revolution. What is left to examine here is how the dynamic distributional power of mass schooling deeply embeds these qualities of knowledge in human society and to such a degree that they now seem fully "natural and normal," as if no other form could ever have been valid, or will be. Through its curricula the schooled society promulgates this distinct epistemology and its wide enactment, and in so doing shapes a worldwide culture dominated by, in a sense, "schooled knowledge," or knowledge that education as an institution generates, legitimates, selects, classifies, distributes, transmits, and evaluates (Bernstein 1971; Benavot et al. 1991; Sadovnik 1995). There are at least three major dimensions that figure prominently in forming school curricula that are a consequence of this academically driven epistemology, and since these have been extensively discussed earlier, here the discussion considers only how each one articulates with knowledge and truth claims.

The first major dimension is the *culture of cognition*: the education revolution increasingly narrows the status of human capabilities towards cognitive performance. Of course, all education and knowledge at any point in history involve cognition, but as the earlier-discussed rise in fluid IQ among schooled populations across the world demonstrates, the schooled society constructs and celebrates a particular set of cognitive skills and elevates them to a heightened status. With the development and flourishing of academic intelligence, traditional mental skills such as recitation, disputation, memorization, formalistic debate, formulae application, rote accuracy, and authoritative text reading and exegesis have been pushed aside as mental problem-solving, effortful reasoning, abstraction and higher-order thinking, and the active use of intelligence take center stage. The latter skills have become the explicit, overarching epistemological leitmotif of modern education, and there is evidence that a culture of cognition continues to intensify in its importance both within and without schools and universities.

The second major epistemological dimension is the *culture of science*. As described in the rise of science in the Western university over the second Western millennium, first rational scholarship then science came to be the dominant truth claim of modern society (Drori, Meyer, Ramirez, and Schofer 2003). Further too, the rise of the social sciences in the university has shaped authoritative knowledge as a science about humans and their societies (Frank and Gabler 2006). This is not to say that all people, including intellectuals, read science or do scientific experiments or consider themselves scientists; in fact, the overwhelming majority do none of these. But the core ideas of science as an epistemological system—knowing as a rational process and knowledge as rationalized through the connection between theory and empirical evidence—transform all knowledge, even that which is not explicitly about science or social science.

The third major dimension, *universalism*, has two epistemological qualities that have become extremely salient for the qualities of knowledge in the schooled society. First, when authoritative knowledge privileges universality, then the particular, the local, the time-bounded qualities of knowledge become less important than the universal, the global, and the timeless truth-like qualities. The emerging epistemology assumes that all knowledge can and should take on universalistic qualities, and the university is chartered to study and apply its authoritative science and rationalized scholarship to everything (Lenhardt 2002). Second, authoritative knowledge based on universalism comes to include universalization of humans themselves (Meyer and Jepperson 2000; Frank and Meyer 2007). The schooled society imbues knowledge with an ideology of the equality of humans and societies, constructed along the norms of universal social justice that have been widely observed over the past fifty years to be included in schooling curricula globally, regardless of the traditional cultures of nations (Baker and LeTendre 2005; Fiala 2006; Fiala and Lansford 1987).

The three dimensions of cognitivism, scientism, and universalism shape a curriculum for children and youth that is remarkably different from what was taught even fifty years ago, and has both widened and intensified the impact of the schooled society on humans' ideas of knowledge and truth claims. The degree of transformation brought about by these dimensions is illustrated by the findings from a set of neo-institutional studies on the historical development of the curricula of primary and secondary schooling. In simple terms, the school curriculum from the earliest grades up through graduate study is based on this new concept of knowledge and its underlying qualities, and by virtue of mass education the cultural reality that it creates is spread to all. Vestiges of older forms of education and knowledge remain, of course, but increasingly they are pushed aside by the worldwide mass schooling curriculum in the primary and secondary grades as it works its way through ever larger proportions of the world's population for longer periods of the individual's lifespan. Three lines of research illustrate the rise of the current education epistemology. Following these, the consequences of cognitivism, scientism, and universalism in two major historical changes in the objectives of curricula—classicism and vocationalism—are described.

### THE COGNITIVE CURRICULUM

A good way to illustrate the growing focus on cognition in education is to track changes in what was taught in school over a long historical period.[4] A recent study examined a century's worth of primary school mathematics curricula as represented in popular and widely used U.S. textbooks; the study focused on the types of knowledge students were asked to learn and interact with at various points in time (Baker et al. 2010). The analysis of over 28,000 pages from 141 elementary school mathematics texts published between 1900 and 2000 indicates profound shifts of curricula towards increased cognitive demand, particularly from the late 1960s on. Elementary school mathematics education historically progressed from rote memorization and recitation to a greater emphasis on mathematical problem-solving and critical higher-order thinking. Increasingly, young students are asked to engage cognitively in effortful, reasoning-based problem-solving with more complex strategies as opposed to using a memorized computational approach. American textbooks from the 1960s onward also present mathematics as requiring more effortful reasoning, application of novel problem-solving skills, inhibitory control, and use of working memory.

Particularly convincing is the historical rise in the number of ways students are asked to solve mathematics problems and a parallel rise in the conceptual complexity of these methods. This historical change in mathematics knowledge taught to young students is illustrated in Figure 8.1. For example, in increasing cognitive demand, one line shows that the aver-

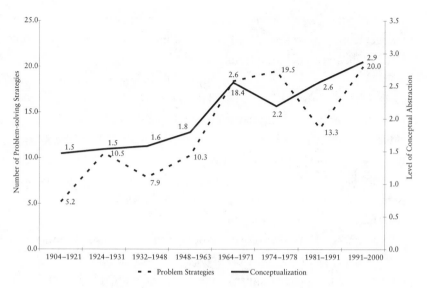

FIGURE 8.1 *Mean number of problem-solving strategies and their conceptual abstraction in U.S. mathematics textbooks.*

Note: First and fourth grades combined from commonly used mathematics textbooks in the United States, 1900–2000.

Source: Reprinted from Baker, Knipe, Cummings, Collins, Leon, Blair, and Gamson (2010). Reprinted with permission from the *Journal of Research on Mathematics Education*. © 2010 by the National Council of Teachers of Mathematics. All rights reserved.

age number of unique problem-solving strategies (versus rote use of a few strategies) the young student was exposed to increased over the century from about five to over twenty. The other line indicates that the mean level of mathematical abstraction of arithmetic problem-solving strategies increased as strategies went from requiring mostly nonconceptual skills, such as memorizing addition tables, to expecting more abstract skills, such as doing addition as a union of sets.

At the turn of the twentieth century, much of the mathematics instruction for children in the upper elementary grades was rigid and formalistic, and emphasized drill and rote memorization. For example, an educator who visited thirty-six urban school systems in the 1890s characterized mathematics instruction as patently absurd: "In no single exercise is a child permitted to think," he exclaimed. "He is told just what to say, and he is drilled not only in what to say, but also in the manner in which he must say it" (Rice 1893, 38). Modern textbooks are much more likely to treat the student as an active mathematician by expecting him not only to solve new types of problems but also to have a deeper understanding of the mathematics behind the solutions.

For example, first- and second-grade mathematics textbooks from 1929 usually depicted situations that placed the reader in a passive role and often in one not even involved in mathematics. Rarely did these textbooks introduce geometric shapes. By late in the twentieth century, textbooks routinely asked students to directly solve problems about geometric shapes. Not only have the problems changed, but the text and pictures of later textbook models show far more active mathematics being undertaken by students (Salinas et al., forthcoming).

The analysis from this research goes on to present many similar examples and supporting material showing how over the past forty years the presented curricula have required students to use more frequent effortful, reasoning-based problem-solving with more complex strategies in learning all types of mathematics, including even basic arithmetic. Implicit in the curriculum is the accompanying message that the student is empowered to use his or her own cognitive skills, even to the point of deciding and justifying which mathematical approach to use on each problem (Bromley, Meyer, and Ramirez 2011b). It is likely that education's growing culture of empowered cognition has reached other parts of the curriculum too; for example, similar findings of the growing cognitive demand of the reading curriculum since the late 1960s have recently been presented (Gamson, Lu, and Eckert 2013). Lastly, there is evidence that this trend is moving from higher-income to lower-income nations and, within nations, from more-advantaged to less-advantaged schools (Cueto, Ramirez, and Leon 2006).

## ELITE KNOWLEDGE FOR THE MASSES

In a series of cross-national studies, David Kamens, Aaron Benavot, and John Meyer with others have shown the historical rise of mathematics and science as subjects intended for all (Kamens and Benavot 1991; Kamens, Meyer, and Benavot 1996). Most study of the historical development of the qualities of knowledge reflected in school curricula tends to examine single national cases and a single subject at a time. To overcome the obvious limitations of this approach, these researchers collected an extensive set of official curriculum listings and instructional time requirements by academic subject for all nations with such records going back to the beginning of the nineteenth century (and in some cases into the eighteenth century)—thus forming a cross-national, historical archive of what was taught in schools over the rise of mass education. This is a sweeping picture showing when subjects entered national curricula and how much instructional time they received; more broadly, it shows the scientization of a mass curriculum.

From the traditional perspective on education and society it is assumed that knowledge of mathematics and science was always part of elite education, and that with their growing application in a technical world they "naturally" traveled down from higher education into the schooling curriculum as necessary skills for a wider range of students. Similarly, one might also assume that on the way down the schooling levels these subjects became watered down, or even dumbed down, for the wider masses. But neither of these assumptions proves to be correct when compared against the actual historical record.

Mathematics, of course, is an ancient subject and a major part of elite knowledge in the West fueled also by earlier major discoveries by Islamic scholars. For example, the study of Euclid's mathematics was part of the medieval university's quadrivium, and base skills in mathematics such as the fundamentals of arithmetic were as standard in the education of the young Thomas More in the fifteenth century as they are today in primary schooling. But as an overall academic subject, mathematics was often associated with the "vulgar practice of commercialism" in many places in the world before the beginning of mass schooling; so too, in the academies of early Western antiquity mathematics was at times considered "below stairs, as preparatory subjects" for the higher and most valued pursuits of philosophy (Marrou 1956, 97). It was not until the nineteenth century, and in some cases quite late in that century, that basic mathematics became a standard curricular subject throughout education systems (Kamens and Benavot 1991).

Science, a comparatively newer academic subject, has an even more checkered curricular past. While teaching at least some basic arithmetic was seen as useful throughout the history of schooling, in the eighteenth century science was considered suspect (questioning too many established truths of theology and the established social order), or too advanced for the common mind, or too technical and narrow to waste "more important" classically trained minds on (Kamens and Benavot 1991). Yet these negative images vanished over the next two centuries, and along with mathematics science became a central truth claim and generator of valid knowledge, usually as the product of university-based scholarship.

As mass schooling spread, mathematics and science—including social and behavioral sciences—became a major part of the new epistemology. Most people, prior to the advent of mass schooling, had very little contact with this kind of knowledge, but by late in the last century all over the world secondary and primary students were routinely exposed to heavy doses of mathematics and science. Today, across 163 national secondary systems, about a third have a program that focuses intensively on mathematics and science (Kamens, Meyer, and Benavot 1996). Along with language skills, these two subjects have come to dominate all types of primary and secondary schooling curricular programs (Kamens and Benavot 1991). The curricular archive clearly shows that the three now make up the cornerstone of the mass school curriculum from the earliest grades on.

Interestingly, the rise of mathematics and science has happened across most nations with very little if any influence from specific national characteristics. In other words, the shift towards mathematics and science for all students reflects a deeper change in the idea of knowledge and what should be taught, which is unaffected by cultural heritage and organizational, political, and technological conditions of particular nations. These studies also show that along with mathematics and science, the secondary school curriculum has increasingly become taught in a comprehensive secondary school—a school that was designed initially in the United States to teach all subjects under one roof and with as similar a curriculum for all students as possible (Hammack 2004). For example, while secondary education programs in classical training declined from the early part of the twentieth century, by 1980 comprehensive programs including a range of curricula dominated by modern language, mathematics, and science made up 90 percent of all secondary schooling worldwide (Kamens, Meyer, and Benavot 1996).

Another indicator of this trend is the proportion of upper secondary (tenth through twelfth grades in the United States) curricular tracks, or sequenced sets of courses, that students could embark on across the world (Kamens and Benavot 2006). Figure 8.2 provides a snapshot of the world-wide structure of the secondary school curriculum at three time points over the last century. Again, the rise in comprehensive tracks is obvious, but so too is the shifting knowledge emphasis of tracks in specific areas of the curriculum. Note the parallel between the changes from 1930 to 1980 here and in earlier discussions on ideas about society and science arising out of the university. Also at the secondary level, classics reigned supreme in the 1930s, but just five decades later it had declined to less than 10 percent of school subjects, while mathematics and science tracks and social sciences tracks increased. With mass schooling, then, the notion that all students, regardless of the occupations they end up taking, should be exposed to mathematics and science became standard. Further, the comprehensive school represented the underlying idea that all children and youth should have access to the same knowledge and truth claims.

What is often underappreciated about this new form of schooling content is that it is more than a simple organizational change; rather, it is the direct manifestation of the change in cultural understandings about knowledge,

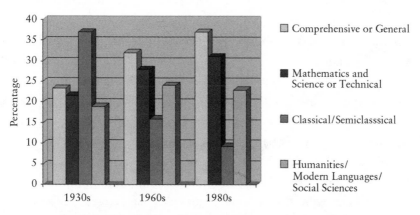

FIGURE 8.2 *Distribution of upper secondary academic tracks/programs worldwide, by historical period.*

Source: Kamens, Meyer, and Benavot (1996). © 1996 by the Comparative and International Education Society. All rights reserved. Used by permission.

and universal access to it, that runs through the entire curriculum of the schooled society described here. As Michael Young observes, a powerful message about knowledge is to offer what were once elite subjects to all students in the common setting of the comprehensive school.

This change is often overlooked in the inevitable concerns about whether this new education is appropriate for all students (the conservative complaint) or whether adequate educational quality is provided so that all students can learn the curriculum (the progressive complaint). In their rush to critique, both positions miss the amazing transformation of qualities of knowledge and the massive access to knowledge that have been brought forth in the schooled society. The same is true about the universal quality of knowledge itself and the impact universalistic knowledge has had on how children and youth are asked to learn about the world.

### UNIVERSALISM AND THE CURRICULUM

The university's role in the promotion of universalism as a desirable quality of knowledge and knowing was described in Part I. So it is not surprising that neo-institutional research finds that universalism has also worked its way into the school curriculum, not just in a preference for scientific explanation and theory, but also in perhaps the most particular of topics— the history and uniqueness of specific peoples and their geopolitical living arrangements. In addition to mathematics and science, the school curriculum increasingly includes a social science version of the history of human societies (often called social studies), which contains important metamessages about knowledge and its relationship to the world. One interesting example is of the decline of nationalism and the rise of the notion of the universal citizen living in the universal society.

The transformation of the nature of scholarship on human history is illustrative of the universalistic trend in knowledge about the geopolitical world. First, undeniably the modern nation-state has been the single most avid supporter (and funder) of mass schooling from the earliest beginnings of the education revolution until now (e.g., Fuller and Rubinson 1992). And there is interesting historical analysis suggesting that early in the twentieth century mass schooling systems and what they taught legitimated the decline of empire as a political goal and supported the rise of the modern nation as the singular geopolitical organization of people and their land masses (e.g., Ramirez and Boli 1987). Second, several studies of the long-term change in university-based scholarship on history and its role in the university curriculum from 1900 to the end of the twentieth century by David Frank and colleagues find the emergence of a dramatic new emphasis and approach to histories of peoples, geopolitical organization, and human endeavors (Frank, Schofer, and Torres 1994; Frank, Wong, Meyer, and Ramirez 2000).

There are four major parts to the new universalistic historical account. First is the demise of the idea of civilization as a grand historical narrative, and in its place is put the superiority of the evolution of the nation. Second is the lessening of the centrality of particular nations (and related metropolitan centers) as origins of civilization, along with the implication that social progress is universal. Third is the shift to human and geopolitical history written and taught as part of a "rationalized social system," or history as sociological history.[5] And lastly is the spread of this approach to a growing number of smaller time periods, geographic areas, and peoples. Therefore, the history curriculum (and its corresponding scholarship) in an American university at the turn of the nineteenth century would almost exclusively focus on the United States as a legacy of the development of the European (mostly Anglo-Saxon) civilization in particular and the West (Greco-Roman civilizations) in general. By the end of the twentieth century this same university would likely have a history department with scholars and courses representing all regions of the world across shorter time periods, a variegated view of American history and its people, and history applied in a universal framework to a wide range of social components of society, such as war, women, or ethnicity. Finally, these neo-institutional studies find that this expanded and universalized history is part of the scholarly discourse and curriculum at universities around the world.

To appreciate the implications of these findings one must return to Michael Young's argument about the social construction of knowledge. Certainly, the past is the past, but how the story of the past is researched and communicated constructs contemporary knowledge of the past. A common assumption is that historical accounts change as "new facts" are found. In a sense this is true, but the social construction of what new facts are important to find and what ways are valid to find them is an essential part of the study of history. This construction has been thoroughly scientized and universalized within the schooled society. Thus, the new character of historical knowledge has made its way into lower levels of schooling, reaching mass proportions of students. Using the historical curricular archive, this is what a cross-national analysis of social and political curricula in secondary schooling from 1900 to 1986 by sociologist Suk-Ying Wong finds (1991). The overarching trend is moving away from courses and course content that are explicitly related to national histories and nationalism (allegiance to and superiority of a nation), and towards a concept of all nations as a universal society, whose citizens are not nationalistic proponents of one nation but components of a society underlying all nations.

For example, Wong finds across all types of nations in all regions of the world a precipitous drop in courses and content on the specific geography, civic structure, and isolated history of a particular nation. Counter to this, she identifies a rising trend in social science courses and content that teach a universalistic notion of humans and society, including their histories—thus, a universal historical sociological narrative emerges within the curriculum. Social sciences in official curricula were evident in only 11 percent of nations in the 1920s, yet had increased to 60 percent of nations by the 1980s. Wong also finds that the later-twentieth-century social science curriculum is remarkably similar in content across nations. This transformation of knowledge about the polity and geopolitical realities of the world is in direct parallel to what David Frank and Jay Gabler find in the rise of social science in the university (2006).

Not only do courses in social science replace traditional geography, civics, and history, but the content of these courses changes toward a distinct focus on universalistic knowledge about humans and societies. For example, national geography is transformed towards universal knowledge: memorizing cities and unique geological features such as rivers, oceans, and mountain ranges is replaced by universalistic knowledge about earth's environmental systems, geoscience, and a notion of the interdependence of all nations' environments. As an analysis of the scientific literacy and attitudes of fifteen-year-olds in about sixty nations shows, by the beginning of the twenty-first century most secondary students from a large range of nations think precisely along these universalistic lines about the social and physical nature of the earth and its environments (OECD 2009b). Similarly, as will be explored in a later chapter, the curriculum of civics shifts from a narrower focus on a particular nation's governance to generalized knowledge about democratic citizenship, which in theory (and this is a major part of the taught message) is transferable to all nations. Consequently, as cross-national research finds, aggressive and singular nationalistic attitudes and beliefs among contemporary secondary students declines, while universalistic notions of membership in a world polity emerges (Rauner 1998; Schissler and Soysal 2005; Wiseman, Astiz, Fabrega, and Baker 2011). Similarly, the spread of instruction in English for the purpose of making the supranational citizen is spreading across the curricular policies of many nations (Cha and Ham 2011). Modern schooling vanquishes parochialism, including to a degree the specific nation, because it replaces it with the widely valued notion of a *universalistic, panworld society.*

In addition to history and social studies, other neo-institutional studies of curricular areas find a growing curricular approach to the universalism of knowledge, including for mathematics and science (Kamens and Benavot 1991; McEneaney 2005), foreign languages (Cha 1991; Cha and Ham 2008), environmental studies (Bromley, Meyer, and Ramirez 2011b), and global awareness and human rights education (Soysal and Wong 2007; Suárez 2007; Suárez and Bromley 2012). Again, this is not likely a consequence of some overt organizational plan on the part of schools or curricular specialists who develop course content (although they are carriers of the larger associated cultural messages). Rather, it is an outcome of a shifting cultural understanding about the preferred quality of knowledge over the course of the education revolution. Of course, in all societies prior to the schooled society, knowledge could be thought of as universal, but over the course of the development of the university an explicit universality of knowledge and truth claims has been intensified, and is now a symbiotic dimension of the cognitively empowered individual in a scientized world.

The preferred nature of knowledge and truth claims of the schooled society plus the way in which mass education exposes more of the world's population to these creates significant change. Perhaps most evident of this is the profound shift away from two prominent cultural ideologies that supported education prior to the maturing of the education revolution. First is the appreciation of classical knowledge and its associated truth claims as the ultimate educational objective of advanced education; and second is the teaching of skills for a vocation as the educational object for all other kinds of schooling.

## THE DEATH OF CLASSICISM AS TRUTH

Consider the following reported event:

Departing from its practice during the 230 years of its existence, Yale University announced today that hereafter the study of the classics is not required for the degree of bachelor of arts, and the degree of bachelor of philosophy will be discontinued . . . [Greek, Latin, and Hebrew] will be replaced by modern languages. Yale News predicts that "when no longer tied to academic apron strings Greek and Hebrew [would fall] . . . and the rigors of [a] competitive and practical age will exact their toll upon Latin." Freshman celebrated by holding a parade which ended with a huge bonfire into which they tossed Latin and Greek grammars. (*New York Herald Tribune*, 2006)

This incident is not the product of the supposed dumbing down of the university of the past few decades, nor is it a product of the presumed academic irreverence of the late 1960s. The classics text-burners were Yale freshmen in 1931, and while the bonfire is no doubt attributable to collegiate spontaneity, the university's decision was part of a sweeping change in the nature of academic knowledge that had been a long time coming and by now has thoroughly saturated secondary and primary schooling.

At the midpoint of the nineteenth century, just before the education revolution took off, most secondary schools in nations that had such schooling routinely offered instruction in the classical languages of Greek and Latin, and to some extent Hebrew, as an essential part of the curriculum.[6] Yet by the end of the twentieth century, instruction in these languages in most countries was relegated to specialty courses for very few students. The importance of this change reaches far beyond language instruction. The classical languages, particularly Latin, were for centuries considered the essential key to unlocking the secrets of classical knowledge, which along with theology was valued as the most important of all knowledge. Of course, Latin was the language of the Church and university-educated elites and thus also of the earliest universities; the Latin Quarter in Paris was the original neighborhood of scholars and students at the first Western university. Latin was not just for scholarship; it was fully utilitarian as the language of all feudal European elites, religious and secular alike. So the decline of Latin and other classical languages marks a major transformation of the idea of knowledge and truth claims.

The neo-institutional sociologist of education Yun-Kyung Cha used the cross-national, historical curricular archive described earlier to undertake an extensive study of the changing language requirements in national curricula around the world from 1850 to 1986; Cha found a trend of replacement of classical Greek and Latin with modern foreign languages (i.e., languages other than national languages) (Cha 1991). In Figure 8.3 Cha's data show crisscrossing trends. Once universally taught, classical languages have been in steady decline within both primary and secondary language curricula over the last century, dropping to inclusion in less than

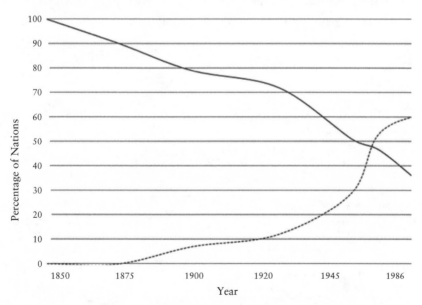

FIGURE 8.3 *Decline of classical language and rise of foreign languages taught in national curricula worldwide.*

Source: Cha (1991, 23). Reproduced by permission of ASA and the author.

30 percent of national curricula in the 1980s. Further too, Cha finds, in the middle of the nineteenth century Greek and Latin instruction took about a third of the entire instructional time for all subjects in secondary schools worldwide, but by the 1980s this had dropped to a mere one percent!

At the same time, instruction in modern foreign languages entered the curriculum modestly from the end of the nineteenth century, and by the late 1950s began a steady climb to inclusion in over 60 percent of national curricula by the 1980s. There is no evidence that these opposing trends have stopped. Some exposure to linguistic organization, taught along with a major foreign language, is now routine in the mass schooling curricula, while classical Greek and Latin are only "necessary" for those very few students who are headed to a life of scholarship on antiquity and related studies (Kamens and Benavot 1991). This has occurred worldwide, as shown in Figure 8.4, which displays the prevalence of foreign language instruction (other than official languages in multilingual nations) by grade level. By the middle grades (known internationally as lower secondary) most nations' school systems provide instruction in at least one foreign language.

In the United States at the turn of the twentieth century over half of all secondary students studied Latin, and during the rest of the century this

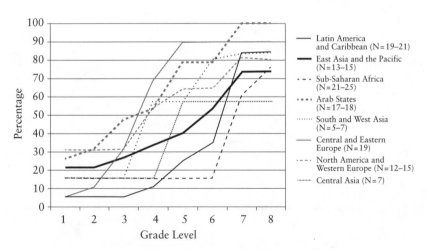

FIGURE 8.4  *Prevalence of foreign language education in grades 1 to 8, circa 2000, by world region.*
Source: UNESCO Institute for Statistics

proportion steadily eroded. While recently there have been some minor increases in Latin study among students, much of this is an overt cognitive strategy to master Latin roots, not as a step to classical knowledge but rather for assistance in learning English vocabulary, specifically for tests like the SAT and GRE aimed at obtaining more educational opportunity; for example, school texts such as *Vocabulary from Latin and Greek Roots: A Study of Word Families* are specifically written for this limited application of classical languages (Osborne 2004). A related analysis of the historical curricular archive reveals that in addition to classical languages, classical knowledge in general has dropped substantially in secondary school curricula worldwide from the 1930s, when over a third of all national secondary curricula were essentially based on a classicist approach to knowledge, to only 9 percent by 1980 (Kamens, Meyer, and Benavot 1996).

Classicism, with its emphasis on the knowledge and truth claims from antiquity as well as early Western philosophical thought and Christian theology, is reflected in texts by centuries-old scholars, which were to be slavishly memorized and eloquently recited in the classical languages of Greek and Latin. This education, which made up so much of Augustine's fourth-century education and Thomas More's elite formal education in late-fifteenth-century London, has been mostly wiped out by the assumptions behind the education revolution that now drive the world's curricula. This research documents one of the most transforming influences that mass education has had on the nature of knowledge: the death of classical knowledge as the foundation not only of schooling, but of society itself. This is not to say that primary and secondary schooling all by themselves killed classicism; rather, that the ideas hatched in the university over the course of the eighteenth and nineteenth centuries slowly shut off classicism and subsequently worked their way down into the foundation of the school curriculum. Related factors in various nations intensified this shift; for example, classical knowledge in the nineteenth-century American curriculum, which was aligned with traditional cultural values, gave way to a preference for scientific knowledge symbolizing a culture of nation-building during that era (Richardson 2009). Most people going through modern schooling, particularly since the middle decades of the twentieth century, have never come into contact with the classical languages or a classicist approach to knowledge. The reach of the transformation of authoritative knowledge in the schooled society means that current students find the intellectual tools and truth claims of classicism, once so common, at least among elites, to be strange and alienating.

Older intellectual objectives, such as learning the set pieces of classical questions and answers, and the proper consumption and display of this learned dialogue, are replaced by knowledge originating out of the truth claims of the three epistemological dimensions described earlier. Thus, the once celebrated trivium—grammar, rhetoric, and dialectics (formalistic argumentation)—has given way, ironically, to skills that were thought of as pedestrian and beneath classical forms, such as the cognitive skills of mathematical and rational analysis, new problem-solving, and original theorizing and reasoning by the student. As these new ideas about knowledge and truth claims make their way through the culture, they become known as the "natural and modern way" to think about any academic subject from health to history. A limited universalism of Latin, Greek, and Hebrew, along with classical knowledge and the rhetorical skills to display it, gave way to a much wider universalism and explicitly cognitive orientation of knowledge through the schooled curriculum.

Consider in this regard the modern study of literature. Skills of close text exegesis, starting first with memorization of classical literature and debate over the "true," original meaning of the text, which were once the main definition of authoritative knowledge, are replaced in the schooled society by understanding and appreciating theory applied to texts, the latter serving as a form of data or empirical observation. Social context and significance of the societal history, such as the historical period and social conditions at the time the text was written, become the way to "learn" the truth of the text rather than its claim to be an ageless classic.

Importantly too, the new focus on social context is not particular; instead, it is universalized in the sense of social theory applied to the author, her historical time period, and what social science has learned about social development. Social theory, essentially the same truth claims used by the social sciences, pours into the instruction in literature for even the youngest of students. Literature becomes universalized, and the way to study it takes on considerable qualities of the social sciences as well as references to general cultural contexts. Hence, the predictable negative reactions to an image of the closed canons of literature, often cast as a reaction to dominance by Western classicism, become disturbing only to the classically educated (e.g., Bloom 1987). Instead, the accepted truth of the schooled society is that all of human society is valid for study, and therefore all types of literature by all types of authors become meaningful; further, as often argued within the academy, such an epistemological stance is morally superior to the exclusion of any cultural heritage (e.g., Said 1978).

Literary criticism too becomes less a dialogue about actual books and more an exercise of general cultural critique without much direct reference to the literature at all. Compare, for example, Alfred Kazin's 1942 highly acclaimed *On Native Grounds*, where throughout his masterful discussion of the interplay between a series of American novels and culture the former always remains the subject, with Terry Eagleton's remark in the epigraph, or any other of successful postmodern literary critics, where literature, if mentioned at all, is increasingly merely a pretext for the analysis of culture. Hence, as neo-instituionalist David Frank once quipped, "with ever growing mass higher education soon there will be more people who have written a book than actually read one!"[7] Being anathema to the classicist approach to education, all students are now invited (some would say forced) to act like a mathematician, an author, a poet, a literary critic, and so forth.

The old distinction between artists who produce the art and critics who critique it breaks down, not because, as the critics would have it, there is now such a crisis of culture to which they must offer their advice, but because of the ideas of self-empowerment combined with wide access to all knowledge, including the academic study of art, that mass education from kindergarten to university pushes in so many subtle, yet pervasive ways. This effectively melds artist with critic so that art becomes an empirical theory of culture (or more accurately, competing theories of culture) and at the same time uses itself as a type of empirical observation to validate theory. Older forms of artistic and epistemological distinctions among artists, writers, scientists, and mathematicians versus the rest of humanity become, with mass education, ever more taboo as useless and socially unjust hierarchical (nonuniversal) distinctions (Frank, Schofer, and Torres 1994).

Traditional education taught the classical canon to the masses (not really all the masses but the beginnings of such) as elevated art and knowledge to be correctly appreciated and held in appropriate awe; the highest forms being recitation of famous poems, copies of great visual art, and memorization of plot lines and characters of famous novels. But this has radically changed. Across all parts of the curriculum, modeled in form on the qualities of a scientific theory, ideas such as the value of empirical information, openness to revision based on new ideas and data, competition with other theories, students as enactors of knowledge, and usefulness in solving everyday problems (mass expertise) are all part of the pervasive message now carried more or less uniformly throughout educational curricula from pre-K to the advanced levels of the university. The curricular shift away from classical philosophy, theology, and classical literature towards an emphasis on universalistic scientific theory is not only evident among science curricula, but now theoretical knowledge, including meta-knowledge about theory in general, is increasingly the conceptual architecture of curricula in the humanities, such as history, certainly in language arts, and even in applied courses on social relationships with peers.

Predictably, current classics departments at the university no longer do classicism as it once was practiced, that is, as the centerpiece of all higher forms of knowledge. Note the description of a common type of course found in classics departments' curricula in the contemporary university:

From the domestication of animals and the dawn of agriculture to the development and socialization of monotheism, the world of the first civilizations led to that of the Bible and ancient Israel. This course, involving a critical view of Biblical texts in light of other ancient sources, archaeology and historical methods, explains the nature and the evolution of society, religion and thought in the Biblical era. Learn how civilization arose, and how the state appropriated religion and applied it for its purposes. How the science of administration developed and deployed ideological tools to further its own ideas as the West developed. This course is deeply subversive, particularly of religious and academic shibboleths. The only authority in this class is that of the most persuasive reader, and doctrines, whether religious or political, will have to be checked at the door. (Pennsylvania State University course catalog of the Classics and Ancient Mediterranean Studies Department, 2008)

Described here is essentially a course based on social science and universalistic historical analysis of the classical world, not on classical knowledge itself. There is no mention of the absolute truth of classic forms, nor any requirement to be able to reproduce such forms, nor an appreciation of their application to the world today, which marked so much of classicism as a knowledge system before mass education. Much the opposite is evident; the ancient classical world can and should be submitted to modern social analysis (read scientific and universalistic), and implicit here is the assumed superiority of the applicability of social theories to society, theories which developed within the Western universities of the eighteenth and nineteenth centuries.

Likewise, modern schooling vanquishes the trappings and tools that were once the essential doorway to classical intellectualism, and it replaces these with the idea of "intellectual competencies" for knowing the full world here and now. Knowing the once-assumed essential languages of classical Hebrew, Greek, and Latin is no longer a marker of the well-educated individual. Instead, some understanding of one or two modern languages is seen as a general competency with which to enter the world as an educated individual. Gone too are the much celebrated mystical qualities and secrecy around authoritative knowledge before the schooled society brought forth the idea that knowledge is open (although often technically dense and opaque, but not purposely hidden) and should be accessible to all, not just those who know the code of Latin, Greek, and Hebrew. The onetime epitome of classical education—the polyglot polymath—is a nearly extinct species of academia (Marrou 1956). So, too, the old parts of the trivium die out: grammar is now seen as a human development pursuit in the enrichment of the ability to communicate; rhetoric as a skill and form of knowledge hardly survives, but mass public-speaking courses in secondary school and the university are taught for civic empowerment; and logic is dominated by mathematics and scientific models of human cognition (i.e., by a broader swath than the classically trained dialectician).

Even though this change is extensive and now nearly complete, a steady stream of laments about classicism's death is nevertheless published by scholars pining away for the old days, and these writings are often accompanied by dire predictions of nothing less than the impending fall of human civilization (e.g., Bloom 1987). What is rarely understood though is that mass formal education has killed classicism, not because mass schooling and the mass university are blundering, uncouth institutional simpletons, but rather because over time academic knowledge coming out of universities created a new image of society, along with new ideas about how knowledge should be generated and used in this new society (e.g., Frank and Gabler 2006). Pouring forth in the 1960s, the explicitly cognitive American mathematics curriculum is a good example of what has replaced classicist approaches to learning. The subject is still mathematics, of course, but even the youngest of learners are exposed to mathematical knowledge as theory to be actively used in everyday problem-solving. Generalized cognitive skill replaces formulistic classical learning. The death of classics as a foundation of knowledge and education is a major change brought on by the schooled society; the other side of the same process is the equally dramatic decline of vocationalism, once the central epistemological goal of education for the masses.

## THE OBSOLESCENCE OF VOCATIONALISM

In the early 1990s the author was part of an international delegation from the World Bank to a Latin American nation to assess a package of organizational reforms aimed at improving the nation's rapidly growing secondary school system as part of a request for a large national development loan from the bank. At a crucial juncture in the meetings the delegation was shown the state of vocational secondary school training in the nation by way of a visit to two schools. At the first, considered a good example of the usual vocational training in the country, a classroom full of teenage students took apart analogue rotary-dial phones and put them back together over and over again; both the students and their teacher displayed great pride in this accomplishment. When it was gently noted that the rotary-dial phone would soon be outdated technology, the director of the school defended the curriculum as providing simple hands-on skills that "eventually will add up to job training." At the second school, noted as one of the nation's top vocational schools, teenage boys in a large open-air factory were working hard on fixing engine chassis from American Chevys circa the 1960s. When it was pointed out that automobile technology had moved considerably beyond the 1960s, the director of the school acknowledged this but added that the real value of the experience was that the instructors could judge the attitudes and work habits of the students and pass on their recommendations to hiring firms.

Both the idea of simple skill transfer as used in the first school and industrial apprenticeship as used in the second have largely been replaced worldwide. It is not just a matter of technology updating; the change goes much deeper, right to the heart of the meaning of education in the schooled society. Ministry of Education officials from the host nation were fully critical of the curriculum used by both schools, and in fact, the point of the trip was to persuade the delegation of the need for reformed secondary education for the future of this nation. Their vision was a comprehensive secondary system for all students that would be completely based on an academic curriculum, including the central assumption that the cognitive skills such a curriculum would instill would be generalizable to all work. This, they had come to believe, was the best preparation of the entire population for the nation's future.

Over just a half century, the idea that schooling for most students should be training for specific vocational skills has died and been replaced by the idea that schooling is about the cognitive and social development of the actualized, multifaceted, cognitively effortful, universal individual. As more aspects of human life become the domain of education, the schooled society constructs the image of the student as far more than just a future worker. Certainly, the notion of schooling as preparation for the future is still part of the educational ideology, but it is now envisioned as a much broader package, less focused on particular kinds of jobs and skill acquisition, and based more on cognitive and social enhancement for all kinds of activities after the educational experience. It is not only that enrollment in vocational training has declined, but also that the very idea of vocationalism has been replaced.

Usually, the decline in vocational training is chalked up to an assumed failure of schooling to "keep up" with the rapid technology changes of the past century, as if schooling is somehow incapable of teaching advanced technologies. And indeed that is one way to consider the example above. But is schooling really incapable? Or, on further consideration of the example, is it more that this narrow vocational instruction was motivated by an older and now outmoded pedagogical goal of transferring simple skills for the world of work and inculcating youth with the work habits of the workplace? The fact that the leaders of the educational establishment of that nation viewed their own vocational curriculum as no longer useful, or even, as one official lamented, as "a waste of precious human talent," says a lot about the decline of vocationalism in general. Although they easily could have designed updated technical training, ministry officials did not seek a World Bank loan in order to increase the level of technology in vocational training to high-tech digital phones and automobiles. Rather, they wanted the loan to do away with this kind of training altogether and replace it with academic cognitive development; and the World Bank's delegation could not have agreed more. That is a telling and ironic change given the once strong focus on vocational training among all kinds of multilateral agencies, including the World Bank, involved in education and national development (Heyneman 2005).

In two studies, comparative sociologist Aaron Benavot (1983, 2006) dissects worldwide trends in vocational secondary education, and convincingly tells a story of a fast rise followed by a long free fall. When mass schooling began in North America and Western Europe at the beginning of the twentieth century, vocationalism was one of its core ideas. Before public schooling, formal education had for the most part been an exclusive experience for the children of the elite, sometimes combined with a small, rising mercantile sector (the future middle class). Mass education meant that schooling was becoming more accessible to the children of the working class, who made up the large ranks of the industrial workforce in rapidly industrializing nations. The idea of vocationalism materialized in most nations into a range of vocational secondary schooling aimed at making the new workers for the coming industrial age (Baker 1999).

This history is reflected in what Benavot finds: by 1950, a third of all secondary students in North America and Western Europe were enrolled in vocational programs, and worldwide about a fourth of secondary enrollments were in vocational education (in Eastern Europe it was a full 50%). But 1950 was the tipping point, as these were the largest enrollment shares vocational education was to have for the rest of the century.

By 1975, it had dropped worldwide to 16 percent, and it kept declining to where vocational training now makes up only about 10 percent of all secondary school programs. Further, Benavot finds that this drop was uniform across most nations, and neither the level of industrial output nor the size of the industrial labor force in nations slowed the decline. This means that the death of vocationalism is a result of a shift in the central values and ideas behind schooling and its curricula, more than it is a reaction to the rhythms of industrialization. Tellingly, even existing vocational programs are less likely to grant terminal degrees (i.e., for a specific job) and are themselves more broadly academically cognitive, including an emphasis on participants gaining yet more (academic) education in their futures (Benavot 2006). A similar study by the U.S. Department of Education shows that in the United States the downward trend in vocational education continues. The percentage of public secondary school students concentrating in an occupational curriculum declined from the early 1980s through the 1990s (U.S. Department of Education, NCES 2003). With the exception of computer technology, all types of curricular areas geared to occupations were declining within the overall secondary curriculum. At the same time, student concentration in academic courses increased, and the content of the remaining vocational courses increasingly included academic material.

The broader idea of vocationalism—that is, its notion of preparing students for a set of fixed and somewhat differentiated positions in society, with the accompanying assumption that the most valuable knowledge is parochial and specific for a particular role in the workplace—gave way to a profound universalism, which was applied first to knowledge and then to schooling itself. As noted in Part I, the university built upon its original feudal vocational mission to ultimately transcend vocationalism, and this is certainly one causal factor behind the decline of vocationalism throughout mass schooling over the past century. Also, of course, this feeds directly into the rise of the educated worker and workplace, as well as the extensive use of educational degrees as occupational credentials. That this has happened in such a sweeping and rapid fashion clearly illustrates the empirical weakness of the traditional perspective on schooling and society. If education mostly follows external forces, it is unlikely that nations with significant industrial labor forces (particularly newly industrializing nations) would drop vocationalism as a main goal of education; yet they have done so, and continue to.

Much of this process bears directly on the influence of qualities and beliefs about knowledge in the schooled society. External social forces tend not to vocationalize the university, as many incorrectly assume. Instead, the university expands its unique scholarly and scientific epistemology to include an ever increasing range of the activities of vocations. In the current full manifestation of the schooled society, the university has universalized many things vocational, mostly away from older notions of long-term fixed jobs having a stable set of skills that can be imparted through vocational training. For example, even the world's largest penal system, that of the United States, has turned away from vocational education and considerably towards access to knowledge and general academic education; for example, 80 percent of federal prisons offer college courses to inmates (U.S. Department of Justice 2003). The schooled society orders up academics for prisoners, even if education programs have a dubious effect on recidivism rates (Harer 1995).

Another way to appreciate the decline of vocationalism is to compare it to what organizations, both private and public, do to train their employees after schooling. On-the-job training, or training in the knowledge needed for the job, is also transformed by the culture of education. If schooling merely followed societal trends, one might assume that as education levels rose in populations, on-the-job training would decrease; in other words, highly schooled workers would not "need" more training. The exact opposite has occurred. The continually educating employee is seen as a major asset to the organization. As a result, training programs in work organizations have grown and now are widely institutionalized in all types of workplaces. While it is hard to find complete enrollment and course offerings across workplaces, a study of training by Richard Scott and John Meyer in the early 1990s estimates that

by any criterion training conducted by U.S. work organizations is a sizable enterprise, involving in any given year more than half again as many students as are enrolled in four-year college and universities and consum[ing] from a quarter to a third of all resources expended on traditional higher education programs. (1991, 301)

By their estimates literally millions of training courses occur every year, attended by a huge proportion of the workforce. At the same time, the ideas of useful knowledge and the multifaceted person shaped by this knowledge in the schooled society change the course content of on-the-job training. While there is still narrow technical training, the real growth has been in the spread of more diffuse education, from human relations skills to self-enhancement techniques, including cognitive skills (Monhan, Meyer, and Scott 1994). Paralleling the emergence of the educated workplace, the training of workers is less vocational in a narrow sense and aimed more at broad human development and cognitive problem-solving.

Teaching the student the specific skills of a job, such as carpentry, has dropped in value, but not because there is no more carpentry or because there is some vocational training crisis; rather, it is because the idea runs against the deeper logic spread by the education revolution throughout the culture. Knowledge as specific vocational skill, which was so prominent in non-elite (nonclassical) education some seventy-five years ago, has faded, not because of a change in technology but because greatly expanded formal education promotes the assumption of the extensive educability of all people in cognitive, scientific, and universal qualities of knowledge that are assumed to be valuable for all activities, including carpentry. Modern schooling overturns the assumed necessity and immediacy of specific vocational skills, because it replaces them with *cognitive tools* assumed to be essential in performing any job and solving any problem. It also replaces vocationalism with the idea that education is universal and hence universally beneficial to all aspects of life. One can endlessly read this type of rhetoric throughout multinational agencies' policy recommendations for education and economic development (e.g., Rychen and Salganik 2003). And this relatively new educational goal has spread worldwide; certainly this was the idea behind the education leadership of the World Bank mission wanting to reform vocational training in the early 1990s.

Even among vocationalism's last bastions educational ideas are shifting. For example, German sociologists Justin Powell and Heike Solga convincingly argue that in Germany, where vocationalism and education are still publicly praised, it is mostly a mythical belief that stems from the nation's anachronistic approach to higher education expansion and education in general, and is now less connected to the current realities of the education system and labor market (Powell and Solga 2011; Baker and Lenhardt 2008). From time to time, often with reference to Germany, American educationalists suggest that a return to vocationalism would profit the nation, but they misunderstand both the extent to which vocationalism now makes little sense within a schooled society and how far education has transformed society away from these essentially nineteenth-century ideas about individuals and occupations, even in Germany (Hamilton and Hurrelmann 1994).

## THE KNOWLEDGE SOCIETY
## AS THE SCHOOLED SOCIETY

A strong case can be made that the epistemological foundation of the schooled society underpins a knowledge society, including its corresponding information economy (Cha and Ham 2011; Richardson 2009). This is certainly reflected in the rapid spread of instruction in schools and universities in the information and communication technology curriculum, which Ham and Cha show to be at first a function of the size of a nation's science productivity (university knowledge conglomerate), and then, once begun, a dissemination into education systems in all types of nations (2011). But the schooled society and the knowledge society are linked not only because of the ability of mass education to develop knowledge comprehension, technological communication skills, and demand for such training among large segments of the population. Additionally and crucially, the schooled society creates the basic cultural understanding of knowledge as accessible, humanly constructible, applicable to human progress, and rational. These qualities underlie the deep extent of knowledge production and its value in postindustrial society. The schooled society constructs a reality that is conducive to holding knowledge production in high esteem, and this includes considerable belief in the idea that more universal knowledge is better for human society. This secular trust in knowledge and social progress stems from the culture developed by the university, is spread widely by the dynamics of the education revolution, and underpins the culture of intense applications of knowledge. Although the debate continues over whether the knowledge society is a historically distinctive social order, a central and often overlooked confirming fact in this direction is that the knowledge society rests upon the historically distinctive emergence of the schooled society (Lyon 1988; Webster 1995).

Expansive formal education not only produces the capacity to generate even more knowledge, but it also produces the cultural values that reinforce this large-scale effort. It is no wonder then that formal education as it is widely practiced today is forever under some criticism from proponents of older intellectual models of knowledge and truth claims. Education in the postindustrial society sits between bookends of shrill criticism and charges of unmet expectations. On one side, the conservative elite frets over declining classical standards and past glories of traditional educational methods, or as Bloom called it, the closing of the mind. On the other side, the business community pounds out a constant refrain of caution about irrelevant curricula leading to a lack of specific skills among graduates. The effect is a dizzying set of complaints, seemingly from all sides at once. But instead of being inept or falling behind, the educational institution has, for better or worse, changed the culture through transforming the kinds of knowledge and truth claims that are the most respected in and vital to society.

Accompanying this is an ideology promoted in education that from the youngest grades the student is an individual empowered to know, use, and even create knowledge. A recent analysis of textbooks across nations from the 1970s until the present finds this metamessage embedded in a host of curricular content that asserts the rights of students as children, and that emphasizes an empowered human agency, promoting active participation as well as the capacities and interests of the student (Bromley, Meyer, and Ramirez 2011b). These textbooks are full of invitations to the student to think (metacognition) about knowledge and most tellingly to "decide" (self-empowerment) how to use and critique it. Mass schooling and mass attendance in higher education insert a historically unique cultural form of student-centeredness into the knowledge process. The child in school and the youth in university are thought to be made a fuller person if they understand in a participatory fashion the "true" scientific and scholarly process behind the knowing of nature and society (Frank and Gabler 2006; Frank and Meyer 2007). Vocationalism and classicism are supplanted by a set of ideas supporting the rise of ever greater cognitization of human capabilities and the now widely held belief that all humans must master an academic curriculum dominated by science, mathematics, social science, and a general cosmopolitan outlook on the world. Images of elite knowledge, as well as the exclusiveness of education in elite settings, become as antiquated as the Latin textbooks the Yale students once threw into the fire.

Once the logic of the unfolding education revolution established the right of everyone to enter the institution of education, it became powerfully normative for everyone to become in a sense a scholar. By definition all have the right and are encouraged to consider themselves intellectuals, poets, mathematicians, scientists, psychologists, and so forth regardless of their skills and talents. And that is how the schooled society has come to conceptualize and organize knowing and knowledge. It is open and purposely accessible to all. It is to be tried on or taken for a test drive around the block by any and all, not just celebrated by an awestruck audience or reserved in formalistic secrecy for the powerful few.

CHAPTER 9

# Failure, Redemption,
# and the Construction of the Self

In modern society education allocates its dropouts to failure . . . non-graduates are socialized through life experience to the meaning of their failure just as graduates are socialized to the meaning of their success.

JOHN MEYER, *American Journal of Sociology*, 1977

Those taking the GED are so excited about the program that they are willing to talk about it with others and encourage them to join. They see it as something to be proud of.

Director of an adult education program in Florida, 2006

ANYONE CLOSE to an educationally challenged child, or who was one themselves, knows the pain and frustration of not doing well in school. Schooling has become such an all-encompassing phenomenon in the lives of children and youth that it takes on important meaning well beyond just a route to an occupation, to the point that a person's educational status has come to form a considerable portion of his public *and* private self. Not only has educational attainment eclipsed all other factors leading to most people's eventual public social status; it has become a major defining element of the private, subjective self. Increasingly, the whole construction of the "successful life" includes significant normative pressure for academic participation and successful attainment (e.g., Meyer 1986, 1992; Pallas 2002, 2003).

Relative success or failure in school reflects upon the whole of the individual and even her family. As an institution, the educational process has come to define the terms of personal success and failure to a degree unknown before the education revolution, producing a world where a person's self-image is routinely formed vis-à-vis educational status well before any posteducational achievement as an adult. This is a remarkable cultural change over a short historical period. Like the backward educational credentialing of successful business executives, earlier formal education greatly legitimizes adult performance. Academic performance becomes more than just an allocation of students to a future education and occupational opportunity; it becomes a major status in and of itself that is carried into adulthood, where it becomes deeply rooted within the subjective self. The old notion of educational selection and pruning of the population has been significantly devalued by the image of formal education creating a crucial cognitive, psychological, and to a degree moral developmental experience for all, even up through the university. Before the education revolution began, an inability to do academics was for most, high- and low-born alike, not necessarily a major barrier to outward or inward success. It was seen as a deficit, to be sure, but not one with much long-term effect on the individual's social chances, and there was little stigma attached to it, if any. But this has all changed.

A good way to see both formal education's pervasive institutional power to define personal success and how it enters deeply into the cultural construction of self-image in the schooled society is in the story of the widely imagined social problem of the school dropout in American society, along with the invention of a mass educational program to "solve the problem."

### THE DROPOUT AS DEVIANT

"Dropout" is the American term applied to students who leave school without finishing a degree. It was initially applied mostly to high school leavers, but the term, or some close variation on it, will no doubt shortly be widely applied to those who quit *higher education* as well. The dropout as a socially meaningful category—that is, where the idea came from, and how it has been used in discussions about education and, most important, as a target of social programs—is not just a notable historical development; it also illustrates the degree to which the spread of mass schooling and its greater institutionalization within society form new definitions of people, their performances, and increasingly their whole self. The term "dropout" has come to mean nothing short of a summative measure of the lack of worth of a person. "Dropout" is the inverse of "school graduate," and taken together they define educational status, which no one in the schooled society can now escape. One is either a graduate of the normal amount of schooling at a particular time, or one is a dropout. The development of this all-encompassing educational status is telling. So too was the public appearance in the 1960s of the dropout problem, the sister of the overeducation crisis debate; ironically, the former argued that society was threatened by too little education, while the latter feared too much. Proponents of both positions, however, misunderstood the nature of the emerging schooled society.

With the spread of mass schooling demographically to larger proportions of cohorts of children and developmentally for longer periods of the child's life, educational officials came to worry about children who did not attend when they could have, or attended for less time than needed to finish. Excellent social histories and institutional analyses describe the creation in the late nineteenth and early twentieth centuries of administrative regulations and compulsory attendance laws to prevent truancy, which came to support and enforce the idea that all children should attend primary schooling (e.g., Boli and Thomas 1985; Richardson 1994). But while being an extension of this trend, the image of the dropout has since been so intensified as to be qualitatively different; and crucial for the story here, the dropout intensified as a meaningful status long after schooling was made compulsory, during a period when most children were finishing elementary schooling and most youth enrolling in secondary schooling.

Once hatched as a social phenomenon in the 1960s, the act of dropping out of high school mushroomed in public media attention, drawing much political concern and therefore rapidly taking on qualities of a menace to the collective (Dorn 1996).[1] Similarly, intellectuals and influential educators took up the problem from the perspective of negative social consequences. For example, Harvard University's president and education reformer James Conant weighed in on dropouts in 1961:

[The dropout is] not likely to become a constructive citizen of his community. [Instead,] as a frustrated individual he is likely to be anti-social and rebellious, and may well become a juvenile delinquent. The adverse influence of the street is largely a consequence of gangs of such youths, out of school and unemployed. (Conant 1961, 35, as quoted in Dorn 1996)

Popular media and professional literatures of the period also brimmed with images of pending social chaos at the hands of teenagers who quit school before graduating. Even the then faddish popularized version of Freudian analysis, including the fear of castration, was applied to the problem, as a study of dropouts in 1962 proclaimed:

To the inhibited boys, seeking competence in any of these areas [like sports] unconsciously represented becoming better than their fathers and carried the threat of castration. They were consciously afraid that they could not be successful and would get hurt in the process of trying to achieve. Much more security and safety lay . . . in being nonachievers. (Scholarship and Guidance Association 1962, as quoted in Dorn 1996)

The Ford Foundation, a philanthropic promoter of education for the common good and a beacon of rationalized social reform along the lines of social science and progressive intervention, funded in 1961 a research and advocacy center within the National Education Association (NEA) with the explicit purpose of organizing a public dissemination campaign about the dropout problem. Professional education journals at the time published several hundred articles on dropouts, and exposure to the idea of the dropout as a major national problem was nearly unavoidable for Americans. Dorn's (1996) bibliographical analysis of periodicals over the 1960s shows that once the term emerged into the public, a burst of articles in all types of popular print media followed. Most historians of the period agree that once it was reified by university-based research and turned into public commentary widely disseminated through mass media, the idea of the dropout merged the act of leaving school prematurely with personal failure and became a lasting fixture within modern culture (Papagiannis, Bickel, and Fuller 1983).

Heading into the 1960s, America resonated with the dropout problem, as the period became the "decade of the dropout" and in the public's eye was quickly connected to a host of related youth problems. It seemed all at once that the nation was faced with an alien and violent youth culture emerging as the baby boomers hit adolescence, and dropping out of school was thought to be a leading cause of the problem. What is now considered obvious to most about the links among poverty, urbanization, and youthful delinquency was just being "learned" by politicians and a rapidly expanding middle class. Added to the mix was the transformation of many northern cities as the mass movement of impoverished southern African

Americans met considerable residential and economic racism (Lemann 1992). Of course, these kinds of conditions and their pernicious interconnections have been around ever since humans first began to live together in large numbers, and indeed many of the families of the new American middle class heading for the suburbs had just emerged from urban neighborhoods with close proximity to these very same conditions. But there was a distinct refocusing on these social trends in the early 1960s, and with the help of emerging language from social science within the university, it led to a reshaping of the dropout phenomenon as a widespread social problem to be addressed by society for the common good.

For example, here is how one contemporary observer of the trend considered the long-term, dire consequences of many adolescents not finishing high school in the late 1960s:

> It is from this hard core of dropouts that a high proportion of the gangsters, hoodlums, drug addicted, government-dependent-prone, irresponsible and illegitimate parents of tomorrow will be predictably recruited. (Cervantes 1965, 197)

It was a time ripe for the notion of threatening, unruly youth, even celebrated in a fashion. To the melodious strains and titillating gyrations of the Jets and Sharks in Leonard Bernstein's *West Side Story*, a rendition of Shakespeare's *Romeo and Juliet* in the language and images of urban gangs and troubled youth, Americans added the teenage dropout to their list of societal threats. Not surprisingly, sophisticated analyses of the dropout discourse have accurately noted that in the 1960s (and perhaps even more so today) the ranks of dropouts were disproportionally filled with youth from marginalized and oppressed racial, social-class, and linguistic groups (Dorn 1996; Fine 1991).

What every historian of the dropout trend points out with a great sense of irony (misplaced irony, as argued below) is that the school dropout came onto the public scene precisely at the time when high school graduation rates were starting their largest ascent in U.S. history (and in other developed nations). The rate of graduation, the inverse of the dropout rate, significantly increased from the 1940s through the rest of the century. As shown in Figure 9.1, the decades of the 1950s, 1960s, and 1970s showed large growth in high school graduation rates, the greatest absolute growth

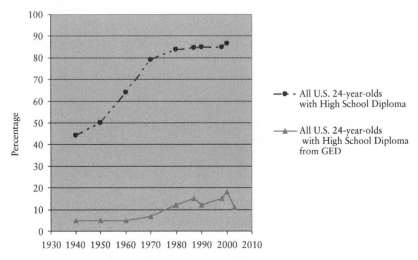

FIGURE 9.1   *U.S. high school regular diploma and GED completion rates by age 24, 1930–2000.*
Source: U.S. Census Public Use Samples

being in the 1960s. In twenty years, the nation went from just 50 percent of American twenty-four-year-olds achieving a high school diploma in 1950 to 80 percent in 1970. The same is true of graduation rates among young African Americans, which astonishingly grew from 20 percent in 1950 to 60 percent by 1970.

With this great expansion of the American secondary school, inequalities in graduation rates between social groups dramatically declined as well. For example, while at the beginning of the dropout decade female students were twice as likely as male students to finish high school, by 1970 rising rates among males had lowered this disparity by 30 percent. An average African American youth in 1940 was a full two-thirds less likely than an average white youth to finish high school, but by 1970 completion rates were equal across race (Dorn 1996).

In fact, one could easily portray the main transformation of American youth over the entire twentieth century as one of increasingly delayed entry into the labor market because school was attended for longer periods of their lives. Across the historical arc of this major social trend, the 1960s was the tipping point when the nation took a huge turn towards becoming a schooled society. Why then was it at precisely this time in American history, when mass secondary education was booming, that school dropouts became such a publicized problem? The usual answer is that the paradox between soaring graduation rates and the emergence of the dropout problem is the result of the media's having driven a phony issue into a frenzy. This turns out not to be the case.

## WHAT CREATED THE DROPOUT AS A SOCIAL PROBLEM?

To answer this question one must first consider the timing of the emergence of the dropout issue. From the perspective of the schooled society, it occurred exactly at a point in history when one would expect the creation of this kind of social problem: the intensifying ideas behind the education revolution symbiotically joined the growing normative pressure to finish secondary school and the image of the dropout into what became a deep cultural transformation of how people think about themselves and others in a schooled society. Changing a person's behavior and deeply held beliefs is not trivial, and when this happens across millions of people in hundreds of thousands of families over a relatively short period it is substantial. In human terms, what the statistical graduation/dropout rates above indicate is a steady and deepening shift in how large segments of the population came to think about themselves relative to schooling and its value in life. Like an unseen seismological event under an ocean causing a very observable tidal wave, so too can an unseen fundamental change in an underlying cultural notion about society bring on a demographic tidal wave like the expansion of secondary school completion during the 1960s. So the right question is not, Why did the social problem of the dropout in the United Stats seemingly fall from the sky in the early 1960s? Instead, the more theoretically productive question to ask is, What caused the underlying historical shift in people's thinking on what is normal regarding who goes to school and for how long? And from this perspective, what then is a dropout?

As described in Part I, at the core of the main wave of the education revolution is an accretion over the last century and a half of now implacable beliefs in the values of "education for all" and "the more education in a life, the better." The school dropout then becomes a mass problem at exactly the time when the number of people dropping out (not finishing) declines, because dropping out is not really a problem of numbers; it is an identification of "deviant behavior" in the schooled society. As a social problem, dropping out seemingly falls from the sky, not because it is a made-up problem, as some intellectuals believed at the time (and still do), but rather because it heralds the breakthrough of a new cultural order with sufficiently widespread acceptance to matter in how most people think and behave (Parsons 1971).

As with the growing taboo against educational credential fraud, the nature of deviance defines the normative order. So it is not that declining numbers of school-leavers unmask an invented social problem; instead, it is the opposite. A very real social construction is formed by the ubiquitous increase in high school graduates, most saliently by the rise in the number of youth who are at risk of dropping out of school—that is, *attending school but at risk of becoming an educational deviant*. A change over just two decades from 50 to 80 percent of all youth taking on the arduous academic task of completing four years of secondary school indicates a considerable shift in the normative culture of schooling and society. It is not surprising that it is at this point within the United States—the education revolution's advance outpost—that the schooled society comes to maturity by defining deviance *educationally*.[2]

This social fact is lost on those who think about education from the traditional perspective, likening the dropout to a phony "social construction" (e.g., Cervantes 1965; Papagiannis, Bickel, and Fuller 1983). Their notion is that since the term "dropout" is made up, so too is the phenomenon a made-up social problem. But this rests on a flimsy view of social construction, short on theory and long on supposed debunking of the media and popular culture. Instead of recognizing the construction of educational deviance as marking a substantive shift in the cultural model of schooling in society, they see the problem of the dropout as a myth in the sense of a falsehood. For them, dropout, as a term and then as a category of people, was somehow foisted onto society, apparently while nobody was looking. Such a notion of social construction, however, trivializes social forces and often completely misunderstands them. Unfortunately, this historically debunked version of the school dropout is what intellectuals and the public alike have come to believe, and thus they too miss the real sociological significance of the emerging new social order of the schooled society in the United States during the 1960s.[3]

A debunked social problem could not be further from the real process of the social construction of educational deviance, yet it is easy to appreciate how such a misinterpretation comes about. In observing something's historical development, particularly something as ubiquitous and thus elusive as widespread cultural understandings, it is tempting to conclude that the trumpeters of the deeper cultural shift are the actual cause of change. And so a deeper cultural change appears to be brought on by a rather tepid process of little more than media attention. Obviously, a cultural shift cannot speak for itself; the people who live it and observe it speak, often through the media. But the government, employers, mass media, and even the foundation committed to disseminating the news of the problem did not generate the idea that to drop out of school is to be deviant. Instead, they summarized and transmitted the deep and robust cultural shift occurring at the roots of the schooled society—namely, that *a new model of society holds that secondary education has become necessary to be a modern person.*

This core value is far more than the notion of technical training for the labor market; it includes this, of course, but the notion of the dropout as a serious problem mirrors the moral foundation of modern society as a collection of individuals who are developed in full chiefly through their participation in formal education. This participation extends well into the years of early adulthood and even beyond, as seen in "lifelong learning" slogans promoting quasi-formal education for all adults. Therefore, the teenage high school dropout was the central metaphor by which the nation wrestled with an emerging model of society where all youth should undertake comprehensive secondary education (e.g., Hammack 2004).

Some public discourse about the dropout issue at the time among various elites and social observers showed exactly this process. Consider how Daniel Schreiber, the head of the then new and high-profile NEA center on dropouts, described the dropout as

"running away from work half-done, from *school half-completed*," he declared: "How *American education* solves the problem of school dropouts . . . may well determine America's future." (Schreiber 1962b, 234, emphasis added; as quoted in Dorn 1996, 66)

This image from the leading intellectual center charged with examining the dropout problem squarely places the issue within the context of mass education, both in the nature of the deviance and in the solution's lying within education as an institution. Schreiber very clearly indicates that the real challenge faced by the nation is not the dropout as the cause of rising crime and violence per se, but how the schooled society will be successfully achieved for all.

Another example of rumblings heard from the deeper cultural shift is a description of what today would be called the "human capital" model of education, appearing in a 1962 article in the widely circulated *Saturday Evening Post*:

We waste more than a million kids a year. As we once wasted natural gas and forests and topsoil, today we waste our most valuable natural resource—the *productive power of young brains* and muscles, the creative power of young imaginations and emotions. (Kohler and Fontaine, p. 16, emphasis added; as quoted in Dorn 1996, 66)

The warning is about wasting collective young brain power through undereducation. Earlier in the century, before the large growth in secondary education and the beliefs driving it, this kind of public language would have been far less prevalent and meaningful.

A further excellent example of the underlying normative change in the schooled society reflected through public discussion of the dropout was the focus on what was called the "crisis of the capable dropout." A plethora of studies at the time attempted to find and separate out from all dropouts those with higher academic abilities. These became known as "capable dropouts," and were the focus of much expert discussion (for a summary see Voss, Wendling, and Elliott 1966). Note the strong normative message underlying these researchers' description of the capable dropout:

[Even with] adequate reading ability and IQ, his grades may, in fact, be primarily D's and F's. In such cases, the *capable dropout* is "flunking" for reasons connected with *citizenship, school attendance.* . . . It is the capable dropout that is considered a contemporary social problem, because his abilities and potentialities are not realized, and this constitutes a *societal waste*. (Voss, Wendling, and Elliott 1966, 367, emphasis added)

Here is represented the singular mortal sin in the schooled society: *to have academic talent and yet to drop out of school.* This is the purist case of the "dropout as deviant of the schooled society."

Here also, the pairing of educational failure with the lack of participatory citizenship in schooling is a critical addition to the scenario of the dropout problem. The problem is not defined as purely technical (students with low academic abilities); instead, it is defined as a problem of adherence to the new educational order. What makes this normative environment even more remarkable is that estimates at the time found that anywhere from one half to three-fourths of all dropouts were judged to have the ability to finish high school. This one idea on top of the emerging schooled society created a large class of educational deviants of the worst kind (Voss, Wendling, and Elliott 1966).

In a few instances the discussion in the 1960s of the dropout issue did go so far as to consider early school leaving as pure deviance in and of itself. For example, one astute professional observer at the time pointed out that "the reasons for drop-outs are practically the same as the cause for delinquency" (O'Neill 1963, 157). But this was as close as the discussion got to the underlying truth about the cultural shift to a schooled society. The broader context of the normative shift towards mass secondary education was not widely addressed; therefore, the real implications of the expansion—that dropping out is itself the main deviant act, not so much what happens afterwards—was often lost in the shuffle of interpretations at the time. Youth delinquency, obviously a type of deviant status, and its links to dropping out, was very much part of the professional and public rhetoric of the time, yet it was mostly a limited discussion about the tendency of a school dropout to *then become* a delinquent youth. And that link turns out not to be very strong, as leaving school early does not seem to lead to criminal delinquency in and of itself, or at least the relationship is more complicated than just dropping out leading to crime (e.g., Jarjoura 1993; Staff and Krieger 2008).

If what was really behind education's cultural power to equate personal failure with academic shortcomings was the large-scale shift towards a full-blown schooled society, then one should be able to find a significant discussion about what was happening in schools as the underlying norms changed. And this is indeed the case. The struggle with this major expansion is fully obvious in how educators of the time evaluated the pressure placed on the school by the dropout problem. This is best summarized by the dean of history of American education Lawrence Cremin:

The growing comprehensive nature of secondary institutions has saddled high schools with the expectation of universal education. Only the success of high schools in becoming mass institutions has made the idea of a "dropout problem" possible, yet it still suggests that high schools have failed in some basic task. (1990, 12)

Dropout and graduate are two halves of the same unitary and universal status, an inescapable status in the emerging schooled society of the midtwentieth century. If dropping out is the sin that reflects the virtue of completing high school, then ironically the much intellectually maligned GED is the road to redemption.

### BACK INTO SOCIETY WITH A GED

What the famous entertainer Bill Cosby, the late founder of Wendy's hamburger chain Dave Thomas, the former Delaware lieutenant governor Ruth Ann Minner, the actor Christian Slater, and the former U.S. senator Ben Nighthorse Campbell have in common is that these successful, public individuals all earned a high school diploma through the GED test. The stories of these people and their GED success, and other stories like them, are repeated over and over on numerous informational websites and advertisements from adult education programs related to the GED. Like a mantra, the message intones that the GED is a path to more education, better jobs, and general success. Once heard, the moral of the story is obvious to everyone. All of these successful people were at one time failures, but by passing the GED and receiving a secondary school diploma they got back on life's track, and this alternative avenue to a secondary school credential made it possible for them to go on to achieve significant success.

Slightly more subtly conveyed by these famous and influential people's stories is the message that there is no lasting stigma from educational redemption through the GED. Furthermore, as the gushing comments from these GED celebrities attest, they are proud of the action they took to get back into life's pursuit of (educationally defined) success. The final message portrayed through these short testimonials is that had these celebrities not taken the steps to complete the GED, they were most assuredly headed for lifelong failure. The one notable exception is the story of Dave Thomas, who attained the GED long after he became a millionaire. His story thus communicates what is perhaps the overarching central message: the GED is about shedding the dropout deviant status and rejoining the schooled society, regardless of one's postschool experiences in the world.

The GED, commonly called by these initials, stands for the bureaucratic-sounding General Educational Development test. Even in semi-official literature one can come across the GED misnamed the General Equivalence Diploma, because that is more in line with what it has become—an equivalent for a high school diploma. Anyone who has dropped out of high school and is eighteen years or older can pay no more than $200 and sit for a seven-and-a-half-hour test on a range of five academic subjects—reading, writing, mathematics, science, and social studies.[4] If they pass it, test-takers are awarded a GED diploma that is by and large substitutable for a regular high school diploma; the GED diploma is routinely referred to in applications for jobs and higher education as the "high school equivalency degree." The test is also made available to students younger than eighteen who cannot attend all four years of high school for various reasons, such as pregnancy, health, or family hardship. The United States is not the only nation to have an equivalency examination for earning a diploma; for example, China has the Entrance Examination of Adult Higher Education.[5]

Administered by the American Council of Education (ACE), the GED has grown substantially since its inception during the Second World War, when it was a device to move returning soldiers into higher education or the job market without sending them back to finish high school. Originally, it was a type of benefit for service to the country, but the GED has since morphed into an all-purpose method for all types of people to finish high school. For example, in the large states of California and Florida one in four awarded high school diplomas are through the GED (Smith 2000). The ACE estimates that one in every seven Americans with high school credentials received the GED, as well as one in twenty college students.

Often thought of as only an inexpensive means to assist the dropout as an individual, the GED program is more broadly a mechanism that helps to support the norms of the schooled society. The GED credential's full equivalency to a high school diploma is widely proclaimed in public. Here is how the agency that is responsible for administering the test, the GED Testing Service (1993), describes the purpose and credential status of the test:

To provide an opportunity for adults who have not graduated from high school to earn a high-school level educational diploma by demonstrating the attainment of developed abilities normally acquired through completion of a high school program of study. . . . the credential provided by passing the GED may be used in a manner identical to a school diploma.

How did a bureaucratic, military expedient conceived for a narrow purpose and intended to last only a short time become such a stable and large undertaking for so many types of people? And what does the GED in general illustrate about formal education in the schooled society?

Thomas Smith, a sociologist of education at Vanderbilt University, undertook a comprehensive analysis of the GED from the perspective proposed here (Smith 2000, 2003). He assessed the existing empirical research on the use and payoffs of the GED, and added his own analyses of data from large national samples of youth followed over a decade. What he found is an interesting paradox about the role the GED now plays in American education, the solution of which goes a long way to explaining the GED phenomenon.

The paradox is that the GED's popularity continues in the face of low immediate economic payoff as a credential in the labor force (e.g., Heckman and Cameron 1993; Cameron and Heckman 1994; Gareth, Jing, and Kutner 1995; Maloney 1992). Not only does the average worker with a high school diploma awarded through the GED make less than the average worker with a regular diploma, but the GED-holder's income does not differ much from lifelong dropouts'. Smith summarizes the technical research as follows:

While surveys of employers have shown that they generally consider the GED as equivalent to the traditional diploma in hiring decisions, much of the literature on the economic returns to GED attainment indicate that these returns are significantly below those of traditional high school graduate and . . . not much better than [the income of] dropouts who have not earned a high school equivalency diploma. (2000, 64)

Yet even in the face of low immediate benefits, roughly one million Americans without a high school diploma attempted the GED in 2005. In just a quarter of a century, from 1972 to 1995, seventeen million people attempted to pass the GED, ten million of whom received the GED diploma (GED Testing Service 1993). And in 2008 nationwide a half a million dropouts passed the GED, amounting to 12 percent of all high school credentials issued that year (Heckman, Humphries, and Mader 2010). Why do so many people undertake a full day of testing, requiring study and preparation on the part of most test-takers?

Considering only the low immediate payoff may lead one down the wrong path to conclude that a great many people acted, or were forced or tricked to act, foolishly. Instead, the absence of immediate payoff in the labor market actually highlights the real process at hand. As the flip-side of the deviant status of the dropout in the schooled society, the GED is the process by which educational failures can get on track and back into the schooled society, and perhaps most saliently, achieve a basic status that defines the normal self. Therefore, the historical pattern of the GED's growth verifies the same cultural shift described above. As displayed in Figure 9.1, the GED grew into a much traveled route to the high school degree at the same time that rates of high school attendance (and completion) surged, and hence there was a growing number of youth going to secondary school and at risk of becoming dropouts. After its original use following the Second World War, the GED lingered on the educational landscape, contributing only 5 percent of all diplomas; but by 1970 the GED's share in diplomas began to climb and did so rapidly to a high of 18 percent of all secondary degrees in the nation in 2001 (Smith 2000).

Not surprisingly, many detractors of the GED argue that it is only a cheap imitation of a "real" high school diploma and that it dupes marginalized people into thinking they are acquiring an educational credential, which does not in fact deliver true benefits personally or collectively. Such an assessment is akin to the education-as-myth argument described before. On a policy level the same detractors suggest that the increased use of GED attainment as a measurable goal by welfare programs, social programs, and even penal institutions, as a cheap and easy way to prove their continued effectiveness, has unnecessarily propped up the GED as a kind of political collective myth (see Smith 2000 for a summary). In fact, these concerns were what led to the flurry of studies of the economic payoffs of the GED in the mid-1990s, noted above. Much like the tendency to debunk the dropout problem in the late 1960s, the initial facts about the GED can lead to a similar conclusion. But the detractors and debunkers miss the larger institutional picture of the GED, for which there is a lot of evidence.

## EDUCATIONAL REDEMPTION AND SELF-WORTH

If the GED is directly related to leaving a deviant status and rejoining the larger educational order, this should be reflected in how test-takers think about their status vis-à-vis the GED. First, they should be aware that the path back from educational failure is not so much about a hope for some immediate payoff in their current jobs as it is about their futures. Second, plans for additional education made possible after attaining a high school credential should be prominent among their reasons for pursuing the GED. Lastly and most importantly, successful completion of the GED should produce a strong positive reaction in their self-worth. As John Meyer points out about failure in a schooled society (see epigraph), coming back from educational deviance through the GED, as minimal as it might seem in comparison to other educational attainments happening around these test-takers, is not just a narrow strategy for a limited future; it is an affirmation of reentering the moral order of the schooled society. These predictions are precisely what the data indicate.

As Smith (2003) documents across a number of surveys of GED test-takers, when asked why they are pursuing the degree, most test-takers answer that it is not for reasons of their immediate job. Just as technical studies have recently helped policy-makers understand, most who take the GED test are not duped by false promises that a GED will instantly pay off, and not surprisingly, these people understand firsthand that the jobs they have now will not be influenced very much. Instead, test-takers' expectations are overwhelmingly a mixture of pursuing future education *and* regaining an acceptable educational status for their own self-worth in a highly educated society. Estimates of up to one third see the GED reintegrating them into the education system through access to higher education, trade school, or job training (Baldwin 1991). Another third see the most important benefit of the GED as a way to "feel better about themselves as people." And the last third see the GED as leading to some future job enhancement. This pattern of motivation on the part of those who are willing to take a five-battery, seven-and-a-half-hour test, in many cases long after dropping out of any academic environment, and who know they are clearly educational failures (63% of test-takers have completed only two years of high school or less) is a strong indicator of the relief that the GED offers in restoring a normative standing in the schooled society. Test-takers' future education plans are not just wishful thinking: one half of all who pass the GED go on to study in higher education (Smith 2003). These expectations for more education are nourished by commercials on GED-related websites full of pop-up windows advising on everything from applying to college to shopping for the right clothes for the collegiate experience.

The feelings of self-worth among those who pass and receive the GED are even more pronounced than the test-takers' and have a ripple effect on the social standing of the whole person. A number of surveys of GED-holders report that upwards of 70 to 90 percent of them feel significantly better about themselves as people for having earned the degree (Darkenwald and Valentine 1985; Iowa Department of Education 1992; Mally and Charuhas 1977). For example, in one such survey of GED-holders in Maryland, 73 percent report feeling greater self-confidence in their abilities; 93 percent feel that the GED gave them a second chance; and one half report that their lives now have more direction, that they are willing to assume more responsibility, and that their families are pleased with their performance (Reed 1985). Although the GED is often marginalized in analyses of American education, one would hardly find such widespread positive feelings if for the millions who take and pass the test it was only a trivial accomplishment.

In reality the GED is not a minimal accomplishment (at least beyond the technical taking of a test) for either the individual or the collective; it is as much about leaving the deviant status of dropout as it is about getting back on track within the schooled society. The GED's resurgence in the last forty years is borne out of a cultural shift towards the ever greater value placed on education in American society and what that does to those who for any reason cannot finish secondary schooling. As would be predicted, for many GED-holders the degree leads to more formal education and job training, and these have been shown to have both an economic and a social payoff in the long run (Murnane, Willett, and Boudett 1994; Gareth, Jing, and Kutner 1995; Kroll and Qi 1995). Gaining self-worth within the schooled society is a major change for these GED-holders and indicates how much the institution of education has come to construct the self.

At this point in the story GED debunkers are always quick to point out that far fewer people with the GED diploma complete higher education's baccalaureate degree than do those with regular secondary school diplomas. And this is true; for example, estimates from the early 1990s show that by age twenty-seven only 5 percent of GED-holders have the BA compared to 25 percent of high school completers (Smith 2000). The rate of completion of a two-year associate degree by age twenty-seven, however, is more similar across the two groups; the associate degree is where over 40 percent of all students in higher education now begin. At the same time, though, receiving a GED is a key means to secure financial aid eligibility for more education, as funding agencies use a GED as proof of the ability to benefit from higher education. Also, the GED has been used by youth who want to go to higher education before the age of eighteen, and American home-schoolers, of course, regularly use the degree as verification of their readiness for postsecondary education. Given the social and economic circumstances that most GED-holders come from, it is quite an accomplishment that about half of them move on to try higher education (estimates suggest that two-thirds of GED-holders have plans for more education sometime in their lives; GED Testing Service 2001).

Even if by early adulthood not many have finished the BA, they themselves know that they can pursue more education without any stigma—and perhaps with financial aid.

That the GED is a form of salvation within the schooled society is also reflected in the widespread enthusiasm for the process which greets the prospective test-taker on numerous websites. Plus, the GED articulates perfectly with the burgeoning enterprise of adult education. Illustrative of this is one adult GED recipient's reaction to passing the test:

I think that was one of the most important days of my life when I got that [GED] diploma in the mail. It was better than my wedding day, it was better than giving birth. It was, it was such an accomplishment that I've never topped before, you know, so it was a really, really good feeling. (Prins and Toso 2008; see also Snider 2009)

Even the way the GED operates as a general educational undertaking speaks to its primary role of reintegrating the individual, beyond just a technical educational certification. If the value of reentry into the schooled society were merely a matter of assessing the technical competence of minimally educated workers, one could imagine a very different process from the GED. For example, official recognition could be given to dropouts for the number of credits completed in high school, and these would be taken into the labor market as a type of partial certification. Further, a test could be used, but it would be far more vocational in nature, and scores on the test would also be taken into the labor market. Yet neither of these technically reasonable methods is employed in the American society as a way to move dropouts into the labor force.

The GED is now organized as a fully valid educational credential with all the social meaning afforded a regular high school degree, and this is even evident in the general academic nature of the test. Over the test's history its materials have remained oriented towards general academic subjects, and just like the epistemological shifts in school curricula, the test has been modified to include more cognitive material, such as problems explicitly demanding the academic intelligence skills of higher-order thinking and problem solving (Smith 2000, 2003). Test scores are not taken into the labor market or higher education; instead, the GED acts as a regular secondary school credential. This subtle but telling transformation is further reflected in the fact that the ACE continues to make the test more difficult to pass—in the 1940s, levels were set so that about 90 percent of all test-takers would pass; in recent times the cut-off point has been moved to about 70 percent.

One would expect that if the GED is truly a normative process leading the fallen individual back into the schooled society, it would be undertaken by dropouts with the most to lose by remaining in a deviant status and the most to gain from reintegrating into the educational order. This appears to be the case. As Smith (2003) describes, there has been a notable shift towards younger test-takers (ages nineteen to twenty-two) in recent decades, even though adult education continues to enroll many older students who also try to pass the GED. Further, compared to those remaining in the dropout status, those with the GED do enter better the norms of a schooled society, as they have more civic participation (Reder 1994), lower criminal recidivism rates (Nuttall, Hollmen, and Staley 2003), and a more complete internalization of social norms (Smith 2000). Perhaps most telling is that the GED-holders are more academically capable than dropouts (Cameron and Heckman 1994).

While taking the GED is just plain easier for some of these people, there has also been a marked rise in the number of people who study very hard for the test. In just nine years, from 1980 to 1989, the number of test-takers preparing one hundred hours or more doubled to about one quarter of all test-takers, a national study finds, and while the average amount of preparation is much lower, there has been a general increase in study preparation overall (Boesel, Alsalam, and Smith 1998). One hundred hours of instruction and learning in reading, it is interesting to note, is enough to advance the average high school student one grade level (Mickulecky 1990). But this is not to say that the GED directly adds massively to one's human capital—that is, learned skills; rather, it serves as an official gate to additional education and, importantly, as a way out of a deviant status, with all of the attendant positive impact on the individual (Smith 2000).

Instead of thinking about the GED as a cheap degree fooling the marginal in society, one could turn that on its head by comparing the GED to possible alternatives that could have materialized but did not. In a social order based less on formal education one could easily imagine a process by which individuals, particularly from disadvantaged groups, were relegated to permanent academic failure. In Germany, for example, a nation that is further behind the United States in fully embracing the cultural implications of the education revolution, the lowest secondary track (*Hauptschule*), ending after just the ninth grade, has a credential of low value in the labor market, and these individuals are more or less defined as permanent academic failures. Plus, there is little way for many of them to change this; not surprisingly, many children of foreign-born parents end up in the *Hauptschule*.[6] Or too, one could imagine a process by which small numbers of academically talented dropouts were identified and given special assistance to continue on educationally. Tellingly, Germany has such a small-sized program of talent-based promotion out of the *Hauptschule*.

The real stigma in the schooled society is dropping out of school, not reentering it with a GED; the GED is redemption from this negative status. Neither a dead end nor a narrow talent search, the GED is a mass program purposively made as accessible as possible (e.g., tests are regularly administered in penal institutions), and while the test may be "easier" for test-takers with more academic ability, the goal of the program is to offer a way by which as many people as possible can obtain the same secondary school credential.

It is not surprising then that the GED is heavily used by individuals in minority racial groups which have relatively high dropout rates. As Figure 9.2 illustrates, about a fifth of African Americans and Hispanics who achieve a high school diploma after completing at least their sophomore year of secondary schooling do so through the GED. The GED is also used overwhelmingly by economically disadvantaged people of all racial and ethnic groups (Smith 2000). Many social programs—Job Corp, Even Start, and programs for the homeless—aimed at the most disadvantaged in American society help individuals attain a secondary education degree through the GED.

This use of the GED as a form of mass reentry into the schooled society by disadvantaged and racial minorities is made even more notable in that the entire GED program is sponsored by the American Council of

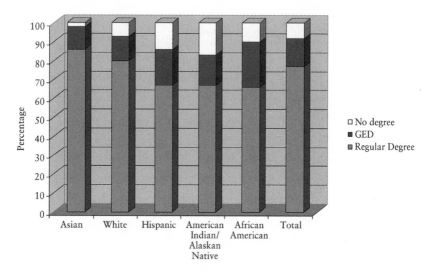

FIGURE 9.2  *Attainment of high school diploma by 1992 of national sample of*
*1980 U.S. high school sophomores, by race.*
Source: U.S. Department of Education, National Center for Education Statistics (1995)

Education, the large, venerable association of most higher education and related institutions in the United States. The ACE proudly claims to serve a *unifying voice for all of higher education*, and one part of that voice is the GED program. Not trade unions, not firms interested in training more workers, not even the secondary education system, rather American higher education is the primary organizational force behind the maintenance and revitalization of the GED. If the GED were limited to only a technical certification process, it is doubtful that the top American association of universities and colleges would have been its main supporter for the last sixty years.

After completing its original mission of enrolling many returning soldiers into higher education, the GED could have easily been discarded. What extended the program is the general institutional logic of the education revolution—to produce more potential students—and this idea fits perfectly within the democratic mission of American higher education. In fact, if one can get past the stigma the GED holds for many educational analysts (seemingly the only group in American society to hold this negative view), then the GED can be seen as an amazing societal educational accomplishment, one that could only be pulled off by the considerable institutional power of universities and colleges in the society where the education revolution is at its most advanced.

## THE EDUCATED SELF IN THE SCHOOLED SOCIETY

Predictably, with the expansion of higher education, higher education completion rates have become a public policy issue as more students are at risk of being a "higher education dropout." As sociologists of social movements would note, the dropout issue is already a well-worn "social frame," so its application to higher education leavers, and then even to graduate program leavers some time later, will be relatively rapid.[7] Right on cue, experts within the university have already started to apply the dropout frame to completion rates in higher education; widespread use of the term "college dropout" is just around the corner. Educationalists, sociologists, psychologists, and human development experts have started to herald the newest expansion of the schooled society—college and university for all—by examining the who, what, and where of BA completion rates (e.g., Grodsky and Jackson 2009; Hess, Schneider, Carey, and Kelly 2009; and see Pervin and Rubin 1967, for an earlier forecast of the issue as baby boomers enrolled in higher education).

While the completion rate of the BA among youth is only about a third of what the high school completion rate was in the mid-1960s, when the high school dropout problem was widely proclaimed, the proportion of those with high school diplomas trying higher education has soared in recent years. Now over half (57%) of all twenty-five- to twenty-nine-year-olds with a high school diploma (regular or GED) attend some amount of higher education in two-year and four-year institutions, and this has grown steadily over the past decade in the United States as well as many other nations (U.S. Department of Education, NCES 2006; Schofer and Meyer 2005). If not yet graduating, then at least attending college and university is rapidly becoming the normative model of what one does after secondary school. Interesting too, as the BA becomes more normative, the original function of the GED could weaken as the U.S. federal government makes secondary education completion rates a responsibility of the schools themselves.[8]

In a thorough review of the research on higher education completion rates, sociologists of higher education Regina Deil-Amen and Ruth López Turley (2007) document a growing flow of published major studies from a trickle of a half dozen in the mid-1980s to a steady stream of over two dozen from the mid-1990s until now; this is a similar frequency to that just prior to the emergence of the high school drop problem in the public media of the 1960s (Dorn 1996). Predictably, these studies address the characteristics of who does not finish, what factors of institutions may impede completion, and what to do about the problem. As Deil-Amen and Turley summarize, the findings are not a surprise. With one notable difference, the description of those entering and not completing the BA degree is exactly the same as the description of the high school dropouts forty years ago. Higher education students who are from minorities, students with poorer and less educated parents, and students with academic problems in high school are less likely to finish the BA as youth (although some will likely finish as adults).

Unlike the secondary school dropout phenomenon, the emerging college dropout is slightly different given the exceptional growth in two-year higher education institutions. Sociologist Kevin Dougherty (1992, 1994) finds across several studies a substantial gap of 11 to 19 percent in BA completion between community college entrants and comparable four-year college students. He goes on to list a number of qualities of the community college and its atmosphere that lower the chances of students to transfer, such as lower opportunities for social integration, difficulties obtaining financial aid, and loss of credits in transferring to four-year institutions. Just as the GED is often referred to as marginal, so too are the two-year colleges; yet like the GED, the environment of two-year institutions drips with the message that continuing on to the BA has become more essential for the individual (Fleishman and Baker 2012). Upon completing a study of high school guidance counselors' advice to students, sociologist of education James Rosenbaum (2001) describes a pervasive "college-for-all" norm communicated regardless of the student's achievement, effort, and preparedness, and this message is also widely evident in the community college itself (see also Deil-Amen and Rosenbaum 2002; Labaree 1990).

Both the GED and the expanding two-year institutions have been referred to as forms of a "cooling out" of educational ambitions. This term raises the larger, long-discussed issue in the sociology of education about whether education systems do produce such mechanisms to "cool out" individuals who are incapable of meeting rising educational norms; therefore, the topic is germane to the growth of the schooled society (e.g., Alexander, Bozick, and Entwisle 2008; Brint and Karabel 1989; Clark 1960, 1980; Deil-Amen 2006; Dougherty 1994). With the initial growth in two-year institutions, the term has come to represent several contrasting hypotheses about education and society. On one hand, for those who see education as myth, the cooling-out hypothesis suggests that the two-year institution and the GED placate those of lower socioeconomic status by giving them an educational experience that mostly shepherds them into working-class jobs and lives (e.g., Brint and Karabel 1989). But all of the conceptual and empirical problems with this social reproduction hypothesis, discussed earlier, apply here as well and need not be repeated.

On the other hand, the original hypothesis about the "cooling out" of the two-year sector's educational experience is closer to the argument here, though it requires an important addition. The late sociologist of higher education Burton Clark coined the term in 1960, not as a phony or social reproductive process but as a way to talk about the coming schooled society, its relative democratic openness to comprehensive secondary education, and possible challenges to society because of rising norms of education (see also Hammack 2004). Clark saw these as potential problems for society to solve on its way to a schooled society; he predicted that rising educational norms were here to stay and upper levels of the education system would be required to include all youth. And of course he was right; yet what he missed, but later acknowledged, is that the overeducation crisis did not materialize, because education also transformed many other institutions. The two-year sector has grown extensively and has gotten more academic and connected to the four-year over time. Thus, rising educational norms present less of a societal challenge than originally thought; further, the two-year institutions did more to extend education than to decrease it. Lastly, like the GED, these institutions have been shown to "warm up" academic ambitions among some students as much as they cool them in others (Deil-Amen 2006; Fleishman 2013).

In research and policy discussions about two-year higher education

institutions one sees the former cooling-out metaphor meeting the normative order of the schooled society head on. If the kind of encouragement
given out in these institutions is a duping cooling-out, it is of an uninten-
tional sort, and understandably, since as in all normative orders there are
difficulties for individuals who cannot conform and for education systems
themselves. As Deil-Amen and Rosenbaum (2002) also point out, faculty
in community colleges encourage even the weakest of students to attempt
to earn the BA through taking college courses at the two-year institution
and then transferring to a four-year school; yet such students are frequently
not made aware of the academic challenges they would face and the low
likelihood of completion.

Is this collective deception, aimed at reproducing social inequalities, or
is it sound advice (admittedly incomplete) based on the present realities of
the schooled society? The triumph of the academic culture has for the most
part eliminated vocational training (the narrowest form of vocationalism),
and the nature of a growing number of jobs in the United States is not one
of a stable, narrow technical vocation. Educational credentials continue
to establish their centrality in the labor market and students know this to
some degree, as a growing income return of the BA degree in American
society and elsewhere is discussed in the mass media on a regular basis.
Given the powerful logic behind greater education's potential to develop
the individual in the schooled society, it is very likely that both attendance
and completion rates of the BA will continue to rise. Along with this rise
will be a deepening crisis of the deviant college dropout—essentially a re-
play of the 1960s high school dropout.

A common complaint heard about the notion of "higher education for
all" is that not all individuals are capable of such academic accomplishment.
This, of course, was exactly the same widely voiced concern just before
high school completion became nearly universal in the 1970s—a concern
that in current discussions is either conveniently forgotten or assumed to
have gone away with instructional advances. But in fact, then as now, the
cultural logic of the schooled society is powerful enough to construct a
reality where mass schooling at each successive level wins out. There is
little to suggest that this will not continue to be the case as higher education expands worldwide. For example, widespread use of remedial courses

at most universities will now "bring students up to collegiate standards," something that occurs at the most elite institutions too. Also, the recent creation of programs of study for cognitively impaired students at some universities demonstrates the pervasiveness of the norms of mass higher education (Schmidt 2005). Much like what occurred in the case of mass secondary education, there will likely be a mutual accommodation between the masses of youth going to higher education and the institutions themselves—the point being that just like finishing secondary schooling now, a similar norm will emerge in the near future for higher education degrees.

Given all this, will the normative drive to a BA degree for all young adults generate something like the GED for higher education? Probably not in the exact form, though a similar logic and need will exist. One can easily imagine (and there is some real movement towards this already in the United States) a more standardized method of credit transfer between and among two- and four-year institutions. In fact, universities and other higher education institutions across the European Union have developed a common credit system, which was first used in the academic year 2006–2007. Also, there are already many online programs for BA completion. One can also imagine a test designed to establish earned credit towards the BA degree for learning "in life" or, more likely, for material learned through commercial tutoring companies and online courses (Davies, Quirke, and Aurini 2006). It is very likely that the institution of higher education, in the midst of its ongoing expansion of *post*baccalaureate education, will be the coordinator and sponsor of such a process (e.g., González 2012).

The dropout and the GED illustrate theoretically how formal education constructs the social order of the schooled society and thus has a major impact on perceptions of the normal process towards a functioning self. The perspective advanced here solves three commonly observed paradoxes about educational expansion and school-leavers. First, it is now clear why the dropout problem never goes away even in the face of continued swift growth in schooling throughout the population: the dropout as a social issue is the clarification (as deviance) of the expanding moral order of normative formal education for all. Second, it also becomes clear why even though schooling demands ever more academic sophistication on the part of students, the mildly challenging GED (and likely future mechanisms for higher education dropouts) only grows in legitimacy: the GED is an education-based way back into the moral order. And finally, one can start to appreciate why formal education becomes society's source for solutions to the non-educational problems of individuals (e.g., violence, sexual problems, irresponsible parenting, drug addition): in a schooled social order the ameliorative intervention that is thought to be the most effective is an ever-elaborated application of the educational model of enhanced human development.

### CHAPTER 10

# An Educated Polity

## The Universal Solvent and the Political Paradox

The educated man is a different political actor from the uneducated man.

GABRIEL ALMOND AND SIDNEY VERBA, *The Civic Culture*, 1963

The numbers drive the dollars.

OLD WASHINGTON, D.C., ADAGE about how governmental funding follows technical analysis of population change; quoted by Republican Representative Thomas Sawyer of Ohio in 1993, who subsequently lost the 2006 election because of Democratic redistricting driven by census data (Wright 1994)

AS IN SO MUCH OF LIFE in postindustrial society, education is the single most determining factor in an individual's political motivation, capability, and proclivity to undertake civic involvement. Starting from the earliest systematic empirical studies of political behavior in democracies over sixty years ago and continuing up to current research, education is consistently reported as a powerful influence on a person's political competence and involvement (e.g., Lazarfeld, Berelson, and Gaudet 1944; Almond and Verba 1963; Nie, Junn, and Stehlik-Barry 1996). Not only is educational attainment far and away more salient than any other demographic characteristic of an individual; its effect is also larger than the impact of growing up in nations with radically different political cultures and heritages (Wiseman, Astiz, Fabrega, and Baker 2011). The association between formal education and all things political about individuals is so consistently found in studies that education has long been referred to as the "universal solvent," meaning in a double sense that education weakens old patterns of political behavior in unschooled, traditional society, and that it also weakens the effects of non-educational characteristics on the political qualities of modern individuals (Converse 1972). As powerful as education's effect on politics has been, the relationship turns out to be far more complex, and to have unexpected outcomes.

## THE EDUCATION-DEMOCRACY PARADOX

As the education revolution was beginning to intensify, just before the middle of the twentieth century, political scientists were finding ever more evidence of the association between education and political behavior, and they attempted to predict what would happen with educated polities in the world's emerging constitutional democracies. Paradoxically, these extrapolations from trends among individuals to society-wide politics proved markedly wrong. Though compared to less-educated individuals the educated were, and still are, more politically oriented, societal levels of voting, expressions of patriotic nationalism, and other traditional citizenship activities and attitudes have remained stagnant or have even declined with rising educational attainment across nations. Since the 1960s, formal democracy has been "downsized" in the sense of less participation in political parties at the national level in the United States and elsewhere (Crenson and Ginsberg 2004; Kamens 2009); there are many observations that a majority of the working class and lower-middle classes have seceded from American politics and public life (e.g., Brody 1978; Burnham 1984; Luttbeg 1984; Ladd 1978, 1979; Piven and Cloward 1988; G. B. Powell 1986; Teixeira and Rogers 2000; Wolfinger and Rosenstone 1980); and fewer Americans report "feeling at home" in the polarized politics of the post-1960s era (e.g., DiMaggio, Evans, and Bryson 1996; Lane 2001; Teixeira 1990). These trends create the widely discussed education-democracy paradox: *As the universal solvent of education is so powerful among individuals, why has this not led to more collective traditional citizenry in democracies?*

For the most part, prior attempts to solve the paradox have asked why educated individuals do not actively engage more in traditional citizenship roles. In a book devoted to the subject, political scientists Norman Nie, Jane Junn, and Kenneth Stehlik-Barry start from the common assumption that "aggregate levels of education can change, but the number and rank of seats in *the political theater are fixed*" (1996, 100, emphasis added). This is how prior scholarship on education and politics imagines it—a changed individual held up against a more or less constant political norm of citizenship in democratic society. Not surprisingly, at the core of this image is the traditional model of education and society; hence, the authors' suggested solution to the paradox is that the education effect occurs mostly as a zero-sum competition: as educational attainment expands, membership among the politically engaged elite and their networks shifts upward to higher levels of education, and those of the masses who attain what were formerly elite levels of education will nevertheless continue to act as less-politicized non-elites. But there are a number of problems with this thesis, not least of which is the overwhelming research indicating that absolute levels of education have consistent influences on educated individuals which leave them anything but less politicized. Also, it fails to explain why the educated are less involved in traditional citizenry, or what has caused the rise in a new and intensified type of collective political action, described below. The schooled society perspective on education and society suggests that the way to solve the paradox is to ask what an educated polity does to the dimensions of politics in the postindustrial society. Contrary to Nie and colleagues' imagery, recent research on education as a primary institution shows that as a polity becomes more educated, *it tears down the old political theater and erects an entirely different one in its place.*

In their comprehensive review of over four thousand studies completed across three decades of research on the effects of American higher education (college and university attendance and degree completion) on individuals, higher education researchers Ernest Pascarella and Patrick Terenzini document a wide array of educational influences related to politics (2005).[1] Of course some of the reviewed research verifies what others have found in terms of the education-democracy paradox in the United States. Compared to its other influences, higher education's association with increased likelihood to vote is modest; however, as often noted, voting provides only a limited opportunity to participate in politics. So too, there is not much evidence that higher education radicalizes the large majority of students towards either left or right partisanship and party affiliation, although there is recent evidence that higher cognitive achievement is associated with more-progressive attitudes and greater trust in the political process, though not in political authority (e.g., Astin 1993; Schoon et al. 2010).

What is often overlooked, however, is the ample evidence of "hyper–

civic involvement" that results from higher education. Individuals are not necessarily made more liberal or conservative by the university experience; instead, they acquire many cognitive abilities and attitudes that enable them to become involved in a broad way with community and political issues, regardless of their overall ideological orientation. As Pascarella and Terenzini's complete review convincingly demonstrates, a large volume of research conveys that university students, compared to less-educated young adults, are more willing to be "publicly active," more able to challenge traditional political positions, and more committed to influencing social values and the makeup of the political structure. Also, attending college or university substantially enhances individuals' academic intelligence and general cognitive abilities to think through abstract organizational strategies for political change; and it increases their specific political knowledge about who holds offices, governmental roles, and constitutional principles (e.g., Dalton 2008; Emler and Frazer 1999; Fiske, Lau, and Smith 1990).

There are many indicators of education's contribution to the skills necessary for effective civic and community involvement. For example, one reviewed study reports that individuals with a BA are 30 percent more likely to volunteer for a community service group than individuals with no postsecondary education (Kuh et al. 2001). Crucially, there is evidence that a university experience tends to instill a greater sense of "empowerment and social efficacy"; thus, educated individuals are more likely to be of the opinion that they can make a difference in their community and beyond (e.g., Sax and Astin and Sax 1998). Related to this is the effect of greater education on instituting a worldview of doubt or skepticism, which is bound up in a general reflexivity stemming from the student's exposure to scientific methods and authoritative knowledge production of the university (Giddens 1991).[2] The educated are open to this worldview, one aspect of which is having less trust in established political authority, and hence a willingness to question authority openly. Lastly, individuals with a higher education are more likely to have greater social capital in terms of network density and quality, which can be turned into political resources and stimulate political actions (Emler and Frazer 1999).

All of this research leads to the speculation that an educated citizenry actually changes politics and transforms fundamental dimensions of citizenship, nationally and globally. For example, it can be argued that much of the impetus and planning for the Arab Spring of 2011 was a result of widespread importation of modern education development into these populations over the past twenty years. Apparently, the repressive regimes of the region were more aware of the human capital benefits of education than they were of threats to their survival from an educated polity.

The exact hypothesis outlined here has been developed and tested by David Kamens, a neo-institutional sociologist interested in the intersection between education and politics. His study of the consequences of expanding university education on politics in postindustrial society is fully compatible with the evidence of educational effects on individuals, and although most of his examples are American, his research findings are easily applied worldwide. Kamens argues that the schooled society expands and mobilizes the polity in many directions not experienced in traditional society:

Expanding higher education creates an expanded and mobilized polity in democratic societies. The result is high levels of political action outside the boundaries of the conventional political system. . . . The end result is a more inclusive political system and a more highly mobilized society, *all turbo charged by rampant individual empowerment*. (2009, 99–100, emphasis added)

His study goes on to illustrate an association between the effects of an educated polity and the nature of politics in the twenty-first century, which is made up of two significant new developments. The first is the expansion of the polity itself in the sense of increasing societal capacity for more, and more complex, collective action. Social movements, including advocacy organizations and professional social movement organizations, with their now elaborate organizational and political tactics, occur frequently in postindustrial society (e.g., Minkoff and McCarthy 2005; Schofer and Longhofer 2011; Walker 1991). The nature of politics enacted through social movement tactics has become more technocratic, often based on methods and assumptions found in social sciences, and thus reinforces a greater affinity between the effects of higher education and political action (e.g., Dobbin and Kelly 2007; McAdam 1982). Much like the expansion of formal organizations for the educational transformation of work, described earlier, millions of university-educated individuals worldwide possess tremendous capacity for generating and sustaining sophisticated social movements that can cause profound political transformations (Smith and Wiest 2012). The second development is that this greater capacity for politicized collective action is aimed at ever more topics; innumerable aspects of life become politicized, much as they have become (and because they have become) incorporated into the university's knowledge conglomerate.

A good example of both qualities of the new educated politics is the politicization of sexual identity. Although governments have always regulated some manifest aspects of sex, from a public perspective perhaps nothing is more nonpolitical than sexual activity. But since the 1970s a robust and growing wave of global social movements has aimed at politicizing this most intimate side of everyday life. This is succinctly illustrated by a call to political action by the new "sexual citizen":

The sexual citizen could be male or female, young or old, black or white, rich or poor, straight or gay: could be anyone in fact, but for one key characteristic. The sexual citizen exists because of the new primacy given to sexual subjectivity in the contemporary world . . . this *new personage is a harbinger of a new politics of intimacy and everyday life.* (Weeks 1999, 35, emphasis added)

"A new politics of intimacy and everyday life" is witnessed in countless political actions worldwide aimed at the rights, issues, and public recognition of the now public *and* political statuses of lesbian, gay, bisexual, transgendered, questioning, and allied citizens, or "LGBTQA" in the parlance of American campus student groups assisting in politicizing sexual passions and affinities. And, of course, as the list suggests, sexually politicized interest groups can expand effortlessly. Sometimes, too, one politicized topic merges with another, forming particularly supercharged political and social action. For example, sexual-identity politics mixes potently with the politics of AIDS treatment. Also, and predictable from the research review of Pascarella and Terenzini, traditionally left or right political parties do not fully capture sexual politics, as groups and movements have come from a range of overarching ideologies and even mix more conventional ideologies within one sexual-identity movement (Bell and Binnie 2000). While sexual-identity politics at times intersects with conventional party politics, it is very much an independent political phenomenon. A few of the many other examples of the politicizing of traditionally nonpolitical areas of life are people's relationship to the natural environment (Longhofer and Schofer 2010), to animals (Jepperson and Meyer 2007), and to the rights of children (Suárez 2007).

The education revolution has played a major part in the formation of this new, endlessly expandable polity supported by extensive capacity within the population to undertake political actions. This occurs through the symbiotic effects among the parts of the education revolution already described in earlier chapters. Therefore, in contrast to how the education-democracy paradox would have it, the educated generation does not lack interest or motivation to take political action; instead, it is considerably more capable and inclined to be political about ever more aspects of life than were former, less-educated generations. However, the new generation does this in less conventional ways, which are often misperceived as apolitical, or even antipolitical. A world awash in nontraditional civic mobilization and group formation at every level of civil society is precisely in parallel to the influence of higher education on the political behavior and capabilities of individuals, which Pascarella and Terenzini's massive review documents. In all likelihood there is no education-democracy paradox; instead, mass enrollment in advanced education, the "universal solvent," is also an intensified meta-solvent, which on the collective level transforms politics itself.

## POLITICS IN THE SCHOOLED SOCIETY

Kamens reassesses the key trends in American political life in light of the interaction of individual and collective effects of education. As he notes, these trends are frequently publicly bemoaned as disturbing and dangerously antipolitical, and all are assumed to be the consequence of a politically disengaged generation. Whether these trends are in fact a civic problem is up for debate, but what is clear is that they are *not caused* by a lack of political mobilization; rather, they are likely caused in large part by the new, turbo-charged politics of the schooled society.

The first trend is the high frequency of polarized and contentious public debates in contemporary developed societies, including more discourse about global and abstract topics such as environmentalism, economic globalization, and human rights (e.g., PEW Research Center for People and the Press 2004a, 2004b; Saunders and Abramovitz 2003). If education expands the polity in both individual capacity and incorporation of more topics, it is logical that it would also expand public discourse. As noted, education does not necessarily make for a more conservative or liberal populace, but it does raise political capacity for all ideologies to the degree that extensive collective action from various sides of an issue can be mounted—so much so that contentiousness is ever more present in public discourse. The constant rise of more-sophisticated media technologies is often given credit for this trend, but to a large extent it is the educated political professionals behind the use of mass media technology plus the news demands of increasingly educated audiences that deserve the credit. Also, the curricular and scholarly content of the education revolution increasingly invites the educated to be empowered members of the world, to think more abstractly and less narrowly, and to be open to universalization of all kinds of social problems solvable through human action. With this educated sensibility spread across ever larger proportions of populations, all varieties of global issues can stir political action, even those unrelated to actual local problems.

The second frequently observed trend is the erosion of conventional participation in formal democracy, such as voting, political party membership, and union membership (e.g., Crenson and Ginsberg 2004; Reich 1994; Skocpol 1997). An educated polity is made up of individuals who see themselves as having the right and entitlement to pick and choose issues relevant to their own interests, salient identities, and personalities; they feel empowered to act on these, often at the expense of participation in conventional, formal party politics (Frank and Meyer 2002; Judd and Downing 1990). Other research points to the twin effects of advanced education leading to less reverence for external authority and greater independence of thought (e.g., Kohn and Schooler 1969; Meier 1982). Illustrative of this is an innovative cross-national study that finds an association between national cultures that are based on individualism and the rise and growth of professionalized (read academic) psychology (Frank, Meyer, and Miyahara 1995). Nations that have had a longer history of political elites who support an ideology of economic and social gain through scientifically guided progress tend to develop deeper cultures of professional psychology resting on the notion of the individual as the principal actor in society.

In the schooled society, a culture of individualized-identity political mobilization supplants conventional politics: formal citizenship defined by conventional participation downsizes, while a broader capacity for collective, issue-based, political mobilization occurs throughout society. In undertaking an extensive cross-national analysis of factors that encourage the formation of formal, nongovernmental, voluntary associations, Schofer and Longhofer (2011) find that, accounting for wealth and other characteristics, the higher the overall level of education in a nation, the more associations were created, from 1970 to 2006. As widely noted, a high density of voluntary associations feeds directly into politicized social movements influencing national politics and policy making (e.g., Minkoff, Aisenbrey, and Agnone 2008; Minkoff and McCarthy 2005; Skocpol 2003; Reger and Staggenborg 2006).

The third trend is the much discussed decline of the nation-state as the singularly supreme political entity. Overt nationalism is receding and with it the public's belief in the nation-state's ability to achieve social and economic progress. The political right panics at the former, while the left is bewildered by the latter (Fourcade 2006; Fourcade-Gourinchas and Babb 2002; Pierson and Skocpol 2007). But again, both parts of this process likely have their origin in the influence of an educated polity.

For example, the author and colleagues completed an analysis of a survey of secondary school students' political and civic knowledge and engagement in twenty-seven nations (Wiseman, Astiz, Fabrega, and Baker 2011). Compared to results of studies done several decades ago, among these students nationalistic ideals and sentiments have fallen, and they have fallen the farthest among the most academically accomplished. As expected, more academically accomplished students participating in civic education show evidence of increased capacity to engage in collective action; plus, they are more likely to hold positive attitudes about civic involvement for issues beyond nation-states, such as universal human rights, the global environment, and gender equality (e.g., OECD 2009b). There is evidence of a generalized world polity forming among these students—one that is shaped by formal education rather than being a product of unique national political histories. Therefore, although educational achievement is associated with students' support for democratic processes, with their political knowledge, and with their civic attitudes, ideas, proclivity to act, and behaviors, there is little variation among students from different nations on these things even though the study compared students from Western democracies and many former Eastern Bloc nations, where historical experience with democratic traditions are weak. In other words, educated students are similar in their readiness for political mobilization regardless of the nation they live in (Castillo 2013). Related to this point are the detailed historical studies of the messages communicated through university and school curricula about the geopolitical world, which were described earlier in the educational transformation of knowledge (see also Sobe 2011).

Also, this trend presents some irony given the original role of the nation-state in mass education. In the nineteenth century and early parts of the twentieth, during the development of constitutional democracies in Western Europe and North America, basic mass education played an important role in support of the nation-state (Ramirez and Boli 1987). And of course, the strengthening democratic state became the main funder and political supporter of mass education (Fuller and Rubinson 1992). But the education revolution has expanded the scope of this process from national to global, a predictable outcome in light of the global dimensions and content of education.

The fourth trend is the political demobilization of some segments of populations (Brody 1978; Crenson and Ginsberg 2004; Nie, Junn, and Stehlik-Barry 1996; D. Powell 1986; Skocpol 2003; Wuthnow 2002). What is telling about this trend is that it is most intense among the less educated, creating a rising gap in civic mobilization by education level. If the intensified politics of the schooled society rests on advanced capabilities, attitudes, and empowerment derived through education, then people having less of these are more likely to find themselves alienated from the new politics generated by an educated polity. So too, political movements such as the Tea Party in the United States and anger in Europe over the European Union project can be seen as reactions of the less educated (organized, of course, by small numbers of the highly educated) against the privileges and political sensibilities of the more educated (Cahn and Carbone 2010; Fligstein 2008). The reverse trend is also evident: an expanding educated polity becomes a political ally of further dimensions of the education revolution. A good illustration of this comes from the Eastern Bloc in the late 1970s. In reaction to a rising politically astute educated generation advocating still more education for its children, the old revolutionary guard in communist Eastern Europe put into place draconian policies to cut back on rapidly expanding higher education enrollments; this in turn caused a backlash among educated citizens, which contributed significantly to the growing crisis of legitimacy in regimes and to their eventual downfall two decades later (Baker, Köhler, and Stock 2007; Reisz and Stock 2007).

## THE FUTURE OF EDUCATED POLITICS

The evidence here suggests that the education revolution has played a significant role in shaping the ongoing democratic revolution. The institution's leveraging of human capabilities has expanded politics in a number of surprising directions, and the penetrating culture of education has changed ideas and values about politics. Both of these processes will likely continue into the future. While it is clear that the education revolution has an impact on individuals' political and civic capacity, its impact on the nature of politics is less obvious and merits additional speculation.

What will likely continue into the near future is the intense synergy among the expanding knowledge conglomerate of the university, sophisticated flexible social movements, and politicization of ever more aspects of life. Reflected in the words of former representative Thomas Sawyer (see epigraph), the exportation of tools and ideas from social and behavioral sciences into political strategies and policy making is a result of an affinity between the university-generated ideas of a socially progressive, humanly constructed, and scientifically studied society and a parallel logic in democratic polities. It is not just that social and behavioral sciences offer tactical tools for the new politics; more fundamental are the similar cultural assumptions behind both. The charter of the university to study (and scientize) everything spills over into the mass democratic political arena and reinforces the latter's tendency to politicize everything. At the same time, the social movement as political strategy wins out over more inflexible political structures, such as political parties, because movements are well suited to an environment of expanding politicization; plus, they can rapidly organize around social frames that stem from the university's charter, mobilize growing numbers of educated citizens, and harness their capacity in this type of political action. It is likely that digitally supported forms of "liquid-democratic" political movements popping up in national societies is a function of high rates of advanced education across populations.[3] This process is further supported by the expectations and understandings that an increasingly educated public brings to politics. This three-way symbiosis among the university knowledge conglomerate, the flexible social movement, and the politicization of everyday life makes for interesting speculation on how far the current political environment will intensify into the future. As distasteful as some find these current trends in politics, they are likely here to stay.

Consider one last example of the power of the university to shape the frames upon which life is politicized through social movements. Over four tragic days in 1952 heavy coal smog trapped by an inversion layer of cold air rapidly killed an estimated four thousand Londoners; over eight thousand more were to die in the ensuing weeks. At the time, this major signal about society's use of natural resources was seen mostly as an episodic problem. The British Parliament did enact the Clean Air Act in 1956, but nevertheless, the implications were not anything like they would be today with the existence of what might be called the global environmental ideology (a now standard frame for action) and its parallel social and political mobilization (e.g., the green movement). David Frank's insightful historical analysis shows that the global politicization of the natural environment stemmed from a shifting conception of human society and its relationship to nature: from one of separateness and opposition in the nineteenth century, to a vision of exploitable resources, to the more recent scientized version of an ecosystem in which humans and the environment are interdependent (1997). Along with this ideology, the university defined and produced authoritative knowledge, which was enacted by a cadre of geoscientists and related scholars. The whole process was ripe for politicization. Frank goes on to find that this redefinition of nature and human society by university-fueled scientific associations was a key factor in the greater politicization of environmental issues that has now spread globally through social movements, mobilized political actions, and formal state reactions (e.g., Frank, Hironaka, and Schofer 2000; Long-hofer and Schofer 2010). As expected, this reconception and its pairing with political action is distributed as a commonly accepted phenomenon to the next generation of students through primary and secondary educa-tion (Pizmony-Levy 2011).

Skeptics of this argument will no doubt reply that environmentalism only became a worldwide issue when science produced an understanding through some natural progression of knowledge. Yet this misses the larger picture of the university as a constructor of knowledge. It also assumes a natural progress of truth and knowledge that is disembodied from social institutions, a notion that has run into much philosophical and sociologi-cal criticism (e.g., Young 2008). This is not to argue for an overly relative notion of truth, as there are many examples of older knowledge replaced by newer (and by implication "truer") knowledge. The point is that the deepening charter of the university in society heavily influences this whole process, including what becomes politicized.

The argument here does not assume that mass education is the only cause of change in politics in postindustrial society. Across nations there are certainly a number of other contributing factors. For example, in the United States, behind some of the trends noted earlier are too the struc-tural, constitutionally specified articulation among branches of government, which can increase political conflict and frustration within the polity (e.g., when a sitting president from one party and a majority in the legislature from another party are locked in a stalemate) (Linz 1990). But as with other consequences of the education revolution, the point is not that edu-cation becomes a singular cause; rather, it becomes a *major* cause of the transformation of many institutions composing society. Future research could explore how various political structures might intensify or mediate the educational effects described here.

The universal solvent of education has occurred in politics, but its broad transforming qualities have been misperceived. Instead of what was once predicted to evolve into an orderly, rationalized, conventional political life, the schooled society creates a passionate and supercharged civic culture having much the opposite qualities. Consequently, in place of the last century's large ideological battles between, say, fascism and communism, today smaller ideological differences are scattered across a wide array of issues and fought over with increased political mobilization, competence, and intensity. To the degree that a decline in monumental ideological battles represents a kind of "end of history," an argument can be made that the education revolution has played a major role (Fukuyama 1992). Yet at the same time, the coming of the schooled society has ensured that the end of expanding politics is nowhere in sight.

### CHAPTER 11

# An Educated Laity

## The Education-Religion Paradox

I believe in an America where the separation of church and state is absolute; where no Catholic prelate would tell the President—should he be Catholic—how to act, and no Protestant minister would tell his parishioners for whom to vote.

Presidential candidate and Roman Catholic JOHN F. KENNEDY,
Address to the Greater Houston Ministerial Association, September 12, 1960

IF ANYTHING IS ASSUMED to be antithetical to a deeply educated society, it is widespread belief in religion. Yet if the United States can be considered an originator and sustainer of the schooled society, then the opposite is true. American society is among the most churched and religious of developed nations in the world, and it has gotten more so over the course of the education revolution. At the beginning of the American Revolution in 1775 only 17 percent of the total population adhered to a religion, but by the end of the twentieth century church membership had grown to 60 percent and a full 95 percent of Americans claimed to believe in a God (Finke and Stark 1992; Froese and Bader 2008). There is no evidence of a decline of either education or religion in sight (Greeley 2001). Like the education-democracy paradox, the demographic expansion of both education and religion in the United States presents an interesting paradox with which to consider the impact of the schooled society on religion.

### THE EDUCATION-RELIGION PARADOX

The education-religion paradox is different from that of education and democracy because education, particularly in advanced forms, was for many reasons assumed to eliminate adherence to religion in postindustrial society. As described earlier, the major epistemological revolution brought about by the university over the eighteenth and nineteenth centuries was the far-reaching idea that society is humanly constructed and that knowledge about it can be accumulated by empirical scientific inquiry without any reference to deistic influence (Frank and Gabler 2006; Shermer 2002; Watson 2010). As one of the most influential originators of this epistemology, Karl Marx, stated, "The criticism of religion ends with the precept that the Supreme Being for man is man" (as quoted in Bell 1977, 421). Similarly, other university-based, founding social theorists such as Max Weber and Émile Durkheim predicted that religion would decline as a function of the rise of the ideas promulgated by the Western university. By this logic, the role of the university in the initiation of the education revolution makes it the most secular and secularizing of institutions; even when there is direct religious administrative control within modern universities, the reigning scientific worldview is usually at the core of the curriculum (Cherry, DeBerg, and Porterfield 2001).

Coinciding as it did with the birth and rise of the social sciences, the hypothesis that religious authority declines as education spreads became habitually assumed to be true. Religious authority in postindustrial society has in fact declined, or at least it must share the stage with science, secular political states, and many other nonreligious authorities, including educational ones (e.g., Chaves 1994). For example, note in the epigraph the lengths to which John Kennedy went in 1960 to promote a secular limit on papal authority (much to the displeasure of the Roman Catholic establishment at the time), as well as publicly challenging Protestant, anti-Catholic tendencies deeply rooted in American institutions. But though this process of desacralization—removing religious authority from other social institutions—is a major feature of postindustrial society, religion lives on and even thrives in the schooled society; hence, the education-religion paradox.

Given the worldwide extent of the education revolution, it is remarkable how incorrect the hypothesis was that mass schooling would cause religion to decline within populations. This incorrect prediction was based on the presumption that two things would happen in heavily schooled societies. One, well-established mainline religions would decline in membership; and two, small ephemeral cults and sects would spring up, and die off as quickly. Eventually, the argument reasoned, these two processes would bring forth a fully secular society, where religion, if it survived at all, would remain on the outer margins. Instead, much the opposite occurred in the United States and in many other nations.

In *The Churching of America, 1776–1990*, the seminal sociological study of the rise, fall, and rebirth of American religious denominations, sociologists of religion Roger Finke and Rodney Stark (1992) find a historical repetition of a common life cycle of organized religions: spiritual groups start as small, upstart sects before the more successful of them become established churches, which in some instances become massive "mainline" denominations. In most cases, after a peak in membership and popularity, mainline denominations go into an extended period of significant decline, while other churches, in earlier stages of their life cycle, rise to surpass them. Also, certain splinters of established denominations may revitalize as sects again. Finke and Stark argue that this churning at the heart of what they liken to a religious market offers individuals many spiritual options among many religious organizations competing for their membership. This dynamic is the likely cause of the historical growth in the proportion of Americans joining religious organizations. In the absence of governmental prohibition on the founding of churches, literally thousands of sects, unaffiliated churches, and spiritual congregations now operate in the United States, offering all kinds of religious theologies. Of course, many of these die as small ephemera, but others rapidly replace them, and some will grow into megachurches, large spiritual movements, or even fully established denominational religions (Stark and Bainbridge 1985).

Continual, overlapping cycles of *birth, growth, decline, and revitalization* is the opposite of what many intellectuals predicted would happen as education expanded. But the historical record of religion in the United States strongly supports what Finke and Stark hypothesize. For example, by the middle of the nineteenth century, the membership of the colonial upstart sects of Baptists and Methodists eclipsed the founding denominations of Congregationalists (originally the Puritans), Episcopalians, and Presbyterians. Another example is the late-nineteenth-century upstart sect of the African American Pentecostal Church of God in Christ, which has grown to now twice the size of the large American Baptist denomination. The same organizational life cycle occurs for non-Christian religions as well. Currently, there are about 1,500 established denominations in the United States, about twenty-five of which have over one million members; all are supported by billions of dollars in annual donations and volunteer involvement (Melton 1989). In parallel with the course of the American education revolution, Finke and Stark paint a picture of a growing, vibrant religious culture, which many intellectuals had predicted could never occur in advanced, postindustrial, highly educated societies.

## SOLVING THE EDUCATION-RELIGION PARADOX

The central challenge to solving the education-religion paradox is to explain how powerful but contradictory ideas about central aspects of life can coexist. Perhaps the main reason that modern education and religion are frequently thought to be incompatible is because the education revolution teaches a worldview based on science, rationality, and the human construction of society, while religion is based in revelation, faith, and the existence of a supernatural being. Fundamentally, religions are sets of ideas, and if nonreligious ideas about the same phenomena take on powerful meanings in society they may devalue the religious ones. Since the highly educated are more exposed to secular ideologies than the less educated, they should be the most likely to turn away from religion; thus, as society is populated with ever more highly educated people, religion will supposedly die out. Yet education, with its ideas about rational inquiry and humanly constructed societies, and religion, with its ideas about the supernatural in human life, increasingly coexist.

Simply stated, the education-religion paradox results from a miscalculation of what mass education means for religion in postindustrial society. Contrary to the topics analyzed in other chapters, the problem behind this paradox is not an overreliance on the traditional model of education as a secondary institution, but is ironically a miscalculation of the effects of education as a primary, robust institution. It is obvious why intellectuals predicted that education would cause religious decline, and certainly as an institution education has played a significant role in supplying the ideas for the desacralization of other social institutions. But what is emerging from sophisticated research is that education does not end religion; rather, it changes beliefs in a direction compatible with some of the central ideas of the education revolution. Importantly, a case can be made that the education revolution actually increases the potential for new types of religious organizations to flourish.

As noted before, almost all Americans believe in a God, but what is telling is the difference in the qualities of God across individuals with different
amounts of education. Sociologists of religion Paul Froese and Christopher
Bader's extensive study of Americans' images of their God shows this clearly
(2010). Compared to the less educated, those with at least a BA degree are
twice as likely to believe in a "distant God," who is more abstract, cosmic,
sexless, mysterious, and forgiving of human weakness. At the other end
of the spectrum, individuals with a high school degree or less are twice as
likely to believe in an animated "authoritarian God," who is perceived to
be a strict, father-like, supernatural being, concrete, active, and wrathful.

What the Froese and Bader study additionally reveals about the coexistence of ideas from the education revolution and religion is that about
one half of educated individuals believe in a God who is thought to have
started the universe yet is mostly, if not entirely, inactive in everyday affairs. At the same time, a sizable majority of the less educated worship a
God who is perceived to be minutely active in everyday affairs, who can
directly intervene in individuals' lives, and who will even cause bad things
to get the attention of humans. For those who believe in a mostly inactive God, the central secular idea promoted by the education revolution
that society is humanly constructed presents little contradiction. So too,
the idea that science is a rational method to understand the world (God's
world included, as was the case in early universities) is also not hard to
accept by believers of a relatively inactive God; unexplained things need
not be considered supernatural acts, because for these educated believers
such occurrences will eventually be explained by rational, scientific inquiry.
Indeed, although there is some recent evidence to the contrary, American
scientists are about as religious as their similarly educated counterparts;
and while there are more atheists among social scientists, the latter are not
as a whole unreligious even though their intellectual enterprise squarely
rests on the assumption of a humanly constructed society (Ecklund, Park,
and Veliz 2008; Stark and Finke 2000).

Many educated individuals believe in a God that on the one hand is
supernatural, and the creator of a moral code for life, but on the other
hand tends to have fewer qualities that present major contradictions around
core secular ideas about society. Conversely, the God of many of the less

educated is mostly incompatible with the ideology of the schooled society. Hence, the less educated are also more likely to believe in the existence of paranormal phenomena, which have little or no basis in science (Bader, Mencken, and Baker 2010).

Sociologist of religion Philip Schwadel has completed the most extensive studies of the influence of education on American Christianity. His analysis of the beliefs and religious behaviors of large, nationally representative samples of American Christians fully corroborates the findings about educated individuals' images of God (2011, 2003). By substantial amounts, college- and postgraduate-educated Christians are less likely to hold beliefs that contradict culturally verified reality in that they tend *not* to believe that the Bible is the literal and true word of God, that an individual can be possessed by the Devil, or that the biblical account of the origins of human life is literally correct. Also, he finds that the long-noted trend of higher education leading to disaffiliation from organized religion has in recent decades reversed. Again, this evidence suggests that advanced education does not wipe out religious belief, but it probably reshapes it in a form that is compatible with central secular ideas of postindustrial society.

It should be noted that neither the Schwadel nor the Froese and Bader studies followed subjects over their life, so one cannot know for sure whether more education leads to belief in a more abstract, inactive God, or whether belief in this kind of God leads to more education. But as argued generally throughout this book, it is likely that education is the driver. This argument is supported by Pascarella and Terenzini's survey of research on the effects of college attendance on religiousness (2005). They reviewed studies that followed large samples of students over their time at college, and all studies reported that the higher education experience does *not* lead to abandonment of religion, but rather leads to a strengthening of the level of precollege spirituality (e.g., Graham and Donaldson 1996; Lee 2002). At the same time, the college experience does lead religious individuals to less trust in religious authority, less conformity to traditional denominations, and greater refinement of individual religious values. All of these are brought by an educated laity to the expanding number of churches unaffiliated with established denominational hierarchies (see also Hout and Fischer 2002).

Another good indicator that education and religion can exist together is that when Americans are asked why they might doubt their religion, traditional reasons, such as evidence of evil and suffering in the world and personal tragedies, are often listed, while science and secular ideas about the human construction of society are only infrequently cited (Smith 1998). Even among the 5 to 10 percent of Americans who claim no religious connection, most are not irreligious, as they often pray and believe in a supernatural being (Stark and Finke 2000).

In the heavily churched, heavily schooled American society, it is not atheism that the educated turn to. In fact, while the most educated are more likely to be atheistic, atheists account for only about 5 percent of all the college- and university-educated. Instead, the educated worship a God that is in many ways compatible, or at least not very contradictory, with the ideas of postindustrial society that have been shaped so profoundly and spread so widely by the education revolution. As many sociologists of religion persuasively argue, belief in a supernatural being does not preclude effective participation in a rationalized world (e.g., Stark and Finke 2000). Most people are able to keep belief in a supernatural being and belief in a humanly constructed society separate enough to avoid disruptive spiritual dissonance in their lives. Education is not necessarily a barrier to the idea of a supernatural being; instead, the image of God is changed in the schooled society. And such change should not be construed as a degradation of religious theology—in fact, an educated laity and what it believes do much to strengthen religion in the postindustrial culture.

### EDUCATED LAITY
### AND A ROBUST RELIGIOUS CULTURE

Ruling out the assumption that education and religion are mutually exclusive clears the way to appreciate a number of advantages that a culture of education and an educated laity bring to a rich religious culture, at least in the United States and perhaps many other places as well. The first advantage is that the greater participatory nature of more-educated individuals applies to their religious behavior. For example, Schwadel finds that higher-educated Christians are more likely to participate in the organized activities of their churches, including religious services (2003).

This trend is found even after holding constant many other characteristics of individuals, such as gender and financial resources. Schwadel's data on Christians, as well as studies of non-Christians, persuasively show that the very same skills and motivation driving greater civic participation, such as public speaking, proclivity to challenge authority, ability to organize people and resources, autonomy of action, and self-efficacy, all described in the preceding chapter, also make educated individuals, on average, more effective members of religious organizations (Stark and Finke 2000). And this is the case even though the educated are less likely to agree with all the tenets of a particular religion (Finke 2003). Therefore, in the United States the education revolution has directly propelled the churning religious market. Because new sects and religions can be easily started, entrepreneurship and many other skills and attitudes acquired from advanced education are rewarded in the competition for survival of sects. An educated laity and clergy are better equipped to organize and mobilize religious groups.

A second advantage of an educated society for religion flows from ideas that are injected by the education revolution into society at large. Sociologists of religion now have evidence that the main reason for the decline of mainline denominations in postindustrial society is that they weakened core spiritual messages yet rigidly preserved traditional (pre-modern) approaches to church management and recruitment. In contrast, the most successful segments of the American religious market have taken the opposite selective accommodation to a desacralized society; namely, adopting and innovating modern organizational approaches while preserving core messages (Finke 2003).[1] Some examples of how an educated laity and clergy have used ideas growing out of the education revolution to enhance the American religious culture illustrate the positive impact of education on religion.

The first example is the phenomenal growth of Christian churches unaffiliated with established denominations. These are known as independent churches, and there are now over 1,200 of them with an average weekly service attendance of at least 2,000, which as a whole are fulfilling the spiritual needs of millions of Americans. A number of these have developed into megachurches averaging over 35,000 in weekly attendance (Hartford Institute for Religion Research n.d.). Most megachurches are evangelical in spiritual style and stem from variations on basic Protestant theology, and each takes religious organization to a level unknown just fifty years ago. As argued here, education elevates societal capacity to produce more formal organizations and more of greater size and complexity, and this applies equally to religious organizations.

In their aptly titled book, *Holy Mavericks: Evangelical Innovators and the Spiritual Marketplace*, sociologists Shayne Lee and Phillip Sinitiere document the rise of megachurches and the organizational size and complexity to which they have grown through managerial, marketing, and membership-participation innovations (2009). For example, the Lakewood Church of Houston, Texas, led by the innovative "smiling preacher," Joel Osteen, is the largest megachurch in the nation with weekly attendance of over 43,000 at various worship services held in the church's $90 million renovated sports arena. Managing and recruiting for an organization this large depends on a sophisticated and educated staff, and Lakewood has 350 paid staff members mobilizing five thousand volunteers weekly to pull off its service program, including simultaneous Spanish translations. Additionally, Lakewood, like many other megachurches, employs sophisticated technology to reach beyond its already massive number of attendees. The church produces its own audio podcast, which is downloaded by 52 million people, and its television broadcast program reaches a weekly audience estimated at over seven million people in nearly one hundred countries; the program is rated number one by Nielsen Media Research in the inspirational category (Scheitle and Finke 2012). This is not to imply that evangelical movements attract only, or even mostly, higher-educated worshipers, but given the size of these movements they likely do have at least a moderately educated laity. Notably, many of the innovations used by Lakewood and its peer megachurches rely on both an educated staff and a high degree of volunteering among the membership, a behavior that is far more prevalent among more-educated members.

Intellectuals frequently write off these kinds of religious organizations as little more than the operations of hucksters out for money, or as lowbrow, marginal spirituality. While a few independent churches do fit this caricature, in the main large independent churches provide for the daily spiritual needs of a growing number of mainstream Americans, and they are exceedingly well organized. Starting as small sects and tending to keep to a more traditional message about religion, megachurches have attracted large segments of the population, including sizable shares of the educated. They have done this by embracing and applying concepts of modern organizational theory, management, marketing, the psychology of group participation, and social movement technology, all of which have their foundations in university knowledge production over the past century.

Beyond bringing organizational ideas, an educated laity enhances the ability of megachurches to be run by staffs of specialized experts, believers themselves who command a high degree of volunteerism among members. Megachurches have succeeded in the schooled society because they have shown great innovation in organizational design, recruitment of members, worship, leadership selection, and many others strategies, while keeping core beliefs mostly intact (Finke 2003). In many cases, the willingness of these complex organizations to innovate along modern managerial and organizing paradigms has led them to invent new organizational techniques, which have flowed out into nonreligious enterprises. For example, a case study designed to train MBA students, published in the *Harvard Business Review*, centers on the organizational innovations developed by Willow Creek Community Church, an early megachurch, to attract "unchurched" individuals (Schlesinger and Mellado 1991). And noted earlier is the example of the Academy of Management, the main professional association of scholars and social scientists of organizational management, which includes an interest group named "Management, Spirituality and Religion."

A second example of the positive impact of education on the religious culture in the United States is found among innovative mass religious movements. Some of these successful movements employ a different accommodation to the desacralized postindustrial society from that of megachurches. Like many evangelistic megachurches they use modern and innovative organizing methods, but instead of holding more rigidly to a core religious message, they accommodate their spiritual message to a postindustrial, heavily educated society. A good illustration of this is the Emerging Church movement, which is developing a theology that is explicitly spiritual *and* compatible with the qualities of belief preferred by many educated individuals. In this case, a group of like-minded evangelical theologians, clerics, and practitioners came together to explore how to be Christian in the postindustrial, schooled society, and they have formed a leadership network called Emergent, whose members share both theological and organizational strategies and tactics. Emergent's widely stated goal is to merge the intensity of evangelic spirituality with the theological sensibilities of more-educated individuals, and then spread this message using some of the organizational techniques that megachurches have developed. For example, some of the Emergent leaders advocate a "healthy marriage between science and Christianity" (Lee and Sinitiere 2009, 93). Here is how Lee and Sinitiere summarize the approach of a founding leader of the Emerging Church movement, Brian McLaren:

Rather than rejecting postmodernism for its excesses, McLaren urges Christians to embrace its moral intentions and form a progressive Christian faith that promotes recognition and repentance of the West's colonial history and arrogance. (89)

Although it is a challenge to estimate the number of followers in such a movement, the authors present indications that the Emerging Church has become a popular religious alternative for many. This approach is also found among non-Christian religions as well; Jewish leaders affiliated with the emerging movement of Synagogue 3000 explicitly aim to express ancient faith in a postindustrial cultural setting.

A final effect of widespread education on religious culture is, from a religious point of view, a highly ironic one. If it were not for education's major role in supplying and disseminating the ideas validating desacralization, the thriving religious culture in postindustrial America, and elsewhere in the world, might never have occurred. Before the advent of modern society and the education revolution, societies tended to have one dominant religion intertwined with their core cultural ideas and social organization. The influence of education as a social institution has shifted society from a religious basis to a secular one, and in the process has desacralized societal institutions. But the process of desacralization has not so much wiped out religion as it has led to extensive religious pluralism—many faiths existing at once, more or less equally.

By their very nature, all religions claim the one truth as their own. Therefore, prior to extensive desacralization, human history is filled with the persecution of religions that deviate from the single established be-lief. Tragically common in the historical record are political persecutions and military warfare fueled by religious differences between and within societies—such as the seventeenth-century Thirty Years' War in Europe. Desacralization, however, breaks the tight link between the one true faith and all other institutions in a society. This process has long been consid-ered a form of secularization (Chaves 1994). But desacralization does not necessarily lead to a fully secular society; surprisingly, it may set the con-ditions for religious pluralism.

Similar to their assumptions about education, some intellectuals assume that religious pluralism within a society eventually brings down all religions. How can people think that there is one true religion when so many different types exist at once? Nevertheless, several decades of research on religion convincingly show that religious pluralism leads to greater overall religious adherence. This happens for a number of reasons, including open competi-tion for followers (Smith 1998). In fact, this relationship is at the heart of Stark and Finke's religious marketplace model, which is now widely used to explain the flourishing culture of religion in the United States (2000). Recent sociological studies confirm the hypothesis that the proliferation of religious groups does not speed secularization; instead, it increases overall adherence to a religion across a population. For example, Christiano (1987) and Stark and Finke (2000) find at various time points in the United States that the greater the religious pluralism, the more denominations grow and the greater the numbers of individuals who regularly attend religious services of all kinds. The same relationship holds for minority, non-Christian religions, such as Judaism (Silberstein, Rabinowitz, Ritterband, and Kosmin 1987).

## AN AMERICAN EXCEPTION
## OR A WORLD PHENOMENON?

It is often noted that a main cause of the United States' religious plural-ity and dynamic religious market is the lack of a monopoly on religious supply controlled by a state-sanctioned official church. Along with the nation's constitutional insurance of the separation of church and state, the American environment is particularly conducive to religious growth and change. One could speculate that such factors could even override other secularizing cultural factors such as the often-assumed debilitating effects of education on religion. In short, the American case could be an exception, and thus in fact education in other places might retard religious adherence and religious organizational innovation. But a growing set of evidence indicates that religion has not declined as the education revolution spreads worldwide (Stark and Finke 2000). Along with desacralization, the same kinds of changes in religions observed in the United States as a function of widespread education occur elsewhere too; and there is no discernible trend towards a fully secular world society. The vigorous culture of the American schooled society and its symbiotic influences on religion may herald a future world than represent an exception.

Probably the most cited case of the widely educated and supposedly secular society are the nations of Western Europe. Even here though is there evidence of religious belief throughout populations, albeit moderated by state churches and state authorities that stifle the religious market. The best case of this might be Iceland, a highly educated society with a Lutheran state church and one of the lowest average weekly church attendance levels, at just 2 percent. But in-depth research of various kinds finds that even in this formally secularized society, 80 percent believe in life after death and in the human soul, and frequently pray to a supernatural being, and only just over 2 percent of adults say they are "convinced atheists" (Stark and Finke 2000; Swatos 1984). Some scholars of religion in the postindustrial world now consider Europe to be the exception to an otherwise still largely religious world; there is evidence that even China is becoming more religious over time (Jenkins 2007). So too, extreme systematic attempts to stamp out religion, as in past communist societies, have never been successful, and in some cases these actions may have enhanced religious adherence (Froese 2008). Plus, there is evidence that similar to American religious movements, other religious revivals, such as a current one among Muslims, depend on the leadership and financial support of the highly educated in these societies (Martin 1991).

Finally, the long historical relationship between the rise of the university and the Catholic Church, plus the role of the university in the education revolution, have done more than produce a unique educational institution. The core values at the very heart of the educational institution are in essence religious ones closely related to Judeo-Christian morality (Baker forthcoming). This is not to say that mass education promulgates transcendental belief and the existence of a supernatural being—it clearly does not—but it does deeply instill a message about human development, societal development, and social justice that is morally compatible with many religious theologies, which continue to flourish in the schooled society (Meyer 2000; Ramirez, Bromley, and Russell 2009).

# Conclusion

## The Schooled Society and Beyond:
## Ubiquitous, Formidable, and Noisy

Education is a secular religion in modern societies . . . it provides a legitimating account of the competence of citizens, the authority of elites, and the sources of the adequacy of the social system to maintain itself in the face of uncertainty.

JOHN MEYER, *American Journal of Sociology*, 1977

FROM ITS ORIGINS over the long development of the Western university, up through widespread mass primary and secondary schooling, and now well into the spread of mass higher education, the education revolution has transformed individuals, social institutions, and human society. The extensive body of evidence examined here shows that instead of subserviently following other institutions, formal education has developed into a primary institution with its own independent influence on society, constructing more than it reproduces. The robust and extensive ideology, or culture, of education is mostly a product of its own success as an institution; in other words, it is not a creation of an overeducation crisis, educational credential inflation, a fooled public, a plot to reproduce social class, runaway populism, technological advance, media hype, or any other of the supposed external reasons often suggested. Like other founding social institutions currently at the heart of human society, the massive undertaking of formal education commands a significant share of cultural understandings that influence life globally, deeply permeating many non-educational dimensions. Seen this way, the indefatigable expansion of schooling across the world's population and the rising normative levels of educational attainment across successive generations can enrich the understanding of ascendant aspects of late-modern society, many qualities of the subsequent postindustrial society, and likely scenarios for the future of global society.

Broadly speaking, the empirical evidence reveals two concurrent processes driving the education revolution, which account for the institution's stunning success in postindustrial society. The first is the independent, aggregated influence of massive numbers of educated individuals on society. This most obvious outcome of the education revolution originates in, and is sustained by the second process, in which the cultural ideas underpinning the institution influence the further development of the content, meaning, and function of education itself and permeate other major social institutions. As demonstrated in the analyses of education's influence on other social institutions, the two processes intricately interact with one another to considerable synergetic effect, which is now ubiquitous and formidable and certainly should not be quietly or under-appreciated in intellectual accounts of postindustrial society and its future, as it has been.

### THE UBIQUITOUS EDUCATED INDIVIDUAL

The first process, expansion of education to include all individuals, is often commented on only in terms of its impact on someone's individual life or as a prelude to overeducation imagery, while mass education's potential aggregate influence is virtually ignored. But the evidence assembled in this book points to a broad set of consequences from the worldwide spread of a common form of mass schooling. Schooling's ubiquitous influence on a vast majority of all humans is a central part of the education revolution's impact.

Chiefly because of the demographic reach of mass education, the "new modern people" that Alex Inkeles found among developing nations' peasantry in the 1960s have become the norm worldwide (1996). It is a distinctly different world when wide access to even a few years of primary school pushes most people away from sources of traditional authority, such as clans, tribes, and religious leaders, and instead leads them to believe that worldly authority is not absolute, that it is natural to apply instrumental (means-ends) rationality to all aspects of one's life, that one should embrace the notion of social progress and refrain from fatalism, accept science as a major source of truth, and include a cosmopolitan global perspective. The world's population is now made up of waves of individuals empowered along these dimensions, who compared to members of past societies have considerable academic cognitive skills, and who feel entitled to apply them. This is not to say that everyone does equally well in pursuit of formal educational attainment or is equally transformed, but compared to a century ago when most were unschooled and illiterate, today's educated world population changes society in many unexpected and substantial ways.[1]

The educated worker, citizen, or believer transforms the nature of labor and profit-making, politics, or religion. When most and soon all people in many parts of the world are educated, these changes fundamentally reconstruct other institutions, although not often in the ways that the original enthusiasts of mass education predicted. For those who are educated and already live in the advanced form of the schooled society, the teaching of a child to read, write, do some mathematics, and have a beginner's understanding of science and social science seems by comparison to the great complexity of society a relatively basic undertaking, even a sociologically trivial one. But compared to an unschooled traditional society, schooling whole cohorts permeates every facet of life.[2] The relatively simple act of teaching basic academic skills has the potent unintended effect of creating a new type of societal member. Although recent research on how literacy, numeracy, and the general schooling experience add up to a radically different human is beyond the scope here, the scientific conclusion emerging is that the educational transformation of individuals, even at very basic scholastic levels, intensifies and enhances profound cognitive and emotional development, which cascades into substantial development of the overall individual, to an extent not often undertaken among unschooled individuals (e.g., Baker, Salinas, and Eslinger 2012). And as there are now waves of such people, their combined presence changes society.

In addition to the six social arenas examined in the second half of the book, many more dimensions of society are just as profoundly changed by the influence of large aggregates of at least minimally educated individuals. From consumption patterns to intimate sexual behavior to recreational activities, one after another body of research on behavior, attitudes, frames of reference, and values reports strong associations with educational attainment, which almost always overshadow associations with other demographic characteristics, such as gender, race, ethnic background, age, religion, political orientation, and economic resources, even though these non-educational factors are routinely considered by social scientists to be the more defining characteristics of individuals.

For reasons described earlier, the ascendance of large-scale educational attainment downgrades the saliency of many characteristics of individuals in understanding their actions, beliefs, and general orientation to life, so that in a relatively short historical period the most accurate demographic predictor of most dimensions of the individual has come to be formal education. If one were asked today to choose the single best demographic characteristic to predict the nature of an unknown, unseen individual, a mountain of research strongly nominates educational attainment. The flip side is reflected in the profound ways educational attainment enters the overall self-definition of individuals and the ways educational deviance and redemption shape perceptions of the self in the schooled society. Importantly, educational attainment's efficacy as a key demographic characteristic is not chiefly the opportunities or future status that a particular educational degree enables; rather, it is directly a function of how education transforms the individual's ways of thinking, feeling, and acting and thus permeates significant aspects of psychological development. Certainly, the public legitimacy of educational attainment as the almost singular route to future opportunities and later status is part of this process, but the full effect of the schooling experience on the individual goes well beyond.

If, for example, as early sociologist Auguste Comte allegedly noted, "demography is destiny," then our destiny is educationally transformed demography. Although not specifically reviewed here, much research indicates that formal education strongly associates with (and likely changes) cardinal processes that aggregate into demographic transitions of populations. It is probable that the education revolution played a significant role in changing patterns at the heart of changing population dynamics since the nineteenth century, such as mate selection, family formation, fertility, child survival, health and mortality, and immigration. Related to this is the empirical finding that educationally derived human capital in populations influences nations' economic growth (e.g., Birdsall, Pinckney, and Sabot 2008; de Barros, Ferreira, Vega, and Chanduvi 2009; Hanushek and Woessmann 2007; Pritchett 2001; Ramirez, Luo, Schofer, and Meyer 2006). Certainly, the mostly predetermined qualities of age and gender continue to play major roles, but it can be argued that education is now the master social variable in demography (e.g., Baker et al. 2011; Lutz and Samir 2011;

Lutz, Sanderson, and Šerbov 2004). Further, large aggregates of educated individuals entail consequences that transcend particular social institutions and population dynamics.

Over the past 150 years, the education revolution has been the great homogenizer of the world's population. As formal education has increasingly become homogenized in its intent, content, and function across all places, its influence on individuals is itself homogenizing, even in the face of considerable differences across local cultures (Baker and LeTendre 2005; Inkeles 1996). Thus, as a greater proportion of the world's population undertakes the same transforming experience, people everywhere become more alike across many facets influenced by education. Also, the education revolution has certainly caused greater elaboration of dimensions of the individual, but these too are consistent across similar education levels. Compared to the status of clans, families, and other primary groupings in traditional society, the education revolution has been a major cause behind the rise, intensification, standardization, and cultural celebration of the individual (including the celebration of small individual differences) as the *legitimate* social entity and most efficacious form of social actor (Jepperson and Meyer 2007). All manner of aspects of the individual are associated with education level; consequently, individuals with the same educational experiences act, think, feel, and believe in broadly similar ways. There are many ramifications. Just one example is the described rise of academic intelligence and its standardizing of cognitive skills across demographic backgrounds and occupations, at least among cohorts born after the intensification of the education revolution (Weakliem, McQuillan, and Schauer 1995). The education revolution has already muffled the influences of local traditional culture, and appears to be on the way to muffling even the influences of imagined national cultures as well (e.g., Wiseman, Astiz, Fabrega, and Baker 2011). All of these prodigious influences of an aggregation of educated individuals are themselves sustained and intensified by the education revolution's formidable impact on culture.

## CULTURAL TRANSFORMATION

When theorizing about social institutions was first popular, sociologist Lewis Coser (1974) coined the term "greedy institution," referring to an institution that seeks to dominate all aspects of social life. Unlike religion in many traditional societies, education was not intended to be all-encompassing by original design, but by virtue of its ensuing cultural success, it has become institutionally greedy. This is John Meyer's point in the epigraph; education is like a secular religion, its cultural impact transcending its own technical qualities. This process, the theme of the first half of the book, goes well beyond the qualities of educated individuals to include the emergence of core understandings, meanings, and values of the institution that now have far-reaching implications for all cultural dimensions of postindustrial society. Compared to less formally educated societies, over the past century and a half once-novel cultural ideas about education and humans have become bedrock understandings of the schooled society: "education is human actualization"; "educational development of individuals is a central source of the collective good"; "academically instilled higher-order thinking is the superior human capacity," and so forth. These form a powerful, much believed ideology that underpins the further growth and centrality of education as an institution. So too, the qualities of universal authoritative knowledge supported by the knowledge conglomerate create a knowledge and scientized society rooted firmly in the belief that such knowledge is preferable for everything from occupations to intellectual inquiry to human fulfillment.

The institution's impact on cultural meanings about what education should be in a postindustrial society, and how it contributes to society at large, goes well beyond the connection between the educational status and occupational status of individuals. For example, first, the beliefs that education is a human right and that cognitive ability is the supreme skill combine to create three overarching understandings about education: one, the belief that all children and youth (and now all adults too) can and should learn in formal academic settings; two, that these settings should be open to all abilities; and lastly, that the skills of higher-order cognition are the most valuable to instill in all people. A second example is the combination of the beliefs that education is a human right and that schooling individuals contributes to the common good. This belief sustains the tendency of education to expand across the life course by the logic that educational investment in individuals is the central route to social progress. A final example is the synergistic influence of the ideas of meritocratic academic achievement, universal knowledge, and cognitive skills on the rising saliency of academic intelligence and the decline of the older, entrenched forms of vocationalism and classicism as educational objectives. Although still pined for by some intellectuals, the classical form of Thomas More's fifteenth-century education and the vocationalism permeating educational goals of later centuries are in fact rapidly fading and will not likely return as long as the current institutional logic of education continues to capture so much cultural legitimation.

The evolution and intensification of the institution generate even more elaborate cultural products that permeate postindustrial society, such as academic intelligence as a privileged human capacity and academic achievement as meritocratic and socially just. These and similar cultural ideas, plus the synergy among them, figure prominently in the analysis of the consequences of the education revolution for other social institutions, as demonstrated in the transformation of jobs and work, occupational credentials, and the knowledge economy. Similarly, it can be argued that the schooled society forms the basis for any number of recently observed social trends, such as the rise of a creative class, new economies, and significant parts of globalization (Florida 2001; Reich 2010). As these values and cultural meanings expand, they tend to be self-reinforcing and to shape further cultural understandings. This expanding process is illustrated in the rise of the school dropout issue and the GED phenomenon as part of the construction of personal identity in a heavily schooled society. These kinds of constructive capacities of education as an institution propel it further into the center of contemporary society.

In addition to education's impact as an institution on selected noneducational institutions, described in the preceding chapters, there are many other institutions ripe for analysis, which when completed will help evaluate the full dimensions of the schooled society. For example, as noted above, a significant amount of empirical evidence shows that the education revolution has transformed the health of human populations, as well as many other demographic processes. It is also likely that a rising educated population influences the institution of the family in terms of marriage, divorce, and courtship. Similarly, parenting and childhood have been significantly changed by the education revolution (e.g., Schaub 2010). And there is much more to be investigated, such as social movements in modern society, the military, the justice system, the modern personality, and the social construction of the life course, to name a few. While most of the evidence reported by social scientists consists of associations between educational attainment and individuals' skills, behavior, attitudes, and thoughts across different activities of life, these often herald a larger story of how a particular institution is being reshaped by the values and ideas brought forth by the education revolution. Educational effects on individuals and institutions go hand in hand; as seen in uncovering the educational transformation of politics and religion, the task is often a matter of piecing together the bigger story.

In addition to education's influence on non-educational institutions, many general processes, such as social problems and their solutions, which occur across a range of institutions, will continue to be "educationalized" as well. It is a major cultural change to assume that the best way to handle deviance, and all kinds of human problems, is to educate deviants and those with problems and then educate society at large about the social problem. Pushing aside many traditional strategies, such as shunning, physical punishment, banishment, and religious solutions, the education revolution has made educational strategies the assumed most efficacious way to bring individuals back into the moral order of society, plus to prepare society to meet future challenges. It is a significant institutional achievement that formal education as an ameliorative activity is deeply imbued within the culture of the schooled society. All of this awaits additional analysis of the institutional influence of education.

## A FOUNDING INSTITUTION
## OF POSTINDUSTRIAL SOCIETY

The cultural impact of the education revolution is less obvious than individual effects because all successful institutions increase the naturalness and taken-for-granted quality of the concepts, values, and meanings that they help to construct. This fact no doubt also reinforces a persistent intellectual underappreciation of the cultural influence of the schooled society. Yet what has been dubbed a "quiet revolution" because of its relative absence from accounts of the origins of modern society is in its totality of influence a very loud social phenomenon that requires full integration into new sociological models of the history of societal change.

As described in some detail in the first half of the book, a lasting consequence of the epistemological revolution developed within universities is the recognition that human society is socially constructed, and this conception has in turn fueled the grandest of intellectual endeavors about society, namely, to identify key causal factors behind the worldwide death of traditional society in all of its forms and the rise, globalization, and intensity of modern society. From the midnineteenth century on, this project led to the founding of the discipline of sociology and other social and behavioral sciences (Collins and Makowsky 1998). Creators of sociological inquiry, including Karl Marx, Émile Durkheim, and Max Weber, spent their careers wrestling with understanding this transition, and their general insights, if not specific empirical arguments, set the leitmotifs of investigation for the great expansion of the social sciences over the course of the twentieth century (Frank and Gabler 2006). It is ironic then that these intellectuals' work was too early to recognize the implications of the growing institution of education; instead, economic and political factors received the lion's share of credit.[3]

Even though the cultural influences behind the education revolution were set in place by the same epistemological development, the demographic process of mass schooling was in its infancy as the extensive intellectual project about societal transition took off. Therefore, the main implications of the education revolution were late for inclusion in original formative scholarship on the origins of late-modern and postindustrial societies. But given all of the evidence reviewed here on just a selected set of social institutions, the extensive educational culture of postindustrial society cannot merely be a derivative of collective economic production or the necessity for political solidarity. The rapid demographic growth in education is similar in its impact to the rapid growth of large-scale capitalism and the democratic nation-state. The educational institution is directly tied to both of these, of course, but it can also be seen as a founding institution responsible for significant parts of the great social transformation away from traditional forms of society.

Along with a handful of prominent analysts of the university in post–Second World War America, the leading sociological theorist of his time, Talcott Parsons, who coined the term "education revolution," was on to this exact point, but it was soon lost in the ensuing rejection of functional sociological theory along with the field's embrace of Marxism and its focus on economic conflict and inequality. Consequently, the institution of education was relegated to the limited role of social reproduction, the process through which the advantaged pass on their class advantage to the next generation, and the less advantaged are socialized to complacency and low-status labor positions. Of course, formal education always involves some degree of reproduction, but this is not the only, or even chief way in which the institution now influences society. As explained before, the institution's class-reproductive qualities are declining in the face of direct construction of status by educational performance alone. The education revolution has led education to surpass social reproduction and enter into direct social production. It has changed the terms of status attainment and the nature of social hierarchies to the point that traditional theories of social class structure should be reinvestigated with the schooled society in mind.

## NEO-INSTITUTIONAL THEORY OF EDUCATION AND SOCIETY

The full story of the transition from traditional to modern to postindustrial society awaits, and a major challenge for sociology and related inquiry is to incorporate the cultural impact of the education revolution in understanding the evolving postindustrial society. Considerable theoretical inertia must be overcome. The schooled society argument fits under the larger conceptual umbrella of neo-institutionalism, which itself is related to original functional theorizing about society. Functional theories attempt to explain the processes by which humans construct and sustain societies. While functional theories recognize conflict as one major process, economic class-based conflict (or any social conflict) is not the singular driving force. Following this general theoretical line, neo-institutional theory attempts to improve upon some well-known weaknesses of the original functional perspective. First, it fully embraces the notion of social construction and does away with any reference to technical or natural or even universal needs in the making of society. Second, it trades heavily on the notion of institutionalization as the essential process producing and sustaining culture. Third, it theorizes that the inner workings of social institutions consist of the impact of values, ideas, constructs, and meanings through their manifestations of cognitive maps, scripts, schemata, and common understandings of individuals acting within a particular societal sector. And last, neo-institutional theory strives to account for the exponential growth in the complexity of societies, which purely material or overt-political-power processes cannot fully explain. From a neo-institutional perspective, social change occurs with greater or less institutionalization of particular sectors of meaning and social activity.

All of these themes have been used here in the exploration of the schooled society. First, it has been shown that there was nothing natural, technically functional, or inevitable in the origins of the education revolution. If the Western version of the university had not happened, a different model of education would have likely developed, including a far more limited version of formal schooling than now. Indeed, the anthropological norm across the record of organized societies before 150 years ago has been to provide formal schooling for the very few and in highly specialized forms (e.g., religious elite training). Second, along with the demography of mass schooling, the main consequence of the education revolution has been a greater capacity to produce and sustain cultural ideas. Third, much of the story behind the educational transformation of other institutions shows a process by which cultural products, in the form of values, ideas, constructs, and meanings around education, interact and synergistically increase societal complexity and propel themselves into many dimension of postindustrial life. Lastly, the greater institutionalization of formal education as reflected in these products is the driving force behind the impact of the education revolution.

In addition to addressing weaknesses of earlier functional and Marxian theories of education and society, the schooled society perspective is also an improvement on the human capital theory as a way to think about education and society. Although human capital thinking came out of economics, not sociology, it has in many ways become the theory of choice for sociologists attempting to explain educational phenomena beyond social reproduction. It has been successful in this, but in a limited way. The educational transformation of work and labor market credentials illustrates how a neo-institutional framework adds to human capital theory education's transforming effect on individuals, firms, and profit-seeking. With this new perspective, the insights of human capital theory about investment in formal education can be incorporated into a broader institutional perspective on education and society.

Much writing about neo-institutional theory in general is about how organizations within the same societal sector tend to take on considerable isomorphism in structure and operating details; and this has also been applied to schools and schooling (e.g., Baker and LeTendre 2005; Jepperson 2002). The argument here shifts to the lesser-examined but equally central process by which particular institutions become powerful enough to generate significant isomorphic pressure in the first place. The fact that this focus has not been so prominent in neo-institutional research about education has tended to narrow the debate to one of degrees and forms of isomorphism. More research on how education has come to construct so much of the reality of postindustrial society will be an important challenge in the testing of the theory.

Like all successful theories, the neo-institutional theory of education and society will remain useful until it is not. Until then, it is an improvement over all types of theories relying on the traditional perspective, as these leave substantial amounts of educational phenomena and their consequences unaccounted for. It is also a reasonably parsimonious way to think about the full societal impact of a strong education sector. One need not turn to overly complicated theory about the saliency of one outcome of schooling over another; they all form the package that has such a summative influence on society. Similarly, the argument integrates cognitive and psychological dimensions of schooling with its influence on a highly legitimated status-attainment process and cultural understandings, into one theory that recognizes too the potential for synergistic effects across all of these. Further, the schooled society perspective opens a way to recognize the less-appreciated absolute effects of schooling at certain levels of education (e.g., two years versus six years of schooling) along with the more commonly analyzed relative differences (more schooling versus less schooling, regardless of absolute attainment); the former effect has been mostly lost in sociological analyses and the latter has received too much singular attention.

Lastly, the argument and research examined here demonstrate the intellectual weaknesses of the traditional perspective on education and society in all of its various versions. It is now obvious that the traditional perspective fails to explain a wealth of educational phenomena, and its narrow vision leads to unjustified cynicism about education and society. From such a perspective, origins of oppression within society are attributed to education whether or not there is evidence to support this hypothesis; and everything else about education, beyond its social reproduction of inequality, must therefore be mostly myth. Hence, education is completely corrupted, at least in comparison to some perfect, and unattainable, hypothetical form. Such a position becomes nearly absurd in light of even the simplest liberating effects of teaching individuals basic academics. Similarly, for those who see education as only a part of a mechanically constructed world revolving around technical advance, education is valued but in a narrow and secondary fashion; therefore, education as an institution must also follow the technical requirements of the collective. When it instead constructs many new cultural understandings, these must be cynically chalked up to institutional incompetence and ignored sociologically, economically, psychologically, and so forth.

Once again, then, the media are full of experts, who saw a looming overeducation crisis after the 2008 market devaluation; so too, rising costs of higher education spur on discussions of "who really needs" advanced education. The traditional perspective hosts, like clockwork, this time-worn punditry of a looming education crisis. But now as then, this stems from a limited and now mostly inaccurate model of education and society. This is not to say that large changes in the economy and other primary institutions cannot influence the course of education, for clearly they can and will continue to do so; but starting from the premise that education is now a primary institution of society enables an accurate assessment of what trends and crises in other parts of society will do to education and its broader institutional impact.

If the schooled society brought about by the education revolution will likely continue into the foreseeable future, what will its impact on individuals look like? What will the future of its founding institution, the university, be? And what will be the schooled society's influence on the future of non-educational aspects of human life?

## THE FUTURE OF THE SCHOOLED SOCIETY

As many consequences of mass education became apparent in the 1970s, John Meyer put forth the beginnings of the schooled society perspective, in which the education revolution sustains itself and will gain greater social saliency into the future (1977). Foreseeing a robust institution, Meyer's insights were prophetic and stimulated three decades of neo-institutional research integrated here. To make his point, Meyer hypothesized that the education revolution was bringing about two mutually reinforcing societal processes that together generate significant institutional power. One is the effect of a growing allocative legitimacy of education, and the other is the effect of intensifying academic intelligence.[4] As described in the second chapter, allocation is sociological shorthand for the role formal education performs in the attainment of social status; academic intelligence stands for the change in thinking processes and self-identities through the effects of (1) learning the manifest curriculum; (2) developing domain-general cognitive skills such as deeper reasoning, problem solving, and rational thought; and (3) expanding conceptual images of the self and the world along the lines of Inkeles's newly educated peasant that is now intensified with mass advanced education.

Specifically, Meyer hypothesized that over time and across more and more individuals, allocative and academic intelligence consequences of schooling will reinforce one another and form a significant ideology about the centrality of formal education, which in turn will intensify the future legitimacy of each process. As illustrated by the analyses of the dimensions and consequences of the education revolution throughout the book, this hypothesis is very plausible. Accepting this self-reinforcing nature of formal education also easily leads to the prediction that the educational culture of postindustrial society will likely intensify into the future. The mutually reinforcing relationship between the rising allocative power of formal education and the intense privileging of academic intelligence reaches into every part of the postindustrial society analyzed here. This early insight by Meyer has not been fully explored, even by neo-institutionalists, yet this relationship is at the heart of the schooled society and it can explain a wide range of phenomena. While Meyer chose perhaps the two most obvious transforming processes of the education revolution, his hypothesis can be extended to other major cultural dimensions of the schooled society, as discussed above. Applying this logic points to a future dominated by the effects of formal education on individuals, the global culture, and their synergistic combinations.

For individuals, predicting such a future begs the question of how far education attendance and degree attainment will expand into the average life-course. Many would suggest that there must be some natural limit, yet past waves of expansion of secondary education and higher education did not stop at what then was thought to be the natural limit on the time individuals would spend in school. While the future will not likely hold the creation of new advanced degrees beyond the Ph.D. and professional degrees, the nature of future expansion is already clear. Ever greater numbers of youth enrolling in higher education and taking on multiple majors, growing programs of BA-graduate degree combinations as well as secondary school–BA degree combinations, the earning of multiple graduate degrees, and the enrolling in lifelong learning as adults are all examples of the many ways education is likely to expand into individuals' lives in the near future. At the other end of the life-course one can already see significant growth of mass early childhood education (pre-kindergarten); and even if its eventual form is still unclear, there is already a supporting ideology for early childhood education that is full of the general ideas of the education revolution, with little to stop their enactment (Schaub 2009). As noted above, as social problems and their solutions are increasingly defined through the values of the schooled society, ever more social interventions will be essentially educational and school-like in their content and goals, thus exposing and re-exposing many people to educational values and processes across many aspects of their lives. Together, these emerging innovative expansions of education suggest that it makes little sense to argue about some natural limit; at both ends of the life-course, formal education continues to expand in a number of ways, and as long as the values and cultural meanings continue to hold significance, there will be deeper participation of individuals in education into the future.

It should also be noted that the schooled society is still relatively young and has a way to go on its current path towards the norm of some higher education for all youth. Even in the heavily schooled United States, over half of the entire population has only a high school degree or less. But the demographic march of generations and the expanding norms of education will change this rapidly in the near future. Although many pundits and educators continue to speculate on some limit to educational expansion, education as an institution has proved elusive to control by other institutions and even professional educators. Its central meanings are so highly valued in contemporary society as to give the institution a measure of immunity to external control. While there are, and will continue to be intensive public debates about all aspects of education and from many different political ideologies, these rarely if ever conclude that less education for individuals and the collective is the best path. What inevitably happens as a result of these kinds of debates is an intensification of education's ubiquity, content, and meaning in society (e.g., Rury 2013; Tyack and Cuban 1995).

Over the past decade, human capital economists discovered cognitive skills and neuroscience, and this research has been used in a growing number of policy debates about when it is optimal to invest in cognitive skill enhancement through formal educational programs—early in life versus later; for early high-achievers versus remedial students, and so forth (e.g., Cunha, Heckman, and Schennach 2010). To the point here, what is assumed in these debates is some ability and motivation of society to ration or limit educational expansion, but this is not likely to happen. For all of the reasons and empirical trends described in earlier chapters, the education revolution has made limiting formal education to some at the expense of education for others a widely held anathema, to the point that it is unrealistic to assume that governments could, or would, attempt this to any real degree. Also as noted above, there are powerful, positive values about education merged with ideas about the actualized, developed human that actively prompt educational expansion of all types.

The prediction here, though, should not be construed to mean that no forces in contemporary society could retard the continued growth of the schooled society. Education as an institution is not invincible or completely impervious to other institutions. There are competing cultural meanings and power struggles throughout society; capitalism's frequent conflict with the state is one good example of how two primary institutions compete for power. There are many examples of accommodation and competition between education and other institutions. These have been purposefully left unexplored here because they are often misconstrued to mean that education is a secondary institution, and this would have hindered the main proposed argument. From a schooled society perspective, however, the dynamics of competition and conflict between education and other primary institutions should be part of future analyses of education and society.

Lastly and ironically, much-noted scholarship on the coming of an intensive globalization has also tended to ignore the role of the education revolution in this phenomenon. The relatively homogenous practice of education from the earliest grades up through graduate training worldwide is not the product of globalization; instead, mass education and its historically increasing homogeneity of values, ideas, and assumptions increase the capacity for globalization, creating a world in which the university (as it always did in a more geographically limited way from its beginnings) continues to provide central ideologies.

### THE FUTURE OF THE UNIVERSITY

Parsons's insight was right: the Western form of the university has transformed global culture to an extensive degree (Meyer, Ramirez, Frank, and Schofer 2008). Nevertheless, this transformation is not so readily obvious, because it is has been incremental and its effects are now so ubiquitous. The university has created a powerful ideology that has intensified over the past century, where human society, the physical universe, religion, and in short, all things of life can be understood through rational universal scholarship, which includes theory and scientific methods. The university, and education in general, is widely assumed to be the most appropriate institution for people to learn this ideology and then enact it through their educational development. As noted before, it is not argued here that the university creates every idea; instead, it creates, and imbues society with, the axial principles and qualities of knowledge. And if these powers were not enough, the university has legitimated many other cultural products of education. For example, the notion and importance of academic intelligence and a highly cognitive approach to life is manifestly supported by the university's knowledge conglomerate in educational psychology, neuroscience, artificial intelligence, information technology, cognitive psychology, and so forth. Thus, society becomes a reflection of formal education, and the university sets the main dimensions of this reflection.

The university is thus the model for, and the institutional catalyst behind the education revolution. The nation-state certainly fostered mass primary and then secondary education, but it did not originate the ideas behind what formal education has become, nor did industrialization, urbanization, democratization, capitalism, or growing social complexity. The unique multifaceted charter of the university created the ideology behind the demographic expansion at lower schooling levels that has now come around to higher education. Combining authoritative knowledge production with the ability to create educational degrees that certify individuals as empowered to enact this knowledge in everyday life is a far-reaching model, which lies at the foundation of the schooled society. The history of the university is the history of the education revolution, and the whole story of the latter can be summed up as an evolving grand inclusion of all people, all occupations, and central cultural meanings into the university. In many ways the future of the university is the future of the schooled society itself.

What is often missed in discussions predicting the future of the university is a full appreciation of the scale of its transforming powers. These tend to be considered too narrowly, whether the discussion is about technical knowledge or instilling democratic values. Both of these are certainly part of the overall story, but the scope of the university charter remains underestimated. The educational transformation of work, profit strategies, job content, and credentials nicely illustrates the broad effect of the university and mass higher education on society. Also, the influence of the university on the nature and content of knowledge further illustrates this profound transformation. Authoritative knowledge takes on distinct characteristics such as being universal and general instead of particularistic and local; theoretical and systematic instead of idiosyncratic (i.e., relying on know-how). Whether it is ice cream, gender, management, or nanoscience, the university, in addition to expanding the actual content of a subject, shapes the fundamental understandings of society, its physical universe, and its origins. Those who predicted the coming of a Mode 2 knowledge conglomerate with a receding role for the university misunderstood this charter; instead, a vital hyper–Mode 1 knowledge production evolved with the epistemological ideology of the university and the expansion of higher education at its heart. These will likely continue into the future.

This sturdy charter in contemporary society was already obvious to observers of the early research university, who understood the growing potential of the university to produce authoritative knowledge and to change individuals who worked within it, namely, university-based scholars and by extension the students trained by them. For example, at the turn of the eighteenth century, the German intellectual and educationalist Wilhelm von Humboldt wrote about how the rising German research university production of authoritative knowledge significantly transformed the scholar and the student towards the *modern autonomous mind* (Lenhardt 2005). As higher education enrollments include increasing proportions of society, greater exposure to scholarship and authoritative knowledge yields greater personal autonomy to use one's modern mind; this moves from a quality of the few to a widely agreed-on social norm for most people, spilling over into all other societal institutions.

Is the university the only institution creating significant knowledge in society? Obviously no, but there are only a handful of others, and in the current highly educated state of society, the university continues to ascend in importance in creating meaning throughout society. Other institutions, of course, have major roles in the making of postindustrial society: large-scale capitalism, including the free market and its organizational domination, and constitutional representative democracy also shape important ideologies and continue to ascend in legitimization as well. But even these two powerful institutions have only a limited charter on creating knowledge and expertise. This is not to deny that there are innumerable other activities in human life where ideas are generated and discussed; certainly, ideas come from lots of places throughout society, but currently the university is the central and independent institution intentionally producing authoritative knowledge through a process of creating, reformulating, defining, scrutinizing, and systematizing ideas into ideologies. The university produces the backbone of reigning ideologies that shape so much of the rest of postindustrial culture, and since this institution's power is within an educational context, it forms the bedrock conditions for a social order based on a culture of education.

Once one rejects the hypothesis that education just blindly follows other institutions, the power of the university and its role in creating the education revolution become clear. As the research indicates, the authoritative knowledge field of management science, the establishment of the MBA degree, and its expansion to mass proportions did not chiefly happen because capitalist enterprises demanded, or even required it. Although the muscular institution of capitalism did naturally set the stage for this development, management science and the MBA degree are distinctly educational products of the university that have transformed the dimensions of capitalism, and in so doing reinforce future demand from firms for more of the same from the university.

Lastly, one can already see developments that point to the future of the university within the schooled society. Higher education continues to expand enrollments, and the debate about universal higher education is ongoing, albeit sporadically. Higher education institutions (including American two-year institutions) that are not typical universities will tend to take on as many university-like qualities as they can. Similarly, all universities will move towards the qualities of the super research university whenever possible. The notion of a highly differentiated higher education sector will probably not occur at the level once thought, as all higher education institutions will tend to move towards the one dominant model of the university. It is also likely that rigid boundaries between lower education and higher education will blur, as the latter will reach down into the former. The boundary between undergraduate and graduate education will also continue to blur, as is now evident in the growth of combined BA/MA programs, and the many online degrees available. Curricula will continue to take on active, scholarship-type qualities and grow ever more cognitive. Because of the strength of the university model in the schooled society, it is unlikely that "corporatization" of the university will happen, at least not through the much-predicted dominance of a corporate model. Nor will the university go back to a past of classicism or embrace an old form of vocationalism; instead, the scientific study of humans and their environment will intensify as a central motivation of all scholarship and curricula.

### THE SCHOOLED SOCIETY, GOOD OR EVIL?

There is endless debate over whether the conditions of contemporary society are morally better than those of past societies or imagined future ones. While the debate is an important one for the future of society in general, it often spills over into sociological theorizing, causing confusion. Theory attempts to explain how society is, not how it necessarily should be. This confusion between scientific theory and a moral position on the education revolution and society is a barrier to a fair appraisal of the schooled society. For example, since the Marxist-postmodern perspective considers education as a conductor of capitalist oppression, when neo-institutionalism rejects this argument on theoretical and empirical grounds, it is often charged that the theory is morally bankrupt for embracing education and ignoring inequality, neither of which is true.

So too, if economics is the dismal science, education research is surely the Pollyanna science. Because the many researchers, along with the public and policy-makers, who are intent on improving the techniques of schooling assume formal education to be such a positive good, skeptical intellectuals almost instinctually suspect excessively optimistic prophesying of some morally superior world to come. Of course, the positive belief in education is an outcome of the schooled society itself, but that does not mean that a strong culture of education is necessarily morally good or bad. This commingling of scientific theory and moral assertion is harmful to future scholarship and a balanced assessment of the costs and benefits of the education revolution.

As with all successful institutions, there are significant moral assumptions behind education's central values, but this does not mean that the scientific study of these values is a promotion of a particular moral order. Adding to the confusion, the writings of neo-institutionalists are not particularly explicit about this; nevertheless, the schooled society perspective, like all sociological theory, assumes no moral judgment. Problematically too, three decades of terminology used by neo-institutionalists, including the author, to describe the education revolution and its societal consequences—words like rise, triumph, expansion, construction, robust—lend an unintended impression of positive moral overtones. This lexicon began innocently as an attempt to call sociological attention to what had previously been considered mundane and thus intellectually underappreciated, but the impression remains that the theory includes a moral argument. Further complicating this is the fact that the neo-institutional perspective has used the same terminology to empirically document the positive moral stature that education as an institution holds in postindustrial society. Also, a crucial feature of the institution of education is its ability to change the moral understandings not only of schooling but of society itself. Education is a dominating moral process in society, which any theory of education and society must account (not advocate) for. Regardless of its sometimes over-the-top terminology, the schooled society perspective is a scientific argument, not a moral assessment.

Going beyond sociology and setting aside theory and its moral neutrality, it is nevertheless fitting to end this exploration of education in postindustrial society with some reflection on whether the education revolution has been a positive development for society. To start, most would choose a schooled world over a formally uneducated one for any number of rational reasons. The liberating and empowering effect of even basic academic training is hard to see as a negative, and the same is true for the more elaborate effects of higher education. The overall positives of the education revolution are obvious, and in the opinion of most, they greatly outweigh the negatives. But along with these much-lauded effects of the education revolution come some pernicious qualities, three of which illustrate the darker side of the schooled society.

First and foremost, all normative social orders are by definition oppressive to a degree. Regardless of which ideas and human capacities are constructed into a dominant institution, other ideas and capacities are pushed aside, made trivial, and as shown earlier, even made taboo. But in keeping with the overall argument here, to the degree that the educational institution is oppressive, it is more about its own version of oppression than as a mere conveyer of other institutions' power. This is readily observable in the schooled society's celebration of academic intelligence. The education revolution devalues institutionalization of other capabilities, such as physical labor, acuity in warfare, religious charisma, craftsmanship, and sexual prowess, which have all been dominant sources of power in earlier human society. The stronger the cultural effects of the ideas and understandings generated by education, the weaker other types of meanings become, and this means by definition some oppression by its own normative order.

For individuals, these kinds of costs are evident: those who do not do well within dominating institutions of society suffer. Hence, extensive activity and industry to meet the central pressures and demands of schooling have penetrated all strata of society, including everything from old-fashioned tutoring to psychological intervention to pharmaceutically aided learning (e.g., Baker and Mori 2010). The same motivation also drives the legitimating proliferation of what is known as "special education" within the operation of schooling and among the research interests of learning-scientists; this schooling is adapted to students who experience a range of challenges in developing academic intelligence (and now also to students who are very adept at academic intelligence, for extra advantages) (e.g., Hibel, Farkas, and Morgan 2010). As normative pressures of the institution mount, norms of parenting, childhood, formation of the self, and even the operation of schooling are pressured to change, creating stress and cultural strain as education is ever more institutionalized (LeTendre 2002; Schaub 2013).

Predictable are the popular cultural inventions that attempt to counter the education revolution's normative pressure. For example, if educational psychologist Howard Gardner had not invented the notion of "multiple intelligences," someone else would have had to (1983). His provocative hypothesis is that a range of human capabilities has intelligence-like qualities and that these are equally part of one's overall intelligence. While some of these capabilities, such as mathematic, logical, spatial, and linguistic, articulate with the components of academic intelligence so favored by education, others such as intra- and interpersonal and musical do not. Gardner's argument is still a long way from an empirically based new theory of human intelligence; but its popularity among many educators and the general public is likely because it directly counters the domination of academic intelligence in schooling. Belief in multiple intelligences offers some "face-saving" within the schooled society—someone who is unsuccessful at school, with its now dominant and singular construction of intelligence, might still be considered intelligent, which is itself a highly celebrated normative value for individuals because of the education revolution. Thus, ironically, even though the imagery of multiple intelligences is a reaction to the cultural power of education, by equating separate intelligences in terms of cognitive ability, it inadvertently intensifies the notion of human capabilities within education's conceptual framework.

Second, like all known societies, the schooled society produces and legitimates a social hierarchy, and along with it unequal distribution of social and material goods, including scarce privileged rights. Indeed, one of the central points made here is that in the schooled society stratification has been transformed from older forms into a form that follows the institutional logic of formal education. Furthermore, the postindustrial culture now equates academic hierarchy with an expression of *socially just* merit, although this yields a number of consequences that may not be very socially just. For example, the schooled society readily expands demand and supply of high-end services such as financial, legal, and health services often at the expense of basic services for all kinds of people. The growing professions supplying these are among the best-paid positions in developed nations, thus creating inequality among the upper parts of the labor market; plus, variation across educational credentials is a main causal factor in inequality among all salaries. This educational effect on creating endless demand also feeds into a growing capitalist system of consumption, which of course has some well-known negative societal consequences. Expanding formal education helps to lift many out of absolute poverty, a feat that most economists find more beneficial to society than eliminating relative inequality, but nevertheless, advanced forms of the schooled society can create and maintain damaging inequalities. For instance, many would cast the rise of a creative class as a positive, but this obvious consequence of the schooled society also comes with exclusivity among social groups to a considerable degree (Florida 2001).

Lastly, it has become clear that mass education's transformative processes have in some instances been employed for immoral goals. For example, the technology of schooling has been purposefully enlisted to achieve political oppression. Tyrannical regimes of all political stripes have used formal mass education to justify their existence and fool the public into accepting their vision of national societies (e.g., Jansen 1990; Arnove 1995; Peterson, Hayhoe, and Lu 2001; Walker and Archung 2003). Even democratic nations have at times used mass education in forced indoctrination of ethnic, language, religious, and other minorities into a common citizenry, often with disastrous effects on children (Adams 1995). So too, as already described, the education revolution as a founding institution of late-modern society played a major role in the death of traditional society and many unique ways of human life along with it.

While these negative qualities are clearly costs of the education revolution and have been the focus of much scholarship, the overall transforming process of education is somehow resistant to total corruption, at least if the basic academic learning process is included. As described, an educated polity, even if its schooling includes totalitarian distortions of truth, is harder to dominate than a severely undereducated population; educated members of minorities, once they have overcome barriers to access to the university, often lead the way in preserving their distinct cultures; and the same is true about the academic collection, systemization, celebration, and distribution of knowledge about traditional societies.

Overwhelmingly, the education revolution's main ideology has changed the terms of the social contract worldwide to include the social rights and educated capabilities of a far greater proportion of populations than ever before. Unlike the Marxists and postmodern moralists, one need not hope for some far-off liberating form of mass education; it is already happening, and it promises substantial societal consequences into the future.

# Reference Matter

# Notes

1. The distinction here between primary and secondary institutions applies to the difference in their role in creating society, not to the older sociological idea of face-to-face versus formally organized.

2. The word "institution" here should not be confused with the conventional meaning of a specific place made of bricks and mortar, as in, "Mercy Hospital is an institution." Instead, sociology conceives society as made up of social institutions that gather, distribute, and control a set of rules for behavior and social roles to be played out in a particular sector of life.

3. The original institutional theoretical perspective formed the conceptual backbone of functional theory of society and culture.

4. Since it is predicted that a significant contribution to the institutional power of education is its global reach and tendency towards rapid globalization, each exploration here of the consequences of the education revolution attempts to examine evidence from all regions of the world. But the considerably larger volume of research in the U.S. case limits this effort (itself a function of the success of the American version of the research university described in Chapters 3–5). This is somewhat offset, however, by the fact that in many ways the United States represents an advanced form of the schooled society and likely foreshadows the future worldwide.

## CHAPTER 1

1. It should be pointed out that widespread enrollment does not imply equal quality of schooling, and there is still considerable variation among the school experiences of students from different nations and social groups within nations.

2. Enrollment rates for the United States can be somewhat misleading as to when the system achieved universal enrollment in primary and secondary schooling. The nation has a rather high dropout rate for eighteen-year-olds, often as high as one in four in disadvantaged rural and urban neighborhoods. But through the GED and a number of other programs aimed at helping dropouts finish high school, U.S. completion rates by the age of twenty-four are among the highest in the world. See Chapter 9 for an analysis of these nontraditional education paths.

## CHAPTER 2

1. Also, the Flynn effect has been shown with data from wide administrations of the Weschler test.

2. Torche also found some evidence suggesting that among the Americans who are earning postgraduate degrees, social origin again explains some portion of adult status. While yet to be replicated, the finding does raise speculation about the interaction between allocation processes and expansion of new educational degrees.

## CHAPTER 3

1. The difference between the numerous colleges in the United States (and now elsewhere) and universities is sometimes misunderstood. The university is the older and main form of higher education, and hence all universities have what Americans refer to as graduate education (postbaccalaureate); while the college was originally an internal subunit of the university and only became a stand-alone educational organization in the American system of higher education in the late eighteenth century (Durkheim 1938/1977). American colleges conform to a large degree to the same institutional model, but with a focus on undergraduate preparation. Hence the full institutional package of the Western university, not the stand-alone college, is the main form of interest here.

2. In formulating a sort of manpower planning scheme for the schooled society, Clark Kerr (e.g., 2001) developed some of the same ideas as here in the early 1960s with his idea of a "multiversity." But his assumption that the university could and should be the top-down commanding entity in the knowledge society missed the mark, and as a consequence his insightful ideas about the implications of the early development of the American knowledge conglomerate had diminished intellectual impact—until they were revised by Roger Geiger, a historian of the research university, much later (1993).

3. Islamic universities were significantly older than the first Western ones, with Al-Azhar in Cairo claiming to be the oldest continuous university in the world. But for a number of reasons, such as a tradition of wealthy patronage, Islam's theological message and loose organizational structure, and geopolitical forces, the Eastern version of the university remained limited in that it was rarely copied outside of the Middle East. And now even in the Middle East there are many Western-style universities.

4. The University of Paris was the forerunner to the currently operating Sorbonne, which was originally a college of the former (Durkheim 1938/1977).

5. This function continues to the present. For example, Pope Benedict XVI, then a cardinal in the Curia, successfully lobbied against the advancement of an up-and-coming papal favorite to archbishop because the candidate held only a Ph.D. in philosophy. The eventual appointee held a Ph.D. in theology, which the future Pope reasoned to be more suitable training for solving theological disputes ("Future Pope Tried to Get Fuller Inquiry in Abuse Case," *New York Times*, April 27, 2010).

6. Universalism should not be thought of as coming from the term "university"; the latter meant something close to "corporation" in medieval society and was used to describe early feudal corporations of scholars.

7. The same is true of former Eastern Bloc academies of science, which were once more powerful than universities under communist regimes. After the fall of the Iron Curtain, in Estonia, for example, one such academy was given three years to essentially transform itself into a university to compete with others for central funds for graduate training and research—or else perish.

8. In the context of a different era, this is essentially the underlying historical story behind the rise of the American super research university discussed in the next chapter.

9. Funding won for research is the most common way to measure overall research activity. Of course, it is not a perfect indicator as some funds produce more knowledge output than others, but on average funds and output are assumed to be closely related.

## CHAPTER 4

1. Einstein made his earliest discoveries while employed at the patent office in Bern, but after he completed the Ph.D., he was soon a professor at a university for the rest of his life.

2. The term "world-class university" is also used in the literature; in contrast, "super research university" is used here to denote the intensification of the knowledge conglomerate instead of a global ranking.

3. Interestingly, there is hardly any systematic evidence about the relative costs and benefits of the super RU model.

4. Research productivity and quality are difficult to measure. A frequently used statistical indicator, and the one used here, is the citation rate of a university's faculty's work in other published research.

5. This is not to imply that the United States, or any other nation, has achieved full openness to higher education. But in comparison, the U.S. education system, for all its faults, has reduced many barriers to education so that the average education level grows with each new generation. Witness, for example, the rich conversation in the American legal systems about the extent to which the higher education system is open in fact as well as in principle to all, regardless of race, class, and other demographic categories in which students from minority groups have been historically underrepresented.

6. Illustratively, manpower planning imagery was, and still is, so evident in German culture that oppositional liberal reformers in conjunction with the rising middle class had to campaign for a constitutional change outlawing the official use of such ideas in education and labor market policies by the government.

7. The oft invoked heavy emphasis on collegiate sports in some American institutions only fuels the process rather than causing it, as many colleges and some universities having low-level sports programs also have similar levels of alumni support (Kirp 2003).

8. Furthermore, academic universalistic development, not some form of expanded vocational training, led the way inside the university. The much later spread of the university-trained professional as an expert wielding authoritative knowledge was suppressed over a long period, during which the antithesis of the expert—the "cultivated man" as a polymath steeped in the classics—was the main goal of a university education, this being before the intensification of the education revolution. For example, Max Weber astutely observed that over much of its history up to the nineteenth century, the university aimed at "a knightly or ascetic type, at a literary (as in China) or at a gymnastic-humanist type (as in Hellas), or at a conventional 'gentleman' type of a Anglo-Saxon type" (Weber 1978, 1001). These essentially prebureaucratic, prerationalized forms of cultural training of an elite dominated, and stand in sharp relief against the rise of the specialized expert, particularly in the way expertise has spread over the twentieth century, forming so much of the current model of university training. The implications of the university's cultural expansion by merging the idea of universalism of knowledge and inquiry with professionalism are taken up in the third chapter (Chapter 5) on the university and the education revolution.

9. These are referred to as "1st Profession Degree" in the education statistics literature.

10. In other words, a significant share of the multiple graduate degrees was not just completing a master's on the way to a Ph.D.

CHAPTER 5

1. An example from education: following a Pennsylvania public school board's decision to place intelligent design (essentially divine creationism) into its science curriculum alongside evolution, a federal court sided with a citizens group's suit to remove it from the curriculum on the basis of legal findings that the material had religious intent *and* was not recognizable as science.

2. The disenchantment of the authority of religion has progressed into our culture so

that by the turn of the twenty-first century a secular-university president or a CEO of a firm can believe and profess in a religious explanation of the world, but if she were to publicly assert and demonstrate that she believed with fervor that an organizational problem is the work of a god and therefore out of her hands, there would be a quickly called meeting of the institution's governing board. Note, for example, the legal troubles and credibility problems encountered by Thomas Monaghan, the Domino's Pizza billionaire, when he publicly said that the Virgin Mary had directed him to develop a town in Florida and move his newly founded Ave Maria Law School there (*Chronicle of Higher Education*, November 2, 2007, 6).

3. The same universities were followed over the entire time period, but as new nations were formed in the middle of the twentieth century new universities were added.

4. See Foucault (1974) and Hoskin's (1990) essay on Foucault as a crypto-educationalist for a similar, but socially darker version of this process.

5. "Peachy Paterno" remains a popular flavor even in the wake of the child abuse scandal over one of the football program's former assistant coaches.

6. This estimate comes from the website run by Joan Korenman out of the University of Maryland–Baltimore County Women's Studies Program, which organizes the most comprehensive listing of women's studies programs, departments, and research centers in the United States and in other countries. Included also are units termed "gender studies." See http://research.umbc.edu/korenman/wmst/programs.html

7. Wotipka and Ramirez did not have a measure of the proportion of a nation's higher education faculty that was female, which would be the best test of the insurgency argument.

8. An interesting exception is found in the enlightened absolutism of the eighteenth century, when cameralism, or the science of public finance, was developed in the German university (Lenhardt 2005).

9. For an oppositional critique of the argument here, see Khurana 2007.

10. Boolean algebra, of course, was an important step towards the first computation machines as forerunners of the modern computer.

11. Later, the Germans followed the French and broke off a strong university-based research capacity into elite non-university institutes. This has led to some of the current crisis in this nation's university system in its attempts to mount significant super research universities (Baker and Lenhardt 2008).

CHAPTER 6

1. The overeducation literature focused only on males, but if more attention had been paid to the telling combination of factors behind the similarly skyrocketing enrollments of females, these experts might have realized that there is more behind the education revolution than just a narrow competition for jobs (e.g., Baker and LeTendre 2005).

2. I am indebted to the succinct conceptual insights of Mark Blaug (1970), Richard Rubinson and Irene Browne (1994), and Peter Wiles (1974); although dated, these writings ring as true now as they did then.

3. In the original conception of human capital there were other kinds of investments such as willingness to move to areas with new jobs and on-the-job training, but over time formal education has proved to be the main investment (Teixeira 2009).

4. Those familiar with current debates about educational accountability policies and the extensive use of testing, such as those that make up the No Child Left Behind laws in the United States, will recognize Dore's complaints.

5. The one small difference found was in job satisfaction for very highly educated people working in menial jobs.

6. Obviously growing numbers of university students in some nations led social and political protest, but the dynamic here was not alienation from education–job mismatch, rather in and of themselves student revolts are another institutional effect of education on society (e.g. Meyer and Rubinson 1972).

7. Differences among estimates are due to different methods. Clogg and Shockey use a relative overeducation measure with no anchoring in job skills, while B. H. Burris uses a measure of difference between education level and directly observed job skill requirements.

8. I am indebted to Peter Meyer, also of the Bureau of Labor Statistics, for leading me to this research.

9. See Abbott (1988) for the argument that the formal organization destroys professionalization in the more narrow traditional sense.

10. Berg 1971, 99, table V-2.

11. "GeD" stands for "general educational development," a measure used by the U.S. Department of Labor to categorize skills requirements of jobs. It should not be confused with the GED, or the General Educational Development tests, which award an alternative secondary school diploma in the United States.

### CHAPTER 7

1. This leads to Collins's idea of education as status competition, which many sociologists frequently associate with *The Credential Society*.

2. Even for the "experience then education" route to licensure, the candidate has to have worked with a licensed (i.e., educationally credentialed) architect.

3. The formulation of backward credentialing as reflecting the growing normative nature of forward educational credentialing stems from conversations with John McCarthy and the archival research assistance of John Crist.

4. For example, see Purdue University's Executive Education Program in the 1990s.

5. For example, standard treatments of the history of American higher education (such as Brubacher and Rudy's 1958 authoritative *Higher Education in Transition: An American History: 1636–1956*, which devotes less than three pages to *Honoris Causa*) have surprisingly little to say about honorary degrees; and what is the standard reference, Stephen Epler's *Honorary Degrees: A Survey of Their Use and Abuse* (1943), is now seventy years old. Interesting cases would include Benjamin Franklin, who terminated his formal schooling at the end of the second grade but used the title "Dr." throughout his life. This was in part justified by several honorary degrees, the first from Harvard College and others from European scholarly societies, rather than universities. And too, Johns Hopkins University president Daniel Coit Gilman, who in 1887 claimed that unearned degrees were "a sham and a shame," was on his way to accepting nine honorary degrees for himself (David Bills, personal communication, January 2010).

6. Details about each of these examples can be found on the *Wall Street Journal*'s website under "Careers," November 13, 2008, which summarizes original articles in the *Wall Street Journal*.

7. The respondent's father's education could be considered a type of educational factor, but because it does not measure the respondent's educational attainment it is more accurately considered a non-educational factor. The author thanks Emily Smith Greenaway for assistance in estimating the model.

8. The unusual ordering of returns of degrees is most likely due to the fact that because there were not GSS (General Social Survey) data at the middle of the twentieth century, these

estimates are derived from the 1977 data for older respondents who were entering the labor market in the 1950s and reflect some unknown degree of advancement in occupations.

9. In fact, this is so much the case that now modern militaries themselves prefer educational credentials as prior training to be an effective solider (Army.com 2009).

### CHAPTER 8

1. The larger size of the papal library was the result of its extensive collection of liturgical texts, whereas the king's collection held relatively few of these.

2. Not to be confused with Michael D. Young, mentioned in Chapter 7.

3. Down through the ages, of course, a prodigious philosophical literature on the nature of knowledge has accrued, containing many schools of thought that have, to varying degrees, influenced the sociology of knowledge; however, a discussion of this is beyond the present scope.

4. Indeed, despite the widespread misconception that the quality of American schools has declined in recent decades, in addition to curricula national assessments of mathematics indicate that the reverse is true, as a long-term trend analysis of mathematics achievement scores finds that mathematics achievement in 1999 was higher than in 1973 for all three assessed groups—nine-year-olds, thirteen-year-olds, and seventeen-year-olds (Campbell, Hombo, and Mazzeo [National Center for Education Statistics] 2000).

5. This trend is no doubt partly rooted in the Annales School of history.

6. Most nations outside of Western Europe and North America did not develop secondary schooling until later in the next century.

7. The growth in online blogging, particularly the rising popularity of blogged novels, can be seen as a result of this trend of the educational epistemology.

### CHAPTER 9

1. Throughout this chapter the author is indebted to the thorough chronicling of the school dropout issue by Sherman Dorn's *Creating the Dropout: An Institutional and Social History of School Failure*, and although the discussion in this chapter arrives at a different conclusion, the author's scholarship rests on the book's solid foundation.

2. There have been earlier incidents like this, such as the Massachusetts Bay Colony's first North American compulsory education law, the Olde Deluder Satan Law of 1647, which followed on a 1642 law that required every head of household to ensure the literacy of all children resident in that home. However, the dropout phenomenon of the 1960s both intensified and broadened the meaning of "educational deviant" to a level not seen before in modern society.

3. A real irony is that the predilection of many people in the schooled society to resonate with the debunking of social problems as merely false myths is itself a function of widespread education, which leads to mass consumption of a crude "sociologicalization" of society found in the media and, dare one say, in mass academic sociology courses too.

4. The test costs vary from state to state from free to $200.

5. In 2007, 2.92 million Chinese adults undertook the exam, and 2 million of them earned a diploma.

6. It is reasonable to predict that as the education revolution continues to influence world culture, nations that have lagged behind for whatever reasons will move towards larger redemptive measures for individuals to continue more formal education. In fact, Germany appears to be on the verge of one such transformation of its lowest-level secondary school.

7. Now most universities officially monitor statistics about the average "time to degree"

in their graduate programs, the implication being that noncompleters and laggard graduate students are a problem, an idea that would have been less meaningful just fifty years ago.

8. For example, No Child Left Behind legislation did not allow schools to count the GED as progress towards lowering their dropout rate.

### CHAPTER 10

1. Of course higher education attendance is not a random experiment, but Pascarella and Terenzini's thoroughness in examining both cross-sectional and longitudinal studies, often with considerable statistical conditioning on other individual factors, suggests that the major trends they find across numerous studies represent actual higher education effects in a causal sense.

2. Because key processes in his theorized dynamics of modernity are related to the argument developed here, it is unfortunate that Giddens did not consider the education revolution in his insightful writings about modernity and self-identity.

3. An example is the new digital, liquid-democratic Pirate Party in Germany (*The Economist*, April 24, 2012, 60).

### CHAPTER 11

1. And to be fair it should be noted that there are some cases in which dominant denominations have declined because a highly educated clergy chose the accommodation strategy of weakened (secularizing) core theological messages while retaining ineffective traditional organizational methods (Finke 2003).

### CONCLUSION

1. Whether the schooling effect on individuals is exactly monotonically linear with increasing attainment is a question requiring further research, but what evidence there is indicates this to be the case (e.g., Pascarella and Terenzini 2005).

2. This is not to imply that there is no informal education in traditional societies, but formal education that is now prevalent worldwide leads to many distinctly different outcomes not present in traditional informal education.

3. Of course, as mentioned in the story of the university and the education revolution, both Durkheim and Weber included some examination of the role of the university and science in their analyses of the great transition of society, but they could not be expected to have seen formal education's independent and future massive role in this transformation worldwide, or its intensification (e.g., Durkheim 1938/1977; Weber 1958).

4. "Academic intelligence" replaces Meyer's original use of the word "socialization," because the former more accurately represents what schooling does, and the latter is an older term now rarely used, which conveys other unneeded meanings.

7

# References

Abbott, Andrew. 2001. *Chaos of Disciplines*. Chicago: University of Chicago Press.
——. 1988. *The System of Professions*. Chicago: University of Chicago Press.
Academy of Management. 2012. http://www.aomonline.org
Acemoglu, Daron. 1998. "Why Do New Technologies Complement Skills? Directed Technical Change and Wage Inequality." *Quarterly Journal of Economics* 113, no. 4: 1055–89.
Ackroyd, Peter. 1999. *The Life of Thomas More*. New York: Anchor Books.
Adams, David Wallace. 1995. *Education for Extinction: American Indians and the Boarding School Experience, 1876–1928*. Lawrence: University Press of Kansas.
Alexander, Karl, Robert Bozick, and Doris Entwisle. 2008. "Warming Up, Cooling Out, or Holding Steady? Persistence and Change in Educational Expectations After High School." *Sociology of Education* 81, no. 4: 371–96.
Almond, Gabriel A., and Sidney Verba. 1963. *The Civic Culture: Political Attitudes and Democracy in Five Nations*. Newbury Park, CA: Sage.
Altbach, Philip G., and Jamil Salmi, eds. 2011. *The Road to Academic Excellence: The Making of World-Class Research Universities*. Washington, DC: World Bank.
Anderson, Benedict. 1991. *Imagined Communities*. London: Verso.
Andrews, Rhys, and George Boyne. 2010. "Better Public Services." *Public Management Review* 12, no. 2: 307–21.
Apple, Michael W. 1990. *Ideology and Curriculum*, 2nd ed. London: Routledge.
Archer, Margaret S. 1979. *Social Origins of Educational Systems*. Beverly Hills, CA: Sage.
Aries, Philippe. 1962. *Centuries of Childhood: A Social History of Family Life*. New York: Vintage Books.
Army.com. 2009. "Army Knowledge Online." http://www.army.com/enlist/active-duty-requirements.html
Arnove, Robert F. 1995. "Education as Contested Terrain in Nicaragua." *Comparative Education Review* 39, no. 1: 28–53.
Arum, Richard, and Josipa Roksa. 2011. *Academically Adrift: Limited Learning on College Campuses*. Chicago: University of Chicago Press.
Astin, Alexander W. 1993. *What Matters in College?* San Francisco: Jossey-Bass.
Astin, Alexander W., and Linda J. Sax. 1998. "How Undergraduates Are Affected by Service Participation." *Journal of College Student Development* 39, no. 3: 251–63.
Autor, David H., Lawrence F. Katz, and Alan B. Krueger. 1998. "Computing Inequality: Have Computers Changed the Labor Market?" *Quarterly Journal of Economics* 113, no. 4: 1169–213.
"The Ayes Have It; Germany's Pirate Party." 2012. *The Economist*, April 28, 60.
Bader, Christopher D., F. Carson Mencken, and Joseph O. Baker. 2010. *Paranormal America: Ghost Encounters, UFO Sightings, Bigfoot Hunts, and Other Curiosities in Religion and Culture*. New York: New York University Press.

Baker, David P. 1999. "Schooling All the Masses: Reconsidering the Origins of American Schooling in the Postbellum Era." *Sociology of Education* 72, no. 4: 197–215.

———. 2008a. "Mass Higher Education and the Super Research University: A Symbiotic Relationship." *International Higher Education* 2, Fall: 36–53.

———. 2008b. "Privatization, Mass Higher Education, and the Super Research University: Symbiotic or Zero-Sum Trends?" *Die Hochschule* 2: 36–52.

———. 2009. "The Educational Transformation of Work: Towards a New Synthesis." *Journal of Education and Work* 22, no. 3: 163–91.

———. 2011. "Forward and Backward, Horizontal and Vertical: Transformation of Occupational Credentialing in the Schooled Society." *Research in Social Stratification and Mobility: A Journal of the International Sociological Association* 29, no. 1: 5–29.

———. forthcoming. "The Great Antagonism That Never Was: Flourishing Religion in the Schooled Society."

Baker, David P., Hilary Knipe, Eric Cummings, John M. Collins, Juan Leon, Clancy Blair, and David Gamson. 2010. "One Hundred Years of American Primary School Mathematics: A Content Analysis and Cognitive Assessment of Textbooks from 1900 to 2000." *Journal of Research on Mathematics Education* 41, no. 4: 383–423.

Baker, David P., Helmut Köhler, and Manfred Stock. 2007. "Socialist Ideology and the Contraction of Higher Education: Institutional Consequences of State Manpower and Education Planning in the Former East Germany." *Comparative Education Review* 51, no. 3: 353–77.

Baker, David P., and Gero Lenhardt. 2008. "The Institutional Crisis of the German Research University." *Higher Education Policy* 21: 49–64.

Baker, David P., Juan Leon, and John M. Collins. 2010. "Facts, Attitudes, and Health Reasoning About HIV and AIDS: Explaining the Education Effect on Condom Use Among Adults in Sub-Saharan Africa." *AIDS and Behavior*: 1–9. DOI 10.1007/s10461-010-9717-9

Baker, David P., Juan Leon, Emily G. Smith Greenaway, John Collins, and Marcela Movit. 2011. "The Education Effect on Population Health: A Reassessment." *Population and Development Review* 37, no. 2: 307–32.

Baker, David P., and Gerald K. LeTendre. 2005. *National Differences, Global Similarities: World Culture and the Future of Schooling.* Stanford, CA: Stanford University Press.

Baker, David P., and Izumi Mori. 2010. "The Origin of Universal Shadow Education: What the Supplemental Education Phenomenon Tells Us About the Postmodern Institution of Education." *Asia Pacific Education Review* 11, no. 1: 36–48.

Baker, David P., Daniel Salinas, and Paul J. Eslinger. 2012. "An Envisioned Bridge: Schooling as a Neurocognitive Developmental Institution." *Developmental Cognitive Neuroscience* 2: 6–17.

Baldwin, Janet. 1991. "Schooling, Study, and Academic Goals: The Education of GED Candidates." *GED Profiles: Adults in Transition*, no. 2. Washington, DC: American Council on Education.

Baldwin, Lionel V. 1991. "Higher-Education Partnerships in Engineering and Science." *Annals of the American Academy of Political and Social Science* 514, no. 1: 76–91.

Bastedo, Michael N., and Patricia J. Gumport. 2003. "Access to What? Mission Differentiation and Academic Stratification in US Public Higher Education." *Higher Education* 46, no. 3: 341–59.

Becker, Gary S. 1993. *Human Capital: A Theoretical and Empirical Analysis, with Special Reference to Education.* Chicago: University of Chicago Press.

Bell, Daniel. 1977. "The Return of the Sacred? The Argument on the Future of Religion." *British Journal of Sociology* 28, no. 4: 419–49.

Bell, David, and Jon Binnie. 2000. *The Sexual Citizen: Queer Politics and Beyond*. Cambridge, UK: Polity Press.

Ben-David, Joseph. 1971. *The Scientist's Role in Society*. Englewood Cliffs, NJ: Prentice Hall.

Ben-David, Joseph, and Awraham Zloczower. 1991. "Universities and Academic Systems in Modern Societies." *European Journal of Sociology* 3: 45–84.

Benavot, Aaron. 1983. "The Rise and Decline of Vocational Education." *Sociology of Education* 56, no. 2: 63–76.

———. 2006. "A Global Study of Intended Instructional Time and Official School Curricula." http://ns.worldbank.org.ru/ecaedu/bg/Global_Curriculum_text_Eng.pdf

Benavot, Aaron, Yun-Kyung Cha, David Kamens, John W. Meyer, and Suk-Ying Wong. 1991. "Knowledge for the Masses: World Models and National Curricula, 1920–1986." *American Sociological Review* 56, no. 1 (February): 85–100.

Benavot, Aaron, and Phyllis Riddle. 1988. "The Expansion of Primary Education, 1870–1940: Trends and Issues." *Sociology of Education* 61, no. 3: 191–210.

Bennhold, Katrin. 2010. "Future Pope's Role in Abuse Case Was Complex." *New York Times*, April 26, 2010.

Berg, Ivar. 1971. *Education and Jobs: The Great Training Robbery*. New York: Praeger.

Berger, Peter, Brigette Berger, and Hansfried Kellner. 1974. *The Homeless Mind: Modernization and Consciousness*. New York: Vintage.

Berger, Peter, and Thomas Luckmann. 1966. *The Social Construction of Reality: A Treatise in the Sociology of Knowledge*. Garden City, NY: Anchor Books.

Berkovitch, Nitza, and Karen Bradley. 1999. "The Globalization of Women's Status: Consensus/Dissensus in the World Polity." *Sociological Perspectives*: 481–98.

Berman, Eli, John Bound, and Stephen Machin. 1998. "Implications of Skill-Biased Technological Change: International Evidence." *Quarterly Journal of Economics* 113, no. 4: 1245–79.

Bernstein, Basil. 1971. "On the Classification and Framing of Educational Knowledge." In *Knowledge and Control*, ed. M. Young. London: Collier-Macmillan.

Bills, David B. 1988. "Educational Credentials and Promotions: Does Schooling Do More Than Get You in the Door?" *Sociology of Education* 61, no. 1: 52–60.

———. 2003. "Credentials, Signals, and Screens: Explaining the Relationship Between Schooling and Job Assignment." *Review of Educational Research* 73, no. 4 (Winter): 441–49.

———. 2004. *Sociology of Education and Work*. Malden, MA: Blackwell.

Birdsall, Nancy, Thomas Pinckney, and Richard Sabot. 2008. "Natural Resources, Human Capital, and Growth." In *Resource Abundance and Economic Development*, ed. R. M. Auty. Oxford, UK: Oxford University Press.

Blair, Clancy, David Gamson, Steven Thorne, and David Baker. 2005. "Rising Mean IQ: Cognitive Demand of Mathematics Education for Young Children, Population Exposure to Formal Schooling, and the Neurobiology of the Prefrontal Cortex." *Intelligence* 33, no. 1: 93–106.

Blau, Peter M., and Otis D. Duncan. 1967. *The American Occupational Structure*. New York: Wiley.

Blaug, Mark. 1970. *An Introduction to Economics of Education*. London: Penguin.

Bledstein, Burton. 1976. "The Culture of Professionalism: The Middle Class and the Development of Higher Education in America." New York: Norton.

Bloom, Allan. 1987. *The Closing of the American Mind*. New York: Simon & Schuster.

Blumberg, Paul, and James M. Murtha. 1977. "College Graduates and the American Dream." *Dissent* 24, no. 1: 45–53.

Boesel, David, Nabeel Alsalam, and Thomas M Smith. 1998. *Educational and Labor Market Performance of GED Recipients.* Washington, DC: National Library of Education.

Boli, John, and George Thomas. 1985. "Explaining the Origins and Expansion of Mass Education." *Comparative Education Review* 29, no. 2 (May): 145–70.

Boli, John, and George Thomas. 1999. *Constructing World Culture: International Non-Governmental Organizations Since 1875.* Stanford, CA: Stanford University Press.

Bourdieu, Pierre, and Jean-Claude Passeron. 1977. *Reproduction in Education, Society, and Culture.* Cambridge, UK: Cambridge University Press.

Bowles, Samuel, and Herbert Gintis. 1976. *Schooling in Capitalist America: Educational Reform and the Contradictions of Economic Life.* New York: Basic Books.

Boxer, Marilyn Jacoby. 1998. *When Women Ask the Questions: Creating Women's Studies in America.* Baltimore: Johns Hopkins University Press.

Brand, Jennie E., and Yu Xie. 2010. "Who Benefits Most from College? Evidence for Negative Selection in Heterogeneous Economic Returns to Higher Education." *American Sociological Review* 75, no. 2 (April 1): 273–302.

Breen, Richard, and Jon O. Jonsson. 2007. "Explaining Change in Social Fluidity: Educational Equalization and Educational Expansion in Twentieth-Century Sweden." *American Journal of Sociology* 112, no. 6: 1775–810.

Breen, Richard, and Ruud Luijkx. 2007. "Social Mobility and Education: A Comparative Analysis of Period and Cohort Trends in Britain and Germany." In *Trends and Mechanisms in Social Stratification Research*, ed. R. Pollak S. Scherer, G. Otte, and M. Gangl, 102–24. New York: Campus.

Bremner, William J., and David M. de Kretser. 1975. "Contraceptives for Males." *Signs* 1, no. 2: 387–96.

Brint, Steven. 1996. *In an Age of Experts: The Changing Role of Professionals in Politics and Public Life.* Princeton, NJ: Princeton University Press.

———, ed. 2002. *The Future of the City of Intellect: The Changing American University.* Stanford, CA: Stanford University Press.

Brint, Steven, and Jerome Karabel. 1989. *The Diverted Dream: Community Colleges and the Promise of Educational Opportunity in America, 1900–1985.* New York: Oxford University Press.

Brody, Richard. 1978. "The Puzzle of Political Participation in America." In *The New American Political System*, ed. Anthony King, 287–324. Washington, DC: American Enterprise Institute.

Bromley, Patricia, John W. Meyer, and Francisco O. Ramirez. 2011a. "Student-Centeredness in Social Science Textbooks, 1970–2008: A Cross-National Study." *Social Forces* 90, no. 2: 547–70.

Bromley, Patricia, John W. Meyer, and Francisco O. Ramirez. 2011b. "The Worldwide Spread of Environmental Discourse in Social Studies, History, and Civics Textbooks, 1970–2008." *Comparative Education Review* 55, no. 4: 517–45.

Brooks, David. 2011. "The Quest for Dignity." *New York Times*, February 1.

Brown, Peter. 2000. *Augustine of Hippo: A Biography.* Berkeley: University of California Press.

Brown, Phillip, and Hugh Lauder. 2009. "Economic Globalisation, Skill Formation and the Consequences for Higher Education." In *The Routledge International Handbook of the Sociology of Education.* London: Routledge.

Brubacher, John S., and Willis Rudy. 1958. *Higher Education in Transition: An American History, 1636–1956*. New York: Harper & Brothers.

Burnham, Walter Dean. 1984. "The Appearance and Disappearance of the American Voter." In *Electoral Participation: A Comparative Analysis*, ed. R. Rose. Beverly Hills, CA: Sage.

Burris, Beverly H. 1983. *No Room at the Top*. New York: Praeger.

Burris, Val. 1983. "The Social and Political Consequences of Overeducation." *American Sociological Review* 48, no. 4: 454–67.

Byun, Soo-Yong, and David P. Baker. 2013. "Shadow Education." In *Emerging Trends in the Social and Behavioral Sciences*, ed. R. A. Scott and S. M. Kosslyn. Thousand Oaks, CA: Sage.

Cahn, Naomi, and June Carbone. 2010. *Red Families v. Blue Families: Legal Polarization and the Creation of Culture*. Oxford, UK: Oxford University Press.

Cameron, Stephen, and James J. Heckman. 1994. "Determinants of Young Males' Schooling and Training Choices." In *Training and the Private Sector*, ed. Lisa M. Lynch. Chicago: University of Chicago Press.

Camic, Charles, Neil Gross, and Michèle Lamont. 2011. *Social Knowledge in the Making*. Chicago: University of Chicago Press.

Campbell, Jay R., Catherine M. Hombo, and John Mazzeo. 2000. "NAEP 1999 Trends in Academic Progress: Three Decades of Student Performance." Washington, DC: National Center for Education Statistics.

Carnevale, Anthony P., and Stephen J. Rose. 2011. "The Undereducated American." Washington, DC: Georgetown University, Center on Education and the Workforce.

Carroll, Glenn R., and Michael T. Hannan. 1999. *The Demography of Corporations and Industries*. Princeton, NJ: Princeton University Press.

Castells, Manuel. 1996. *The Rise of the Network Society: The Information Age: Economy, Society and Culture*, vol. 1. Malden, MA: Blackwell.

Castillo, Milagros. 2013. "Liberally Educating Students: Developing African American and Latino Undergraduates' Sociopolitical Capacity in Introductory Sociology." Doctoral dissertation. Teachers College, Columbia University.

Ceci, Stephen J. 1991. "How Much Does Schooling Influence General Intelligence and Its Cognitive Components? A Reassessment of the Evidence." *Developmental Psychology* 27, no. 5: 703–22.

Centre Daily Times (State College, PA). 2009. "Babin Wants to Stay in Jail to Get GED Before Release, Man Will Have to Resolve Drug Case from July." December 14, 5.

Cervantes, Lucius Ferdinand. 1965. *The Dropout: Causes and Cures*. Ann Arbor: University of Michigan Press.

Cha, Yun-Kyung. 1991. "Effect of the Global System on Language Instruction, 1850–1986." *Sociology of Education* 64, no. 1: 19–32.

Cha, Yun-Kyung, and Seung-Hwan Ham. 2008. "The Impact of English on the School Curriculum." In *The Handbook of Educational Linguistics*, ed. B. Spolsky and F. Hult, 313–28. London: Blackwell.

Cha, Yun-Kyung, and Seung-Hwan Ham. 2011. "Educating Supranational Citizens: The Incorporation of English Language Education into Curriculum Policies." *American Journal of Education* 117, no. 2: 183–209.

Chait, Richard. 2002. *The Questions of Tenure*. Cambridge, MA: Harvard University Press.

Chandler, Alfred D. 1977. *The Visible Hand: The Managerial Revolution in American Business*. Cambridge, MA: Belknap Press.

Chandler, Alfred D., and Bruce Mazlish. 2005. *Leviathans: Multinational Corporations and the New Global History*. Cambridge, UK: Cambridge University Press.

Chaves, Mark. 1994. "Secularization as Declining Religious Authority." *Social Forces* 72, no. 3: 749–74.

Chaves, Mark, and James C. Cavendish. 1994. "More Evidence on US Catholic Church Attendance." *Journal for the Scientific Study of Religion* 33, no. 4: 376–81.

Cherry, Conrad, Betty A. DeBerg, and Amanda Porterfield. 2001. *Religion on Campus*. Chapel Hill: University of North Carolina Press.

Chevalier, Arnaud. 2000. "Graduate Over-Education in the UK." Discussion Paper, no. 7. London: London School of Economics and Political Science, Centre for the Economics of Education.

Christiano, Kevin J. 1987. *Religious Diversity and Social Change: American Cities, 1890–1906*. Cambridge, UK: Cambridge University Press.

Clark, Burton R. 1960. "The 'Cooling-Out' Function in Higher Education." *American Journal of Sociology* 65, no. 6: 569–76.

———. 1962. *Educating the Expert*. San Francisco: Chandler.

———. 1980. "The 'Cooling Out' Function Revisited." *New Directions for Community Colleges* 32: 15–31.

Clogg, Clifford. 1979. *Measuring Underemployment: Demographic Indicators for the United States*. New York: Academic Press.

Clogg, Clifford C., and James W. Shockey. 1984. "Mismatch Between Occupation and Schooling: A Prevalence Measure, Recent Trends and Demographic Analysis." *Demography* 21, no. 2: 235–57.

Cobban, Alan B. 1975. *The Medieval Universities: Their Development and Organization*. New York: Methuen, dist. Harper & Row, Barnes & Noble Import Division.

Cole, Jonathan R. 2009. *The Great American University: Its Rise to Preeminence, Its Indispensable National Role, Why It Must Be Protected*. New York: Public Affairs.

Cole, Micheal. 1996. *Cultural Psychology: A Once and Future Discipline*. Cambridge, MA: Belknap Press of Harvard University Press.

Collins, David. 1998. *Organizational Change: Sociological Perspectives*. New York: Routledge.

Collins, Randall. 1979. *The Credential Society*. New York: Academic Press.

———. 1998. *The Sociology of Philosophies: A Global Theory of Intellectual Change*. Cambridge, MA: Harvard University Press.

———. 2002. "Credential Inflation and the Future of Universities." In *The Future of the City of Intellect*, ed. S. Brint, 23–46. Stanford, CA: Stanford University Press.

Collins, Randall, and Michael Makowsky. 1998. *The Discovery of Society*. New York: McGraw-Hill.

Converse, Philip E. 1972. "Change in American Electorate." In *The Human Meaning of Social Change*, ed. Angus Campbell and Philip E. Converse, 307–17. New York: Russell Sage Foundation.

Coser, Lewis A. 1974. *Greedy Institutions: Patterns of Undivided Commitment*. New York: Free Press.

Craig, John E. 1981. "The Expansion of Education." *Review of Research in Education* 9: 151–213.

Cremin, Lawrence A. 1990. *Popular Education and Its Discontents*. New York: Harper & Row.

Crenson, Matthew A., and Benjamin Ginsberg. 2004. *Downsizing Democracy: How America Sidelined Its Citizens and Privatized Its Public*. Baltimore: Johns Hopkins University Press.

Crespo Cuaresma, Jesús, Wolfgang Lutz, and Warren Sanderson. 2014."Is the Demographic Dividend an Education Dividend?" *Demography* 51, no. 1: 299–315.

Cuban, Larry. 1993. *How Teachers Taught: Constancy and Change in American Classrooms, 1890–1990.* New York: Teachers College Press.

———. 2009. *Hugging the Middle: How Teachers Teach in an Era of Testing and Accountability.* New York: Teachers College Press.

Cuban, Larry, and Dorothy Shipps. 2000. *Reconstructing the Common Good in Education: Coping with Intractable American Dilemmas.* Stanford, CA: Stanford University Press.

Cueto, Santiago, Cecilia Ramirez, and Juan Leon. 2006. "Opportunities to Learn and Achievement in Mathematics in a Sample of Sixth Grade Students in Lima, Peru." *Educational Studies in Mathematics* 62: 25–55.

Cunha, Flavio, James J. Heckman, and Susanne M. Schennach. 2010. "Estimating the Technology of Cognitive and Noncognitive Skill Formation." *Econometrica* 78, no. 3: 883–931.

Dalton, Russell J. 2008. *The Good Citizen: How a Younger Generation Is Reshaping American Politics.* Washington, DC: CQ Press.

Darkenwald, Gordon G., and Thomas Valentine. 1985. "Factor Structure of Deterrents to Public Participation in Adult Education." *Adult Education Quarterly* 35, no. 4: 177–93.

"Data, Data Everywhere." 2010. *The Economist,* February 27, 4.

Davies, Scott, Linda Quirke, and Janice Aurini. 2006. "The New Institutionalism Goes to the Market: The Challenge of Rapid Growth in Private K-12 Education." In *The New Institutionalism in Education,* ed. Heinz Dieter-Meyer and Brian Rowan, 103–22. Albany: State University of New York Press.

de Barros, Ricardo P., Francisco H.G. Ferreira, Jose R. Molinas Vega, and Jaime S. Chanduvi. 2009. *Inequality of Opportunity in Educational Achievement in Five Latin American Countries Measuring Inequality of Opportunities in Latin America and the Caribbean.* Washington, DC: World Bank.

Deil-Amen, Regina. 2006. "'Warming Up' the Aspirations of Community College Students." In *After Admission: From College Access to College Success,* ed. James E. Rosenbaum, Regina Deil-Amen, and Ann E. Person, 40–65. New York: Russell Sage Foundation.

Deil-Amen, Regina, and James E. Rosenbaum. 2002. "The Unintended Consequences of Stigma-Free Remediation." *Sociology of Education* 75, no. 3 (July): 249–68.

Deil-Amen, Regina, and Ruth López Turley. 2007. "A Review of the Transition to College Literature in Sociology." *Teachers College Record* 109, no. 10: 2324–66.

Denny, Kevin J., and Colm P. Harmon. 2001. "Testing for Sheepskin Effects in Earnings Equations: Evidence for Five Countries." *Applied Economics Letters* 8, no. 9: 635–37.

de Solla Price, Derek J. 1963. *Little Science, Big Science.* New York: Columbia University Press.

DiMaggio, Paul. 1997. "Culture and Cognition." *Annual Review of Sociology* 23: 263–87.

DiMaggio, Paul, John Evans, and Bethany Bryson. 1996. "Have Americans' Social Attitudes Become More Polarized?" *American Journal of Sociology* 3, November: 690–755.

Dobbin, Frank, and Erin L. Kelly. 2007. "How to Stop Harassment: Professional Construction of Legal Compliance in Organizations." *American Journal of Sociology* 112, no. 4: 1203–43.

Dobbin, Frank, John Meyer, and Richard Scott. 1993. "Equal Opportunity Law and the Construction of Internal Labor Markets." *American Journal of Sociology* 104, no. 2: 441–76.

Dohm, Arlene, and Lynn Shniper. 2007. "Occupational Employment Projections to 2016." *Monthly Labor Review* 130, no. 11 (November): 86–125.

Dom, Mark, Timothy Dunne, and Kenneth R. Troske. 1997. "Workers, Wage, and Technology." *Quarterly Journal of Economics* 112, no. 1: 253–90.

Dore, Ronald P. 1976. *The Diploma Disease: Education, Qualification and Development.* Berkeley: University of California Press.

Dorius, Shawn F. 2013. "The Rise and Fall of Worldwide Education Inequality from 1870 to 2010: Measurement and Trends." *Sociology of Education* 86, no. 2: 158–73.

Dorn, Sherman. 1996. *Creating the Dropout: An Institutional and Social History of School Failure.* Westport, CT: Praeger.

Dougherty, Kevin J. 1992. "Community Colleges and Baccalaureate Attainment." *Journal of Higher Education* 2, March: 188–214.

———. 1994. *The Contradictory College: The Conflicting Origins, Impacts and Futures of the Community Colleges.* Albany: State University of New York Press.

Downey, Douglas B., Paul T. von Hippel, and Beckett A. Broh. 2004. "Are Schools the Great Equalizer? Cognitive Inequality During the Summer Months and the School Year." *American Sociological Review* 69, no. 5 (October 1): 613–35.

Dreeben, R. 1968. *On What Is Learned in School.* Reading, MA: Addison-Wesley.

Drori, Gili S., John W. Meyer, and Hokyu Hwang. 2006. *Globalization and Organization: World Society and Organizational Change.* Oxford, UK: Oxford University Press.

Drori, Gili S., John W. Meyer, Francisco O. Ramirez, and Evan Schofer. 2003. *Science in the Modern World Polity: Institutionalization and Globalization.* Stanford, CA: Stanford University Press.

Drori, Gili S., and Hyeyoung Moon. 2006. "The Changing Nature of Tertiary Education: Neo-Institutional Perspectives on Cross-National Trends in Disciplinary Enrollment, 1965–1995." In *The Impact of Comparative Education Research on Institutional Theory,* ed. David P. Baker and Alex Wiseman. Greenwich, CT: JAI.

Dugger, Celia W. 2009. "Eager Students Fall Prey to Apartheid's Legacy." *New York Times,* September 29.

Duncan, Greg J., and Richard Murnane, eds. 2011. *Whither Opportunity: Rising Inequality, Schools, and Children's Life Chances.* New York: Russell Sage Foundation.

Dunne, Timothy, and James A. Schmitz, Jr. 1995. "Wages, Employment Structure and Employer Size-Wage Premia: Their Relationship to Advanced-Technology Usage at US Manufacturing Establishments." *Economica* 62, no. 245: 89–107.

Durkheim, Émile. 1938. "The Birth of the University." In *The Evolution of Educational Thoughts: Lectures on the Formation and Development of Secondary Education in France,* trans. and ed. Peter Collins, 75–87. Boston: Routledge & Kegan Paul.

———. 1938/1977. *The Evolution of Educational Thought: Lectures on the Formation and Development of Secondary Education in France.* Trans. and ed. Peter Collins. Boston: Routledge & Kegan Paul.

Ecklund, Elaine Howard, Jerry Z. Park, and Phil Todd Veliz. 2008. "Secularization and Religious Change Among Elite Scientists." *Social Forces* 86, no. 4: 1805–39.

Eicholz, Robert E., Phares G. O'Daffer, and C. R. Fleenor. 1991. *Addison-Wesley Mathematics.* Menlo Park, CA: Addison-Wesley.

Emler, Nicholas, and Elizabeth Frazer. 1999. "Politics: The Education Effect." *Oxford Review of Education* 25, no. 1–2: 251–73.

Enders, Jürgen, Barbara M. Kehm, and Uwe Schimank. 2002. "Structures and Problems of Research in German Higher Education: An Overview and an Agenda for Further Studies." In *Trends in American and German Higher Education,* ed. Robert McAdams. Cambridge, MA: American Academy of Arts and Sciences.

Enders, Jürgen, and Ulrich Teichler. 1995. *Der Hochschullehrerberuf im Internationalen Vergleich*. Bonn: Bundesministerium für Bildung, Wissenschaft, Forschung und Technologie.

Epler, Stephen E. 1943. *Honorary Degrees: A Survey of Their Use and Abuse*. Washington, DC: American Council on Public Affairs.

Eslinger, Paul J. 1998. "Neurological and Neuropsychological Bases of Empathy." *European Neurology* 39: 193–99.

Ezell, Allen, and John Bear. 2005. *Degree Mills: The Billion-Dollar Industry That Has Sold over a Million Fake Diplomas*. Amherst, NY: Prometheus Books.

Faia, Michael A. 1981. "Selection by Certification: A Neglected Variable in Stratification Research." *American Journal of Sociology*: 1093–111.

Ferrer, Ana M., and Craig Riddell. 2002. "The Role of Credentials in the Canadian Labour Market." *Canadian Journal of Economics/Revue canadienne d'économique* 35, no. 4: 879–905.

Fiala, Robert. 2006. "Educational Ideology and the School Curriculum." In *School Knowledge in Comparative and Historical Perspective*, ed. Aaron Benavot and Cecilia Braslavsky, 1–20. Hong Kong: Springer.

Fiala, Robert, and Audri G. Lansford. 1987. "Educational Ideology and the World Educational Revolution, 1950–1970." *Comparative Education Review* 31, no. 3: 315–32.

Filkins, Dexter. 2009a. "Afghan Girls, Scarred by Acid, Defy Terror, Embracing School." *New York Times*, January 14.

———. 2009b. "A School Bus for Shamsia." *New York Times*, August 7.

Fine, Michelle. 1991. *Framing Dropouts: Notes on the Politics of an Urban Public High School*. Albany: State University of New York Press.

Fine, Sidney A. 1968. "The Use of the Dictionary of Occupational Titles as a Source of Estimates of Educational and Training Requirements." *Journal of Human Resources* 3, no. 3: 363–75.

Finke, Roger. 2001. "The New Holy Clubs: Testing Church-to-Sect Propositions." *Sociology of Religion* 62, no. 2: 175.

———. 2003. "Spiritual Capital: Definitions, Applications, and New Frontiers." Prepared for the Spiritual Capital Planning Meeting, October 10–11.

Finke, Roger, and Rodney Stark. 1992. *The Churching of America, 1776–1990: Winners and Losers in Our Religious Economy*. New Brunswick, NJ: Rutgers University Press.

Fiske, Susan T., Richard R. Lau, and Richard A. Smith. 1990. "On the Varieties and Utilities of Political Expertise." *Social Cognition* 8, no. 1: 31–48.

Fleishman, Shannon S. 2013. "Community Colleges in the Lives of Contemporary Youth: Educational Expansion, Steady Expectations, and Inter-Institutional Attendance." Doctoral dissertation. Pennsylvania State University.

Fleishman, Shannon S., and David P. Baker. 2012. "Community Colleges: Past, Present, and Future." Association for the Study of Higher Education, annual conference, November 15–17, Las Vegas, NV.

Fligstein, N. 2008. *Euroclash: The EU, European Identity, and the Future of Europe*. Oxford, UK: Oxford University Press.

Florida, Richard. 2001. *The Rise of the Creative Class*. New York: Basic Books.

Flynn, James R. 1984. "The Mean IQ of Americans: Massive Gains 1932 to 1978." *Psychological Bulletin* 95: 29–51.

———. 1987. "Massive IQ Gains in 14 Nations: What IQ Tests Really Measure." *Psychological Bulletin* 101: 171–91.

———. 1998. "IQ Gains over Time: Toward Finding the Causes." In *The Rising Curve:*

*Long Term Gains in IQ and Related Measures*, ed. U. Neisser, 25–66. Washington, DC: American Psychological Association.

————. 1999. "The Changing Cultural Content of the Nation-State: A World Society Perspective." In *State/Culture: State Formation After the Cultural Turn*, ed. G. Steinmetz, 123–43. Ithaca, NY: Cornell University Press.

Fogarty, Timothy. 1997. "The Education of Accountants in the U.S.: Reason and Its Limits at the Turn of the Century." *Critical Perspectives on Accounting* 8: 45–68.

Foucault, Michel. 1974. *The Order of Things*. London: Tavistock.

Fourcade, Marion. 2006. "The Construction of a Global Profession: The Transnationalization of Economics." *American Journal of Sociology* 112, no. 1: 145–94.

Fourcade-Gourinchas, Marion, and Sarah L. Babb. 2002. "The Rebirth of the Liberal Creed: Paths to Neoliberalism in Four Countries." *American Journal of Sociology* 108, no. 3: 533–79.

Frank, David J. 1997. "Science, Nature, and the Globalization of the Environment, 1870–1990." *Social Forces* 76, no. 2: 409–35.

Frank, David, and Jay Gabler. 2006. *Reconstructing the University: Worldwide Shifts in Academia in the 20th Century*. Stanford, CA: Stanford University Press.

Frank, David. J., Ann Hironaka, and Evan Schofer. 2000. "The Nation-State and the Natural Environment over the Twentieth Century." *American Sociological Review* 65, February: 96–116.

Frank, David J., and John W. Meyer. 2002. "The Profusion of Individual Roles and Identities in the Postwar Period." *Sociological Theory* 20, no. 1: 86–105.

Frank, David J., and John W. Meyer. 2007. "University Expansion and the Knowledge Society." *Theory and Society* 36, no. 4: 287–311.

Frank, David J., John W. Meyer, and D. Miyahara. 1995. "The Individualist Polity and the Prevalence of Professionalized Psychology: A Cross-National Study." *American Sociological Review*: 360–77.

Frank, David J., Evan Schofer, and John Charles Torres. 1994. "Rethinking History: Change in the University Curriculum, 1910–90." *Sociology of Education* 67, no. 4 (October): 231–42.

Frank, David J., Suk-Ying Wong, John W. Meyer, and Francisco O. Ramirez. 2000. "What Counts as History: A Cross-National and Longitudinal Study of University Curricula." *Comparative Education Review* 44, no. 1: 29–53.

Freeman, Richard B. 1975. "Overinvestment in College Training?" *Journal of Human Resources* 10, no. 3: 287–311.

————. 1976. *The Overeducated American*. New York: Academic Press.

Frey, Carl Benedikt, and Michael A. Osborne. 2013. "The Future of Employment: How Susceptible Are Jobs to Computerisation?" www.oxfordmartin.ox.ac.uk

Froese, Paul. 2008. *The Plot to Kill God: Findings from the Soviet Experiment in Secularization*. Berkeley: University of California Press.

Froese, Paul, and Christopher Bader. 2008. "Unraveling Religious Worldviews: The Relationship Between Images of God and Political Ideology in a Cross Cultural Analysis." *Sociological Quarterly* 49, no. 4: 689–718.

Froese, Paul, and Christopher Bader. 2010. *America's Four Gods: What We Say About God—And What That Says About Us*. New York: Oxford University Press.

Fukuyama, Francis. 1992. *The End of History and the Last Man*. New York: Free Press.

Fuller, Bruce, and Richard Rubinson, eds. 1992. *The Political Construction of Education: The State, School Expansion, and Economic Change*. New York: Praeger.

Gamson, David. A., Xiaofei Lu, and Sarah A. Eckert. 2013. "Challenging the Research Base of the Common Core State Standards: A Historical Reanalysis of Text Complexity." *Educational Researcher* 42, no. 7: 381–91.

Gardner, Howard. 1983. *Frames of Mind: The Theory of Multiple Intelligences.* New York: Basic Books.

Gareth, Michael S., Zhongren Jing, and Mark Kutner. 1995. *The Labor Market Effects of Completing the GED: Asking the Right Questions.* Washington, DC: American Institutes for Research.

GED Testing Service. 1993. "The Tests of General Educational Development: Technical Manual." Washington, DC: American Council on Education.

———. 2001. "Who Took the GED? GED 2000 Statistical Report." Washington, DC: American Council on Education, GED Testing Service.

Geiger, Roger L. 1993. *Research and Relevant Knowledge: American Research Universities Since World War II.* New York: Oxford University Press.

———. 2004. *Knowledge and Money: Research Universities and the Paradox of the Marketplace.* Stanford, CA: Stanford University Press.

Geiger, Roger L., and Creso M. Sá. 2008. *Tapping the Riches of Science: Universities and the Promise of Economic Growth.* Cambridge, MA: Harvard University Press.

German Federal Ministry of Education and Research. 1996. "Federal Research Report." Federal Parliament of Germany Printed Paper 13/4554. August 5. Bonn/Berlin.

Gibbons, Michael, Camille Limoges, Helga Nowotny, Simon Schwartzman, Peter Scott, and Martin Trow. 1994. *The New Production of Knowledge: The Dynamics of Science and Research in Contemporary Societies.* London: Sage.

Giddens, Anthony. 1991. *Modernity and Self-Identity: Self and Society in Late Modern Age.* Cambridge, UK: Polity Press.

Giroux, Henry A. 2000. "Postmodern Education and Disposable Youth." In *Revolutionary Pedagogies: Cultural Politics, Instituting Education, and the Discourse of Theory*, ed. P. P. Trifonas, 174–95. New York: Routledge Falmer.

Goldin, Claudia, and Lawrence F. Katz. 1996. "Technology, Skill, and the Wage Structure: Insights from the Past." *American Economic Review* 86, no. 2: 252–57.

Goldin, Claudia, and Lawrence F. Katz. 1998. "The Origins of Technology-Skill Complementarity." *Quarterly Journal of Economics* 113, no. 3: 693–732.

Goldin, Claudia, and Lawrence F. Katz. 2008. *The Race Between Education and Technology.* Cambridge, MA: Harvard University Press.

González, Jennifer. 2012. "National Network Will Help Apprentices Earn a College Degree." *Chronicle of Higher Education.*

Gottschalk, Peter, and Mary Joyce. 1998. "Cross-National Differences in the Rise in Earnings Inequality: Market and Institutional Factors." *Review of Economics and Statistics* 80, no. 4: 489–502.

Graham, Steve, and Joe Donaldson. 1996. "Assessing Personal Growth for Adults Enrolled in Higher Education." *Journal of Continuing Higher Education* 44: 7–22.

Grant, Edward. 1986. "Science and Theology in the Middle Ages." In *God and Nature: Historical Essays on the Encounter Between Christianity and Science*, ed. David C. Lindberg, Ronald L. Numbers, 49–75. Berkeley: University of California Press.

Greeley, Andrew. 2001. "The Future of Religion in America." *Society* 38, no. 3: 32–37.

Grodsky, Eric, and Erika Jackson. 2009. *Social Stratification in Higher Education.* New York: Teachers College Press.

Grubb, W. Norton, and Marvin Lazerson. 2005. "Vocationalism in Higher Education: The Triumph of the Education Gospel." *Journal of Higher Education* 76: 227–40.

Gumport, Patricia J. 2002. *Academic Pathfinders: Knowledge Creation and Feminist Scholarship*. Westport, CT: Greenwood Press.

Gumport, Patricia J., and Michael N. Bastedo. 2001. "Academic Stratification and Endemic Conflict: Remedial Education Policy at CUNY." *Review of Higher Education* 24, no. 4: 333–50.

Ham, Seung?Hwan, and Yun?Kyung Cha. 2009. "Positioning Education in the Information Society: The Transnational Diffusion of the Information and Communication Technology Curriculum." *Comparative Education Review* 53, no. 4: 535–57.

Hamilton, Stephen F., and Klaus Hurrelmann. 1994. "The School-to-Career Transition in Germany and the United States." *Teachers College Record* 96: 329–44.

Hammack, Floyd M. 2004. *The Comprehensive High School Today*. New York: Teachers College Press.

———. 2012. "Paths to Legislation or Litigation for Educational Privilege: New York and San Francisco Compared." *American Journal of Education* 116: 371–95.

Hammock, Robert C., and Ralph S. Owings. 2005. *Supervising Instruction in Secondary Schools*. New York: McGraw-Hill.

Hanson, Gordon H., and Ann E. Harrison. 1995. "Trade, Technology, and Wage Inequality." Working paper, no. W55110. Cambridge, MA: National Bureau of Economic Research.

Hanushek, Eric A., and Ludger Woessmann. 2007. *The Role of Education Quality in Economic Growth*. Washington, DC: World Bank.

Harer, Miles D. 1995. "Recidivism Among Federal Prisoners Released in 1987." *Journal of Correctional Education* 46, no. 3: 98–128.

Harris, Seymour E. 1949. *The Market for College Graduates and Related Aspects of Education and Income*. Cambridge, MA: Harvard University Press.

Hartford Institute for Religion Research. n.d. "Database of Megachurches in the U.S." http://hirr.hartsem.edu/megachurch/database.html

Hecker, Daniel. 2005. "Occupational Employment Projections to 2014." *Monthly Labor Review* 128, no. 11 (November): 86–125.

Heckman, James J., and Stephen V. Cameron. 1993. "The Nonequivalence of High School Equivalents." *Journal of Labor Economics* 11, no. 1: 1–47.

Heckman, James J., John E. Humphries, and Nicholas S. Mader. 2010. "The GED." Working paper, no. 16064. Cambridge, MA: National Bureau of Economic Research.

Hegna, Kristinn, and Ingrid Smette. 2010. "Educational Horizons: The Role of Agency, Class and Gender in the Choice of Upper Secondary Education." Working paper. Oslo: Research Council of Norway.

Hess, Frederick M., Mark Schneider, Kevin Carey, and Andrew P. Kelly. 2009. *Diplomas and Dropouts*. Washington, DC: American Enterprise Institute.

Heyneman, Stephen P. 2005. "The History and Problems in the Making of Education Policy at the World Bank." In *Global Trends in Educational Policy*, ed. David P. Baker and Alexander W. Wiseman. Oxford, UK: Elsevier Science.

Hibel, Jacob, George Farkas, and Paul L. Morgan. 2010. "Who Is Placed into Special Education?" *Sociology of Education* 83, no. 4: 312–32.

Hogan, David. 1996. "'To Better Our Condition': Educational Credentialing and 'The Silent Compulsion of Economic Relations' in the United States, 1830 to the Present." *History of Education Quarterly* 36, no. 3: 243–70.

Holtkamp, Rolf. 1996. *Duale Studienangebote der Fachhochschulen*, 115. Hanover, Germany: HIS, Hochschulplanung.

Hoskin, Keith. 1990. "Foucault Under Examination: The Crypto-Educationalist Unmasked." In *Foucault and Education*, ed. S. Ball. London: Routledge.

———. 1993. "Education and the Genesis of Disciplinarity: The Unexpected Reversal." In *Knowledges: Historical and Critical Studies in Disciplinarity*, ed. Ellen Messer-Davidow and David R. Shumway, 271–304. Charlottesville: University of Virginia Press.

Hout, Michael. 1984. "Status, Autonomy, and Training in Occupational Mobility." *American Journal of Sociology* 89, no. 6: 1379–409.

———. 1988. "More Universalism, Less Structural Mobility: The American Occupational Structure in the 1980s." *American Journal of Sociology* 93, no. 6: 1358–400.

———. 2012. "Social and Economic Returns to College Education in the United States." *Annual Review of Sociology* 38: 379–400.

Hout, Michael, and Thomas A. DiPrete. 2006. "What We Have Learned: RC28's Contributions to Knowledge About Social Stratification." *Research in Social Stratification and Mobility* 24, no. 1: 1–20.

Hout, Michael, and Claude S. Fischer. 2002. "Why More Americans Have No Religious Preference: Politics and Generations." *American Sociological Review* 67: 165–90.

Howe, Florence. 2000. *The Politics of Women's Studies: Testimony from Thirty Founding Mothers*. New York: Feminist Press at the City University of New York.

Howell, David R., and Edward N. Wolff. 1991. "Trends in the Growth and Distribution of Skills in the U.S. Workplace, 1960–1985." *Industrial and Labor Relations Review* 44, no. 3: 486–502.

Huff, Toby E. 1993a. *The Rise of Early Modern Science: Islam, China, and the West*. New York: Cambridge University Press.

———. 1993b. "Science and Civilizations East and West." *Society* 31, no. 1: 77–79.

———. 2011. *Intellectual Curiosity and the Scientific Revolution: A Global Perspective*. New York: Cambridge University Press.

Hussar, William J., and Tabitha M. Bailey. 2011. "Projections of Education Statistics to 2019 (NCES 2011–017)." Washington, DC: National Center for Education Statistics, Institute of Education Sciences.

Inkeles, Alex. 1969. "Participant Citizenship in Six Developing Countries." *American Political Science Review* 63, no. 4: 1120–41.

———. 1974. "School as a Context for Modernization." In *Education and Individual Modernity in Developing Countries*, ed. Alex Inkeles and Donald B. Holsinger, 7–23. Leiden, Netherlands: E. J. Brill.

———. 1996. "Making Men Modern: On the Causes and Consequences of Individual Change in Six Developing Countries." In *Comparing Nations and Cultures: Readings in a Cross-Disciplinary Perspective*, ed. Alex Inkeles and M. Sasaki, 571–85. Englewood Cliffs, NJ: Prentice Hall.

Inkeles, Alex, and David H. Smith. 1974. *Becoming Modern: Individual Change in Six Developing Countries*. Cambridge, MA: Harvard University Press.

Iowa Department of Education. 1992. "What Has Happened to Iowa's GED Graduates? A Two-, Five-, and Ten-Year Follow-up Study, Ed 344–047." Des Moines: Iowa Department of Education.

Ishida, Hirosh. 1993. *Social Mobility in Contemporary Japan: Educational Credentials, Class and the Labour Market in a Cross-National Perspective*. Stanford, CA: Stanford University Press.

Jacobs, Jerry A., and Scott Stoner-Eby. 1998. "Adult Enrollment and Educational Attainment." *Annals of the American Academy of Political and Social Science* 559, no. 1: 91–108.

Jakobi, Anja P. 2009. *International Organizations and Lifelong Learning*. London: Palgrave Macmillan.

Janeway, Elizabeth. 1975. "On the Power of the Weak." *Signs* 1, no. 1: 103–9.

Jansen, Jonathan D. 1990. "Curriculum as a Political Phenomenon: Historical Reflections on Black South African Education." *Journal of Negro Education* 59, no. 2: 195–206.

Jarjoura, G. Roger. 1993. "Does Dropping Out of School Enhance Delinquent Involvement? Results from a Large-Scale, National Probability Sample." *Criminology* 31, no. 2: 149–72.

Jenkins, Philip. 2007. *The Next Christendom: The Coming Global Christianity*. New York: Oxford University Press.

Jepperson, Ronald L., and John W. Meyer. 2007. "Analytical Individualism and the Explanation of Macro Social Change." In *On Capitalism*, ed. Victor Nee and Richard Swedberg. Stanford, CA: Stanford University Press.

Jepperson, Ronald L. 2002. "The Development and Application of Sociological Neoinstitutionalism." In *New Directions in Contemporary Sociological Theory*, ed. Joseph Berger and Morris Zelditch Jr., 229–66. Lanham, MD: Rowman & Littlefield.

The Johns Hopkins University. 2011. "The Johns Hopkins University: Financial Report 2011." http://finance.jhu.edu/pubs/financial_reports/

Judd, Charles M., and James W. Downing. 1990. "Political Expertise and the Development of Attitude Consistency." *Social Cognition* 8, no. 1: 104–24.

Kagan, Jerome. 1974. "On the Uses of the University." *Daedalus* 103, no. 4: 278–81.

Kamens, David H. 2009. "The Expanding Polity: Theorizing the Links Between Expanded Higher Education and the New Politics of the Post-1970s." *American Journal of Education* 116, no. 1: 26.

Kamens, David H., and Aaron Benavot. 1991. "Elite Knowledge for the Masses: The Origins and Spread of Mathematics and Science Education in National Curricula." *American Journal of Education* 2, February: 137–80.

Kamens, David H., and Aaron Benavot. 2006. "Worldwide Models of Secondary Education, 1960–2000." In *School Knowledge in Comparative and Historical Perspective: Changing Curricula in Primary and Secondary Education*, ed. A. Benavot and C. Braslavsky. Amsterdam: Springer.

Kamens, David H., John W. Meyer, and Aaron Benavot. 1996. "Worldwide Patterns in Academic Secondary Education Curricula." *Comparative Education Review* 40, no. 2: 116–38.

Kaufman, Philip, Martha Naomi Alt, and Christopher D. Chapman. 2001. "Dropout Rates in the United States: 2000 (NCES 2002–114)." Washington, DC: National Center for Education Statistics.

Kazin, Alfred. 1942. *On Native Grounds*. New York: Harcourt, Brace, and World.

Keely, Brian. 2007. *Capital humano/Human Capital*. Paris: Publications de l'OCDE.

Kerr, Clark. 1987. "A Critical Age in the University World: Accumulated Heritage Versus Modern Imperatives." *European Journal of Education* 22, no. 2: 183–93.

———. 2001. *The Uses of the University*. Cambridge, MA: Harvard University Press.

Kett, Joseph F. 2013. *Merit: The History of a Founding Ideal from the American Revolution to the Twenty-First Century*. Ithaca, NY: Cornell University Press.

Khurana, Rakesh. 2007. *From Higher Aims to Hired Hands: The Social Transformation of American Business Schools and the Unfulfilled Promise of Management as a Profession*. Princeton, NJ: Princeton University Press.

Kirp, David L. 2003. *Shakespeare, Einstein, and the Bottom Line: The Marketing of Higher Education*. Cambridge, MA: Harvard University Press.

Kleiner, Morris M. 2006. *Licensing Occupations: Ensuring Quality or Restricting Competition?* Kalamazoo, MI: W.E. Upjohn Institute.

Kleiner, Morris M., and Alan B. Krueger. 1998. "The Prevalence and Effects of Occupational Licensing." Working paper. Cambridge, MA: National Bureau of Economic Research.

Kleiner, Morris M., and Alan B. Krueger. 2008. "The Prevalence and Effects of Occupational Licensing." Working paper, no. 14308. Cambridge, MA: National Bureau of Economic Research.

Kleiner, Morris M., and Alan B. Krueger. 2010. "The Prevalance and Effects of Occupational Licensing." *British Journal of Industrial Relations* 48, no.4: 676–87.

Knepper, Edwin Garfield. 1941. *History of Business Education in United States.* Ann Arbor, MI: Edwards Bros., lithoprinters.

Kohn, Melvin, L., and Carmi Schooler. 1969. "Class, Occupation, and Orientation." *American Sociological Review:* 659–78.

Kroll, B. S., and S. Qi. 1995. "A Promise of Empowerment: Results of the GED 1992 Follow-up Survey." Washington, DC: American Council on Education, GED Testing Service.

Kuh, George D., J. C. Hayek, R. M. Carini, J. A. Ouimet, R. M. Gonyea, and J. Kennedy. 2001. "NSSE Technical and Norms Report." Bloomington: Indiana University Center for Postsecondary Research and Planning.

Labaree, David F. 1986. "Curriculum, Credentials, and the Middle Class: A Case Study of a Nineteenth Century High School." *Sociology of Education* 59, no. 1: 42–57.

———. 1990. "From Comprehensive High School to Community College: Politics, Markets, and the Evolution of Educational Opportunity." In *Research in Sociology of Education and Socialization*, vol. 9, ed. R. Corwin. Greenwich, CT: JAI Press.

Ladd, Everett C., Jr. 1978. "The New Lines Are Drawn: Class and Ideology in America." *Public Opinion* 3: 48–53.

———. 1979. "The New Divisions in US Politics." *Fortune* 99, no. 6: 88–96.

LaFraniere, Sharon. 2009. "Files Vanished, Young Chinese Lose the Future." *New York Times*, July 26.

Lane, Robert E. 2001. *The Loss of Happiness in Market Democracies.* New Haven, CT: Yale University Press.

Lauder, Hugh, Michael Young, Harry Daniels, Maria Balarin, and John Lowe. 2012. *Education for the Knowledge Economy? Critical Perspective.* London: Routledge.

Lazarfeld, Paul F., Bernard Berelson, and Hazel Gaudet. 1944. *The People's Choice: How the Voter Makes Up His Mind in a Presidential Campaign.* New York: Columbia University Press.

Le Goff, Jacques, ed. 1993. "Medieval Callings." *History: Reviews of New Books* 21, no. 4: 165–66.

Lee, Jenny J. 2002. "Religion and College Attendance: Change Among Students." *Review of Higher Education* 25, no. 4: 369–84.

Lee, Shayne, and Phillip Luke Sinitiere. 2009. *Holy Mavericks: Evangelical Innovators and the Spiritual Marketplace.* New York: New York University Press.

Lemann, Nicholas. 1992. *The Promised Land: The Great Black Migration and How It Changed America.* New York: Vintage Books.

Lenhardt, Gero. 2002. "Europe and Higher Education Between Universalisation and Materialist Particularism." *European Educational Research Journal* 1, no. 2: 274–89.

———. 2005. *Hochschulen in Deutschland und in den USA.* Wiesbaden, Germany: VS Verlag für Sozialwissenschaften.

Lenzer, Gertrud. 1975. "On Masochism: A Contribution to the History of a Phantasy and Its Theory." *Signs* 1, no. 2: 277–324.

LeTendre, Gerald K. 2002. "Homework and the Quality of Education: A Cross-National Exploration." Working paper. University Park: Pennsylvania State University, Education Policy Studies Department.

Levy, Frank, and Richard J. Murnane. 2012. *The New Division of Labor: How Computers Are Creating the Next Job Market*. Princeton, NJ: Princeton University Press.

Lewin, Keith M. 2009. "Access to Education in Sub?Saharan Africa: Patterns, Problems and Possibilities." *Comparative Education* 45, no. 2: 151–74.

Lewin, Tamar. 2007. "Dean at M.I.T. Resigns, Ending a 28-Year Lie." *New York Times*, April 26.

Lewis, Bernard. 2002. *What Went Wrong? The Clash Between Islam and Modernity in the Middle East*. New York: Oxford University Press.

———. 2004. *From Babel to Dragomans: Interpreting the Middle East*. New York: Oxford University Press.

Lieberson, Stanley. 1980. *A Piece of the Pie: Blacks and White Immigrants Since 1880*. Berkeley: University of California Press.

Linz, Juan J. 1990. "Perils of the Presidency." *Journal of Democracy* 1, no. 1 (Winter): 51–69.

Lipset, Seymour Martin. 1971. *Rebellion in the University*. Boston: Little, Brown.

Locke, Robert R. 1984. *The End of the Practical Man: Entrepreneurship and Higher Education in Germany, France, and Great Britain, 1880–1940*. Greenwich, CT: Jai Press.

———. 1989. *Management and Higher Education Since 1940: The Influence of America and Japan on West Germany, Great Britain, and France*. New York: Cambridge University Press.

Longhofer, Wesley, and Evan Schofer. 2010. "National and Global Origins of Environmental Association." *American Sociological Review* 75, no. 4: 505–33.

Luhmann, Niklas. 2012. *Theory of Society*, vol. 1. Stanford, CA: Stanford University Press.

Luo, Xiaowei. 2006. "The Spread of a 'Human Resources' Culture: Institutional Individualism and the Rise of Personal Development Training." In *Globalization and Organization: World Society and Organizational Change*, ed. J. Meyer, G. Drori, and H. Hwang, 225–40. Oxford, UK: Oxford University Press.

Luria, Aleksandr Romanovich. 1976. *Cognitive Development: Its Cultural and Social Foundations*. Cambridge, MA: Harvard University Press.

Luttbeg, Norman R. 1984. "Differential Voting Turnout Decline in the American States, 1960–82." *Social Science Quarterly* 65, no. 1: 60–73.

Lutz, Wolfgang, and Samir K. C. 2011. "Global Human Capital: Integrating Education and Population." *Science* 333, no. 6042: 587–92.

Lutz, Wolfgang, Warren C. Sanderson, and Sergei Šerbov (eds.) 2004. *The End of World Population Growth in the 21st Century: New Challenges for Human Capital Formation and Sustainable Development*. Oxford, UK: Earthscan.

Lyon, David. 1988. *The Information Society: Issues and Illusions*. New York: Polity Press.

MacLeod, Jay. 2009. *Ain't No Makin' It*. Boulder, CO: Westview Press.

Mally, Neil, and Mary Charuhas. 1977. *A Survey: Perceptions of the College of Lake County's GED Program as Seen by Former Students and Area Personnel Managers*. Lake County, IL: College of Lake County.

Maloney, Tim. 1992. "Estimating the Returns to a Secondary Education for Female Dropouts." Working paper, no. 100. Auckland, NZ: University of Auckland, Department of Economics.

Mangan, Katherine. 2007. "Ave Maria Law Professors File Whistle-Blower Suit." *Chronicle of Higher Education*, November 2, 6.

Mann, Charles C. 2005. *1491: New Revelations of the Americas Before Columbus*. New York: Alfred A. Knopf.

March, James G., and Herbert A. Simon. 1993. "Organizations Revisited." *Industrial and Corporate Change* 2, no. 1: 299–316.

Marrou, Henri I. 1956. *A History of Education in Antiquity*. Madison: University of Wisconsin Press.

Martin, David. 1991. "The Secularization Issue: Prospect and Retrospect." *British Journal of Sociology* 43, no. 3: 465–74.

Martinez, Michael E. 2000. *Education as the Cultivation of Intelligence*. Hillsdale, NJ: Erlbaum Associates.

Massey, Douglas, and Deborah Hirst. 1998. "From Escalator to Hourglass: Changes in the US Occupational Wage Structure 1949–1989." *Social Science Research* 27, no. 1: 51–71.

Mazza, Carmelo, Kerstin Sahlin-Andersson, and Jesper Strandgaard Pedersen. 2005. "European Constructions of an American Model Developments of Four MBA Programmes." *Management Learning* 36, no. 4: 471–91.

McAdam, Doug. 1982. *Political Process and the Development of Black Insurgency, 1930–1970*. Chicago: University of Chicago Press.

McEneaney, Elizabeth H. 2005. "Elements of a Contemporary Primary School Science." In *Science in the Modern World Polity: Institutionalization and Globalization*, ed. G. S. Drori, J. W. Meyer, F. O. Ramirez, and E. Schofer, 136–54. Stanford, CA: Stanford University Press.

McKenna, Christopher D. 2006. *The World's Newest Profession: Management Consulting in the Twentieth Century*. Cambridge, UK: Cambridge University Press.

Meier, Robert F. 1982. "Perspectives on the Concept of Social Control." *Annual Review of Sociology* 8: 35–55.

Melton, J. Gordon. 1989. *The Churches Speak on AIDS: Official Statements from Religious Bodies and Ecumenical Organizations*. Detroit: Gale Research.

Meyer, John W. 1970. "The Charter: Conditions of Diffuse Socialization in Schools." In *Social Processes and Social Structures*, ed. W. Scott, 564–78. New York: Holt.

———. 1977. "The Effects of Education as an Institution." *American Journal of Sociology* 83, no. 1: 55–77.

———. 1981. "Review Essay: Kings or People." *American Journal of Sociology* 86, no. 4: 895–99.

———. 1986. "The Self and the Life Course: Institutionalization and Its Effects." In *Human Development and the Life Course: Multidisciplinary Perspectives*, ed. A. Sorensen, F. Weinert, and L. Sherrod, 199–217. Hillsdale, NJ: Erlbaum Associates.

———. 1992. "The Life Course as a Professionalized Cultural Construction." In *Institutions and Gatekeeping in the Life Course*, ed. W. Heinz, 83–95. Weinheim, Germany: Deutscher Studien Verlag.

———. 1999. "The Changing Cultural Content of the Nation-State: A World Society Perspective." In *State/Culture: State Formation After the Cultural Turn*, ed. G. Steinmetz, 123–43. Ithaca, NY: Cornell University Press.

———. 2000. "Reflections on Education as Transcendence." In *Reconstructing the Common Good in Education*, ed. L. Cuban and D. Shipps, 206–22. Stanford, CA: Stanford University Press.

Meyer, John W., and Michael T. Hannan. 1979. *National Development and the World System: Educational, Economic, and Political Change, 1950–1970*. Chicago: University of Chicago Press.

Meyer, John W., and Ronald. L. Jepperson. 2000. "The 'Actors' of Modern Society: The Cultural Construction of Social Agency." *Sociological Theory* 18, no. 1: 100–20.

Meyer, John W., Francisco O. Ramirez, David F. Frank, and Evan Schofer. 2008. "Higher Education as an Institution." In *Sociology of Higher Education: Contributions and Their Contexts*, ed. P. Gumport, 187–221. Baltimore: Johns Hopkins University Press.

Meyer, John W., Francisco O. Ramirez, and Yasemin Nuhoğlu Soysal. 1992. "World Expansion of Mass Education, 1870–1980." *Sociology of Education* 65, no. 2 (April): 128–49.

Meyer, John W., and Brian Rowan. 1977. "Institutionalized Organizations: Formal Structure as Myth and Ceremony." *American Journal of Sociology* 83, no. 2: 340–63.

Meyer, John W., and Richard Rubinson. 1972. "Structural Determinants of Student Political Activity: A Comparative Interpretation." *Sociology of Education* 45, no. 1: 23–46.

Mickulecky, Beatrice S. 1990. *A Short Course in Teaching Reading Skill*. New York: Addison-Wesley.

Minkoff, Debra C., Silke Aisenbrey, and Jon Agnone. 2008. "Organizational Diversity in the US Advocacy Sector." *Social Problems* 55, no. 4: 525–48.

Minkoff, Debra C., and John D. McCarthy. 2005. "Reinvigorating the Study of Organizational Processes in Social Movements." *Mobilization: An International Quarterly* 10, no. 2: 289–308.

Mohrman, Kathryn, Wanhua Ma, and David P. Baker. 2007. "The Emerging Global Model of the Research University." In *Higher Education in the New Century: Global Challenges and Innovative Ideas*, ed. P. G. Altbach and P. M. Peterson. Rotterdam, Netherlands: Sense.

Mohrman, Kathryn, Wanhua Ma, and David P. Baker. 2008. "The Research University in Transition: The Emerging Global Model." *Higher Education Policy* 21, no. 1: 5–27.

Monhan, Susanne C., John W. Meyer, and Richard W. Scott. 1994. "Employee Training: The Expansion of Organizational Citizenship." In *Institutional Environments and Organizations*, ed. Richard W. Scott and John W. Meyer. Thousand Oaks, CA: Sage.

Moon, Hyeyoung. 2002. "The Globalization of Professional Management Education, 1881–2000: Its Rise, Expansion, and Implications." Doctoral dissertation. Stanford University.

Mueller, Marnie W. 1975. "Economic Determinants of Volunteer Work by Women." *Signs* 1, no. 2: 325–38.

Murnane, Richard J., and Frank Levy. 1996. "With What Skills Are Computers a Complement?" *American Economic Review* 86, no. 2: 258–62.

Murnane, Richard J., John B. Willett, and Kathryn P Boudett. 1994. "Do High School Dropouts Benefit from Obtaining a GED?" *Education and Policy Analysis* 17, no. 2: 133–47.

Murnane, Richard J., John B. Willett, and Frank Levy. 1994. "The Growing Importance of Cognitive Skills in Wage Determination." *Review of Economics and Statistics* 77, no. 2: 251–66.

National Architectural Accrediting Board. 2012. http://www.naab.org/home.aspx

National Association of Colleges and Employers (NACE). 2011. *Internship and Co-op Survey*. Bethlehem, PA: NACE.

National Council of Architectural Registration Boards. 2012. http://www.ncarb.org

National Science Foundation. 2012. "Science and Engineering Indicators 2012." http://www.nsf.gov/statistics/seind12/c4/c4h.htm#s1

Neisser, Ulric. 1998. "Introduction: Rising Test Scores and What They Mean." In *The Rising Curve: Long Term Gains in IQ and Related Measures*, ed. Ulric Neisser, 3–24. Washington, DC: American Psychological Association.

*New York Herald Tribune*. 2006. "In Our Pages: 100, 75, & 50 years ago, 1931: Yale Ends Era of Classics." May 12.

Nie, Norman H., Jane Junn, and Kenneth Stehlik-Barry. 1996. *Education and Democratic Citizenship in America*. Chicago: University of Chicago Press.

Nisbett, R. 2009. *Intelligence and How to Get It: Why Schools and Cultures Count*. New York: Norton.

Nock, Steven L. 1993. *The Costs of Privacy Surveillance and Reputation in America*. New York: Walter de DeGruyter.

Nowotny, Helga, Peter Scott, and Michael Gibbons. 2001. *Re-Thinking Science: Knowledge and the Public in an Age of Uncertainty*. Oxford, UK: Polity Press.

Nuttall, John, Linda Hollmen, and E. Michele Staley. 2003. "The Effect of Earning a GED on Recidivism Rates." *Journal of Correctional Education* 54, no. 3: 90–94.

OECD (Organisation for Economic Co-operation and Development). 2009a. *Education at a Glance 2009*. Paris: OECD.

———. 2009b. "Green at Fifteen? How 15-Year-Olds Perform in Environmental Science and Geoscience in PISA 2006." Paris: OECD.

"Older and Wiser: A Special Report on Germany." 2010. *The Economist*, March 11, 394.

O'Neill, John H. 1963. "High School Dropouts." *Education* 84: 156–59.

Osborne, Elizabeth. 2004. *Vocabulary from Latin and Greek Roots: A Study of Word Families*. Cheswold, DE: Prestwick House.

Pallas, Aaron M. 2002. "Educational Participation Across the Life Course: Do the Rich Get Richer?" In *New Frontiers in Socialization: Advances in Life Course Research*, ed. Timothy Owens and Richard Settersten Jr., 327–54. Oxford, UK: Elsevier Science.

———. 2003. "Educational Transitions, Trajectories, and Pathways." In *Handbook of the Life Course*, ed. Jeylan T. Mortimer and Michael Shanahan, 165–84. New York: Plenum.

Papagiannis, George J., Robert N. Bickel, and Richard H. Fuller. 1983. "The Social Creation of School Dropouts: Accomplishing the Reproduction of an Underclass." *Youth and Society* 14, no. 3: 363–92.

Park, Jin Heum. 1999. "Estimation of Sheepskin Effects Using the Old and the New Measures of Educational Attainment in the Current Population Survey." *Economics Letters* 62, no. 2: 237–40.

Parsons, Talcott. 1971. "Higher Education as a Theoretical Focus." In *Institutions and Social Exchange: The Sociologies of Talcott Parsons and George C. Homans*, ed. Herman Turk and Richard L. Simpson, 233–52. Indianapolis, IN: Bobbs-Merrill.

Pascarella, Ernest T., and Patrick T. Terenzini. 2005. *How College Affects Students: A Third Decade of Research*. San Francisco: Jossey-Bass.

Pau, Bernard. 2003. "From Knowledge to Innovation: Remodeling Creative and Knowledge Diffusion Processes." In *Universities and Globalization: Private Linkages, Public Trust*, ed. Gilles Breton and Michael Lambert, 12–29. Paris: UNESCO.

Pelikan, Jaroslav, and John H. Newman. 1994. *The Idea of the University: A Reexamination*. New Haven, CT: Yale University Press.

Perrow, Charles. 1986. *Complex Organizations: A Critical Essay*, 3rd ed. New York: Random House.

Pervin, Lawrence A., and Donald B. Rubin. 1967. "Dissatisfaction with College and the College Dropout: A Transactional Approach." *Journal of Social Psychology* 72, no. 2: 285–95.

Peters, Ellen, David P. Baker, Nathan Dieckmann, Juan Leon, and John M. Collins. 2011. "Explaining the Education Effect on Health: A Field-Study from Ghana." *Psychological Science* 21, no. 10: 1369–76.

Peterson, Glen, Ruth Hayhoe, and Yongling Lu, eds. 2001. *China's National Minority Education: Culture, Schooling and Development*. Ann Arbor: University of Michigan Press.

PEW Research Center for People and the Press. 2004a. "New Audiences Increasingly Polarized." Washington, DC: Author.

———. 2004b. "The State of the News Media, 2004: Annual Report on American Journalism." Washington, DC.

Pierson, Paul, and Theda Skocpol. 2007. *The Transformation of American Politics: Activist Government and the Rise of Conservatism*. Princeton, NJ: Princeton University Press.

Piven, Frances F., and Richard A. Cloward. 1988. *Why Americans Don't Vote*. New York: Pantheon Books.

Pizmony-Levy, Oren. 2011. "Bridging the Global and Local in Understanding Curricula Scripts: The Case of Environmental Education." *Comparative Education Review* 55, no. 4: 600–33.

Powell, David. 1986. "The New Liberalism and the Rise of Labour, 1886–1906." *Historical Journal* 29: 369–93.

Powell, G. Bingham. 1986. "American Voter Turnout in Comparative Perspective." *American Political Science Review* 80, no. 1: 17–45.

Powell, Justin J.W., and Heike Solga. 2011. "Why Are Higher Education Participation Rates in Germany So Low? Institutional Barriers to Higher Education Expansion." *Journal of Education and Work* 24, no. 1: 49–68.

Powell, Walter W. 2001. "The Capitalist Firm in the Twenty-First Century: Emerging Patterns in Western Europe." In *The Twenty-First-Century Firm: Changing Economic Organization in International Perspective*, ed. Paul DiMaggio, 33–68. Princeton, NJ: Princeton University Press.

Price, Jason A. 2004. *Executive MBA*. EMBA World.

Prins, Esther, and Blarie W. Toso. 2008. "Defining and Measuring Parenting for Educational Success: A Critical Discourse Analysis of the Parent Education Profile." *American Educational Research Journal* 45, no. 3: 555–96.

Pritchett, Lant. 2001. "Where Has All the Education Gone?" *World Bank Economic Review* 15, no. 3: 367–91.

Ramirez, Francisco O., and John Boli. 1987. "The Political Construction of Mass Schooling: European Origins and Worldwide Institutionalization." *Sociology of Education* 60, no. 1 (January): 2–17.

Ramirez, Francisco, Patricia Bromley, and Susan G. Russell. 2009. "The Valorization of Humanity and Diversity." *Multicultural Education Review* 1: 29–54.

Ramirez, Francisco, Xiaowei Luo, Evan Schofer, and John W. Meyer. 2006. "Student Achievement and National Economic Growth." *American Journal of Education* 113: 1–29.

Ramirez, Francisco O., David Suárez, and John W. Meyer. 2006. "The Worldwide Rise of Human Rights Education." In *School Curricula for Global Citizenship*, ed. A. Benavot and C. Braslavsky, 35–52. Hong Kong: University of Hong Kong/Springer, Comparative Education Research Center.

Rauner, Mary. 1998. "Citizenship in the Curriculum: The Globalization of Civics Education in Anglophone Africa, 1955–1995." In *Public Rights, Public Rules: Constituting Citizens in the World Polity and National Policy*, ed. C. McNeely, 107–24. New York: Routledge.

Reder, Steve. 1994. "The Nature and Impact of GED Training in Oregon." Portland, OR: Northwest Regional Education Laboratory.

Reder, Steve, and K. Wickelund. 1994. "Steps to Success: Literacy Development in a Welfare-to-Work Program. Final Report." Portland, OR: Northwest Regional Educational Laboratory.

Reed, Naomi, V. 1985. *Maryland GED Graduates: Changes in Education, Employment and Perceptions of Self-Worth Two Years Later*. Baltimore: Maryland State Department of Education.

Reger, Jo, and Suzanne Staggenborg. 2006. "Patterns of Mobilization in Local Movement Organizations: Leadership and Strategy in Four National Organization for Women Chapters." *Sociological Perspectives* 49, no. 3: 297–323.

Reich, Michael. 1994. "How Social Structures of Accumulation Decline and Are Built." In *Social Structures of Accumulation: The Political Economy of Growth and Crisis*, ed. D. M. Kotz, T. McDonough, and M. Reich, 29–49. Cambridge, UK: Cambridge University Press.

Reich, Robert, B. 2010. *Aftershock: The Next Economy and America's Future*. New York: Random House.

Reisz, Robert, and Manfred Stock. 2007. *Inklusion in Hochschulen: Beteiligung an der Hochschulbildung und Gesellschaftliche Entwicklung in Europa und in den USA, 1950–2000*. Bonn, Germany: Lemmens Verlags, mbH.

Rice, Joseph M. 1893. *The Public School System of the United States*. New York: Century Press.

Richardson, John G. 1994. "Common, Delinquent, and Special: On the Formalization of Common Schooling in the American States." *American Educational Research Journal* 31: 695–723.

———. 2009. "Institutional Sequences and Curriculum History: Classical vs. Scientific Knowledge and the Formation of a New Nation." In *New Curriculum History*, ed. B. Baker. Rotterdam, Netherlands: Sense.

Richardson, John G., and Justin J. W. Powell. 2011. *Comparing Special Education: Origins to Contemporary Paradoxes*. Stanford, CA: Stanford University Press.

Ridder-Symoens, H. D. 1992. "Mobility." In *A History of the University in Europe: Universities in the Middle Ages*, ed. W. Rüegg and H. de Ridder-Symoens. New York: Cambridge University Press.

Riddle, Phyllis. 1993. "Political Authority and University Formation in Europe, 1200–1800." *Sociological Perspectives* 36, no.1 (Spring): 45–62.

Rojas, F. 2007. *From Black Power to Black Studies: How a Radical Social Movement Became an Academic Discipline*. Baltimore: Johns Hopkins University Press.

Rosenbaum, James E. 2001. *Beyond College for All: Career Paths for the Forgotten Half*. New York: Russell Sage Foundation.

Ross, Earle Dudley. 1942. *Democracy's College: The Land-Grant Movement in the Formative Stage*. Ames: Iowa State College Press.

Ross, Robert J.S. 2004. *Slaves to Fashion: Poverty and Abuse in the New Sweatshops*. Ann Arbor: University of Michigan Press.

Rubenstein, Richard E. 2003. *Aristotle's Children: How Christians, Muslims, and Jews Rediscovered Ancient Wisdom and Illuminated the Dark Ages*. Orlando, FL: Harcourt.

Rubinson, Richard, and Irene Browne. 1994. "Education and the Economy." In *The Handbook of Economic Sociology*, ed. N. J. Smelser and R. Swedberg, 581–99. Princeton, NJ: Princeton University Press.

Rüegg, Walter, A., and Hilde de Ridder-Symoens, eds. 1992. *A History of the University in Europe: Universities in the Middle Ages*. New York: Cambridge University Press.

Rumberger, Russell W. 1981. "The Rising Incidence of Overeducation in the U.S. Labor Market." *Economics of Education Review* 1, no. 3: 293–314.

Rury, John L. 2013. *Education and Social Change: Themes in the History of American Schooling*, 4th ed. Hillsdale, NJ: Erlbaum Associates.

Rury, John L., and Shirley A. Hill. 2012. *The African American Struggle for Secondary Schooling, 1940–1980: Closing the Graduation Gap.* New York: Teachers College Press.

Rychen, Dominique Simone, and Laura Hersh Salganik, eds. 2003. *Key Competencies for a Successful Life and a Well-Functioning Society.* Ashland, OH: Hogrefe & Huber.

Sadovnik, Alan R. 1995. *Knowledge and Pedagogy: The Sociology of Basil Bernstein.* Norwood, NJ: Ablex.

Sahlin-Andersson, Kerstin. 2001. "National, International and Transnational Constructions of New Public Management." In *New Public Management: The Transformation of Ideas and Practice,* ed. Tom Christensen and Per Lægreid, 43–72. Aldershot, UK: Ashgate.

Said, Edward. 1978. *Orientalism.* New York: Pantheon Books.

Said, Edward W. 2001. *The Book, Critical Performance, and the Future of Education,* 9–19. Oxford, UK: Taylor & Francis.

Saunders, Kyle, and Alan Abramovitz. 2003. "Ideological Realignment and Active Partisans in the American Electorate." *American Politics Research* 31, no. 10: 1–25.

Schaub, Maryellen. 2009. "Is Universal Access to Prekindergarten the Next Frontier of Schooling Expansion?" Book review of *The Sandbox Investment: The Preschool Movement and Kids-First Politics* by David Kirp, and *Standardized Childhood: The Political and Cultural Struggle over Early Education* by Bruce Fuller. *American Journal of Education* 115, no. 2: 337–41.

———. 2010. "Parenting for Cognitive Development from 1950 to 2000: The Institutionalization of Mass Education and the Social Construction of Parenting in the United States." *Sociology of Education* 83, no. 1 (January 1): 46–66.

———. 2013. "Is There a Home Advantage in School Readiness for Young Children? Trends in Parent Engagement in Cognitive Activities with Young Children, 1991–2001." *Journal of Early Childhood Research.* DOI 10.1177/1476718X12468122

Scheitle, Christopher P., and Roger Finke. 2012. *Places of Faith: A Road Trip Across America's Religious Landscape.* Oxford, UK: Oxford University Press.

Schissler, Hanna, and Yasemin Nuhoğlu Soysal, eds. 2005. *The Nation, Europe, and the World: Textbooks and Curricula in Transition.* New York: Berghahn Books.

Schlesinger, Leonard A., and James Mellado. 1991. "Willow Creek Community Church." Case. Cambridge, MA: Harvard Business Publishing.

Schmidt, Peter. 2005. "From Special Ed to Higher Ed." *Chronicle of Higher Education,* February 18.

Schofer, Evan, and Wesley Longhofer. 2011. "The Structural Sources of Associational Life." *American Journal of Sociology* 117, no. 2 (September): 539–85.

Schofer, Evan, and John W. Meyer. 2005. "The Worldwide Expansion of Higher Education in the Twentieth Century." *American Sociological Review* 70, no. 6 (December 1): 898–920.

Schoon, Ingrid, Helen Cheng, Catharine R. Gale, G. David Batty, and Ian J. Deary. 2010. "Social Status, Cognitive Ability, and Educational Attainment as Predictors of Liberal Social Attitudes and Political Trust." *Intelligence* 38, no. 1: 144–50.

Schultz, Theodore W. 1960. "Investment in Human Capital." Presidential Address. Paper presented at the Seventy-third Annual Meeting of the American Economic Association, Saint Louis.

———. 1961. "Investment in Human Capital." *American Economic Review* 51, no. 1: 1–17.

Schwadel, Philip. 2003. "The Persistence of Religion: The Effects of Education on American Christianity." Doctoral dissertation. Pennsylvania State University.

———. 2011. "The Effects of Education on Americans' Religious Practices, Beliefs, and Affiliations." *Review of Religious Research* 53, no. 2: 161–82.

Scott, Richard, and John W. Meyer. 1991. "The Rise of Training Programs in Firms and Agencies: An Institutional Perspective." In *Research in Organizational Behavior*, ed. B. Staw and L. Cummings, 287–326. Greenwich, CT: JAI Press.

Seymour, Elaine, Anne-Barrie Hunter, Sandra L. Laursen, and Tracee DeAntoni. 2004. "Establishing the Benefits of Research Experiences for Undergraduates in the Sciences: First Findings from a Three?year Study." *Science Education* 88, no. 4: 493–534.

Shanahan, Suzanne, and Sanjeev Khagram. 2006. "Dynamics of Corporate Responsibility." In *Globalization and Organization: World Society and Organizational Change*, ed. G. S. Drori, J. W. Meyer, and H. Hwang, 196–224. Oxford, UK: Oxford University Press.

Shavit, Yossi, and Hans-Peter Blossfeld. 1993. *Persistent Inequality: Changing Educational Achievement in Thirteen Countries*. Boulder, CO: Westview Press.

Shermer, Michael. 2002. "The Shamans of Scientism." *Scientific American* 286, no. 6: 35.

Sicherman, Nachum. 1991. "'Overeducation' in the Labor Market." *Journal of Labor Economics* 9, no. 2: 101–22.

Silberstein, Richard, Jonathan Rabinowitz, Paul Ritterband, and Barry Kosmin. 1987. *Giving to Jewish Philanthropic Causes: A Preliminary Reconnaissance*. New York: North American Jewish Data Bank.

Skocpol, Theda. 1997. "Building Community Top-Down or Bottom-Up?: America's Voluntary Groups Thrive in a National Network." *Brookings Review* 15, no. 4: 16–29.

———. 2003. *Diminished Democracy: From Membership to Management in American Civic Life*. Norman: University of Oklahoma Press.

Skocpol, Theda, and Morris P. Fiorina. 1999. *Civic Engagement in American Democracy*. Washington, DC: Brookings Institution Press.

Slaughter, Sheila, and Gary Rhoades. 2009. *Academic Capitalism and the New Economy: Markets, State, and Higher Education*. Baltimore: Johns Hopkins University Press.

Sloane, Peter. 2002. "Much Ado About Nothing? What Does the Over-Education Literature Really Tell Us?" In *The International Conference on Over-education in Europe: What Do We Know?* (proceedings). Berlin: Max Planck Institute for Human Development; Maastricht, Netherlands: Maastricht University, Research Center for Education and the Labor Market (ROA).

Smith, Christian. 1998. *American Evangelicalism*. Chicago: University of Chicago Press.

Smith, Herbert L. 1986. "Overeducation and Underemployment: An Agnostic Review." *Sociology of Education* 59, no. 2: 85–99.

Smith, Jackie, and Dawn Wiest. 2012. *Social Movements in the World-System: The Politics of Crisis and Transformation*. New York: Russell Sage Foundation.

Smith, Thomas. 2000. "Who Values the GED? Factors Underlying the Supply and Demand of High School Equivalency Credentials." Doctoral dissertation. Pennsylvania State University.

———. 2003. "Who Values the GED? An Examination of the Paradox Underlying the Demand for the General Educational Development Credential." *Teachers College Record* 105, no. 3: 375–415.

Snider, Susan. 2009. "The Lived Experiences of GED Students: What Do Their Experiences Tell Us?" Doctoral dissertation. Pennsylvania State University.

Snyder, Thomas D. 1993. "120 Years of American Education: A Statistical Portrait." Ed. U.S. Department of Education. Washington, DC: U.S. Government Printing Office.

Sobe, N. W. 2011. "Transnational Governance." In *Youth Studies: Keywords and Movements*, ed. Nancy Lesko and Susan Talburt. New York: Routledge.

Solomon, Deborah. 2007. "Questions for Terry Eagleton: The Believer." *New York Times*, April 22.

Sörlin, Sverker, and Hebe Vessuri. 2007a. "Knowledge Society vs. Knowledge Economy: Knowledge, Power, and Politics." In *Knowledge Society vs. Knowledge Economy: Knowledge, Power and Politics*, ed. S. Sörlin and H. Vessuri. New York: Palgrave Macmillan.

Sörlin, Sverker, and Hebe Vessuri. 2007b. "Introduction: The Democratic Deficit of Knowledge Economies." In *Knowledge Society vs. Knowledge Economy: Knowledge, Power and Politics*, ed. S. Sörlin and H. Vessuri, 1–33. New York: Palgrave Macmillan.

Soysal, Yasemin Nuhoğlu. 1994. *Limits of Citizenship: Migrants and Postnational Membership in Europe*. Chicago: University of Chicago Press.

Soysal, Yasemin Nuhoğlu, and Suk-Ying Wong. 2007. "Educating Future Citizens in Europe and Asia." In *School Knowledge in Comparative and Historical Perspective: Changing Curricula in Primary and Secondary Education*, vol. 18, ed. Aaron Benavot, Cecilia Braslavsky, and Nhung Truong, 73–88. Dordrecht: Springer Netherlands.

Spenner, Kenneth I. 1983. "Deciphering Prometheus: Temporal Change in the Skill Level of Work." *American Sociological Review* 48, no. 6: 824–37.

———. 1988. "Social Stratification, Work, and Personality." *Annual Review of Sociology* 14: 69–97.

Spring, Joel H. 1988. *The Sorting Machine: National Educational Policy Since 1945*. White Plains, NY: Longman.

Staff, Jeremy, and Derek Krieger. 2008. "Too Cool for School? Violence, Peer Status and High School Dropout." *Social Forces* 87, no. 1: 445–71.

Stark, Rodney. 2005. *The Victory of Reason: How Christianity Led to Freedom, Capitalism, and Western Success*. New York: Random House.

Stark, Rodney, and William Simms Bainbridge. 1985. *The Future of Religion: Secularization, Revival, and Cult Formation*. Berkeley: University of California Press.

Stark, Rodney, and Roger Finke. 2000. *Acts of Faith: Explaining the Human Side of Religion*. Berkeley: University of California Press.

Stehr, Nico. 2004. *Knowledge Societies*. Thousand Oaks, CA: Sage.

Stevenson, Harold W., and Chuansheng Chen. 1989. "Schooling and Achievement: A Study of Peruvian Children." *International Journal of Educational Research* 13, no. 8: 883–94.

Stinchcombe, Arthur L., and James March. 1965. *Handbook of Organizations*. Chicago: Rand McNally.

Stone, Frank A. 1973. *The New World of Educational Thought*. NTC Business Books.

Stone, Lawrence. 1972. *The Causes of the English Revolution 1529–1642*. New York: Harper Torchbooks.

Stout, Lee. 2009. *Ice Cream U: The Story of the Nation's Most Successful Collegiate Creamery*. University Park: Pennsylvania State University Press.

Suárez, David. 2007. "Education Professionals and the Construction of Human Rights Education." *Comparative Education Review* 51, no. 1: 48–70.

Suárez, David, and Patricia Bromley. 2012. "Institutionalizing a Global Social Movement: Human Rights as University Knowledge." *American Journal of Education* 118, no. 3: 253–80.

Suen, Hoi K., and Lan Yu. 2006. "Chronic Consequences of High-Stakes Testing? Lessons from the Chinese Civil Service Exam." *Comparative Education Review* 50, no. 1: 46–65.

Swatos, William H., Jr. 1984. "The Relevance of Religion: Iceland and Secularization Theory." *Journal for the Scientific Study of Religion* 23, no. 1 (March): 32–43.

Tanner, Marcus. 2008. *The Raven King: Matthias Corvinus and the Fate of His Lost Library*. New Haven, CT: Yale University Press.

Teixeira, Pedro D. 2009. *Jacob Mincer—The Human Capital Labour Economist*. Oxford, UK: Oxford University Press.

Teixeira, Ruy. 1990. "Things Fall Apart: Americans and Their Political Institutions, 1960–1988." In *Change in Societal Institutions*, ed. Maureen Hallinan, David Klein, and Jennifer Glass. New York: Plenum.

Teixeira, Ruy, and Joel Rogers. 2000. *America's Forgotten Majority: Why the White Working Class Still Matters*. New York: Basic Books.

Thurow, Lester C. 1975. *Generating Inequality: Mechanisms of Distribution in the U.S. Economy*. New York: Basic Books.

Torche, Florencia. 2010. "Is a College Degree Still the Great Equalizer? Intergenerational Mobility Across Levels of Schooling in the U.S." Working paper. New York: New York University Center for Advanced Social Science Research.

Treiman, Donald J., and Harry B.G. Ganzeboom. 1990. "Comparative Status Attainment Research." *Research in Social Stratification and Mobility* 9: 105–27.

Trilateral Commission. 1975. *The Crisis of Democracy*. New York: New York University Press.

Tuchman, Gaye. 2011. *Wannabe U: Inside the Corporate University*. Chicago: University of Chicago Press.

Tulviste, Peeter. 1991. *The Cultural-Historical Development of Verbal Thinking*. Commack, NY: Nova Science.

Tyack, David, and Larry Cuban. 1995. *Tinkering Toward Utopia: Reflections on a Century of Public School Reform*. Cambridge, MA: Harvard University Press.

U.K. Royal Society. 2011. *Knowledge, Networks, and Nations: Global Scientific Collaborations in the 21st Century*. London: U.K. Royal Society.

UNESCO. 2000. "The Right to Education: Towards Education for All Throughout Life." EFA Monitoring Report. Paris: UNESCO.

———. 2001. "Monitoring Report on Education for All." Paris: UNESCO.

———. 2002. "Education for All: Is the World on Track?" EFA Monitoring Report. Paris: UNESCO.

———. 2004. "Gender and Education for All: The Leap to Equality." Paris: UNESCO.

———. 2010. "Reaching the Marginalized." Paris: UNESCO.

UNESCO Institute of Statistics. 2004. *Global Education Digest 2004: Comparing Education Statistics Across the World*. Paris: UNESCO Institute of Statistics.

U.S. Bureau of Labor Statistics. 2011. "Distribution of Private Sector Employment by Firm Size Class: 1993/Q1 Through 2010/Q1." Washington, DC: Author.

U.S. Census Bureau. 2005. "The Institute of Education Sciences, National Center for Education Statistics, Adult Education Survey of the 2005 National Household Education Surveys Program." Ed. U.S. Department of Education. Public-use data file. Washington, DC: Author.

———. 2012. "Educational Attainment in the United States: 2012." Washington, DC: Author. www.census.gov/hhes/socdemo/education/

U.S. Department of Education, NCES (National Center for Education Statistics). 1993. "120 Years of American Education: A Statistical Portrait." Washington, DC: Author.

———. 1995. "High School and Beyond Fourth Follow-up (Sophomore Cohort)." Washington, DC: Author.

———. 2003. "Trends in High School Vocational/Technical Coursetaking: 1982–1998." Ed. K. Levesque. Washington, DC: Author.

———. 2006. "The Condition of Education 2006 (NCES2006–071)." Washington, DC: Author.

———. 2007. "Digest of Education Statistics 2006 (NCES 2007–017)." Washington, DC: Author, at Institute of Education Sciences.

———. 2008. "Digest of Education Statistics 2007 (NCES 2008–022)." Washington, DC: Author, at Institute of Education Sciences.

U.S. Department of Justice. 2003. "Education and Correctional Populations." Washington, DC: Author, at Office of Justice Programs.

U.S. Department of Labor. 1956. "Dictionary of Occupational Titles." Washington, DC: U.S. Government Printing Office.

———. 1965. "Dictionary of Occupational Titles." Washington, DC: U.S. Government Printing Office.

———. 1977. "Dictionary of Occupational Titles." Washington, DC: U.S. Government Printing Office.

Vaisey, Stephen. 2006. "Education and Its Discontents: Overqualification in America, 1972–2002." *Social Forces* 85, no. 2: 835–64.

Valentino, Lauren. 2011. "Internships and the Liberal Arts: Resisting the Vocational, Creating Dilettantes." Bethlehem, PA: National Association of Colleges and Employers.

Vallet, Louis-André. 2004. "Change in Intergenerational Class Mobility in France from the 1970s to the 1990s and Its Explanation: An Analysis Following the Casmin Approach." In *Social Mobility in Europe*, ed. R. Breen. Oxford, UK: Oxford University Press.

Voss, Harwin L., Aubrey Wendling, and Delbert S. Elliott. 1966. "Some Types of High School Dropouts." *Journal of Educational Research* 59, no. 8 (April): 363–68.

Walker, Jack L. 1991. *Mobilizing Interest Groups in America: Patrons, Professions, and Social Movements*. Ann Arbor: University of Michigan Press.

Walker, Vanessa Siddle, and Kim Nesta Archung. 2003. "The Segregated Schooling of Blacks in the Southern United States and South Africa." *Comparative Education Review* 47, no. 1: 21–40.

*Wall Street Journal.* n.d. "Careers." http://online.wsj.com/public/page/news-career-jobs.html

Ward, David. 2005. "Universities as Global Institutions." Speech at the University of Manchester, October 19.

Washburn, Jennifer. 2005. *University, Inc: The Corporate Corruption of Higher Education.* New York: Basic Books.

Watson, David, Robert Hollister, Susan E. Stroud, and Elizabeth Babcock. 2011. *The Engaged University: International Perspectives on Civic Engagement.* New York: Routledge.

Watson, Peter. 2010. *The German Genius: Europe's Third Renaissance, the Second Scientific Revolution, and the Twentieth Century.* New York: HarperCollins.

Weakliem, David, Julia McQuillan, and Tracy Schauer. 1995. "Toward Meritocracy? Changing Social-Class Differences in Intellectual Ability." *Sociology of Education* 68, no. 4: 271–86.

Weber, Max. 1958. "Science as a Vocation." In *From Max Weber: Essays in Sociology*, ed. H. H. Gerth and C. Wright Mills. New York: Oxford University Press.

———. 1978. *Economy and Society: An Outline of Interpretive Sociology.* Berkeley: University of California Press.

Webster, Frank. 1995. *Theories of the Information Society.* New York: Routledge.

Weeks, Wendy. 1999. "Social Capital, Volunteerism and Older Women." In *A Certain Age: Women Growing Older*, ed. Marilyn Poole and Susan Feldman. Crows Nest, Australia: Allen & Unwin.

Wei, Ian P. 2012. *Intellectual Culture in Medieval Paris: Theologians and the University, c. 1100–1330.* Cambridge, UK: Cambridge University Press.

Weintraub, E. Roy. 2002. *How Economics Became a Mathematical Science.* Durham, NC: Duke University Press.

Wilensky, Harold L. 1964. "The Professionalization of Everyone?" *American Journal of Sociology*: 137–58.

Wiles, Peter. 1974. "The Correlation Between Education and Earnings: The External-Test-Not-Content Hypothesis." *Higher Education* 3, no. 1: 43–58.

Willis, Paul E. 1977. *Learning to Labor: How Working Class Kids Get Working Class Jobs.* New York: Columbia University Press.

Wiseman, Alexander W., M. Fernanda Astiz, Rodrigo Fabrega, and David P. Baker. 2011. "Making Citizens of the World: The Political Socialization of Youth in Formal Mass Education Systems." *Compare: A Journal of Comparative and International Education* 41, no. 5: 561–77.

Witmer, David R. 1980. "Has the Golden Age of American Higher Education Come to an Abrupt End?" *Journal of Human Resources* 15, no. 1: 113–20.

Wolfinger, Raymond E., and Steven J. Rosenstone. 1980. *Who Votes?* New Haven, CT: Yale University Press.

Wong, Suk-Ying. 1991. "The Evolution of Social Science Instruction, 1900–86: A Cross-National Study." *Sociology of Education* 64, no. 1 (January): 33–47.

Woods, Mary N. 1991. *From Craft to Profession: The Practice of Architecture in Nineteenth-Century America.* Berkeley: University of California Press.

Wotipka, Christine Min, and Francisco O. Ramirez. 2008. "Women's Studies as a Global Innovation." In *The Worldwide Transformation of Higher Education*, International Perspectives on Education and Society, vol. 9, ed. D. P. Baker and A. Wiseman, 89–110. Bingley, UK: Emerald Group.

Wright, Lawrence. 1994. "One Drop of Blood." *The New Yorker*, July 24.

Wuthnow, Robert. 2002. *Loose Connections: Joining Together in America's Fragmented Communities.* Cambridge, MA: Harvard University Press.

Wyatt, Ian, and Daniel H. Hecker. 2006. "Occupational Changes During the 20th Century." *Monthly Labor Review* 129, no. 3: 35–57.

Young, Jock. 2007. *The Vertigo of Late Modernity.* London: Sage.

Young, Michael D. 1958. *The Rise of the Meritocracy, 1870–2033: The New Elite of Our Social Revolution.* New York: Random House.

Young, Michael. 1971. *Knowledge and Control: New Directions in the Sociology of Education.* London: Collier-Macmillan.

———. 2008. *Bringing the Knowledge Back In: From Social Constructivism to Social Realism in the Sociology of Education.* New York: Routledge.

Young, Michael, and Johan Muller. 2007. "Truth and Truthfulness in the Sociology of Educational Knowledge." *Theory and Research in Education* 5, no. 2: 173–201.

Zuboff, Shoshana. 1988. *In the Age of the Smart Machine.* New York: Basic Books.

# Index

academic intelligence, 36, 41–44, 144–45, 151, 155
Academy of Management, 113, 114, 115
American Cocoa Research Institute, 106
American Council of Education, 231, 239–40
architectural education, 166–72; network of associations of, 167
Association of Pacific Rim Universities, 89
Augustine of Hippo, 37–38

baby boom, 148
Bader, Christopher, 265–66
Benavot, Aaron, 194, 211
Berg, Ivan, 140–43, 146, 147, 154
Bernstein, Leonard, *Westside Story*, 223
Bloom, Harold, 217
Boole, George, 115
British education system, 130
British Parliament, Clean Air Act of 1956, 258
Broh, Beckett, 49
Brooks, David, 55
Burris, Val, 131

census data, 133
Cha, Yun-kyung, 203
Chile: vocational training in, 210–11
China, 146, 273
civic education, 255; civic involvement, 247, 250; civic mobilization, 253; and environmentalism, 253, 259; gap in, 256
Clark, Burton, 243
classicism, death of, 202–10
cognitive demand: jobs, 130; mathematics textbooks, 50; schooling, 49–51
cognitive development, 277; cognitive skills, 144–46, 151–52, 154; cognitivist, 190, 192–94; culture of, 43
Collins, Randall, 147–48, 154, 160–62, 165, 171
common global culture, 72–73
community colleges, 242–45; two-year institutions, 132
complementary technology, 149–50
Comte, Auguste, 278

Conant, James, 221
continuing education and work, 173
cooling out, 242–44
Cosby, William, 230
Coser, Lewis: greedy institution, 279
cosmology, 172; Western classical, 103
credentialing, 156–83; backward, 174–76; changing nature of, 213–15; credentialism, 127, 131, 140–43, 159; credentials, 134, 136–38; *The Credential Society*, 147, 181–83; educational transformation of, 158; forms of, 157–62; forward, 172–74; fraud, 157, 176–79; horizontal institutionalization, 162–65; influence on social stratification, 179–82; qualifications inflation, 129–30; vertical institutionalization, 165–72
Cremin, Lawrence, 230
Cuban, Larry, 138

Deil-Amen, Regina, 242
demographic transition, 278
desacralization, 262, 271–72
*Dictionary of Occupational Titles*, 141–43, 146
*Diploma Disease, The*, 128–33
Dore, Ronald, 125, 128–30, 132–33, 139–40, 147, 154
Dorn, Sherman, 221–25
Dougherty, Kevin, 242
Downey, Douglas, 48
dropout: cause of as social problem, 225–30; college, 241–42, 244–45; high school, 220–30; as social problem in the United States, 225
Drori, Gili, 74–76, 136
dual integration, 86
Durkheim, Emile, 103, 283

Eastern Bloc nations, 256–57
Edison, Thomas, 84
education: changes of, 37–40; human right, 32, 55–57; as an institution, 31–36, 127, 279–80; myth, 126–27, 139–41, 143–44, 146, 151, 154; normative power, 132;

societal solution, 246; universalism of, 32, 35

education effects on: classroom, 138; IQ, 44–48; modern individuals, 5–8, 33; occupations, 143, 155; politics, 247; social development, 129, 145, 152–53; technology, 147–51, 153–54; wages, 126, 132, 140–41, 145, 148, 150, 153; worker skills, 149–50, 153–54

educated laity, 266–68

educated polity, 249, 254

education revolution: xi, 1; American, 25; consequences of, 15–18; cultural products of, 31–36, 41, 65; democratic revolution, 257; disadvantaged children, 28–30; expansion of, 30, 128, 134, 136, 139, 146; origins of, 62–73; as quiet social revolution, 3–4; religion, 242, 264; social epistemological revolution, 189–92; work place, 150–52, 154–55

educational transformation, 277

Einstein, Albert, 84

Emerging Church movement, 270–71

end of history, 260

epistemological revolution, 283

Europe, 273; Erasmus Mundus program of, 89; European Union, 256

feudal vocationalism, 104

Fiala, Robert, 31–32

Finke, Roger, 263, 272

Fisher, Irving, 116

Flynn Effect, 44–48

Ford Foundation, 196, 222

Ford, Rollin, 119–20

Frank, David, 60, 100–103, 199–200, 258

Froese, Paul, 265–66

Gabler, Jay, 100–103

game theory, 116–17

Gardner, Howard, 297

Gates, Bill, 84

GED (General Educational Development test), 52, 230–40, 245–46, 281; as educational redemption, 234

GeD (general educational development of job content), 141–42, 144

Geiger, Roger, 79–80

German schooling: *Gymnasium*, 94; *Hauptschule*, 239

Germany, 293

Gibbons, Michael, 78–79

God, shifting images of, 265–67

Goldin, Claudia, 150–52

Gumport, Patricia, 110, 111

health, 281

Hecker, Daniel, 133–35

high school graduation rates, 223–30

higher education, funding of, 89–90; massification, 61

Hippel, Paul von, 48

historical-institutional school of economics, 115

Hobbes, Thomas, 103

Hogan, David, 156

home-schooling, 236

Hout, Michael, 53

Howell, David, 144–45

human capital, 228, theory of, 126–27, 141–42, 146, 151, 153–55

Humboldt, Wilhelm von, 293

Hwang, Hokyu, 136

ice cream: research and academic degree, 105–7; thermoacoustic research, 107

Iceland, 273

Inkeles, Alex, 5–8, 276, 288

international nongovernmental organizations (INGOs), 56

Jomtien Declaration, 55

*Journal of American Oil Chemists' Society*, 106

*Journal of Food Science*, 106

Junn, Jane, 248

Kamens, David, 194, 251, 253

Katz, Lawrence, 151–52

Kennedy, John, 261–62

knowledge: authoritative, 66, 106, 108, 112, 293–94; definition, 61; dominant forms of, 100; globalization of, 87; land-grant model, research university, 92; production of, 77–79, 80; social construction of, 99, 100, 101, 102

knowledge society, 184, 186–87; as the schooled society, 216–18

Lee, Shayne, 269

Lenhardt, Gero, 69–72

Libraries: Cornell University, 185; Library of Congress, 186; Pennsylvania State University, 185; Raven King, 184–85

literature, in schooled society, 206–7

Locke, Robert, 115, 116, 117, 118–19

Longhofer, Wesley, 255

Lopez Turly, Ruth, 242

Luria, Aleksandr, 48

MacLeod, Jay, 127

managerialism, 139, 144, 154
March, James, 135
marginal utility theory, 116
Marx, Karl, 103, 139, 283; theory, 126–27, 147
mass education, 1; cause of change, 258; enrollment, 24–25; nation-states, 57, 256; nineteenth century and early twentieth century, 256; premodern, 23, 37; workplace, 127, 133, 144, 152, 154
mass media, 254
Master's of Business Administration (MBA), 84, 112–21, 161, 294; executive MBA programs, 174–76; *Harvard Business Review*, 270
mathematics, curriculum and textbooks, 192–94; history and expansion of, 195–97
megachurches, 269; success in schooled society, 270
Meyer, John, 1–2, 60, 74, 121, 136, 194, 214, 234, 280, 288
Minner, Roth Ann, 230
Moon, Hyeyoung, 120
More, Sir Thomas, 38–40, 52, 194, 281
multilateral education agencies, 56
multiple intelligence, 298

National Education Association, 222, 227
nation-state, 255; nationalism, 255; nationalistic control, 71
neoclassical microeconomic theory, 115
neo-Darwinian evolution, 102
neo-institutional theory, xiii, 10–13, 136, 155, 284–88
Neumann, John von, 116
new public management, 121
New Sociology of Education, 187–89
Nie, Norman, 248
Nighthorse Campbell, Ben, 230

occupation, access to: formal education credentialing, 157–62; functional differentiation, 161; traditional forms, 156
occupational licensing, 165–71
occupational mismatch, 132, 142
occupational prestige, 180–81
ontology, Western classical, 103
organizations: education foundation of, 135–37; horizontal structure, 138; increase of employment in, 136; intensive rationalization, 137; personnel professionalism, 136
orientalism, 72; replacement of, 102
Osteen, Joel, 269

overeducation, 125, 127–33, 138–39, 143, 146; societal upheaval, 130–31

papal curia, 66; role in universities, 66–67
Parsons, Talcott, 1, 84, 284, 291
Pascarella, Ernest T., 250, 252–53, 266
Peters, Ellen, 48
political action, 249–53; political and civic capacity, 257; political demobilization, 256; political mobilization, 256
postbaccalaureate training: expansion of, in the United States, 95–97
Powell, Justin, 215–16
Powell, Walter, 136
primary institution, 59, 70
privatization-marketization, 59
professionalization, 127, 133–35; education as cornerstone, 133; personnel professionalism, 136; professionalism, 135, 139, 153–54

*Quarterly Journal of Economics*, 148

Ramirez, Francisco, 74–76, 110
religion, 261–74; behavior of, 267; change through education revolution, 264–72; coexistence with education revolution, 264–67, 272–74; life-cycle of, 263; organization of, 268–70; secularization by education, 261–62, 271
religious pluralism, 271–72
research university, 294; expansion of, 88; knowledge conglomerate, 84–90; mass education, 90–98; model of, 105; research, production of, 76–77, 79–80; "super research university" and intensification of, 87
Riddle, Phyllis, 63–68
Roman Catholic Church, 29, 94, 203, 261; role in development of Western form of university, 66–69; and scholarship, 63–67; and science, 69
Rosenbaum, James, 242
Rousseau, Jean-Jacques, 103

Said, Edward, 72
*Saturday Evening Post*, 228
Sawyer, Thomas, 257
Schofer, Evan, 74–76, 255
schooled society, 8; costs and benefits, 295–99; credentialed society, 181–83; culture of, 30; economic globalization, 253; equality and rights, 31, 35, 55–57, 253–55; future of, 288–95; neo-institutional perspective on, 10–13; politics of,

253–55; traditional perceptive on, 9; work place, 131, 135, 137, 139, 144
Schreiber, Daniel, 227
Schultz, Theodore W., 125
Schwadel, Philip, 266–68
science: basic versus applied, 76–81; and Christianity, 69; early, in universities, 74; in modern world polity, 74–76; origins of, in medieval university, 69; scientism and scientization, 190–91, 195–97
Scott, Richard, 214
secondary institution, 59
sexual identity, LGBTQA, 252; politics of AIDS treatment, 252; politicization of, 252
Signs: A Journal of Women, Culture and Society, Journal of Women Studies, 109
Sinitiere, Phillip, 269
Slater, Christian, 230
Smith, Thomas, 232
social construction, knowledge, reality, 100
social mobility, 128
social movements, 251, 255, 257; Arab Spring, 250; power of university, 258; Tea Party, 256
social status, education attainment, 53–55
sociology of religion, 263–66
special education, 297
Stark, Rodney, 69, 263
Stehlik-Barry, Kenneth, 248
Stinchcombe, Arthur, 135
Synagogue 3000, 271, 300

Terenzini, Patrick, 250, 252–53, 266
theology: American, 266; Catholicism, 273–274; Christianity, 39–40, 261–271; Judaism, 272; Muslims, 273
Thomas, David, 230
Torche, Florencia, 53
Trilateral Commission, 131
tutoring, 297

UNESCO, 57; education for all, 56–57
union membership and decline, 165
United Nations Human Rights' Committee, Elimination of Discrimination Against Women, 110

universalism, 69–70; knowledge, 191, 198–202; in inquiry, 70
university: admissions to elite institutions, 58; authoritative ideologies of, 100, 134; center of cultural production, 72; church and, 66–67; competition and cooperation, 89; cultural institution, 62; cultural power of, 66– 68; earliest founding of universities in Europe, 63–64; epistemological revolution in, 102, 110; features of, 64; future of, 292; German, 93–94; humanities, social science, and natural science balance in, 100–102; intellectually disabled youth, 97; impact on business firms and theory of management, 112–20; institutional triumph of, 104, 118; knowledge conglomerate, 100–101, 104–5; longevity of, 63; medieval, 37, 63–67; original functions of, 81; paradox of, 60; social charters and mission of, xiv, 14, 15, 35, 59–62, 72, 80–84, 100, 114, 121
University of: Bologna, 63; City University of New York, 94; Erlangen, 74; Göttingen, 63; Halle, 63; The Johns Hopkins University, 88, 307; Oxford, 63; Paris, 63; Pennsylvania State University, 208

vocationalism, obsolescence of, 210

Weber, Max, 100, 103, 283
Western democracies, 256; Western Europe and North America, 256
Willis, Paul, 127
Wolff, Edward, 144–45
women studies, 107–12
Wong, Suk-Ying, 200
worker, educated individual, 137
workplace, as classroom, 138
World Bank, 210–11
world polity, forming of, 255
Wotipka, Christine, 110
Wyatt, Ian, 133–35

Young, Michael: knowledge paradox, 187–89; social construction of knowledge, 198, 199